1617 5797   59 95

High-Skilled Immigration in a Global Labor Market

High-Skilled Immigration
in a Global Labor Market

Barry R. Chiswick,
Editor

The AEI Press

Publisher for the American Enterprise Institute
WASHINGTON, D.C.

Distributed by arrangement with the Rowman & Littlefield Publishing Group, 4501 Forbes Boulevard, Suite 200, Lanham, Maryland 20706. To order, call toll free 1-800-462-6420 or 1-717-794-3800. For all other inquiries, please contact AEI Press, 1150 Seventeenth Street, N.W., Washington, D.C. 20036, or call 1-800-862-5801.

Library of Congress Cataloging-in-Publication Data

High-skilled immigration in a global labor market / Barry R. Chiswick, editor.
    p. cm.
Includes bibliographical references and index.
ISBN-13: 978-0-8447-4385-1 (cloth)
ISBN-10: 0-8447-4385-2 (cloth)
ISBN-13: 978-0-8447-4387-5 (ebook)
ISBN-10: 0-8447-4387-9 (ebook)
1. Foreign workers. 2. Skilled labor. 3. Professional employees. 4. Labor market. 5. Emigration and immigration—Economic aspects. I. Chiswick, Barry R.
    HD6300.H54 2010
    331.6'2—dc22

Printed in the United States of America

Contents

List of Illustrations

TABLES

Acknowledgments

This project could not have had a successful conference and produced this conference volume without the support of Henry Olsen, director of the AEI National Research Initiative, and Emily Batman, program manager at the American Enterprise Institute, and the other staff members of the American Enterprise Institute.

In addition to the authors of the papers in this volume, it is important to acknowledge the valuable contribution of the discussants who stimulated the discussion at the conference and whose comments enhanced the quality of the final papers and of the panelists in the last session of the conference who explored the public policy issues regarding high-skilled immigration. Audience members played a similar role during the formal and informal general discussions. The discussants were:

Charles Beach, Queen's University, Canada
Örn Bodvarsson, St. Cloud State University
Barry R. Chiswick, University of Illinois at Chicago
Carmel U. Chiswick, University of Illinois at Chicago
Ira Gang, Rutgers University
Ahn Tram Le, Curtin University
Linda Lesky, George Washington University
Cordelia Reimers, Hunter College, CUNY
Eskil Wadensjö, Stockholm University

The panelists were:

Stuart Anderson, National Foundation for American Policy
Steven A. Camarota, Center for Immigration Studies
Barry R. Chiswick, University of Illinois at Chicago
David Frum (Panel Chair), then of the American Enterprise Institute
Demetrios Papademetriou, Migration Policy Institute

In addition, Laurence Iannaccone, then of George Mason University and now at Chapman University, delivered a lunchtime address, titled "Religion and High-Skilled Immigrants."

The production of this conference volume would not have been possible without the expert and dedicated efforts of Laura Harbold, manager, AEI Press, and Victoria Andrew, freelance editor.

Introduction and Overview
of the Chapters

Barry R. Chiswick

For several decades, academic research, public policy, and media attention on immigration have focused on the migration to the United States of low-skilled workers. Sometimes this is in the context of the growing undocumented (illegal alien) population, sometimes it is in the context of employers' concerns about what they perceive as a shortage of low-skilled workers, and sometimes it is in the context of welfare reform, that is, reducing the extent to which immigrants are eligible for public-income transfers. While this attention had merit in its own right, it has distracted attention from the other end of the distribution of skills: high-skilled immigrants.

As Joseph P. Ferrie notes in his chapter in this volume, the specific set of occupations and skills defining high-skilled workers—native born or immigrant—changes according to time period, location, and the nature of the technologies in use. In colonial America, high-skilled workers were craftsmen and artisans, such as blacksmiths and wheel and barrel makers. The high-skilled immigrants today are in scientific, technical, engineering, and management (STEM) occupations. They tend to have many years of formal schooling, high technical training, strong decision-making talents, and they are often highly entrepreneurial, evident whether they are establishing their own businesses or acting in an innovative capacity in an already established business.

While there has always been some research and policy interest in high-skilled immigrants, in the past, this has taken a back seat to concerns

1

associated with low-skilled immigration. Technological, economic, and political developments in the United States and abroad mean that policies regarding and implications of high-skilled immigration can no longer remain on the back burner.

The immigration of high-skilled workers has several apparent effects on economies. In their various roles, high-skilled immigrants expand the productive potential of the economy in which they reside, thereby increasing the growth rate of total-factor productivity. High-skilled immigration to the United States, therefore, enhances the international competitiveness of the U.S. economy and attracts foreign capital to the country. By enhancing the supply of STEM workers, high-skilled immigration adds workers to the labor force who tend to pay more in taxes than they receive in public benefits (drawn from the public treasury in the form of income transfers, medical benefits, educational costs, and so forth). As a result, they tend to have a positive net fiscal balance that contrasts with the negative net fiscal balance of low-skilled immigrant workers. By increasing the ratio of high-skilled workers to less-skilled workers, their immigration increases the demand for low-skilled workers, thereby increasing both the employment and earnings of the latter. This has the effect of reducing poverty, inequality, and the negative net fiscal balance of lower-skilled workers. At the same time, some might argue that large-scale, high-skilled immigration depresses the wages of high-skilled workers, and, hence, the incentives of native-born workers and the general public to invest in the U.S. education system. Some may ask, "Why grow them if you can import them?" Such an attitude might have particularly negative effects on children from disadvantaged families, whether native born or immigrant.

The value to the economy of high-skilled workers has long been recognized in the United States. In colonial times, the separate colonies frequently subsidized the migration of European artisans, especially when they agreed to move to small towns and rural areas. U.S. immigration policy, however, has never focused on admitting immigrants primarily on the basis of their skills or likely contributions to the economy. When immigration restrictions were first introduced in the late nineteenth century, and even after more severe restrictions were introduced in the 1920s, visas were distributed in accordance with quotas based solely on race, nationality, and ethnicity. When immigration policy was reformed in 1965, visas were primarily distributed to immigrants based on family ties to someone already in the United States; few were based on immigrants' skills or expected economic contributions to the United States.

When the United States was unquestionably the world's technological leader and premier economy, it could afford the luxury of paying little attention to the effects of immigration policy on the skills of the U.S. labor force. This is no longer the case. The United States of the twenty-first century may no longer be the world's leader in science, technology, and economic growth. Among the policy priorities dictated by this new reality is that the United States needs to reconsider the goals and implications of its immigration policy.

Moreover, it is now globally recognized that international competition exists not only for the manufacture of goods and services, primary products, and capital, but also for high-skilled workers. Many countries in the Organisation for Economic Co-operation and Development (OECD) have recognized this fact and have adopted immigration policies accordingly. Some countries—such as Canada, Australia, and New Zealand—that previously felt underpopulated and just wanted to attract immigrants generally, have now implemented policies favoring high-skilled immigrants in particular. Others, particularly in Western Europe, have shifted in the last half-century from being countries with net emigration to countries with net immigration and are developing labor-migration policies to attract high-skilled workers. The United States, despite all its features that attract high-skilled immigrants, will fall behind in this international competition unless it sharply alters its immigration policies.

These public policy concerns, and the scarcity of research on high-skilled immigration to the United States and elsewhere, led to the proposal to organize a two-day conference to present original research papers, held April 22–23, 2009, and to the decision to publish the conference volume. The American Enterprise Institute, which had twice hosted previous conferences and published volumes on international migration (see *The Gateway: U.S. Immigration Issues and Policies* [AEI Press, 1982] and *Immigration, Language, and Ethnicity: Canada and the United States* [AEI Press, 1992], both ed. Barry R. Chiswick), enthusiastically agreed to sponsor this project. This book is the product of that initiative.

The first chapter in this volume, "A Historical Perspective on High-Skilled Immigrants to the United States, 1820–1920," is by Joseph P. Ferrie.

Ferrie's chapter examines the history and effects of high-skilled immigration from the first year in which formal immigration data were recorded through the last decade before the enactment of the national-origins quota system designed to restrict Southern and Eastern European immigration severely. Except for the restrictions on Asian immigration first introduced in the 1880s, this century saw largely unrestricted immigration. Ferrie notes that high-skilled immigration must be defined by the context of the time and the technology in use, and he defines high-skilled immigrants as those possessing the skills in demand by the leading industries in each time period. At the outset of the period he examines, artisans constituted the high-skilled workers; some have suggested that their immigration may have slowed the process of U.S. industrialization, although Ferrie does not find evidence that this is the case. Later in this period, the workers in high demand were professionals with scientific and managerial talents. Their immigration was both encouraged by and a boon to capital inflows and the industrialization of the United States. As later chapters in this volume demonstrate, such STEM workers are still in high demand in the labor market and remain one of the important engines of U.S. economic growth.

Ferrie also compares immigrants' skills upon arrival in the United States with the skills they use in employment in the labor market. The latter, rather than the former, is key to determining immigrants' economic contributions. This theme is followed in chapters in this volume on the contemporary transferability of preimmigration training to U.S., Canadian, and Israeli economies. Finally, Ferrie cautions that the circumstances in the United States in the nineteenth century—largely unrestricted labor mobility, a small role for government, substantial barriers to international trade, and the nature of emerging technologies—differ sharply from those of the twenty-first century. Policy implications relevant for the nineteenth century may not be relevant two centuries later.

In chapter 2, "Rights-Based Politics, Immigration, and the Business Cycle, 1890–2008," James F. Hollifield and Carole J. Wilson note that the peak of restrictionist immigration policy occurred with the implementation of the national-origins quota system in the 1920s (a product of 1921 and 1924 legislation) and that the post–World War II trend has been toward liberalizing and expanding immigration opportunities. The first steps involved minor easing of restrictions against Asian immigrants followed by the abolishment of the national-origins quota system entirely in the 1965 amendments to the Immigration and Nationality Act (which encouraged high-skilled Asian immigration), followed by passage of the Refugee Act of 1980, which broadened the definition of a refugee, the granting of amnesty for nearly 3 million undocumented people in the 1986 Immigration Reform and Control Act (IRCA), and the 1990 Immigration Act, which expanded opportunities for high-skilled foreign individuals to work in the United States with the expansion of employer-sponsored temporary and permanent visas.

Not all post–World War II changes in legislation were liberalizing, however. The 1965 legislation included the first numerical limits on immigrants from the Western Hemisphere. The IRCA introduced sanctions against employers who knowingly hired undocumented workers, although these provisions are seldom enforced. The welfare-reform legislation of 1996 attempted to limit the new immigrants' access to public-income transfers.

In an econometric examination of annual immigration flows from 1890 to 2008, Hollifield and Wilson analyze how immigration legislation and the U.S. business cycle affect immigration. They find that, as economic theory predicts, immigration declines as the U.S. unemployment rate increases, but this effect is muted in the post–World War II period. The effect may be muted because the recessions in the postwar period were shallower and briefer, immigration queues lead immigrants to come when they finally get visas regardless of short-term changes in employment levels, and increased personal, family, and public resources are available for immigrants to finance the early adjustment period.

Hollifield and Wilson conclude that economic factors alone do not dictate immigration flows. Instead, U.S. political, foreign policy, and national security concerns have shaped immigration policy and, consequently, have modified immigration patterns. As a result of these and other factors, the number of people who legally immigrate to the United States each year has increased from about 250,000 annually in the 1950s to over 1 million per year in the first decade of the twenty-first century.

An important source of high-skilled immigrants to the United States is foreign students, that is, natives of other countries who come to the United States on a "temporary" basis to attend institutions of higher education. B. Lindsay Lowell and Pramod Khadka explore "Trends in Foreign-Student

Admissions to the United States: Policy and Competitive Effects" in chapter 3. They note that foreign students have become an important part of higher education, in particular, in graduate-level education in the United States. This has also become true for many other countries in the past decade, including Canada, Australia, and a number of Western European countries. Subsequently, international competition for these students is increasing: there is now a global market for higher education, especially in the sciences and engineering.

Lowell and Khadka's econometric analysis of the flow of foreign students to the United States indicates that the primary determinants are U.S. tuition charges, per-capita income in the origin country (which is positively correlated with an increase in the number of students who study abroad), and alternatives to studying in the United States, including new opportunities to receive higher education both in students' origin country and in other countries outside of the United States. They also examine how higher visa rejection rates, which occurred following the 9/11 terrorist attacks, affected the flow of foreign students to the United States.

Foreign students who study in the United States receive clear benefits, including a high-quality education and the increased probability that they might obtain a temporary or permanent visa to work in the United States. The United States also benefits from having foreign students. Foreign students enrich the educational experience for American students; they provide assistance through working as research assistants, laboratory assistants, and lecturers in U.S. colleges and universities; and their presence in the United States on a temporary basis allows U.S. government officials and employers to choose recipients of temporary and permanent work visas with lower risk, as foreign students have gone through a sort of screening process.

As Ferrie notes in his chapter, not all skilled immigrants find employment in jobs that use their premigration skills. While Ferrie analyzes this in a historical context, Barry R. Chiswick and Paul W. Miller analyze the contemporary situation. Their chapter, "Educational Mismatch: Are High-Skilled Immigrants Really Working in High-Skilled Jobs, and What Price Do They Pay If They Are Not?" uses data from the 2000 U.S. population census. They perform analyses for both foreign-born and native-born adult males with at least a bachelor's degree and, separately, for those with at least a master's degree. They define overeducation as a level of schooling that is greater than the usual or average level of schooling in any given occupation. They find that overeducation is widespread among both foreign-born and native-born high-skilled workers, but it is more prevalent among the foreign-born. Among immigrants, whether only college graduates or those with higher educational levels, the extent of overeducation decreases the longer they stay in the United States as they move up the occupational ladder. Presumably, a longer duration in the country enables immigrants to better fit their language, schooling, and technical skills to the demand in the U.S. labor market and, in the case of some occupations, to acquire necessary licenses or certifications.

Among high-skilled workers—both foreign and native born—there is a high rate of return to years of schooling that are usual or typical in a worker's occupation. Years of schooling in excess of what is usual (surplus schooling) provide a very low economic return in comparison. Indeed among foreign-born men, in their first ten to twenty years in the United States, years of overeducation actually have a negative effect on earnings. Chiswick and Miller find at all high-skill levels that all occupations fail to use excess or surplus schooling effectively. Thus, for high-skilled immigrants, that earnings increase as duration in the United States increases is attributable, at least in part, to their progression into occupations that better match, that is, make more effective use of, their education levels. While education appears to serve as a pathway to occupational attainment, over time, earnings appear to be linked more closely to a worker's actual occupation than to an individual's level of schooling.

Two chapters in this volume address immigrant physicians in the United States and Canada. Linda G. Lesky's chapter is titled "Physician Migration to the United States and Canada: Criteria for Admission," and James Ted McDonald, Casey Warman, and Christopher Worswick authored the chapter "Earnings, Occupations, and Schooling Decisions of Immigrants with Medical Degrees: Evidence for Canada and the United States." Lesky analyzes and outlines the different criteria employed to determine which immigrants with medical degrees may enter the United States and Canada. In both countries, some enter as the relatives of citizens or permanent residents. However, most are granted entry because of their medical degrees, although the criteria differ between the two countries. In the United States, potential immigrants with medical degrees enter the country if they are admitted into medical residency programs. While this provides a temporary visa, it is a pathway to obtaining a license to practice medicine in the United States and to acquiring a permanent-resident visa permitting immigrants to continue in the country as physicians upon completing their residencies. In Canada, however, most immigrants with medical degrees enter under the points system, which takes educational attainment, English- or French-language fluency, and age into account, along with other characteristics. Admission into a medical residency program is not required and does not enter into the computation of points needed for a visa. As a result, foreign nationals with foreign medical degrees can enter Canada with no certainty that they will gain admission to a residency program or be able to obtain a license to practice medicine in Canada. As a result, Canadian immigrants with medical degrees are less likely than native Canadians with medical degrees to be employed as physicians in Canada. Lesky's chapter demonstrates that institutional arrangements matter.

McDonald, Warman, and Worswick note the increasingly important role immigrant physicians are serving in providing primary care and specialized medical care, especially in underserved rural and low-income urban areas in the United States and Canada. They analyze the earnings, occupations, and postmigration schooling of physicians using the 2000 U.S. population census and the 2001 Canadian census. For the United States, they cannot differentiate those holding medical degrees from those holding other professional degrees, and so assume that those with professional degrees working as physicians have medical degrees. Overall, they find significantly lower earnings for immigrant physicians than for native-born physicians. In both countries, recent immigrant doctors have lower earnings than native-born physicians, other variables being the same. Yet, perhaps due to selectivity in migration, immigrants who have been in their destination country for a longer period have higher earnings than their native-born counterparts. However, we cannot ignore the possibility of differences in earnings potential, perhaps due to ability, across cohorts.

Those with medical degrees can be identified in the Canadian data. Holders of foreign medical degrees are much less likely to be working as physicians than those who earned their medical degree in Canada, whether native Canadian or foreign born. Recent Canadian immigrants with foreign medical degrees are more likely to be students than are others with medical degrees in Canada or recent immigrant physicians in the United States. The authors speculate that this may be due to differences between U.S. and Canadian immigration policies, along the lines discussed in Linda Lesky's chapter.

Volker Grossmann and David Stadelmann's chapter, "High-Skilled Immigration: The Link to Public Expenditure and Private Investments," presents their theoretical model, in which they assume that high-skilled immigration increases productivity in the receiving economy by causing an increase in capital. They argue that high-skilled immigration increases the marginal product of capital and, hence, the incentives for investment in both publicly financed infrastructure and private capital. They test their model empirically for OECD countries. Their analysis indicates a positive association between the net immigration of university-trained workers and the level of investment in public infrastructure and in the stock of private physical capital. At the same time, there appears to be no relation between the net immigration of high-skilled workers and public spending that is unrelated to investment. This offers support for their argument that high-skilled immigrants enhance productivity in their destination countries.

In chapter 8, Sarit Cohen-Goldner and Yoram Weiss analyze "High-Skilled Russian Immigrants in the Israeli Labor Market: Adjustment and Impact." During the early 1990s, Israel experienced a massive 15 percent increase in its labor force in just a few years due to the sudden and unexpected immigration to Israel of Jews from the Former Soviet Union (FSU). They were more like refugees than conventional economic migrants. Relative to the Israeli labor force, and by any standard, the population of FSU immigrants to Israel was, on the whole, very high skilled, but the immigrants generally lacked Israel-specific skills, including Hebrew language proficiency. While they tended to find jobs in Israel fairly quickly, they initially experienced substantial downward occupational mobility compared to their jobs in the FSU and earned significantly less than Israelis of the same age and schooling. Typical of the immigrant-adjustment experience, occupational attainment and earnings increased for the FSU immigrants with duration in Israel. These improvements were most pronounced for the more highly skilled and the younger immigrants.

The impact of these immigrants changed as their duration in Israel lengthened. Upon arriving in Israel, when they lacked Israel-specific skills, they were most likely to work low-skill jobs and competed mainly with low-skilled Israeli and foreign workers. As their stay in Israel lengthened, they increased their Israel-specific skills and attained jobs better matched to their educational levels, thereby mitigating the initial negative impact on low-skilled local workers. At the same time, increased foreign investment in the Israeli economy increased the capital stock and cushioned high-skilled Israeli workers from any significant negative impact of the FSU immigrants' entry into high-skill occupations.

Cohen-Goldner and Weiss's finding in this "natural experiment" in Israel that exogenous and unanticipated high-skilled immigration attracts foreign capital is consistent with Grossmann and Stadelmann's analysis regarding capital inflows in the OECD in response to high-skilled immigration. What is less clear empirically is whether low-skilled immigration today might have the same positive effects on public and private capital formation. That is, are the findings for Israel and the OECD on public and private capital investments effects of immigration in general, or might low-skilled immigration become a substitute for private capital investments instead?

The final chapter in this volume is "High-Skilled Immigration Policy in Europe," by Martin Kahanec and Klaus F. Zimmermann. The chapter begins with a discussion of an Institute for the Study of Labor Experts Survey that concluded that economic growth would be enhanced by an increase in high-skilled immigration into the European Union. The chapter outlines the current immigration policies in use across European countries and shows that there is no consistent policy approach within Europe. A closed-door policy had been the general European pattern. With the exception of "temporary" guest workers in the 1960s and early 1970s, repatriation from former colonies, and, more recently, refugees, European countries have tended to view immigrants as unnecessary and have preferred to maintain a sense of population homogeneity within country borders. The opposition to immigration in Europe does seem to be less intense in regard to high-skilled workers, but the general perception that Europe would prefer fewer immigrants has had the effect of encouraging high-skilled international migrants to settle in more hospitable destinations.

In spite of the lack of systematic national policies or coordination among European countries, the share of the foreign-born population is increasing in Europe. The authors call on European countries to reject the "Fortress Europe" mentality and to develop systematic and formal immigration policies, especially regarding high-skilled workers.

The chapters in this volume tell a consistent story. High-skilled immigration is not a new phenomenon in the United States, but its characteristics have varied over time as the nature of the skills in high demand change. STEM workers are in high demand in the labor market of the twenty-first century. In the current economic environment, countries compete internationally for these high-skilled immigrants and those who migrate across borders to acquire this training (foreign students). Not all newly arrived high-skilled immigrants are able to secure jobs commensurate with their training. They are less able to do so than are native-born workers with comparable training. As time in the destination increases, however, many of the high-skilled immigrants acquire the local or destination-specific skills—including language proficiency, labor-market information, and licenses or credentials—necessary to improve their occupational standing in the destination country. Immigration policies can affect which high-skilled immigrants will be more successful in finding employment using their skills. High-skilled immigrants are a magnet for capital investment, in terms both of public and private capital. In addition to yielding a positive fiscal balance (paying more in taxes than they receive in public benefits) and raising the earnings of low-skilled workers (a complementary factor of production), high-skilled immigrants expand the output per capita of the economy through the resulting increases in the capital stock. These benefits of high-skilled immigration have affected immigration policy. Some countries (including Canada, Australia, and New Zealand) have already altered their immigration criteria to attract high-skilled immigrants; others are designing policies they hope will accomplish this objective (including many countries in Western Europe).

For the past four decades, U.S. immigration policy has focused on allocating visas on the basis of kinship ties to a U.S. citizen or permanent-resident alien. It is, thereby, losing ground in the international competition for high-skilled immigrants. Whether it retains current policy or shifts to a policy focused on attracting high-skilled immigrants will play an important role in determining the quality of the American labor force in the coming decades.

PART I

Historical Perspective

1

A Historical Perspective on High-Skilled Immigrants to the United States, 1820–1920

Joseph P. Ferrie

Most of the history of immigration to the United States has focused on less-skilled workers. From the Irish fleeing famine in the late 1840s to Southern and Eastern Europeans escaping poverty and flooding the nation's cities in the early years of the twentieth century, both public discussion and most academic interest have focused on the arrival of laborers and farmers rather than workers with more specific skills. The response to immigration, too, has focused primarily on less-skilled immigrants: nativism and antipathy toward immigrants—seen in the platform of the Know-Nothings in the 1850s and apparent through the immigration-restriction movement that culminated in the imposition of the quota system in the early twentieth century—have most often been directed at immigrants at the lowest skill levels.

The immigration to the United States of high-skilled workers has received far less attention. This chapter examines the characteristics of these arrivals, high-skilled immigrants' responsiveness to the U.S. business cycle, their assimilation into the U.S. labor market, and their impact on the U.S. economy. This analysis relies on two new bodies of data: first, transcriptions of original passenger manifests from ships arriving in New York 1846–1900 from Ireland, Germany, Russia, and Italy (Center for Immigration Research

The author thanks Carmel Chiswick and Barry R. Chiswick for comments on an early draft of this chapter.

1976–2003); and second, a new business-cycle chronology that relies on a continuous, consistent series on physical output quantities rather than nominal data such as commodity prices and vague statements in reports by contemporary observers (Davis 2004).

High-Skilled Immigrants: The Numbers, 1820–1920

To assess the portion of high-skilled immigrants included in the flow of immigrants to the United States in the past requires a definition of "high skilled." It seems reasonable to consider "high skilled" those workers whose skills are in demand in the sectors of the economy that are contributing the most to aggregate economic growth. In the twenty-first century, this category would include physical scientists and engineers, computer scientists, financial-services workers, health care professionals, managers, and teachers. But for the period before 1920, different occupations would have fit this definition.

Before the American Revolution, craft workers were in such great demand that they negotiated terms one year shorter than unskilled workers when they immigrated to the United States as indentured servants (Galenson 1981, 455–56). Though literate immigrants also earned shorter terms, their advantage was not nearly as great as that of craft workers. Around 1850, when only a few industries (textiles, for example) were mechanized and much production still took place in the workshops and small-scale "manufactories" of artisans, the "high-skilled" group would include craft workers, mechanics who kept the machines running in sectors where industrialization had begun, and clerks whose letter-writing and bookkeeping skills were essential to the expansion of trade and the growth in the scale of firms. Around 1850, craft workers earned about 170 percent of the daily wage of unskilled laborers, and clerical workers earned about 200 percent of the daily wage of unskilled workers (Margo 2000). By the end of the nineteenth century, though the differential between the unskilled and the craft and clerical groups had not changed substantially, other categories of workers were in such high demand that they commanded dramatically larger incomes than other workers. These included the engineers, scientists, and, increasingly, professionalized managers, whose work made breakthroughs in production techniques and organization possible and led to unprecedented growth in the scale of manufacturing firms. This narrative suggests that during the early nineteenth century, craftsmen, mechanics, and clerks possessed the most highly sought skills, but in the late nineteenth century, they were surpassed in importance by engineers, scientists, and managers.

The extent to which relatively low-tech sectors dominated the U.S. economy in the decades immediately after 1850 (and thus the extent to which the highest-skilled workers—those in scientific, engineering, and managerial occupations—were less crucial at this time than they later became) can be seen in a simple ranking of the top industries by two measures: annual growth in capital per worker and in output per worker. Table 1-1 reports these rankings calculated at the firm level using data from the manuscripts of the Census of Manufacturers in 1850 and 1880 (Atack, Bateman, and Weiss 2004; Atack and Bateman 2004). By these measures, the leading sectors through 1880 were almost all "old" industries using

TABLE 1-1

PERCENT ANNUAL GROWTH IN CAPITAL PER WORKER AND OUTPUT PER WORKER IN U.S. MANUFACTURING FOR TOP TEN INDUSTRIES, 1850–80

	Capital per Worker, 1850–80			Output per Worker, 1850–80	
Rank	Industry	Annual Growth (Percent)	Rank	Industry	Annual Growth (Percent)
1	Tobacco	3.58	1	Leather	3.72
2	Leather	3.41	2	Textiles	2.70
3	Furniture	3.17	3	Apparel	2.35
4	Apparel	2.75	4	Furniture	1.90
5	Construction	2.51	5	Primary metals	1.84
6	Fabricated metals	2.44	6	Paper	1.52
7	Repair services	2.29	7	Food	1.40
8	Chemicals	1.99	8	Tobacco	1.39
9	Stone, clay, and glass	1.82	9	Transportation equipment	1.09
10	Paper	1.68	10	Construction	1.02

SOURCE: Author's calculations from Jeremy Atack, Fred Bateman, and Thomas Weiss, "National Samples from the Census of Manufacturing: 1850, 1860, and 1870," ICPSR04048-v1, Ann Arbor, MI: Interuniversity Consortium for Political and Social Research (ICPSR), 2004; and Jeremy Atack and Fred Bateman, "National Sample from the 1880 Census of Manufacturing," 2nd ICPSR version, Urbana, IL: University of Illinois; Bloomington, IN: Indiana University; and Ann Arbor, MI: ICPSR, 2004.

proven technologies but scaled up to larger establishment sizes employing machinery, including leather, furniture, and apparel. One of the "new" sectors that later came to dominate much of U.S. industrial output in the early twentieth century—chemicals—experienced rapid growth in capital per worker during this period but did not break into the top ten in output per worker. Prior to 1900, the chemicals industry was only beginning the process that would lead to its later dominance. Though primary metals experienced rapid output growth, most of this was in iron production rather than in steel, for which new technologies were only coming online at the end of the nineteenth century. These were two of the sectors that were to become the most scientifically and technologically advanced in the early twentieth century, and they stood to benefit more than most other industries from an influx of high-skilled workers, especially scientists, engineers, and managers.

The leading positions of industries like tobacco, leather, and textiles and apparel in the 1850–80 period suggest that the skills most in demand during this time were those that facilitated production using mechanized production techniques that were generally a larger-scale version of techniques that had been in use since early in the century. Workers with skills in maintaining machinery (mechanics) and in fabricating parts (blacksmiths) were needed, as were the low-level white-collar workers who handled the paperwork that made these larger firm sizes feasible. By the early twentieth century, however, industries that could benefit from more technically sophisticated workers were growing. Between 1904 and 1909, for example, value added in leather and tobacco grew 3.3 times more than the number of workers in those industries—exactly the same ratio as in blast furnaces, chemicals, and fertilizers—implying that value added per worker was growing at comparable rates across all of these industries by the early twentieth century as newer sectors caught up to older ones.

It is difficult to ascertain how the exact mix of skills employed by the leading industries changed from the late nineteenth to the early twentieth century: though the decennial population censuses reported each worker's occupation, they did not report the industries in which workers were employed until 1910. For the period 1910–1930, however, it is possible to identify which occupations were most prevalent in each leading industry. Table 1-2 shows this distribution for four broad sectors: manufacturing,

TABLE 1-2
PERCENT OF WORKERS IN SEVEN INDUSTRIAL SECTORS
BY OCCUPATION, 1910–30

	Manufac-turing	Processing	Transportation/ Utilities	Retail	Tobacco	Iron and Steel	Chemicals
Professional and Technical	1.9	2.3	1.6	1.9	0.2	1.4	4.2
Clerical, Sales	10.8	15.0	25.5	69.1	9.6	8.2	19.7
Craft	55.7	63.8	42.1	16.2	79.3	61.5	34.8
Unskilled	31.6	19.0	30.8	12.8	10.9	28.9	41.2

SOURCES: U.S. Census Bureau, *Thirteenth Census of the United States,* vol. VIII, Manufactures (Washington, DC: GPO, 1913); U.S. Census Bureau, *Fourteenth Census of the United States,* vol. VIII, Manufactures (Washington, DC: GPO, 1923); U.S. Census Bureau, Fifteenth Census of the United States, Manufactures, vol. I–III (Washington, DC: GPO, 1933).

processing, transportation/utilities, and retail. Within these sectors, if we examine three specific industries (tobacco, iron and steel, and chemicals), the differences between "old" and "new" industries are even more striking: in the iron and steel industry, professional and technical workers were seven times more prevalent than in the tobacco industry, and more than twenty times more prevalent in the chemicals industry than in the tobacco industry.

How did immigrants' occupations compare to these changing skill demands in the U.S. economy over the century from 1820 to 1920? The United States has recorded the occupations of arriving passengers since 1819.[1] At the port of arrival, ship captains were required to provide the U.S. Customs House with a list containing the name, age, sex, occupation, and origin of all individuals on board. Figure 1-1 shows the number of adult males who reported occupations by classification as either high skilled (professional and technical workers and managers, officials, and proprietors), medium skilled (craftsmen and clerks), or low skilled (farmers and common laborers). The high-skilled immigrants can be thought of as the crucial immigrants by the end of the nineteenth century, and the middle-skilled immigrants can be thought of as the crucial immigrants throughout the middle decades of the nineteenth century.

Throughout the era of mass migration (from the late 1840s through 1920), the number of unskilled workers increased with each successive wave of migration, while the number of medium- and high-skilled workers

FIGURE 1-1

IMMIGRATION TO THE UNITED STATES OF ADULT MALES REPORTING AN OCCUPATION BY SKILL LEVEL, 1820–1920

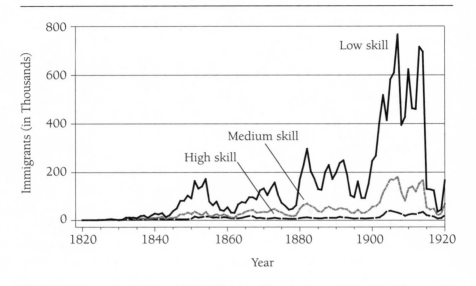

SOURCE: Susan B. Carter et al., eds., *Historical Statistics of the United States: Millennial Edition* (New York: Cambridge University Press, 2006), table AD231–45.

rose less dramatically. Figure 1-2 shows the proportion of immigrants in each group for each year's arrivals. Through 1830, roughly one-third of immigrants came from each group. From the mid-1840s through the mid-1850s—the years which contained the highest-ever rates of immigration into the United States—the share of low-skilled workers increased. In the mid-1850s, dire poverty in Ireland and rural Germany in particular boosted rates of immigration to the United States, increasing the share of low-skilled workers even above the trend increase that had occurred since the 1830s (Hatton and Williamson [2005, 32 and 35–41] attribute this trend increase in part to declining costs of transatlantic transportation). In the second half of the 1850s, however, this trend reversed dramatically: the share of higher-skilled workers rose to nearly 50 percent before the next wave of migration in the 1870s brought the unskilled share back up above 70 percent.

FIGURE 1-2

**IMMIGRATION TO THE UNITED STATES OF ADULT MALES REPORTING
AN OCCUPATION BY SKILL LEVEL, 1820–1920,
PERCENTAGE OF TOTAL IMMIGRATION**

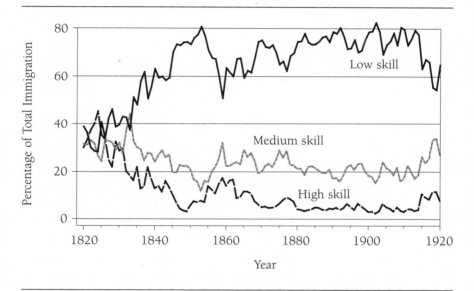

SOURCE: Susan B. Carter et al., eds., *Historical Statistics of the United States: Millennial Edition* (New York: Cambridge University Press, 2006), table AD231–45.

The U.S. Civil War did not deter immigrants—the immigration "bust" at the end of the 1850s was quickly reversed—but the war does mark the high-water mark for high-skilled immigrants in the nineteenth century: their share fell with the outbreak of the war and never recovered. By contrast, the outbreak of World War I in Europe in 1914, though it caused a sharp fall in total migration to the United States, also saw a pronounced rise in the share of medium- and high-skilled immigrants, well in advance of the imposition of the quota system. Meanwhile, the number and proportion of unskilled immigrants to the United States declined during World War I. The difference in the response of the unskilled share between the Civil War and World War I may be accounted for by different circumstances in the source countries: conscription undoubtedly kept many potential migrants in

Europe after 1914; from 1861 until the beginning of World War I, by contrast, there were few impediments to departure from Europe.

By the early 1870s, low-skilled workers again made up 75 percent of total arrivals, and their share consistently remained near this level thereafter. The share of medium- and high-skilled workers fell back to 20 percent and 8 percent respectively. With the imposition of the literacy test under the Immigration Act of 1917, the share of immigrants working low-skilled jobs fell closer to 60 percent and the shares in medium- and high-skilled jobs rose to 30 percent and 10 percent, respectively (see figure 1-2). In the middle decades of the nineteenth century, then, the most important skilled immigrants (middle skilled) seldom made up more than a quarter of the male immigrants with reported occupations, and at the end of the nineteenth century, the most important skilled immigrants (high skilled) never accounted for more than a tenth of the male immigrants with reported occupations.

The published tabulations underlying figures 1-1 and 1-2 do not cross-classify immigrant arrivals by both country of origin and occupation, so it is not possible to see how the mix of high-, medium-, and low-skilled immigrants differs across the countries from which workers emigrated to the United States in the nineteenth century. The original passenger ship lists for more than six million individuals have been transcribed, however, and can be used to shed some light on this issue.[2] Records for Irish (1846–51), German (1850–97), Italian (1855–1900), and Russian (1866–97) arrivals can be grouped into the three broad categories used previously.[3] As figure 1-3 shows, each of the aforementioned countries sent substantial numbers of workers to the United States in the nineteenth century, but the date at which each country's migrant flow peaked varies: Irish immigration peaked around 1850; German immigration peaked in 1855, the mid-1870s, and the early 1880s (each peak corresponds to immigration from a different region within Germany, moving from west to east over time [see Bodnar 1987, 6]); and both Italian and Russian immigration peaked after 1900. The timing of these peaks and of the years for which each country's records have been transcribed means that for both Irish and German arrivals, immigrants at the beginning, middle, and end of the cycle of migration will be observed; for Italy and Russia, only the earliest arrivals are measured.

FIGURE 1-3

IMMIGRANTS TO THE UNITED STATES BY COUNTRY OF ORIGIN, 1820–1920

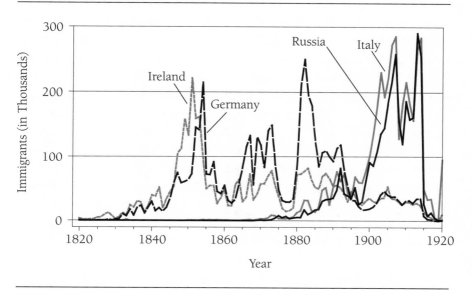

SOURCE: Susan B. Carter et al., eds., *Historical Statistics of the United States: Millennial Edition* (New York: Cambridge University Press, 2006), table AD173–90.

Despite these limitations, it is possible to compare Ireland to Germany and Italy to Russia. Germany sent nearly twice the proportion of medium-skilled immigrants, vital in the mid-nineteenth century, as did Ireland, along with a substantially larger proportion of high-skilled immigrants, who were crucial to the U.S. economy later in the century. Russia sent a larger proportion of both medium- and high-skilled immigrants to the United States than Italy (see figure 1-4). Merely sending a greater share of immigrants with particular occupation designations does not, however, reveal a particular country's contribution to the stock of such workers in the United States. If workers from some countries have difficulty transplanting their skill sets upon arrival, these figures may overestimate those countries' contributions. Conversely, if innate skills were underutilized in a country of origin (perhaps because of restrictions on entry into specific occupations, such as craft trades), but the workers from that country were able to capitalize on those skills after arriving in the United States, figure 1-4 may

FIGURE 1-4

**IRISH, GERMAN, ITALIAN, AND RUSSIAN IMMIGRANTS
TO THE UNITED STATES BY SKILL LEVEL**

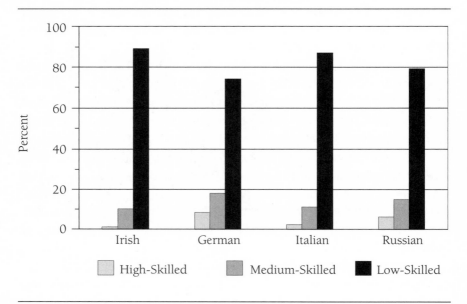

SOURCE: Calculated from U.S. National Archives, Access to Archival Databases (AAD) system, Series GP44.
NOTE: Graph shows Irish immigrants from 1846–51, German immigrants from 1850–97, Italian immigrants from 1855–1900, and Russian immigrants from 1866–97.

underestimate that country's contribution. This issue will be addressed further in the following section.

The differences across these four countries—as well as the overall trend across the nineteenth century—in the proportion of medium- and high-skilled immigrants arriving in the United States do not explain an individual source country's pattern of migration. The mix of skilled and unskilled workers emigrating from a country changes as the stream of migration from that country begins, expands, contracts, and then concludes. The general pattern is one in which the initial emigrants from any country that begins sending workers to the United States are small-scale farmers and petty artisans—the former are displaced by agricultural consolidation, and the latter by modern manufacturing techniques. Both types of worker tend to be somewhat older than less-skilled immigrants, and they often emigrate with their families. As immigration increases from the same source country, passage fares fall and networks of immigrants in the destination country are established, and more unskilled workers find it advantageous to emigrate. At the end of the cycle, even younger workers make the move in large numbers and the proportion of low-skilled immigrants from a source country grows considerably (see Bodnar 1987, 6–16).

The aggregate figures on annual immigration by occupation also make it possible to examine the relative responsiveness of immigrants at different skill levels to economic conditions in the United States. Figures 1-5, 1-6, and 1-7 show the annual numbers of immigrant arrivals in the high-, medium-, and low-skilled categories by year, 1820–1920. The vertical lines superimposed on each figure denote the business-cycle peaks that Davis (2004) identified using a measure of economic activity based on physical quantities of output. This source only extends through 1915, so no post-1915 peaks are shown. Separate figures are generated for each skill level because the vast differences in the scale would obscure sensitivity to business-cycle turning points for the high- and medium-skilled groups.

Before 1900, all three skill levels seem to track U.S. macroeconomic activity similarly: immigration from all three groups declines after each of the four pre–Civil War peaks, and all three groups show little response to the downturn that began in 1864. After 1900, however, some differences emerge: low-skilled immigration falls off sharply after the 1907 peak, but migration by high- and medium-skilled workers continues unabated; and medium- and low-skilled workers respond to the post-1913 downturn, but the number of high-skilled workers had begun to decline nearly three years earlier.

The Process of Assimilation

We now know a great deal about the process of assimilation among immigrants to the United States prior to 1920. Immigrants who arrived prior to 1850 have been followed into the manuscript schedules of the 1850 and 1860 U.S. population censuses, making it possible to assess approximately how long it took immigrants to recover their premigration occupations (Ferrie 1997). This can be done by directly comparing the occupation an immigrant reported in the passenger ship records and the occupation he

FIGURE 1-5

**HIGH-SKILLED IMMIGRATION TO THE UNITED STATES
AND BUSINESS-CYCLE PEAKS, 1820–1920**

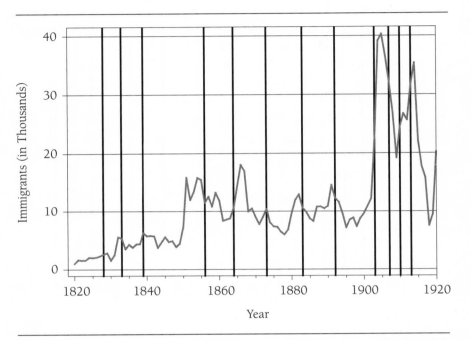

SOURCE: Susan B. Carter et al., eds., *Historical Statistics of the United States: Millennial Edition* (New York: Cambridge University Press, 2006), table AD231–45.

reported in the 1850 and 1860 censuses, together with the number of years between arrival and 1850 or 1860. Immigrants who were enumerated in the U.S. population censuses beginning in 1890 reported the number of years since their arrival in the United States, making it possible to infer how quickly these arrivals came to resemble the native-born U.S. population (Minns 2000).

Figure 1-8 (reproduced from Ferrie 1999, 85) shows that among Germans who arrived in the United States from the high- and middle-skilled groups, more than 75 percent were likely to be employed in a high- or middle-skill occupation almost immediately. British arrivals in these groups were as likely as Germans to be found in high- and middle-skill occupations

FIGURE 1-6

**MEDIUM-SKILLED IMMIGRATION TO THE UNITED STATES
AND BUSINESS-CYCLE PEAKS, 1820–1920**

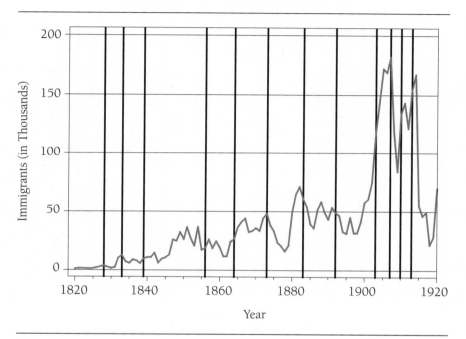

SOURCE: Susan B. Carter et al., eds., *Historical Statistics of the United States: Millennial Edition* (New York: Cambridge University Press, 2006), table AD231–45.

within seven years of living in the United States.[4] However, fewer than half of Irish immigrants who arrived from the high- or middle-skill groups were employed in high- or middle-skill occupations even after ten years in the United States. Ferrie (1999) attributes the poor performance of the Irish more to a lack of economic sophistication and urbanization in Ireland at the time compared to Great Britain and Germany, than to overt discrimination (the notorious "NINA"—"No Irish Need Apply"—signs were actually quite rare; see Jensen 2002) or to the specific skills they reported when they arrived in craft occupations (they were no more likely than the British or Germans to bring skills that were in the process of being displaced by new technologies).

FIGURE 1-7

**LOW-SKILLED IMMIGRATION TO THE UNITED STATES
AND BUSINESS-CYCLE PEAKS, 1820–1920**

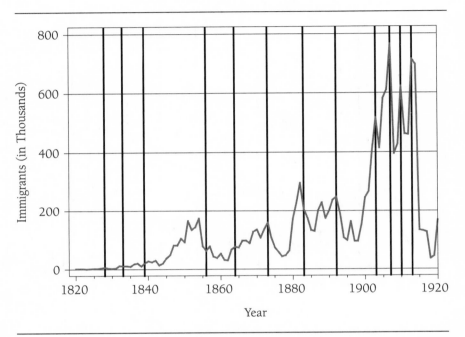

SOURCE: Susan B. Carter et al., eds., *Historical Statistics of the United States: Millennial Edition* (New York: Cambridge University Press, 2006), table AD231–45.

The trajectories depicted in figure 1-8 suggest that for pre–Civil War immigrants, examining only the occupations middle- and high-skilled immigrants reported upon arrival overstates how much they actually added to the stock of middle- and high-skilled workers in the United States (by 25 percent for the Germans and British and by more than 50 percent for the Irish). Even among arrivals from a particular country of origin, it is possible to discern substantial differences in the ability to reattain premigration occupations when comparing immigrants who are identical in most respects. Ferrie (1997, 314) finds that German white-collar, skilled, and semiskilled workers were 50 percent more likely to return to their premigration occupations (controlling for years since arrival) if they arrived in the wake of the

FIGURE 1-8

ESTIMATED PROBABILITY OF AN IMMIGRANT ATTAINING
AN OCCUPATION OTHER THAN UNSKILLED BY YEARS SINCE ARRIVAL,
OCCUPATION AT ARRIVAL, AND SOURCE COUNTRY

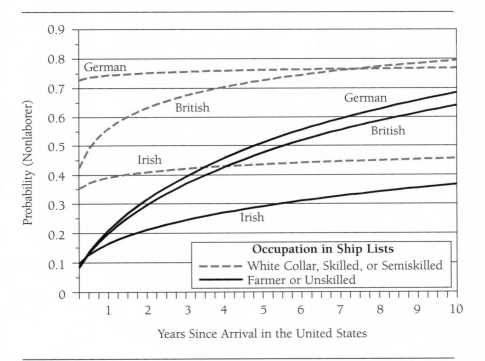

Years Since Arrival in the United States

SOURCE: Joseph P. Ferrie, *Yankeys Now: Immigrants in the Antebellum United States, 1840–60* (New York: Oxford University Press, 1999), 85.

political turbulence that swept across Germany in 1848 than if they arrived prior to 1848; this suggests that conditions in the source country changed to make migration more attractive for many otherwise well-positioned workers (many of these workers were leaders in the "Revolutions of 1848," and had an incentive to emigrate when the uprisings failed).There is a wealth of anecdotal evidence consistent with a pronounced change in the selectivity of German migration to the United States in the wake of the Revolutions of 1848. Levine (1992, 36–37) reports that two-thirds of those who died on Berlin's barricades in the spring of 1848 were urban artisans. A larger fraction of this class of workers had an incentive to migrate after the revolutions because of political concerns, so the population of German emigrants shifted from those who left for primarily economic reasons before the revolutions to a mix of those who left for economic and political reasons after the revolutions. Ferrie (1999, ch. 6) finds that Germans who came to the United States following the revolutions owned less U.S. real estate than other German immigrants, controlling for years since arrival, which is consistent with the sudden, unplanned departure of emigrants who fled Germany after the failure of the revolutions before they had time to liquidate their nonmovable assets. Wittke (1952) documents that Germans who arrived around 1848 tended to be leaders in the German-American community. This suggests that the revolutions, like the Nazi takeover in Germany ninety years later, led many otherwise successful, urban, white-collar and craft workers to flee Germany with little financial capital but substantial human capital, which they used upon arrival in the United States to attain prominence in their communities.

The U.S. censuses of population began to report the number of years since arrival for immigrants in 1890, but these census manuscripts have not survived. Minns (2000) used this information from the 1900 and 1910 census microdata files to assess income growth over the life cycle of immigrants who arrived as adults, controlling for time since arrival. He finds that the effect of years in the United States on income is positive but diminishing as time in the United States increases, even when changes in immigrant quality across successive cohorts are taken into account.[5] Among both white- and blue-collar workers, earnings by immigrant age closely track those for the native born. In the 1910 cross-section, immigrants earn more (controlling for time in the United States) than U.S. natives of the same age (Minns 2000).

The occupations immigrants reported holding in the 1900–1930 censuses can also be used to assess the speed with which immigrants reattained premigration occupations. A focus only on individuals who arrived at ages when they were likely to have acquired their skills in the country of origin (between thirty-five and fifty-five) enables a comparison of the fraction who achieved the occupations previously identified as high-skilled by the start of the twentieth century and the U.S.-born population. This summarizes changes in the quality of arriving immigrants (in part a function of changes in origin countries). To control for the occupation mix in the United States, immigrants are compared to the native-born population. As was the case in the decades before the Civil War, the results in table 1-3 demonstrate that immigrants experienced substantial occupational mobility as their time in the United States increased. The fraction in the highest-skilled occupation group (professional and technical) was higher for immigrants in the United States more than five years than it was for more recent arrivals, though there was no change between those in the United States from five to ten years and those in the United States more than ten years, indicating that most mobility occurred soon after an immigrant's arrival. Similarly, immigrants who have been in the United States for five to ten years are more likely than those who have been in the country fewer than five years to be clerical/sales or craft workers, while the share of immigrants with occupations categorized as unskilled declines by 10.3 percentage points when immigrants in the country for fewer than five years are compared to those in the United States for five to ten years. The change in occupational skill level is less dramatic between immigrants who have been in the United States five to ten years and those who have been in the country for over ten years (in fact, the fraction of immigrants with craft occupations actually declines slightly), suggesting that although immigrants' occupational skill levels improve overall as time in the United States increases, this improvement occurs at a diminishing rate—most of the impact of time in the United States is seen within the first ten years of arrival.

The Impact of High-Skilled Immigrants

We can assess the impact of high-skilled immigrants on the U.S. economy before 1920 in a number of ways. The simplest is to note the extent to which entire industries were transformed by the arrival of particular individuals. After his 1789 arrival to the United States from England, Samuel Slater transformed the U.S. textile industry by introducing the technological innovations that had allowed Britain to dominate the industry in the eighteenth century (Tucker 1981). Henry Burden brought skills from Scotland that he put to use at the National Armory in Springfield, a forerunner

TABLE 1-3

DISTRIBUTION OF NONFARM OCCUPATIONS FOR U.S. BORN AND
IMMIGRANTS BY YEARS IN THE UNITED STATES, 1900–1930 (PERCENT)

Occupation	U.S. Born	Immigrants (by Years in the United States)		
		Under Five Years	Five to Ten Years	Over Ten Years
Profession or Technical	8.2	3.0	3.7	3.7
Clerical/Sales	27.5	8.5	12.4	16.6
Craft	37.9	37.8	43.5	41.8
Unskilled	26.4	50.7	40.4	37.9

SOURCE: Author's calculations from the 1900–1930 Integrated Public Use Microdata Series samples from the U.S. Census of Population manuscripts, Steven J. Ruggles et al., "Integrated Public Use Microdata Series: Version 5.0," Minneapolis: University of Minnesota, 2010.
NOTE: Individuals measured were between thirty-five and sixty-five years old at the time of the census. Immigrants were between thirty-five and fifty-five years old upon arrival in the United States.

of the American machine-tool industry and a vital component of the system of mass production in manufacturing that arose in the mid-nineteenth century. And the foundations of the American chemical industry were laid by a French immigrant to Delaware, Éleuthère Irénée du Pont, whose gunpowder firm not only became one of the world's leading manufacturers but was also a pioneer in business organization (Chandler and Salsbury 1971).

Ferrie and Mokyr (1994) approach this question more systematically: they surveyed entries in the *Dictionary of American Biography* and examined all 1,435 individuals born through 1890 who were active in the United States and reported entrepreneurial occupations (such as industrialist, merchant, banker, financier, capitalist, manufacturer, or businessman) and analyzed their birthplaces. They find that just under 20 percent of these "great entrepreneurs" were born outside the United States at a time when foreign-born individuals made up slightly more than 20 percent of the U.S. white, adult, male population. This demonstrates that immigrants were making noteworthy contributions to the United States in proportion to their representation in the general population. (Of entrepreneurs active in the United States and mentioned in the *Dictionary of American Biography,* nearly a third of those born before 1783 were immigrants.)

A second approach is to examine where immigrants fit into the U.S. occupational structure. We have already examined their skill distribution upon arrival, but were immigrants more or less likely than workers born in the United States to possess high or medium levels of skill? The public use microdata sample file from the 1850–80 and 1900–20 U.S. population censuses can be used to address this question.[6] Figure 1-9 shows the fraction of the U.S. labor force in high- and medium-skilled occupations by place of birth (United States or other). Over the entire seventy-year period, immigrants were nearly as likely as the native born to be in middle-skilled occupations; in fact, in 1880 and 1900, they were just as likely as natives to be in these jobs. Throughout the period, however, immigrants lagged behind natives in holding high-skilled occupations; by the early twentieth century—when these occupations were increasingly crucial to U.S. economic growth—immigrants remained less likely than natives to be found in these jobs. When immigrants are examined separately by country of origin, those who, as a group, most resemble the U.S. native-born workforce are the

FIGURE 1-9

**PERCENTAGE OF WHITE, ADULT MALES IN HIGH- AND MEDIUM-SKILLED
OCCUPATIONS IN THE UNITED STATES, 1850–80 AND 1900–20,
U.S. NATIVES AND IMMIGRANTS**

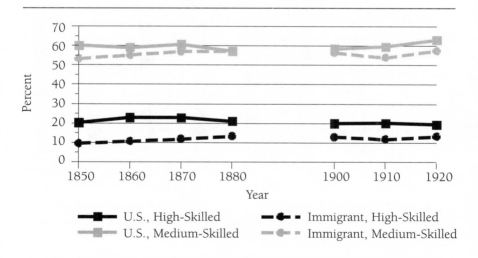

SOURCE: Calculated from the 1850–1920 Integrated Public Use Microdata Series samples from the U.S. Census of Population manuscripts (Ruggles et al., 2010).
NOTE: "Adult" refers to ages twenty to sixty-five.

Russians, who held the largest share of occupations in the high-skilled category. This is consistent with Chiswick's finding (1991) of high achievement among Jewish immigrants to the United States—this group comprises a large fraction of those labeled Russian in figure 1-10.

Uselding (1971–72) provides a more detailed picture of the contribution of skilled immigrants to the U.S. capital stock: he relies on wage differentials by skill level together with the number of immigrants arriving in each year by occupation to estimate the human-capital transfer that immigration entailed.[7] He finds that this transfer amounted to just under 50 percent of the value of gross physical capital formation (GFC) in 1859 alone;

FIGURE 1-10

**PERCENTAGE OF WHITE, ADULT MALES IN HIGH- AND
MEDIUM-SKILLED OCCUPATIONS IN THE UNITED STATES,
1850–80 AND 1900–20, BY ORIGIN**

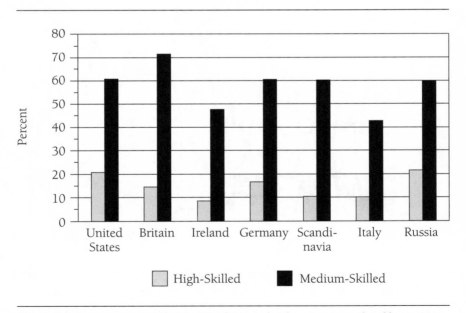

SOURCE: U.S. Census Bureau, "Public Use Microdata Sample Files, 1850–80" and "Public Use Microdata Sample Files, 1900–20," from *Decennial Census* (Washington, DC: National Archives and Records).
NOTE: "Adult" refers to ages twenty to sixty-five.

for some years (for example, 1839, 1849, and 1854) the transfer amounted to more than 75 percent of GFC (Uselding, 1971–72, 57–58). Of the total human-capital transfer in 1859 ($400 million), 24 percent came from the high-skilled group, 32 percent from the medium-skilled group, and 44 percent from the low-skilled group.

Using Uselding's methodology through 1920, the share of the immigration-induced human-capital transfer attributed to each of the three skill groups can be calculated. Figure 1-11 shows this series. The low-skilled group accounted for the majority of the transfer until the imposition of the literacy test in 1917; after the Civil War, the high-skilled group's share remained below 20 percent until the imposition of the literacy test.

FIGURE 1-11

PERCENTAGE OF IMMIGRATION-INDUCED HUMAN-CAPITAL TRANSFER ATTRIBUTED TO EACH SKILL LEVEL UPON ARRIVAL IN THE UNITED STATES

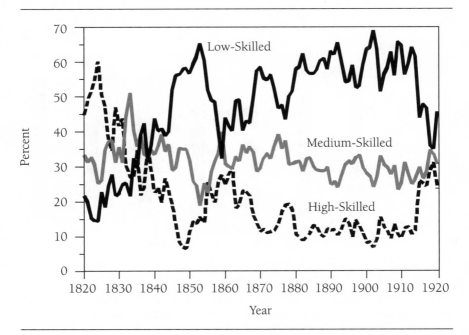

SOURCE: Susan B. Carter et al., eds., *Historical Statistics of the United States: Millennial Edition* (New York: Cambridge University Press, 2006), table AD231–45.

High-Skilled Immigrants and the Transformation of U.S. Industry

The U.S. manufacturing sector underwent a profound transformation over the course of the nineteenth century: small artisan shops using manual techniques were replaced by large factories employing unskilled workers operating increasingly sophisticated machinery. How substantial a role did high-skilled immigrants play in this transformation? In an analysis of the effect immigrant arrivals had on the economic circumstances of native-born workers, Ferrie (1999, 166–82) finds that the arrival of immigrants, particularly of unskilled Irish immigrants, had a large and negative impact on the incomes of craft workers in the urban Northeast between 1850 and 1860. This is consistent with a large body of literature in labor history that assigns immigrants with low skill levels a central role in the process of industrial transformation.

Kim (2007) examines the course of U.S. industrialization after 1850 and concludes that "immigrants not only significantly increased the unskilled to skilled labor endowment, but they also increased the diversity of skills and worker attributes important for division of labor in factories" (23). He also speculates that the pre-1850 immigration of skilled workers from Europe may have hindered the early industrialization of the United States "as many skilled European artisans sought refuge from the spread of European factory production by moving to America" (2).

Ferrie (1999, ch. 8) has examined the occupational mobility of U.S.-born workers over the 1850s (in a sample of individual workers followed from the 1850 census to the 1860 census) and how their fortunes differed according to whether their 1850 county experienced a large influx of foreign-born workers, whether unskilled or craft. An instrumental variables approach was employed to account for the endogeneity of immigrants' location decisions, and the U.S.-born workers were followed to their 1860 locations to account for the full effect of immigrants' arrival (on both performance in the U.S. county of origin and in the destination for those who opted to migrate out of the county). The only negative impact on income (measured as in Minns's work [2000] by occupational income scores) accrued to native-born craft workers in the urban Northeast who moved out of their origin county between 1850 and 1860—this group saw slower income growth than all others. This effect was greatest in counties that saw an influx of largely unskilled Irish workers, suggesting that the transformation of manufacturing from manual to mechanical methods occurred most rapidly in areas where a large, unskilled labor force suddenly became available in the late 1840s and early 1850s.

A substantial body of literature in labor history has described this as a process of "deskilling" in a variety of specific industries. In each case, new techniques were available for adoption by industries previously dominated by small-scale production in artisanal shops. The arrival of unskilled immigrants made the switch to these new techniques cost effective, and native-born craft workers saw their jobs eliminated or downgraded from skilled to semiskilled or unskilled. The reaction to this transformation led to the rise of the Know-Nothing Party, which was the closest the United States ever came to a national, policy-oriented reaction to immigration until the 1890s. The party's base was comprised of just the sort of urban craft workers in the Northeast who were most affected by the process of deskilling. Though the party achieved some electoral successes, its agenda for immigrants never involved anything more extreme than advocating for an extension of the time between immigrants' arrival and their eligibility for citizenship; an outright ban on particular types of immigrants was never on the table.

The more general question of the impact of immigrants' arrival on U.S. manufacturing performance can be investigated systematically by taking advantage of information on the changing mix of occupations for immigrants and natives in each U.S. county and the aforementioned published tabulations on the measures of manufacturing performance: capital per worker and output per worker. In order to account roughly for the endogeneity of the location decisions natives and immigrants made and the importance of unmeasured heterogeneity across counties, the *change* in manufacturing performance measures between time $t + 10$ and time t (for example, between 1880 and 1870) is compared to the *change* in the occupational mix for natives and immigrants between time t and time $t-10$ (for example, between 1870 and 1860).

Figures 1-12 (U.S.-born) and 1-13 (immigrants) show the county-level link between the change in per worker output 1870–80 (on the y-axis) and the change in the share of craft workers in the U.S. labor force 1860–70 (on the x-axis). Counties with a larger rise in the share of U.S.-born workers in craft occupations had higher per worker output growth a decade later than

FIGURE 1-12

CHANGE IN PER WORKER OUTPUT 1870–80 VERSUS CHANGE
IN SHARE OF WORKERS IN CRAFT OCCUPATIONS 1860–70,
U.S.-BORN WORKERS, BY U.S. COUNTY

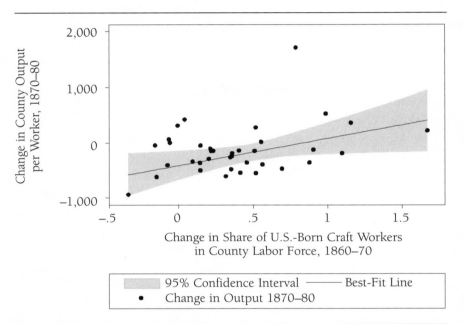

Change in Share of U.S.-Born Craft Workers
in County Labor Force, 1860–70

SOURCE: Calculations based on the 1860, 1870, 1910, and 1920 Integrated Public Use Microdata Series
samples from the U.S. Census of Population manuscripts (Ruggles et al., 2010); and county-level data from
the 1860, 1870, 1880, 1910, 1920, and 1930 U.S. Census of Manufactures (Haines and ICPSR, 2010).

counties with a smaller share. The same effect was not apparent for foreign-
born craft workers. More U.S.-born craft workers were associated with
lower growth of capital per worker (see figure 1-14); again, no effect was
apparent for immigrants (see figure 1-15).

For the early twentieth century, the change in output per worker
1920–30 was unrelated to the change in the share of the county workforce
1910–20 in either craft or professional and technical occupations; this was
true for both U.S.-born and foreign-born workers. Though capital per
worker is not available at the county level in the early twentieth century
data, another measure of economic development, horsepower per worker,

FIGURE 1-13

CHANGE IN PER WORKER OUTPUT 1870–80 VERSUS CHANGE IN SHARE OF WORKERS IN CRAFT OCCUPATIONS 1860–70, FOREIGN-BORN WORKERS, BY U.S. COUNTY

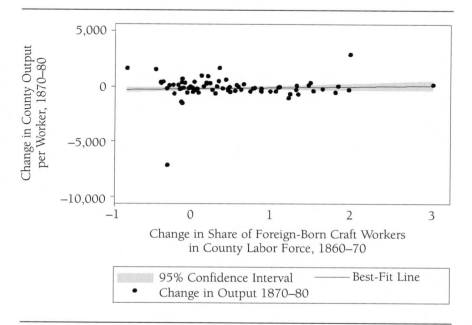

Change in Share of Foreign-Born Craft Workers
in County Labor Force, 1860–70

SOURCE: Calculations based on the 1860, 1870, 1910, and 1920 Integrated Public Use Microdata Series samples from the U.S. Census of Population manuscripts (Ruggles et al., 2010); and county-level data from the 1860, 1870, 1880, 1910, 1920, and 1930 U.S. Census of Manufactures (Haines and ICPSR, 2010).

is an effective substitute. For both U.S.-born and foreign-born workers, an increase in the share of the workforce in craft jobs was associated with an increase in the horsepower used per worker ten years later. The effect was somewhat larger for the U.S.-born population (see figure 1-16) than for the foreign-born population (see figure 1-17). No effect was observed for the highest-skill group (professional and technical).

Taken together, these results demonstrate that throughout the 1860–1930 period, the share of foreign-born workers in craft or professional and technical occupations had less impact on several measures of industrial development (output, capital, and horsepower per worker) than

FIGURE 1-14

**CHANGE IN PER WORKER CAPITAL 1870–80 VERSUS CHANGE
IN SHARE OF WORKERS IN CRAFT OCCUPATIONS 1860–70,
U.S.-BORN WORKERS, BY U.S. COUNTY**

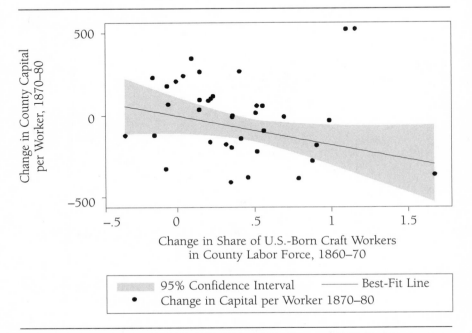

Change in Share of U.S.-Born Craft Workers
in County Labor Force, 1860–70

SOURCE: Calculations based on the 1860, 1870, 1910, and 1920 Integrated Public Use Microdata Series samples from the U.S. Census of Population manuscripts (Ruggles et al., 2010); and county-level data from the 1860, 1870, 1880, 1910, 1920, and 1930 U.S. Census of Manufactures (Haines and ICPSR, 2010).

did the share of U.S.-born workers in these same occupations. Even the impact of changes in the share of U.S.-born craft workers is not entirely clear: an increase in the share of craft workers is associated with a larger increase in output per worker a decade later, but also with a smaller increase in capital per worker. In any case, there is no strong evidence to support the view that the arrival of foreign-born craft workers in the middle of the nineteenth century impeded industrial development. If anything, the evidence cited above from Ferrie (1999, ch. 8) suggests that the arrival of Irish immigrants may have spurred the adoption of new production techniques. The lack of a discernible impact from the highest-skilled groups, among either

FIGURE 1-15

CHANGE IN PER WORKER CAPITAL 1870–80 VERSUS CHANGE
IN SHARE OF WORKERS IN CRAFT OCCUPATIONS 1860–70,
FOREIGN-BORN WORKERS, BY U.S. COUNTY

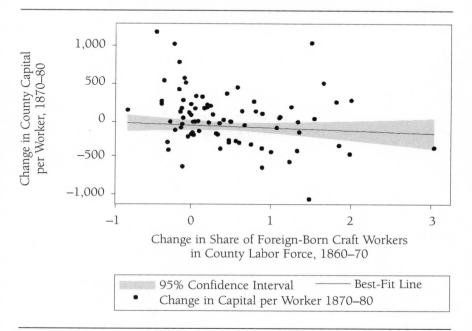

SOURCE: Calculations based on the 1860, 1870, 1910, and 1920 Integrated Public Use Microdata Series samples from the U.S. Census of Population manuscripts (Ruggles et al., 2010); and county-level data from the 1860, 1870, 1880, 1910, 1920, and 1930 U.S. Census of Manufactures (Haines and ICPSR, 2010).

U.S.-born or foreign-born workers, might result from the extremely small sample sizes (the profession and technical groups amounted to no more than 2 percent of the workforce in industry).

Conclusion

The record of high-skilled immigration before the imposition of binding restrictions on entry into the United States in 1921 has been less closely examined than the record of less-skilled immigration. The available evidence suggests that this emphasis has rendered an incomplete view of the

FIGURE 1-16

CHANGE IN PER WORKER HORSEPOWER 1920–30 VERSUS CHANGE
IN SHARE OF WORKERS IN CRAFT OCCUPATIONS 1910–20,
U.S.-BORN WORKERS

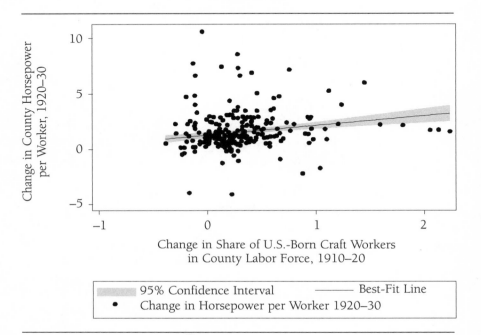

Change in Share of U.S.-Born Craft Workers
in County Labor Force, 1910–20

95% Confidence Interval   ———— Best-Fit Line
•   Change in Horsepower per Worker 1920–30

SOURCE: Calculations based on the 1860, 1870, 1910, and 1920 Integrated Public Use Microdata Series
samples from the U.S. Census of Population manuscripts (Ruggles et al., 2010); and county-level data from
the 1860, 1870, 1880, 1910, 1920, and 1930 U.S. Census of Manufactures (Haines and ICPSR, 2010).

process of immigration. A number of lessons for the formulation of current
immigration policy can be drawn from the slightly more complete picture
presented in this chapter.

The first is that the term "high skilled" needs to be defined within a particular temporal and technological context: from the perspective of
national economic growth, the most desirable immigrants may possess
very different skill sets today than they did in the mid-nineteenth century.
For example, Kim (2007) suggests that low-skilled migration enhanced
and craft-worker migration hindered early U.S. industrialization, though
no evidence for this view was found at the county level. The second lesson

FIGURE 1-17

CHANGE IN PER WORKER HORSEPOWER 1920–30 VERSUS CHANGE IN SHARE OF WORKERS IN CRAFT OCCUPATIONS 1910–20, FOREIGN-BORN WORKERS

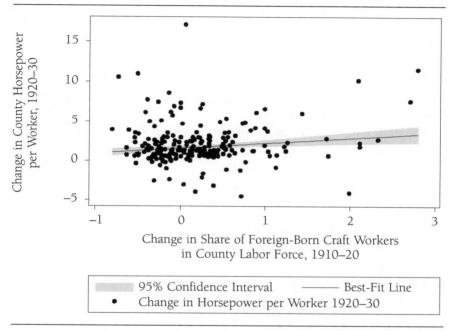

Change in Share of Foreign-Born Craft Workers
in County Labor Force, 1910–20

| 95% Confidence Interval | ——— Best-Fit Line |
| • Change in Horsepower per Worker 1920–30 | |

SOURCE: Calculations based on the 1860, 1870, 1910, and 1920 Integrated Public Use Microdata Series samples from the U.S. Census of Population manuscripts (Ruggles et al., 2010); and county-level data from the 1860, 1870, 1880, 1910, 1920, and 1920 U.S. Census of Manufactures (Haines and ICPSR, 2010).

is that the mix of high- and low-skilled immigrants differs enormously across source countries; even for a particular source country, the mix will differ according to whether the country has just begun sending immigrants or is well into the process of sending immigrants. This mix can also change rapidly in the short run—in fact, the quality of skilled immigrants can change in the short run even within a given mix of skilled and unskilled immigrants—in response to circumstances in the country of origin (for example, see the superior performance of the German skilled workers who came to the United States in the wake of the Revolutions of 1848). Finally, in order to understand the contribution of skilled immigrants to the U.S.

stock of human capital, it is necessary to know more about the process of assimilation and adjustment immigrants experienced: if the skills reported at arrival are not put to use after entry, the benefits of skilled migration will be overstated.

These considerations suggest that a policy to encourage immigration that will supply the skills most in demand at a particular point in time must have three characteristics. First, it must identify the skills that will be in demand in coming years, because after a particular cohort of immigrants arrives—unless those immigrants are admitted as guest workers—the skills the immigrants possess might no longer match those in demand. This is akin to picking which sectors of an economy will be winners and losers, as attempted under the formulation of the "industrial policy" espoused in the last quarter of the twentieth century. That policy was ultimately unable to overcome the challenges posed by trying to predict the future. If immigration policy had been formulated by a benevolent social planner in the middle of the nineteenth century when U.S. cities were inundated with large numbers of unskilled Irish immigrants, it might have seemed reasonable to favor the immigration instead of higher-skilled workers—after all, such craft and clerical workers were the backbone of U.S. manufacturing to that point. But such a policy could have delayed by decades the adoption of new techniques made economical by the arrival of unskilled Irish immigrants.

The second characteristic required of a sound, new, skill-based policy is a high degree of confidence for any particular migrant admitted that the immigrant's skills will actually be employed in the United States, unless entry is explicitly made conditional on employment in a particular high-demand occupation. Workers' particular skills, though adequate on paper, may be a poor match for the actual jobs available to them in the United States. Consider the aforementioned Irish craft workers: though they arrived with the same occupational titles as craft workers from Britain and Germany, they had much more difficulty escaping unskilled work as their time in the United States increased because of unobserved background characteristics (for example, their origins in a much less urban and sophisticated labor market as compared to the origins of the British and Germans). Even if their skills are in demand in the United States, immigrants may choose to take advantage of other employment opportunities if such opportunities had not been available to them in their country of origin. In the absence of a mechanism to ensure that matches between workers' skills and particular jobs persist, a policy of encouraging workers with defined skill sets to enter the United States may not prove effective.

The third characteristic that the policy must possess is insulation from the political process. Three constituencies will arise within the United States in response to immigration, just as they did in the United States in the nineteenth century. As immigrants from a particular origin increase in number in the United States, they will lobby for additional migrants from the same country. As previously noted, the characteristics of migrants from a particular country change as the migration stream from a country begins, matures, and ends, so a policy that simply favors arrivals on the basis of the mix of skills that emigrants from a country possess at one time will not produce a good match with skills in demand in the United States. The second constituency that will arise is employers who become dependent on workers with particular skill sets. As time passes and the businesses are displaced as cutting-edge sectors, other sectors will need to see immigrants with the skills they demand admitted instead. Finally, native-born workers with skills may view immigrants with similar skills as a threat. In the nineteenth century, these problems were muted by a lack of interest in Congress in reducing the stream of immigration at all, let alone in ways that would favor the entry of workers with particular skills. At that time, the U.S. economy was growing rapidly, with cities springing up and industries being transformed in short order. At present, when some resources are seen as more scarce, competition among these three constituencies will place enormous pressure on the institutions in place to foster high-skilled migration.

Some cautions are also in order in drawing policy lessons from the U.S. experience 1820–1920: history does not always provide an adequate guide to policymakers when circumstances have changed dramatically. The evidence on high-skilled immigration to the nineteenth-century United States is from an era when trade in goods was not particularly "free"—this may have skewed patterns of factor prices in ways that led to outcomes that would not be observed today. This was also an era when the United States was growing rapidly, when organized labor was weak, and when new technologies that could make extensive use of unskilled labor were readily available. Finally, the process by which high-skilled immigrants acquire much of the human capital they employ in the United States has changed: in the 1820–1920 period, skills could be acquired in the home country through training and apprenticeship programs and on-the-job experience, and these skills were then brought to the United States; today, many immigrants acquire most of their skills in graduate education programs at U.S. universities (Bound and Walsh 2009). Thus, what we mean today by "skilled" immigrants may no longer be simply a set of well-defined workplace competencies.

Notes

1. For a description of U.S. immigration statistics, as well as the legal context for immigration into the United States, see Carter and Sutch (2006).

2. These records were obtained from the U.S. National Archives, Access to Archival Databases (AAD) system, series GP44.

3. Ibid. The specific occupations appearing in each category are as follows: low-skilled immigrants include farmers and laborers; middle-skilled immigrants include carpenters, blacksmiths, weavers, tailors, masons, and clerks; and high-skilled immigrants include physicians, lawyers, merchants, engineers, and scientists.

4. The figures are based on the three parameters of a continuous-time-duration model with discrete observations and a Weibull hazard (Ferrie 1999, 82–83).

5. Income was not reported for individual U.S. Census respondents until 1940, so Minns (2000) relies on average incomes by occupation to construct these profiles. This procedure necessarily understates the growth of income with time in the United States, as it only measures changes in incomes that occur without crossing occupational boundaries.

6. Individual-level data from the 1890 census manuscripts are missing. The schedules were damaged by fire in 1921 and finally destroyed in 1935.

7. Gallman (1977) criticizes many of the assumptions underlying Uselding's calculations. However, the changes Gallman suggests would mainly alter the level of the human-capital transfer in any particular year, not the distribution of that transfer across occupational categories.

References

Atack, Jeremy, and Fred Bateman. 2004. National Sample from the 1880 Census of Manufacturing. 2nd ICPSR version. Urbana, IL: University of Illinois; Bloomington, IN: Indiana University; and Ann Arbor, MI: Inter-university Consortium for Political and Social Research (ICPSR).

Atack, Jeremy, Fred Bateman, and Thomas Weiss. 2004. National Samples from the Census of Manufacturing: 1850, 1860, and 1870. ICPSR04048-v1. Ann Arbor, MI: ICPSR.

Bodnar, John. 1987. *The Transplanted: A History of Immigrants in Urban America.* Bloomington, IN: Indiana University Press.

Bound, J., S. Turner, and P. Walsh. 2009. Internationalization of U.S. Doctorate Education. National Bureau of Economic Research (NBER) Working Paper 14792, Washington, DC.

Carter, S. B., S. S. Gartner, M. R. Haines, A. L. Olmstead, R. Sutch, and G. Wright, eds. 2006. *Historical Statistics of the United States: Millennial Edition.* New York: Cambridge University Press.

Carter, S. B., and R. Sutch. 2006. International Migration. In *Historical Statistics of the United States: Millennial Edition,* ed. S. B. Carter, S. S. Gartner, M. R. Haines, A. L. Olmstead, R. Sutch, and G. Wright, 1-523–1-652. New York: Cambridge University Press.

Center for Immigration Research. 1976–2003. Records of the Center for Immigration Research, 1976–2003. Washington, DC: National Archives and Records Service, Archival Research Catalog Identifier 566631.

Chandler, A. D. Jr., and S. Salsbury. 1971. *Pierre S. Du Pont and the Making of the Modern Corporation.* New York: Harper and Row.

Chiswick, Barry R. 1991. Jewish Immigrant Skill and Occupational Attainment at the Turn of the Century. *Explorations in Economic History* 28: 64–86.

Davis, J. H. 2004. An Annual Index of U.S. Industrial Production, 1790–1915. *Quarterly Journal of Economics* 119:1177–1215.

Ferrie, Joseph P. 1997. The Entry into the U.S. Labor Market of Antebellum European Immigrants, 1840–1860. *Explorations in Economic History* 34: 295–330.

———. 1999. *Yankeys Now: Immigrants in the Antebellum United States, 1840–60* (New York: Oxford University Press).

Ferrie, Joseph P., and Joel Mokyr. 1994. Immigration and Entrepreneurship in the Nineteenth Century U.S. In *Economic Aspects of International Migration,* ed. H. Giersch, 115–38. New York: Springer-Verlag.

Galenson, D. W. 1981. The Market Evaluation of Human Capital: The Case of Indentured Servitude. *Journal of Political Economy* 89:446–67.

Gallman, R. E. 1977. Human Capital in the First 80 Years of the Republic: How Much Did America Owe the Rest of the World? *American Economic Review* 67:27–31.

Haines, Michael R., and ICPSR. 2010. Historical, Demographic, Economic, and Social Data: The United States, 1790–2002. ICPSR02896-v3. Ann Arbor, MI: ICPSR.

Hatton, Timothy J., and Jeffrey G. Williamson. 2005. *Global Migration and the World Economy: Two Centuries of Policy and Performance*. Cambridge, MA: MIT Press.

Jensen, R. 2002. "No Irish Need Apply": A Myth of Victimization. *Journal of Social History* 36:405–29

Kim, S. 2007. Immigration, Industrial Revolution and Urban Growth in the United States, 1820–1920: Factor Endowments, Technology and Geography. NBER Working Paper 12900, Washington, DC.

Levine, B. 1992. *The Spirit of 1848: German Immigrants, Labor Conflict, and the Coming of the Civil War*. Urbana, IL: University of Illinois Press.

Margo, R. A. 2000. *Wages and Labor Markets in the United States, 1820–1860*. Chicago: University of Chicago Press.

Minns, C. 2000. Income, Cohort Effects, and Occupational Mobility: A New Look at Immigration to the United States at the Turn of the 20th Century. *Explorations in Economic History* 37:326–50.

Ruggles, Steven J., Trent Alexander, Katie Genadek, Ronald Goeken, Matthew B. Schroeder, and Matthew Sobek. 2010. Integrated Public Use Microdata Series: Version 5.0. Minneapolis: University of Minnesota.

Tucker, B. M. 1981. The Merchant, the Manufacturer, and the Factory Manager: The Case of Samuel Slater. *Business History Review* 55:297–313.

Uselding, P. J. 1971–72. Conjectural Estimates of Gross Human Capital Inflows to the American Economy: 1790–1860. *Explorations in Economic History* 10:49–61.

Wittke, C. 1952. *Refugees of Revolution: The German Forty-eighters in America*. Philadelphia: University of Pennsylvania Press.

2

Rights-Based Politics, Immigration, and the Business Cycle, 1890–2008

James F. Hollifield and Carole J. Wilson

Since the end of World War II, immigration to the United States has been steadily increasing. The rise in immigration is a function of market forces (demand-side pull and supply-side push) and of the development of kinship networks, which reduce the transaction costs of moving from one society to another. These economic and sociological forces are necessary conditions for migration to occur, but the sufficient conditions are legal and political. Over time, rights accrue to immigrants—whether they are in the country legally or illegally. How, then, do states regulate immigration in the face of economic and legal forces that push them toward greater openness while security concerns and powerful political forces push them toward closure? The United States is trapped in a "liberal" paradox: to maintain a competitive advantage, the United States, like other liberal democracies with mixed capitalist economies, must remain open to immigration while protecting the social contract and the rights of citizens (Hollifield 1992; 2004).

With the gradual rollback of the national-origins quota system in the 1950s and its eventual repeal in 1965, U.S. immigration policy became increasingly liberal and expansive. The liberalization continued throughout

The authors wish to thank Örn B. Bodvarsson, Barry R. Chiswick, Valerie F. Hunt, Pia Orrenius, and Daniel J. Tichenor for their input and helpful comments. Errors, of course, are the authors' alone.

the 1980s and was reinforced by the passage of the Immigration Reform and Control Act (IRCA) of 1986 and the Immigration Act of 1990, both of which opened the door wider to skilled and unskilled immigration. A new round of restrictive policies began in the 1990s with the passage of Proposition 187 in California, which was designed to limit immigrants' access to public services. Although Prop 187 was struck down on constitutional grounds, it created political momentum for passage of the Illegal Immigration Reform and Immigrant Responsibility Act (IIRAIRA) of 1996, which curtailed some welfare and due process rights of immigrants. Despite these new, more restrictive policies, the fourth wave of immigration in U.S. history continued unabated into the first decade of the twenty-first century, and it has only just begun to slow down as a result of the global economic crisis of 2008–2009. What has sustained this long period of expansion in U.S. immigration in the post-1945 era? How does this period differ from the pre-1945 period, which saw the United States move from an expansive immigration regime marked by the third wave of immigration, which lasted from the 1890s until World War I, to an increasingly closed regime that began with the passage in 1924 of the Johnson-Reed Act (national-origins quota system) and continued through the Great Depression of the 1930s until the end of World War II (Tichenor 2002)?

A casual observer might be tempted to say that throughout the modern and contemporary period, from the third through the fourth wave, immigration has mirrored the business cycle and the performance of the American labor market. However, our findings indicate that economic forces explain only some of the variation in immigration levels in the pre-1945 period, and they are a very poor indicator of immigration in the post-1945 era. From the 1950s through the 2000s, policy effects have had a greater impact on immigration than business cycles. We argue that these expansive policy effects and the break with the business cycle after World War II are linked to the rise of rights-based politics as manifested in "rights-markets" coalitions in Congress (Hollifield 1992; Cornelius, Martin, and Hollifield 1994). We also demonstrate the impact of civil rights politics on immigration and refugee policy, from the Immigration and Nationality Act of 1965 through the 1986 and 1990 acts. The coalitions that formed around the issues of rights and markets (votes on trade and immigration in particular) create strange-bedfellow coalitions of left-liberals (Democrats) and libertarian-conservatives (Republicans). These coalitions helped to sustain liberal immigration and refugee policies until the end of the cold war, but the end of the cold war led to the breakdown of these coalitions (Hollifield, Hunt, and Tichenor 2008).

Politics Matters

In much of the immigration literature, politics is assigned at best a marginal role in migration theory (Hollifield 2008; Portes 1997). According to the push-pull logic, changing economic and demographic conditions (demand-side pull and supply-side push) in sending and receiving countries largely determine levels of immigration to countries like the United States (Martin and Midgley 1994). Similarly the sociological literature on immigration stresses the growth of transnational, informational, and kinship networks, which reduce transaction costs and facilitate cross-border movements (Massey et al. 1987; Sassen 1996; Portes 1996). Since there has been a virtually unlimited supply of migrants ready to cross international borders in the postwar period (a more or less constant supply-side push), most adherents to the economic model contend that shifting demand for foreign labor is the primary determinant of immigration flows (indicating that the demand-side pull varies). By this logic, major shifts in the volume of immigration are driven by labor-market demands and the business cycle in receiving countries. At the same time, economic models assume that policies designed to control immigration are of marginal importance. Either policy interventions merely rubber-stamp labor-market demands and the business cycle as the state is captured by powerful pro-immigration lobbies, or policies are deemed to have no effect because they defy the key economic forces (Freeman 1995; Simon 1989). To some extent, sociological theories of immigration replicate this basic microeconomic push-pull logic, but with the major innovation that international migration is heavily dependent on the development of informational and kinship networks between the sending and receiving communities (Massey et al. 1987; Portes 1996; Massey, Durand, and Malone 2002; Sassen 1988, 1996). Neither economic nor sociological arguments leave much room for policy as a major factor affecting immigration flows.

If politics matters, how can we demonstrate the effects of policy change on immigration while holding economic conditions constant? Employing a time-series model that enables us to separate the economic and policy effects on immigration to the United States from 1890 to 2008, we find that both policy interventions and changing U.S. economic conditions have a significant impact on immigration, although not always in ways we would expect. The model suggests that shifts in unemployment in particular had a sizable and significant effect on levels of legal immigration prior to 1945. During the postwar years of 1946–2008, however, the effects of macroeconomic changes on immigration weaken over time while the impact of policy increases.

These findings are supported by considerable evidence that federal policies, which significantly influenced immigration flows after World War II, won important support from national officials whose goals reached well beyond the demands of the labor market or business cycle. Against the backdrop of cold war politics, executive and congressional officials after 1945 came to view immigration control as an important instrument for advancing American foreign policy objectives (Tichenor 2002). Anticommunism animated contending immigration policy camps in the late 1940s and 1950s. Congressional isolationists successfully defended national-origins quotas and established new ideological exclusions with the McCarren-Walter Act of 1952, despite economic conditions that were conducive to large-scale immigration. By contrast, during and immediately after World War II, internationalists in the White House and Congress expanded refugee admissions and ended Asian exclusion in order to enhance American power and prestige abroad.

By the 1960s, New Frontier and Great Society reformers dismantled restrictive national-origins quotas in the name of advancing racial justice and equal rights (Dudziak 2000; Borstelmann 2003). Immigration reform in 1965 (the Hart-Celler Act) expanded alien admissions to allow for family reunification, to provide a haven for refugees fleeing communist regimes, and to offer new immigration opportunities for ethnic and racial groups long excluded by American law. During the 1980s, new reforms expanded immigration more dramatically. They were propelled by an unlikely coalition of liberal lawmakers, who embraced civil and human rights and ethnic fairness in national immigration policy, and free-market conservatives in

Congress and the executive branch, who saw immigration restriction as antithetical to regulatory relief and open markets. Moreover, the federal courts became increasingly active after the 1960s in protecting the due-process rights of foreigners in admissions, asylum, and deportation proceedings (Schuck 1998). The development of American immigration policy in the postwar era, then, captures changing U.S. economic conditions as often less consequential than policy interventions by various actors in government. Indeed, as we shall see below, national officials have promoted immigration policies that, at times, run counter to economic trends in the United States—the Immigration Act of 1990, for example, was passed in the midst of a recession.

The strong impact of changing U.S. economic conditions on immigration flows before 1945 and the larger significance of state actions in subsequent years underscore the need for greater theoretical balance in the scholarly literature on immigration. In the pages that follow, we examine U.S. immigration trends from the late nineteenth century to 2008 in light of labor-market dynamics and the business cycle.

How does policy influence immigration independent of economic conditions? Figure 2-1 depicts immigration to the United States, as measured by the total number of legal permanent residents (LPRs, or green cards) and status adjustors, which are people who enter the United States under one legal status and then adjust or change to permanent residence while they are in the country (Department of Homeland Security 2009). Immigration decreased from about 600,000 per annum in 1892 to 250,000 by the end of the decade. This decline coincided with the 1893–97 recession, affirming that immigration flows were responsive to economic conditions at the end of the nineteenth century. Immigration rebounded strongly—as did the economy—at the turn of the century, and at the same time unemployment rates were well below the average historically. In short, demand-pull factors were especially conducive to immigration at the turn of the century, and immigration flows reached record levels in the first decade of the twentieth century. The foreign-born share of the population climbed to almost 15 percent in 1910, an all-time high. Yet no major immigration legislation was passed during this period, with the exception of literacy tests Congress imposed a bit later, in 1917—restrictions that were rendered moot by the effects of World War I (1914–18), which abruptly ended the third wave of immigration.

FIGURE 2-1

IMMIGRATION TO THE UNITED STATES, 1890–2008

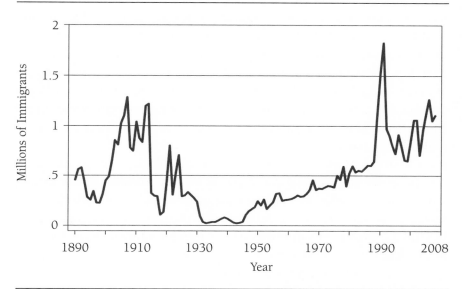

SOURCE: U.S. Department of Homeland Security, *Yearbook of Immigration Statistics,* 2009, available at http://www.dhs.gov/files/statistics/publications/LPR09.shtm (accessed August 2, 2010).
NOTE: Number of immigrants is based on the total number of legal permanent residents and status adjustors in each year.

In the interwar years, immigration revived but fluctuated markedly in reaction to the volatile economic conditions of the Roaring Twenties. The 1924 Immigration and Naturalization Act (also known as the Johnson-Reed Act) brought the nation's first permanent and sweeping numerical limits on immigration. These restrictive measures codified the national-origins quota system, writing a racial hierarchy (in favor of Northern and Western Europeans) into American law (King 2000, 2005). The 1924 law also introduced some skill-based, human-capital criteria into U.S. immigration policy. But by locking in a strong bias in favor of Northern and Western Europeans (and locking out immigrants from Southern and Eastern Europe), the national-origins quota system led to less immigration from Europe and more from the Western Hemisphere, for which the quotas did not apply. Canadians and Mexicans comprised the largest number of newcomers during the 1920s. The onset of the Great Depression in 1929–30 had a powerful effect on immigration flows: demand-pull forces ceased virtually overnight, as the economy shrank and unemployment soared. Annual immigration remained markedly low during the economic difficulties of the 1930s (see figure 2-1).

The recovery of the American economy during World War II led to a rapid decline in unemployment rates and a surge in the gross domestic product (GDP), but no real increase in immigration. Adherents of the push-pull model can account for these outcomes by emphasizing the anomalous and exceptional effects of global warfare that cut the United States off from traditional European sources of immigrant labor. U.S. employers turned increasingly to Mexican and Central American workers to address labor-market demands, especially in agriculture—a trend that was codified in the 1942 *bracero* program that continued until 1963 (Calavita 1992). During the postwar years 1945–2008, as figure 2-1 demonstrates, immigration trended upward for almost the entire period, culminating in the fourth wave of immigration that began in the 1970s and accelerated in the 1980s and 1990s. Strikingly, immigration flows did not expand much in the 1950s (1950 and 1952 witnessed declining immigration numbers) despite significant increases in GDP and new lows in unemployment. Just as intriguing is the gradual increase in immigration during the 1970s and early 1980s, a time when unemployment levels were rising in connection with the two oil shocks and the steep recession that followed. However, immigration began to soar in the late 1980s and has continued unabated through the 1990s and into the 2000s.

Immigration and the Rise of Rights-Based Politics

Throughout its history, the United States has relied heavily upon immigration for westward expansion, settlement, colonization, and economic development. It is no exaggeration to say that immigration has played a critical role in national development, and there have been four great waves of immigration if we count the initial colonization by settlers from the British Isles. In this section, we seek to answer two questions. First, to what extent is immigration in the pre- and postwar periods a function of macroeconomic forces? Second, to what extent was immigration promoted, managed, and regulated by the U.S. government?

From the 1890s through World War II, levels of immigration to the United States corresponded closely with the performance of the American economy. Indeed, the time-series model presented below (see table 2-1) suggests that shifts in levels of unemployment had a significant effect on annual immigration totals before 1945. Yet even as the economic cycles help explain U.S. immigration trends before the mid-twentieth century, the

TABLE 2-1

MODEL PREDICTING LEVELS OF IMMIGRATION, 1890–2008, USING ORDINARY LEAST SQUARES (OLS) REGRESSION

Dependent Variable (Annual Levels of Immigration)	OLS Coefficient	Standard Errors
Economic Effects		
Percent Change in GDP	−524.8	(3,711.6)
Unemployment	−10,232.6[a]	(5,402.1)
Post-1945 Dummy Variable	−221,320.3[a]	(127,441.1)
Percent Change in GDP * Post-1945 Dummy Variable	−4,252.5	(8,452.0)
Unemployment * Post-1945 Dummy Variable	11,644.0	(19,088.0)
Policy Shock Dummy Variables		
1925–40 (1924 Johnson-Reed Act)	−144,230.3[b]	(67,525.8)
1953–65 (1952 McCarren-Walter Act)	20,036.4	(83,864.9)
1966–86 (1965 Hart-Celler Act)	97,721.6	(86,597.6)
1987–90 (1986 IRCA)	429,294.5[b]	(117,838.4)
1991–96 (1990 Immigration Act)	241,212.6[a]	(123,257.0)
1997–2008 (1996 IIRAIRA)	284,031.9	(100,266.4)
Controls		
World War I	−250,760.4[b]	(127,719.3)
World War II	−262,060.7[a]	(97,042.8)
$Y_{(t-1)}$	0.61[b]	(0.077)
Constant	317,631.2[b]	(76,625.9)
Observations	119	
Degrees of Freedom	104	
R-Squared	0.78	
Portmanteau Q	45.53	Not Significant

SOURCE: Authors' calculations.
NOTE: a. $p < 0.1$, b. $p < 0.05$.

unprecedented activism of the U.S. government in these decades had a marked effect on the nature of legal immigration flows. The dramatic decline of immigration during U.S. involvement in World Wars I and II highlights the extent to which immigration is a function of global dynamics that escape the control of the U.S. government. But, if changes in the American labor market and business cycle before the mid-twentieth century go far in explaining *how many* immigrants were admitted in these years (immigration volume), they do little to help us understand significant shifts in *who* was granted entry during these decades (immigration composition).

For most of the nineteenth century, the federal government maintained an essentially laissez-faire immigration policy in which regulatory authority devolved to states and localities (Fuchs 1990; Schuck 1998; Hatton and Williamson 1998; Tichenor 2002). When the federal government first developed the legal and administrative means to regulate immigration in the late nineteenth century, its efforts to control immigration were motivated often as much by a devotion to ethnic and racial hierarchy as by a concern for the country's economic and national security interests (Fuchs 1990; Smith 1997; King 2000, 2005). Against the backdrop of intense electoral competition during the post-Reconstruction period, congressional and executive officials of both parties clamored to curry favor with Sinophobic voters in the western United States by enacting the first Chinese exclusion laws in the 1880s (Mink 1986; King 2000). During the interwar years, the economic impact of immigration figured prominently in the minds of national officials, and they wasted no time in slowing immigration to all but a trickle during the 1920s and 1930s. But the centerpiece of this period's restrictive immigration policies, the national-origins quota system, was deeply informed by a new scientific theory—eugenics—that reinvigorated old distinctions between desirable and unworthy immigrants on the basis of race, ethnicity, and religion (Higham 1955; Fuchs 1990; Smith 1997; King 2000).

The new quota system was explicitly planned to favor Northern and Western European immigrants, and to exclude Asians, Africans, and Southern and Eastern Europeans. At the same time, Mexican migrants were viewed by most officials as a returnable labor force—due to a contiguous border—which could meet the nation's shifting demands for low-skilled labor without allowing these temporary migrants to make permanent claims for membership in U.S. society (Calavita 1992; Garcia y Griego 1989). Only lip service was given to the value of high-skilled immigrants or human capital because immigration during the interwar period was viewed primarily as a source of manpower and population needed to fire the engines of industrialization and farm the land. Until the 1960s, U.S. immigration essentially reflected these policy goals; Northern and Western Europeans comprised most overseas immigration to the country, while Mexican and other Latin American newcomers were typically admitted as guest workers subject to removal whenever their labor was not in demand (Garcia y Griego 1989; Ngai 2004; Zolberg 2006), and Asians were by and large excluded. The U.S. government's influence on immigration flows before 1945, then, captures not only how the government's policies responded to changing economic conditions but also the government's pursuit of foreign policy interests and ascriptive and hierarchical visions of racial order, which cannot be explained simply in economic terms.

Whereas shifts in the U.S. business cycle aligned closely with immigration trends before World War II, they have diverged sharply on several occasions during the past sixty-five years (1945–2010). Despite an impressive postwar economic recovery underscored by low unemployment rates and surges in GDP during the 1950s, the modest levels of U.S. immigration remained relatively stable during that decade. Immigration flows not only failed to keep pace with the postwar economic expansion, they actually declined in the early 1950s. To understand declining immigration amidst economic growth requires knowledge of how government policies shaped immigrant admissions independently of postwar economic developments. Although both the Truman and Eisenhower administrations called for more expansive immigration policies, their efforts were derailed by committee chairs in Congress who preferred more restrictions and vigilantly defended national-origins quotas. During the early 1950s, anticommunist isolationists in Congress secured legislation that reaffirmed national-origins quotas while constructing new immigration barriers intended to tighten national security (Tichenor 1994, 2002; Zolberg 2006). In short, McCarthyism overshadowed economic growth in the immigration realm. Later in the 1950s, the Eisenhower administration took autonomous executive action to grant admissions above the existing quota ceiling, not in response to changing economic conditions but to offer refuge to Hungarians and others fleeing communism, as well as to allow war brides—in this instance foreign policy and humanitarian considerations trumped restrictionist immigration policy.

The first cracks in the national-origins quota policy appeared during and immediately after World War II with the repeal of the Chinese Exclusion Act in 1943, the launch of the *bracero* program in 1942, and the arrival after the war of large numbers of refugees and war brides from Europe and Asia. These groups did not fit within any of the existing quotas (Tichenor 2002). China was an ally in the war against Japan, and Congress decided that the long-standing ban on immigration and naturalization of Chinese nationals was bad for the war effort. Chinese immigrants living in the United States were allowed to naturalize, but strict quotas on Chinese immigration remained in effect. In World War II, the United States was leading the fight against fascism and the racist ideology underpinning it. The contradictions of the American immigration and refugee policy—not to mention segregation and Jim Crow—were increasingly anomalous and at odds with American foreign policy (Smith 1997; Dudziak 2000).

World War II also brought new demands for foreign labor. The *bracero* program was launched to fill gaps in the American labor market resulting from the draft—it was difficult for labor markets and wages to adjust, given that the economy was suddenly on a war footing, and growers were screaming for more labor. This guest-worker program, however, would have major long-term consequences for U.S. immigration policy. The program allowed for the recruitment of tens of thousands of "temporary" workers from Mexico in the 1940s, first in agriculture and subsequently in the railroad and transportation sectors (Calavita 1992). It marked the beginning of large-scale immigration from Mexico that has continued well into the twenty-first century (Garcia y Griego 1989). Attempts were made to reverse the flows with "Operation Wetback" in 1954, in which hundreds of thousands of Mexican workers and their families, including many who were U.S. citizens, were voluntarily repatriated or summarily deported to Mexico. The *bracero* program remained in effect until its repeal in 1964 and the passage of the Immigration and Nationality Act (INA) of 1965.

Public opinion remained suspicious and downright hostile to immigrants and refugees in the 1950s (Fetzer 2000). Congress passed the McCarren-Walter Act in 1952, which made it a felony to "harbor, transport, and conceal illegal immigrants." But under the Texas Proviso, those employing illegal immigrants were exempt from the law. Employers, particularly the growers in the Southwest, had enough political clout to keep cheap Mexican labor flowing into the U.S. market. McCarren-Walter also loosened racial restrictions on immigration ever so slightly, but without repealing the national-origins quota system. Reflecting the fear of communist subversion during the early years of the cold war, McCarren-Walter contained provisions for screening immigrants to catch communists and subversives, a move which was in keeping with McCarthyism and the new red scare. President Harry Truman vetoed the bill, calling it "un-American," but Congress overrode his veto. Congressional efforts to placate xenophobic and McCarthyism-supporting groups made it difficult for the president to ease restrictions on refugees coming from communist countries (Tichenor 2002). Immigration and refugee policy were important foreign policy tools, and the president needed a freer hand to accommodate cold war refugees in particular.

Ultimately the civil rights movement—which had as its primary objective to overturn Jim Crow and achieve equal rights for African Americans—swept away the last vestiges of the racist and discriminatory national-origins quota system, leading to the most radical reform of immigration policy in American history. The 1965 INA, also known as the Hart-Celler Act, was a landmark piece of legislation. It repealed the national-origins quota system, thus eliminating race and ethnicity as the principal criteria for selecting immigrants. It also redefined the relationship between individuals, groups, and the state through a process of political struggle (the civil rights movement) that would sweep away Jim Crow and racial discrimination and, in the process, expand the rights of immigrant and ethnic minorities. A new type of rights-based liberalism was emerging at every level of the polity (Hollifield 1992; Cornelius, Martin, and Hollifield 1994), from partisan and interest-group politics, to the legislature and executive, and especially in the federal judiciary, which became increasingly active in protecting minority rights and civil liberties. Beginning in the 1960s, the courts would play an important role in immigration policymaking through restraining state and local authorities in their treatment of immigrants, helping to consolidate the rights of immigrants and minorities, and reasserting the plenary power doctrine, whereby the federal government (Congress and the executive) has the

FIGURE 2-2

FOREIGN-BORN SHARE OF TOTAL U.S. POPULATION, 1850–2005

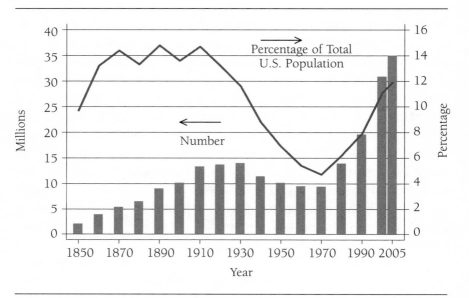

Year

SOURCES: U.S. Census Bureau, "Table 1. Nativity of the Population and Place of Birth of the Native Population: 1850 to 1990," *Technical Paper* 29 (1999), available at http://www.census.gov/population/www/documentation/twps0029/tab01.html (accessed August 2, 2010); U.S. Census Bureau, *Statistical Abstract of the United States: 2004–05,* 2005, available at http://www.census.gov/prod/2004pubs/04statab/pop.pdf (accessed August 2, 2010); U.S. Census Bureau, *Statistical Abstract of the United States: 2007,* 2007, available at http://www.census.gov/prod/2006pubs/07statab/pop.pdf (accessed August 2, 2010).

exclusive authority to regulate immigration as an issue of national sovereignty. Ironically, the Supreme Court's jurisprudence became more interventionist during the civil rights era, not only with respect to state and local governments (see the discussion of *Plyler v. Doe* in Schuck 1998), but also with respect to the federal executive and legislative branches. The INA of 1965 was passed on the heels of the 1964 Civil Rights Act and the Voting Rights Act of 1965. Immigrants were among the most important beneficiaries of the civil rights movement, as laws designed to end racial discrimination against blacks helped open up new political and legal spaces (rights) for immigrant minorities, setting the stage for the fourth (and largest) wave of immigration in American history.

The fourth wave of immigration began slowly in the 1970s, in part because of the severe economic slowdown that was the result of two oil shocks and a steep recession in 1981–82. But as the economy recovered in the 1980s, immigration accelerated rapidly; by the first decade of the twenty-first century, the foreign-born population had climbed to an all-time high of 35 million. The civil rights movement and the INA of 1965 had laid the political and legal groundwork for a more expansive immigration policy, but the soaring American economy in the 1980s and 1990s propelled immigration to new heights. The free-market policies of the Reagan and Clinton administrations made the United States increasingly immigrant-friendly. Demand-pull forces in the U.S. labor market were strong, and an unlimited supply of workers from Mexico, Central America, and Asia were ready to fill this demand.

Strange bedfellow coalitions of civil rights liberals (primarily northern Democrats, many of them—like the late Senator Edward Kennedy of Massachusetts—descendants of the second- and third-wave immigrants) and business-oriented, Wall Street Republicans helped to pass some of the most expansive immigration laws in U.S. history (Hollifield, Hunt, and Tichenor 2008). The Refugee Act of 1980 incorporated the 1951 United Nations (UN) Convention Relating to the Status of Refugees into U.S. law (Zolberg 2006). During most of the cold war period, U.S. policy favored refugees fleeing persecution in communist countries, whereas the UN refugee convention defined a refugee as anyone with a "well-founded fear of persecution." Signatories of the convention were bound by the principle of non-refoulement, whereby any people who met the convention's standard for asylum could not be returned to the country from which they were fleeing. The 1980 Refugee Act brought the United States in line with international law, giving new impetus to a more rights-based approach to immigration and refugee policy. In 1979, just prior to passage of the Refugee Act, Congress established the Select Commission on Immigration and Refugee Policy (SCIRP) under the direction of Lawrence Fuchs. This was the first commission of its kind since the U.S. Immigration Commission, also known as the Dillingham commission, of 1911.

As SCIRP went about its work holding hearings, gathering data, and conducting research in the early 1980s, immigration soared—not only legal immigration, which the INA of 1965 had opened up by making kinship and family ties the primary criterion for admission—but also illegal immigration. The 1965 INA repealed the national-origins quota system, creating avenues for immigration from nontraditional sources, particularly Latin America (especially Mexico), Asia, and eventually Africa and the Middle East. The INA also imposed numerical limits on the number of visas, including the first such limits on immigration from the Western Hemisphere (capped at 120,000 annually). These limitations would lead eventually to a big imbalance between the demand for and supply of visas. Rather than waiting in long queues that could last years, many immigrants chose to come illegally, either slipping across land and sea borders, or entering with a tourist visa and not returning to their original countries after it expired. The majority of illegal immigrants were (and are) visa overstayers, that is, individuals who entered the country on a tourist visa and simply remain in the United States, meld into society, and join a growing black market for labor (Passel and Cohn 2009). By the time the SCIRP made its recommendations to Congress, illegal immigration had become the biggest issue in immigration policy, and the foreign-born population, as a percentage of the total population, was rapidly approaching a historic high (Tichenor 2002). By 2008 foreigners constituted almost 14 percent of the total population—a level not seen since the early twentieth century (see figure 2-2 on page 62). Immigration was reshaping American society, and immigrants were coming to play an increasingly important role in the economy. Immigration policy debates in the 1990s and 2000s would evolve along the following four lines:

1. **Economic:** What are the costs and benefits associated with high levels of immigration, especially illegal immigration?

2. **Social:** How are immigrants to the United States and their children (the second generation) assimilating? Are they learning English? Are they succeeding in the labor market?

3. **Political:** Are new immigrants good citizens? Will they participate in politics, and if so, how? Will they be Democrats or Republicans, liberals or conservatives? Will they constitute a "swing vote?"

4. **Security:** In light of 9/11, what security threats do immigrants pose to the United States? Border enforcement and screening of persons wishing to enter the United States took on a new urgency. How did the terrorists enter the country? Was the attack the result of lax border enforcement and an overly liberal immigration and refugee policy?

Rolling Back Rights to Control Immigration

It was easier to stop or slow immigration and roll back the rights of foreigners and immigrants in earlier periods of history (Hollifield 1999). In the era of rights-based politics, sealing the border, summarily deporting large numbers of immigrants (as happened during Operation Wetback in 1954), stopping family reunification, turning back refugees and asylum seekers, rolling back immigrants' civil rights (due process and equal protection), and cutting their access to social services have ceased to be viable options for addressing immigration concerns. This is exemplified by the fate of California Proposition 187; a federal judge deemed the proposition—intended to prevent illegal immigrants from using public services in California—unconstitutional. In 1986, Congress attempted to better control immigration, especially illegal immigration, with the IRCA. The act, also known as the Simpson-Mazzoli Act, was the result of a compromise between "restrictionists" and "admissionists." Restrictionists wanted to stop illegal immigration; these included Republicans, led by Senator Alan Simpson of Wyoming, and some southern Democrats. Admissionists, who wanted to legalize the large population of illegal immigrants by granting them amnesty, included northern liberal Democrats and were led by Senator Kennedy. In the end, a rights-markets coalition formed in the Senate and the House, and a compromise was struck. The IRCA allowed for the amnesty of illegal immigrants in exchange for imposing sanctions (fines and imprisonment for repeat offenders) on employers who knowingly hired illegal immigrants (Hollifield, Hunt, and Tichenor 2008). Amnesty succeeded in bringing over 2.7 million illegal immigrants out of the shadows. As figure 2-1 shows, this led to a spike in the number of known immigrants (Tichenor 2002). To qualify for amnesty, immigrants had to certify that they were employed and that they had entered the United States prior to January 1, 1982. Opponents of amnesty argued that it created a moral hazard; they argued that more people would be willing to take the risk of immigrating illegally with the hope or expectation that they would receive amnesty at a later date.

The employer sanctions put in place under the IRCA, however, represented the federal government's first attempt to pursue an internal control strategy by using labor laws to control immigration. The IRCA created the I-9 form, which requires all persons seeking employment to present documentary evidence that they are legal residents. Out of concern that the new law could lead to discrimination against job applicants who looked or sounded like foreigners, the IRCA included provisions to ensure that the rights of ethnic minorities would be protected—more evidence of the power of rights-based politics. Under the IRCA, employers were not liable for hiring anyone who presented documents that looked official, and they were not required to verify that the documents were authentic. These provisions made employer sanctions very weak and led to the creation of a new black market for false papers, especially Social Security cards and drivers' licenses (Martin and Midgley 2006). Concerns for privacy and civil liberties have prevented Congress from creating a national identification card, which is common in many other democracies. The American Civil Liberties Union strongly opposes a national ID card (Tichenor 2002).

Agriculture posed a specific regulatory problem because of the informality and seasonal nature of employment in this sector (Martin 2009). In the run-up to the passage of the IRCA, farmers lobbied for a guest-worker program, but labor unions, especially the United Farm Workers of America, cofounded by the charismatic labor leader César Chávez, opposed what they considered a system of bonded labor. The result was the creation of a special agricultural worker legalization program under which 750,000, primarily Mexican farm workers received amnesty. Finally with respect to the impact of the IRCA on overall immigration levels, each person covered by amnesty was able to bring relatives (spouses, parents, brothers, and sisters) into the United States under the family-reunification provisions of the 1965 INA.

The IRCA did little to slow the pace of illegal immigration into the United States. Over the course of the 1990s and into the first decade of the twenty-first century, the number of illegal immigrants rivaled the number of legal immigrants, setting the stage for a backlash against all immigrants, first with California Proposition 187 (1994); then the IIRAIRA (1996); followed by the Border Protection, Antiterrorism, and Illegal Immigration Control Act of 2005, known as the Sensenbrenner Bill; and leading to contemporary debates over what to do about an illegal population estimated to be somewhere between 10 and 12 million people (Passel and Cohn 2009). It is important to keep in mind, however, that not all immigration is illegal, and not all immigrants are unskilled. Illegal immigration dominates the headlines, but while powerful anti-immigration lobbies, like the Federation for American Immigration Reform, seek to reduce immigration drastically, equally powerful pro-immigration lobbies, like the Mexican American Legal Defense Fund and the League of United Latin American Citizens, are devoted to defending the rights and interests of Latinos. Still other organizations in favor of immigration, like the American Chamber of Commerce and various trade associations, represent powerful business interests. Bill Gates, the founder and former head of Microsoft, organized a successful lobbying campaign by high-tech industries to stop Congress from restricting high-skilled immigration while the IIRAIRA was being debated (1995–96) (Tichenor 2002).

We might expect Congress to restrict or slow immigration during times of economic difficulty; but at the start of the relatively mild recession of 1990–91, Congress enacted another expansive immigration reform. The Immigration Act of 1990 was designed to reform legal immigration, and it set an overall annual ceiling of 675,000 immigrants. Because of family reunification and the fact that visas not used in one year can be carried over to the next, on average over 1 million immigrants legally immigrated into the United States each year throughout the 1990s and into the 2000s—a number much higher than that established in the 1990 Immigration Act. Many illegal immigrants are also able to "adjust their status" and become LPRs, or green-card holders, thus adding to the annual totals (see figure 2-1). The Pew Hispanic Center (Passel and Cohn 2009) estimates that over 300,000 people immigrated to the United States illegally each year from 1990 to 2004 (see figure 2-3). In fact the U.S. immigration system relies heavily on status adjustments as a way to deal with enormous backlogs of individuals who find themselves in legal limbo; this system creates demand for immigration lawyers and other specialists who advise millions of immigrants, potential immigrants, and their employers. The American Bar Association, the American Immigration Lawyers Association in particular, is among the most important pro-immigration interest groups. Lawyers are essential for the system to function smoothly: they help to adjudicate and manage hundreds of thousands of cases annually. This gives the American system for managing immigration greater flexibility to deal with admissions on a case-by-case basis, although quotas and quantitative caps on the numbers of visas available for specific nationalities and regions make the system

FIGURE 2-3

ANNUAL NUMBER OF IMMIGRANTS TO THE UNITED STATES
BY LEGAL STATUS, 1990–2004

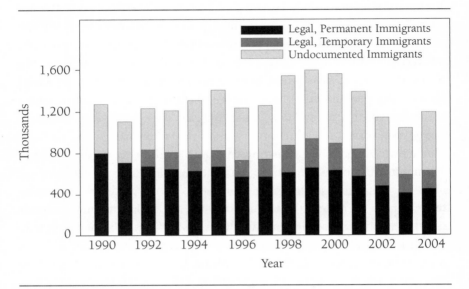

SOURCE: Jeffrey S. Passel and Roberto Suro, *Rise, Peak and Decline: Trends in U.S. Immigration, 1992–2004* (Washington, D.C.: Pew Hispanic Center, 2005), available at http://pewhispanic.org/reports/report. php?ReportID=53 (accessed June 16, 2010).

cumbersome and inefficient (Cornelius, Martin, and Hollifield 1994). The highly individualized nature of this regulatory system is consistent with the broader trend in rights-based politics and policy that began with the civil rights movement.

A New Emphasis on High-Skilled Immigration

The 1990 Immigration Act created a new category of visas (called H1-B) for high-skilled immigrants, thus adding an important economic and human capital (as opposed to family and humanitarian) dimension to U.S. immigration policy. The 1990 act set an annual cap of 65,000 on H1-B visas, but during the high-tech boom of the late 1990s, Congress adjusted the cap in response to higher demand for skilled workers and pressure from business groups. The H1-B visa was designed for high-skilled immigrants, and the act also created H2-A and H2-B visas for nonagricultural seasonal workers. But the number of job-based green cards, whether for unskilled (capped at 10,000 per year) or skilled immigrants (capped at 140,000 per year), was too low to accommodate the demand for skilled immigrant labor (Orrenius and Solomon 2006). Throughout the boom years of the 1990s and into the 2000s, the United States issued more temporary visas (over 600,000 in FY 2005) to fill the gap, while levels of illegal immigration continued to rise (Orrenius and Solomon 2006). It is difficult for Congress to create an employment-based visa system that mirrors the business cycle and perfectly matches the needs of the labor market (see figure 2-4 on page 70). When the high-tech bubble burst in 2001, the demand for H1-B visas declined and Congress reinstated a binding cap of 65,000 H1-B visas per year in 2004, only to see demand rise again in 2004–2007 (Orrenius and Solomon 2006). The bursting of the housing bubble in 2008 and the ensuing financial crisis led to declining demand for unskilled immigrant workers, especially in construction; and unemployment reached 10 percent of the labor force as a whole in 2009 (Martin and Midgley 2010). Because of lags between the demand for and supply of visas, the difficulties of quickly adjusting policy, and the rise of rights-based politics, immigration no longer follows the business cycle (Hollifield, Hunt, and Tichenor 2008).

Immigration and Security Concerns

To combat illegal immigration in the 1990s, the Immigration and Naturalization Service (INS) developed ever more sophisticated strategies for border enforcement (external control), increasing the number of border patrol agents and redeploying them at critical entry points along the U.S.-Mexico border. Operations Hold the Line (Texas, 1993) and Gatekeeper (California 1994) were designed to seal the border in urban areas like El Paso and San Diego and to force illegal crossings away from the cities into remote, desert areas. These external enforcement policies succeeded in redirecting flows, but levels of illegal immigration continued to rise, and thousands of illegal immigrants died in the deserts of the Southwest, leading some to argue that

FIGURE 2-4

NUMBER OF H1-B VISAS ISSUED FOR IMMIGRANTS
TO THE UNITED STATES, 1992–2009

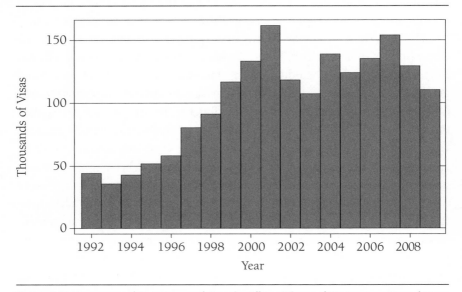

SOURCE: U.S. Department of State, Bureau of Consular Affairs, "Classes of Nonimmigrant Issued Visas-FY1989-2009," detail table, available at http://www.travel.state.gov/visa/statistics/nivstats/nivstats_4582.html (accessed August 2, 2010).

the policies of the Clinton administration were nothing more than symbolic and cynical attempts to show the public that the government was regaining control of the border—an out-of-sight, out-of-mind approach to immigration control—that had deadly consequences for the migrants (Cornelius 2001). The failure of external enforcement policies in the 1990s combined with the terrorist attacks of 9/11 led to a massive reorganization of border control. In 2003, the INS, formerly an agency of the Department of Justice, was reorganized into two agencies—Immigration and Customs Enforcement, and Citizenship and Immigration Services—and placed under the new Department of Homeland Security. A third agency, Customs and Border Protection, was created to coordinate border control. All three agencies were tasked with protecting the United States from another terrorist attack as the security function of immigration and refugee policy came to the fore

(Rudolph 2006). The Real ID Act, passed in 2005, established new standards for drivers' licenses and noncompulsory state identification cards to make them more difficult to counterfeit so it would be more difficult for individuals to obtain false papers. The law was intended to reinforce checks on individual identity while stopping short of creating a national ID card.

The new emphasis on security made travel and immigration to the United States more difficult, especially for anyone coming from a predominantly Muslim country; and U.S. consulates around the world began using greater scrutiny before issuing visas, slowing an already cumbersome and inefficient process with elaborate background checks for visa applicants. Overworked Foreign Service officers (the front line of immigration control) were fearful of admitting someone who might carry out another terrorist attack. The 9/11 hijackers entered the United States legally on tourist and student visas, but seven of the nineteen had false passports and three were on terrorist watch lists, leading the 9/11 Commission—set up to investigate the attacks—to conclude that better immigration and border enforcement might have prevented the terrorists from entering the country in the first place. Security considerations aside, the debate over immigration reform during the George W. Bush administration (2000–2008), as in previous eras, revolved primarily around the economic effects of immigration, especially illegal immigration (Borjas 1990, 1999). In May 2006, Bush proposed "comprehensive immigration reform," to match "willing workers with willing employers," by creating a new guest-worker program, and he proposed an "earned legalization" program for the millions of illegal immigrants already working in the country. Opponents of comprehensive reform charged that it would be a repeat of the IRCA amnesty, creating another situation of moral hazard that would lead to yet higher levels of illegal immigration. The Sensenbrenner Bill of 2005 represented an alternative, "enforcement only" strategy, placing a premium on enforcing existing laws, reinforcing border control, arresting and deporting the millions of illegal immigrants, and criminalizing illegal immigration.

The collapse of the reform effort in 2006 led many state and local governments to take up the cause of immigration control, further dividing communities and the electorate. It was impossible to resurrect the rights-markets coalitions in Congress that enacted earlier reforms during the cold war period (Hollifield, Hunt, and Tichenor 2008). The Republican

Party was divided between a culturally conservative—if not xenophobic—wing that refused to compromise, and a more moderate, business-oriented wing (led by Senator John McCain of Arizona) that wanted to give the Grand Old Party (GOP) a more immigrant-friendly face. Many Republicans, including George W. Bush's deputy chief of staff Karl Rove, feared that demographic changes resulting from high levels of immigration would change the electorate and Hispanics would constitute a swing vote in many key states and districts (Waldman 2007). Some GOP leaders feared ending up on the "wrong side of history" again, as they had in the 1920s when the Republicans ceded third-wave immigrants to the Democratic Party for the better part of two generations. In the run-up to the 2008 presidential election and after their successes in the 2006 midterm elections, Democratic leaders in Congress decided against compromising with moderate Republicans, preferring instead to leave the immigration issue open and to use it against Republicans in 2008. Questions of the extent to which immigration is an issue driving American politics and regarding how the fourth-wave immigrants altered the course of American political development remain unanswered.

Immigration and the Business Cycle

The U.S. government's interests and actions concerning immigration have more than occasionally transcended the economic predictors of the push-pull model and of straight interest-based explanations like those proposed by Freeman (1995; compare to Facchini and Mayda 2009). Reducing U.S. immigration levels to a basic economic causality or to a strict interest group dynamic is inadequate in both explanatory and predictive terms. The United States, like other major immigrant-receiving countries in the post–World War II era, is trapped in a liberal paradox; it needs to maintain adequate supplies of foreign labor (skilled and unskilled), while maintaining control of its borders, preserving the social contract, and protecting the rights of citizens and immigrants (Hollifield 1992). It is not valuable to deny the powerful influence of changing domestic economic conditions over immigration, but understanding the political economy of immigration requires weighing the relative importance of economic and political factors.

To understand and distinguish the influence of economic forces and government actions on U.S. immigration requires a multivariate model that incorporates both economic and political factors.

Using time-series analysis, we separate economic and political effects on immigration flows (see table 2-1 on page 57). (This analysis substantially updates a similar model in Hollifield and others [2008]. The findings, while not identical, are quite similar and thus substantiate the earlier work.) The level of immigration, as measured by LPRs (green cards issued, including status adjustors) serves as the dependent variable in the model. The key economic independent variables are unemployment rates (see Romer 1986; Department of Labor 2009) and percent change in GDP (Carter et al. 2006). These are interacted with a dummy variable coded zero for 1890–1945 and one for the period 1946–2008. In addition, the model includes dummy variables for each of the policy periods, the onset of each is lagged one year (Johnson-Reed Act [1925–40]; McCarren-Walter Act [1953–65]; Hart-Celler Act [1966–86]; the ICRA [1987–90]; 1990 Immigration Act [1991–96]; IIRAIRA [1997–2008]); dummy variables to control for the entire U.S. involvement in World Wars I and II; and a lagged dependent variable to ensure that errors are not serially correlated. Model parameters are estimated using ordinary least squares (OLS) regression.

The first thing to note is that, conforming to the conventional wisdom, economic conditions in the United States have a significant impact on legal immigration flows. Specifically, demand-pull forces, as measured by unemployment rates, have a modest impact on flows in the United States for the period 1890–2008. The coefficient, which assesses the influence of a unit change in unemployment (1 percent in this model) on immigration flows (logged annual immigration), is −10,232.6 and significant at the 10 percent level. In other words, the model predicts that as unemployment increases by 1 percent, the number of legal immigrants entering the United States will decline by 10,233. In the model, we control for a variety of policy interventions (specifically, the five most important immigration acts passed during this time period), as well as the dampening effects of World Wars I and II. Note that labor-market conditions have a much greater impact than changes in the other predictor (percent change in GDP), which is insignificant, meaning that changes in U.S. GDP are unlikely to have any significant effect on the number of immigrants legally entering the country. The argument developed in the first sections of this chapter predicts that economic effects would become weaker over time; that is, as immigration policies change to reflect the rise of rights-based politics, a new legal culture, and more expansive definitions of citizenship and membership—especially during the 1950s and 1960s—political factors would become stronger determinants for immigration flows. Accordingly, we segmented the data into two periods, pre- and postwar (see table 2-1), and, tellingly, we found that macroeconomic conditions (business cycles) have no significant effect on immigration flows during the post-1945 period. After 1945, factors other than business cycles have been driving levels of immigration in the United States.

We also controlled for the effects of World Wars I and II and the 1924 National Origins Act (the Johnson-Reed Act), which made the principle of racial or ethnic exclusivity law in the United States. World War I had an obvious and highly significant negative effect on immigration flows, as did the 1924 policy intervention. The ranges for both World War I and the 1924 Johnson-Reed Act reflect our expectations (see figure 2-5). World War I curtailed flows during this period (as evident by the negative sign); the 1924 act also reduced immigration dramatically (with a coefficient of −144,230.3 indicating that the number of immigrants was reduced by about 144,230 from what would have otherwise been expected), showing the power of the state to restrict immigration flows during this period, which was marked by isolationism (in foreign policy), protectionism (in trade policy), and restriction of immigration. World War II also had a statistically significant negative impact on flows. This is consistent with the hypothesis that as World War II and government policies curtailed immigration flows, these interventions decreased the capacity of prior immigration streams to draw more immigrants into the country.

Table 2-1 also reports the results for the period 1946–2008 (the variables multiplied by the postwar dummy variable). Several interesting and counterintuitive findings stand out. Economic demand-pull effects in the United States continue to weaken and decay over time, despite evidence of a more highly integrated global labor market, associated improvements in transportation and communication, and more efficient migration networks (Massey et al. 1987; Massey, Durand, and Malone 2002; Sassen 1996). Indeed, the coefficients for unemployment and real GDP change show no

FIGURE 2-5

ACTUAL LEVELS OF IMMIGRATION VERSUS THE OLS MODEL PREDICTIONS

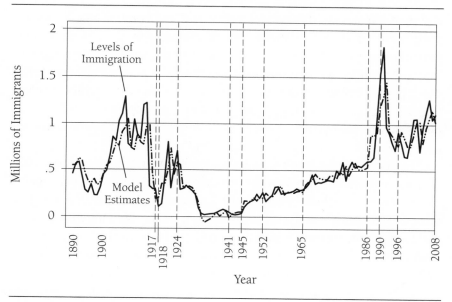

SOURCE: Authors' calculations.

significant effect for the postwar period. The McCarren-Walter Act of 1952 is not statistically significant. The contours of the act corroborate the statistical evidence. The McCarren-Walter Act resulted in only marginal changes to key restrictionist quota provisions of the 1924 Immigration Act that established the national-origins quota system.

A number of policy interventions, by contrast, were significant. Surprisingly, the Immigration and Nationality Act of 1965 (Hart-Celler), often cited as the most important immigration reform since the 1924 law (Reimers 1985), had less of an empirical effect on legal immigration flows than other postwar reforms. The caveat, of course, is that the 1965 act led to a gradual but dramatic change in the composition of these flows by stimulating family unification (which was, after all, the purpose of the law) and encouraging larger flows from non-European sources (an unintended consequence). Two major immigration reforms of the late twentieth century, the

IRCA and the 1990 Immigration Act, however, combined to have an influence on immigration that dwarfed all others.

In sum, the model is a good predictor of immigration levels (it has an R-squared of .78; see table 2-1 and figure 2-5), and it shows the significant influence of economic factors on immigration until 1946 and the growing impact of government actions on flows in the postwar period. This political-economic model of immigration fundamentally challenges presumptions of much of the economic and sociological literature on immigration, specifically that U.S. policy interventions have had at best a marginal effect on immigration levels (Simon 1989). It underscores the influence of both changing economic conditions and government actions on U.S. immigration during the past century. In the post–World War II period, immigration flows are heavily influenced by the rise of what we have termed rights-based politics and the increasing prominence of rights-markets coalitions in U.S. politics, especially during the cold war era (Hollifield, Hunt, and Tichenor 2008).

Conclusion

The last half of the twentieth century marked an important new chapter in the history of globalization. With advances in travel and communications technology, migration has accelerated, reaching levels not seen since the end of the nineteenth century. At the beginning of the twenty-first century, according to the United Nations, roughly 200 million people are living outside their country of birth or citizenship. Even though this figure constitutes less than 3 percent of the world's population, the perception is that international migration is rising at an exponential rate and that it is a permanent feature of the global economy. It seems that economic forces compelling people to move are intensifying. Supply-push forces remain strong, while the ease of communication and travel has reinforced migrant networks, making it easier than ever before for potential migrants to gather the information that they need in order to make a decision about whether to move.

To some extent, supply-push forces are constant or rising and have been for many decades. However, demand-pull forces are variable, and as we can see in the case of the United States, political dynamics have an enormous influence on the direction, composition, and flow of immigrants. The emphasis our model places on markets and rights improves on the prevailing economic and sociological theories. It incorporates economic and policy/legal effects in a manner that distinguishes their relative influence and provides a stronger overall account of immigration flows. Economic forces alone are clearly insufficient to explain immigration flows. Bringing politics into immigration analysis offers greater promise for understanding the direction, composition, and flow of immigration. As we have seen in our analysis of the U.S. case, electoral, foreign policy, and national security interests figure prominently in immigration politics, while focusing on economics and business cycles offers only a partial explanation at best.

A model that integrates immigrants, markets, and rights is more promising than push-pull or transnational models alone in accounting for the volume and composition of immigration flows. These findings are consistent with other studies of the political economy of immigration in Europe (Hollifield 1990, 1992). While they do not contradict the emerging literature in political economy that focuses on interest-based explanations for changes in immigration policy (Freeman 1995; Facchini and Mayda 2009), they do offer us an alternative, rights-based and historical-institutional explanation for the rapid rise in immigration among industrial democracies in the late twentieth century (Brettell and Hollifield 2008). The liberal state has played and will continue to play a vital role in regulating immigration levels.

References

Borjas, G. J. 1990. *Friends or Strangers: The Impact of Immigrants on the U.S. Economy.* New York: Basic Books.

———. 1999. *Heaven's Door: Immigration Policy and the American Economy.* Princeton, NJ: Princeton University Press.

Borstelmann, T. 2003. *The Cold War and the Color Line: American Race Relations in the Global Arena.* Cambridge, MA: Harvard University Press.

Brettell, C. B., and J. F. Hollifield, eds. 2008. *Migration Theory: Talking across Disciplines.* New York: Routledge.

Calavita, K. 1992. *Inside the State: The Bracero Program, Immigration, and the I.N.S.* New York: Routledge.

Carter, S. B., S. S. Gartner, M. R. Haines, A. L. Olmstead, R. Sutch, and G. Wright, eds. 2006. *Historical Statistics of the United States: Millennial Edition.* New York: Cambridge University Press.

Cornelius, W. A. 2001. Death at the Border: The Efficacy and Unintended Consequences of U.S. Immigration Control Policy, 1993–2000. *Population and Development Review* 27 (4): 661–85.

Cornelius, W. A., P. L. Martin, and J. F. Hollifield, eds. 1994. *Controlling Immigration: A Global Perspective.* Stanford, CA: Stanford University Press.

Dudziak, M. L. 2000. *Cold War Civil Rights: Race and the Image of American Democracy.* Princeton, NJ: Princeton University Press.

Facchini, G., and A. M. Mayda. 2009. *The Political Economy of Immigration Policy.* New York: United Nations Development Program, Human Development Reports.

Fetzer, J. S. 2000. *Public Attitudes toward Immigration in the United States, France, and Germany.* Cambridge: Cambridge University Press.

Freeman, G. P. 1995. Modes of Immigration Politics in Liberal Democratic States. *International Migration Review* 22 (Winter): 881–902.

Fuchs, L. 1990. *The American Kaleidoscope: Race, Ethnicity, and the Civic Culture.* Hanover, NH: Wesleyan University and the University Press of New England.

Garcia y Griego, M. 1989. The Mexican Labor Supply, 1990–2010. In *Mexican Migration to the United States: Origins, Consequences, and Policy Options,* ed. W. A. Cornelius and J. A. Bustamente, 49–93. San Diego: Center for U.S.-Mexican Studies, University of California–San Diego Press.

Hatton, T. J., and J. G. Williamson. 1998. *The Age of Mass Migration: Causes and Economic Impact.* New York: Oxford University Press.

Higham, J. 1955. *Strangers in the Land: Patterns of American Nativism, 1860–1925.* New Brunswick, NJ: Rutgers University Press.

Hollifield, J. F. 1990. Immigration and the French State. *Comparative Political Studies* 23 (April): 56–79.

———. 1992. *Immigrants, Markets, and States: The Political Economy of Postwar Europe.* Cambridge, MA: Harvard University Press.

————. 1999. Ideas, Institutions and Civil Society: On the Limits of Immigration Control in Liberal Democracies. *IMIS-Beiträge* 10 (January): 57–90.

————. 2004. The Emerging Migration State. *International Migration Review* 38: 885–912.

————. 2008. The Politics of International Migration: How Can We Bring the State Back In? In *Migration Theory: Talking across Disciplines*, ed. C. Brettell and J. F. Hollifield, 183–237. New York: Routledge.

Hollifield, J. F., V. F. Hunt, and D. J. Tichenor. 2008. Immigrants, Markets, and Rights: The United States as an "Emerging Migration State." *Washington University Journal of Law and Policy* 27: 7–44.

King, D. 2000. *Making Americans: Immigration, Race, and the Origins of the Diverse Democracy*. Cambridge, MA: Harvard University Press.

————. 2005. *The Liberty of Strangers: Making the American Nation*. Oxford: Oxford University Press.

Martin, P. L. 2009. *Importing Poverty? Immigration and the Changing Face of Rural America*. New Haven, CT: Yale University Press.

Martin, P. L., and E. Midgley. 1994. Immigration to the United States: Journey to an Uncertain Destination. *Population Bulletin* 49 (September): 2–45.

————. 2006. Immigration: Shaping and Reshaping America. *Population Reference Bureau* 61(4): 3-27.

————. 2010. Immigration in America 2010. *Population Bulletin Update* (June): 1–6.

Massey, D. S., R. Alarcon, J. Durand, and H. Gonzalez. 1987. *Return to Aztalan*. Berkeley: University of California Press.

Massey, D. S., J. Durand, and N. J. Malone. 2002. *Beyond Smoke and Mirrors: Mexican Immigration in an Era of Economic Integration*. New York: Russell Sage Foundation.

Mink, G. 1986. *Old Labor and New Immigrants in American Political Development: Union, Party, and State, 1875–1920*. Ithaca, NY: Cornell University Press.

Ngai, M. M. 2004. *Impossible Subjects: Illegal Aliens and the Making of Modern America*. Princeton, NJ: Princeton University Press.

Orrenius, P. M., and G. R. Solomon. 2006. How Labor Market Policies Shape Immigrants' Opportunities. *Economic Letter, Federal Reserve Bank of Dallas* (July).

Passel, J. S., and D. Cohn. 2009. A Portrait of Unauthorized Immigrants in the United States. Washington, DC: Pew Hispanic Center. Available at http://pewresearch. org/pubs/1190/portrait-unauthorized-immigrants-states.

Passel, J. S., and R. Suro. 2005. *Rise, Peak and Decline: Trends in U.S. Immigration, 1994–2004*. Washington, DC: Pew Hispanic Center. Available at http://pew hispanic.org/reports/report.php?ReportID=53.

Portes, A. 1996. Transnational Communities: Their Emergence and Significance in the Contemporary World-System. In *Latin America in the World Economy*, ed. R. P. Korzeniewidcz and W. C. Smith, 151–68. Westport, CT: Greenwood Press.

————. 1997. Immigration Theory for a New Century: Some Problems and Opportunities. *International Migration Review* 31: 799–825.

Reimers, D. 1985. *Still the Golden Door*. New York: Columbia University Press.

Romer, C. 1986. Spurious Volatility in Historical Unemployment. *Journal of Political Economy* 94 (1): 1–37

Rudolph, C. 2006. *National Security and Immigration: Policy Development in the United States and Western Europe since 1945.* Stanford: Stanford University Press.

Sassen, S. 1988. *The Mobility of Labor and Capital: A Study in International Investment and Labor Flow.* New York: Cambridge University Press.

———. 1996. *Losing Control? Sovereignty in an Age of Globalization.* New York: Columbia University Press.

Schuck, P. H. 1998. *Citizens, Strangers, and In-betweens.* Boulder, CO: Westview Press.

Simon, J. L. 1989. *The Economic Consequences of Immigration.* Oxford: Basil Blackwell.

Smith, R. M. 1997. *Civic Ideals: Conflicting Visions of Citizenship in U.S. History.* New Haven, CT: Yale University Press.

Tichenor, D. J. 1994. The Politics of Immigration Reform in the United States, 1981–1990. *Polity* 26 (Spring): 333–62.

———. 2002. *Dividing Lines: The Politics of Immigration Control in America.* Princeton, NJ: Princeton University Press.

U.S. Census Bureau. 1999. Table 1. Nativity of the Population and Place of Birth of the Native Population: 1850 to 1990. *Technical Paper 29.* Available at www.census.gov/population/www/documentation/twps0029/tab01.html.

———. 2005. *Statistical Abstract of the United States: 2004–2005.* Available at www.census.gov/prod/2004pubs/04statab/pop.pdf.

———. 2007. *Statistical Abstract of the United States: 2007.* Available at www.census.gov/prod/2006pubs/07statab/pop.pdf.

U.S. Department of Homeland Security. 2009. *Yearbook of Immigration Statistics: 2009.* Available at www.dhs.gov/files/statistics/publications/LPR09.shtm.

U.S. Department of Labor. Bureau of Labor Statistics. 2009. *Household Data Annual Averages: Employment Status of the Civilian, Noninstitutional Population, 1940 to Date.* Available at www.bls.gov/cps/cpsaat1.pdf.

U.S. Department of State. Bureau of Consular Affairs. Classes of Nonimmigrant Issued Visas—FY1989–2009: Detail Table. Available through www.travel.state.gov/visa/statistics/nivstats/nivstats_4582.html.

Waldman, P. 2007. GOP Candidates Alienate Latino Voters. *The American Prospect.* Available at www.prospect.org/cs/articles?article=gop_candidates_alienate_latino_voters.

Zolberg, A. 2006. *A Nation by Design: Immigration Policy in the Fashioning of America.* Cambridge, MA: Harvard University Press and the Russell Sage Foundation.

PART II

From Temporary
to Permanent Status

3

Trends in Foreign-Student Admissions to the United States: Policy and Competitive Effects

B. Lindsay Lowell and Pramod Khadka

International students have become an integral part of higher education in the United States, as well as that of many other countries. International students are in the vanguard of the globalization of high-skilled labor, an evolving system that is closely scrutinized for many reasons. Because of their role in the accumulation of human capital, the international mobility of the highly skilled and of students is linked to the competitiveness of both destination and source countries. U.S. policymakers are concerned about remaining competitive in attracting students in the future, especially since the events of 9/11 led to a sharp drop in students coming to America. Many scholars share these concerns, but the research literature suggests a rather different set of assumptions about how future events may play out.

Policymakers' debates over international students, particularly concerns that policy is a primary hindrance to their mobility, do not fully comport with scholarly inquiry into the impact of economic factors (Doomerrik et al. 2009). Policymakers argue about the attractiveness of migration policies, while the literature on the subject indicates that policies may be no more—or even less—important than perceptions of economic opportunities. At the same time, concerns over international competition and student flows,

The authors appreciate the comments of Barry Chiswick, Cordelia Reimers, and the conference participants.

particularly how they impact America's "market share," have a parallel in scholarly interest in the impact of globalization on educational systems in source countries. Policymakers fear that global competition will lead to dwindling numbers of foreign students, while the evidence suggests that globalization may increase the pool of international students. An increasing number of foreign students could even be coming to the United States for education concurrent with any potential loss of global market share.

Prestigious panels reporting on how policies affected student flows after 9/11—while careful to note improvements in admission procedures after 2003—reflect a general consensus that the policies played a determining role in the drop in numbers (Board of Education and Workforce, National Research Council 2005; American Electronics Association 2005). However, the panels argue that "the downturn has reflected an increased [applicant] denial rate more than a decreased application rate. . . . One can track the changes in nonimmigrant-visa issuance rates directly to changes in visa and immigration policies and structures after the terror attacks of 9-11." (Board of Education and Workforce, National Research Council 2005, 73). Increased security concerns after 9/11 led to greater hurdles for visa applicants, and these procedures effectively deterred students from coming to the United States. Of immediate concern were an increase in applicant refusal rates (wherein consular officials decline the visa application), the newly required applicant interviews for applicants from all countries, security screenings for applicants studying in particular scientific fields or from select countries, and diffident treatment by U.S. officials. Only a small fraction of students faced security backlogs, and most of the systemic delays in processing were reduced within two years. Remarkably, the reports almost uniformly fail to attribute the declines in visa applicants to the 2001 recession and downplay other economic considerations.

Many scholars believe that policies—short of those that explicitly restrict numbers—reflect the political economy and play an indirect role in mobility. Certainly, empirical analyses find that policies matter, although we cannot resolve here the question of whether policies impose a cost affecting migrants' decisions or are a quantity constraint that conditions the impact of push-pull factors (Hatton and Williamson 2003). But analysis suggests that economic pull factors are the driving force of international flows, while an interaction of policies with pull variables suggests that relaxed admission policies increase the power of pull factors (Mayda 2005; Orrenius 2003; Hanson and Spilimbergo 1999). In other words, as long as economic conditions favor migration, easing admission requirements should increase levels of immigration, and tightening admission requirements should decrease immigration levels. The question is the degree to which tightening admission policies restricted the number of foreign students in the United States relative to the effect that economic changes, such as the sharp recession of 2001, had on student migration.

Almost all investigations into the post-9/11 decline in international students cite the globalization of higher education, especially the increasing educational opportunities other developed and developing countries offer to foreign students. "The global competition for talent was already under way when the events of Sept. 11, 2001, disrupted U.S. travel and ravaged the immigration plans of many international graduate students, postdoctoral researchers, and visiting scholars . . . if international students find equally attractive . . . opportunities in other countries, including their own, the difficulty of visiting the United States could gain decisive importance." (Committee on Prospering in the Global Economy of the Twenty-first Century 2007, 3–13). This tempered conclusion is common, recognizing that international competition has been ongoing for some time; still, analysts also believe other countries gained a substantial advantage in the immediate aftermath of 9/11 (Roberts 2006a). At the least, the changes in visa procedures are viewed as having accelerated a loss of foreign students to other countries and to have a potentially long-lasting impact on future competitiveness.

Observers are quick to note that other English-speaking nations have policies that favor foreign-student admissions and market to foreign students. Trends in global education show a remarkable increase in the number of students enrolled in tertiary education, particularly in middle- and upper middle-income countries (Altbach, Reisberg, and Rumbley 2009). Higher-education enrollments in many source countries, China and India in particular, have increased notably in the past decade. This indicates there are more opportunities for potential international students to choose to study in other countries or even to remain at home to complete a college degree. Analysts also believe, however, that the increasing number of students enrolled in programs of higher education is partly a result of opportunities to study abroad in higher-income countries (Bound, Turner, and Walsh 2009; Beine, Docquier, and Rapoport 2009). Rather than a shrinking supply of international students seeking to study in the United States, increasing enrollment rates and the globalization of education may lead to an increase in the number of international students in the United States.

In this chapter, we argue that a confluence of several factors caused the downturn in international student numbers after 2001 (Lowell, Bump, and Martin 2007). First, we discuss historical trends in student numbers and how economic cycles affect these trends; economic cycles are almost always ignored in this context. Next, we discuss trends in U.S. tuition prices after 2001. We then discuss the effects of new visa procedures put in place following 9/11. We will follow that with a discussion of how the globalization of tertiary education and the competitive stance of other countries have affected flows of international students. We then present an econometric analysis of foreign-student visas that controls for changes in per-capita income, the cost of tuition, visa acceptance rates, and international student enrollments. Finally, we conclude that while post-9/11 visa procedures contributed to the decline in student numbers, they were not a primary driver. The changes in visa procedures did not accelerate losses of international students to competing countries; in fact, globalization may increase, not decrease, the future supply of foreign students.

International Students and Economic Cycles

The drop in student numbers, typically referred to as the post-9/11 decline, also occurred in the wake of the worldwide recession of 2001. The best leading indicators of student numbers are "flow" data, such as visa applications or issuances. Relying on "stock" or enrollment data, which responds more slowly to changes, will both show a lag in flow changes and be less volatile. Both flow and stock data refer primarily to the so-called F visa issued to foreign students that permits them to stay in the United States for the duration of their studies. Figure 3-1 shows a 20 percent drop in the number of student visas issued from 2001 to 2002 and another 8 percent drop in 2003. Subsequently, the number of foreign students enrolled in U.S. institutions leveled off in 2002, dropped by 2.4 percent in 2003, and

FIGURE 3-1
Actual and Linear Number of U.S. Foreign-Student Visas and Enrollments in the United States, 1970–2007

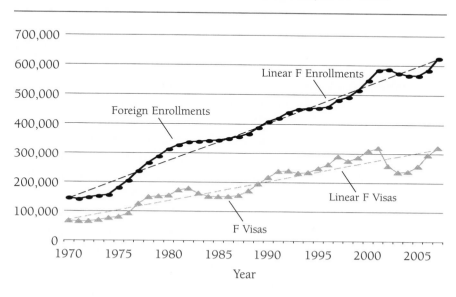

Sources: Institute of International Education (IIE), *Open Doors 2008 Data Tables* (New York: IIE, 2008), available at http://opendoors.iienetwork.org/?p=131530; U.S. Department of State, *Report of the Visa Office* (Washington, D.C.: U.S. Department of State), available at http://www.travel.state.gov/visa/statistics/statistics_1476.html.

dropped a further 1.3 percent in 2004. Visa issuances began to rebound after 2003, and enrollments rebounded soon thereafter.

The initial steep decline that occurred following 9/11 coupled with the tide of complaints over new visa procedures have been taken as de facto evidence that policies have had a predominant impact on foreign-student enrollments in the United States. An explicit belief that post-9/11 admission procedures have continued to depress visa issuances, at least relative to what they would have been otherwise—that the number of foreign students enrolled in U.S. colleges "would have been about 25 percent higher" if the growth rates prior to 9/11 had not been interrupted—also remains (Bush, McLarty, and Alden 2009, 17). This counterfactual assumes that the decline was an aberration attributable to policy mistakes, but it would have been far more surprising if student numbers had not sharply declined due to the recession anyway.

Consider a historic cycle in foreign-student flows from the early 1980s when there were no marked changes in visa processing, as seen in figure 3-1.[1] After several years of strong growth in student visa issuances, a trough followed 1982 that lasted six years. Student visa issuances dropped 15 percent from the high point to the low (two years into the trough), and it took seven years for the number to recover to the linear trend line. The 2001 decline in student admissions was much sharper—it dropped 26 percent by year two—but the recovery started three years into the trough and it took six years for the number to recover to the linear trend line. In other words, while the decline in student flows was deeper in 2001 than in 1982, the rebound and recovery in the 2001 cycle started and finished more quickly.

Faltering economic growth in source countries makes it more difficult for students to afford an education in the United States; when the United States also experiences a recession, the incentive to migrate is reduced. During the 1980s cycle, ten countries were the source of half of all foreign students admitted to the United States for study. Following several years of exceptional growth, gross domestic product (GDP) in these countries dropped 9 percent in 1982 and remained relatively flat until a strong rebound in 1986. In 2000, just seven countries were the source of half of all students; in 2001, the GDP in these seven countries dropped 7 percent (World Bank 2007). U.S. GDP growth also slowed during both student troughs. In the latest cycle, U.S. GDP growth resumed in 2004, the same year student visa issuances first rebounded (World Bank 2007). Given how foreign-student visa issuance has fluctuated with economic cycles in the past, it seems reasonable to attribute the first-order cause of the post-2001 decline to the recession rather than to changes in U.S. policy.

The Cost of College

Most observers have mentioned that a U.S. education is costly, but few have noted that it is costly not only in terms of tuition but also in the amount of time it takes to graduate, and none has taken into account the spike in tuition costs that occurred right after 2001. Historically, international student enrollment across borders was strongly influenced directionally by colonial ties or, later, the cold war (Varghese 2008). Since the 1990s and in today's period of globalization, however, international education has become more market driven. The cost of education may become an increasingly important factor in students' decision-making process, particularly as more countries begin to provide education in English (Verbik and Lasanowski 2007; New Zealand Ministry of Education 2007).

Education for international students costs most in the United Kingdom, and the United States is next in line (Organisation for Economic Co-operation and Development [OECD] 2004). The cost of tuition tends to be lower in many European countries because higher education is heavily subsidized; most charge foreign students the same rate as domestic students, while some actually do not charge foreign students any tuition. Foreign students generate revenue for higher education systems when, as in the United Kingdom, colleges are permitted to charge more for foreign students. In the United States, public institutions charge foreign students out-of-state fees, and private institutions are among the costliest in the world. Adding to the cost, it takes approximately seven and a half years to complete a doctorate in the United States. This is one or two years longer than it takes to earn a doctorate in most countries. One study found that international students pay twelve times more to get a similar degree in the United Kingdom or Australia—eighteen times more in the United States—than they pay in Malaysia, Singapore, or China (Verbik and Lasanowski 2007).

Not only are tuition costs at U.S. colleges relatively high, about three-quarters of all foreign students attend public institutions that increased tuition above the trend line closely timed with the 2001 recession. Figure 3-2 shows that an increase in tuition costs occurred during the period in which foreign-student applications fell most. The trend in tuition and other costs adjusted for inflation in public and private institutions increased constantly over most of two decades. Private institutions, which cost about four times as much as public institutions, saw tuition increases of about 3.4 percent from 2002 to 2005, which was in line with the long-term trend. Public tuition costs increased sharply from 2002 through 2005, however: growth during that time period averaged 7 percent annually, 60 percent more than the annual average rate of increase from 1986 to 2006.

FIGURE 3-2

**CHANGE IN AVERAGE ANNUAL TUITION AND ROOM AND BOARD
AT PUBLIC AND PRIVATE FOUR-YEAR INSTITUTIONS IN
THE UNITED STATES, 1986–2006**

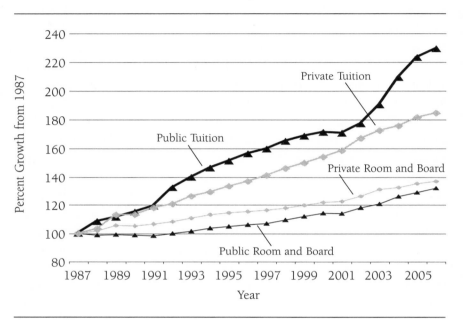

SOURCE: College Board, Trends in College Pricing, *Trends in Higher Education Series* 2009, available at http://www.trends-collegeboard.com/college_pricing/.
NOTE: Tuition is in 2006 dollars (1986 = 100).

Student Policy and Visa Procedures

Changes to visa procedures after 9/11 were generally procedural rather than policy changes; they centered on agencies implementing existing visa regulations in a more comprehensive fashion (Yale-Loehr, Papademetriou, and Cooper 2005). The U.S. policy on foreign students was created in 1952 with the Immigration and Nationality Act (INA). The United States has never placed numerical restrictions on student visas, and has modified only regulatory features (Wassem 2003). To obtain visas, student applicants must demonstrate to consular officers abroad and immigration inspectors at U.S.

ports of entry that they have been accepted by an approved school. They must also not be ineligible on the 1952 INA's grounds of inadmissibility, which include concerns about security, terrorism, health, and crime.

There is a long history of concern in the United States about balancing national security with international students' access to U.S. education. Efforts to control the transfer of sensitive technologies to foreign nationals date back to the 1954 International Traffic in Arms Regulations. The discovery in the wake of the terrorist attack on the World Trade Center in 1993 that one of the conspirators had entered the United States on a student visa and failed to enroll in school prompted concerns about the system (National Commission on Terrorist Attacks upon the United States 2004). This led to the Illegal Immigration Reform and Immigrant Responsibility Act of 1996, which required an electronic system for gathering information on foreign students and the development of an electronic entry-exit system to track migrants. The so-called Visa Mantis program was created in 1998 to screen visa applicants, but a system to track foreign students was not implemented, largely because of resistance from universities (Tierney and Lechuga 2005).

After 9/11, visa processing incorporated security checks for individuals from countries deemed state sponsors of terrorism, increased the use of existing security checks for visa applicants, and mandated that all visa applicants interview at a U.S. Consulate before receiving a visa. The U.S. Congress passed legislation requiring increased cooperation between federal agencies—including the newly created Department of Homeland Security—and the use of entry- and exit-control systems affecting students. The rapid response that was required and problems with interagency systems made for an acute management challenge (Yale-Loehr, Papademetriou, and Cooper 2005). The expanded use of security checks on all visa applications, not just students, also affected the administrative ability to respond (Walker 2004). Delays and uncertainty in processing became an immediate concern for applicants; anecdotes abound of applicants waiting months for interviews and receiving brusque treatment from U.S. officials.

In the aftermath of 9/11, "visa refusal rates" for student applicants were widely tracked as evidence that increased difficulty in obtaining visas was deterring applicants.[2] Applicants may be refused a visa because of poor paperwork, failure to establish that they meet requirements, or because they fail to convince the interviewer that their intentions are appropriate. Indeed, increased scrutiny in the environment of zero tolerance after 9/11 led consular officers to refuse student applicants at higher rates. Student visa refusals increased from about 24 percent in 2000 to 28 percent in 2001 and to 35 percent by 2003. The number of refusals then dropped to roughly 29 percent through 2006, which was still above historical levels.[3] With a lag of about one year, the number of visa applications declined and then rebounded with the increase in the percentage refused. So there is an inverse correlation between the percentage of applicants refused and the number of visa applications.

While the post-9/11 spike in refusals signaled other regulatory changes and doubtless impacted student visa numbers, it is unlikely that they were the major cause of the decline in applicants. Many observers argue that the decline in student applications and enrollments in science and engineering disciplines is associated with the Technology Alert List (Alden 2008).[4] Yet on average, there is no apparent differential refusal rate for, say, Chinese physics students (Todaro 2001). In fact, foreign-student enrollments in physics increased after 2001, while enrollments in computer sciences, the field most affected by decreases in available jobs after graduation due to the recession, plummeted (Lowell, Bump, and Martin 2007). The data demonstrate substantial national variation; there were clear declines in the number of foreign students from Saudi Arabia, which is on the Visa Condor list, but there were also declines in the number of students from Venezuela, Brazil, and Argentina, none of which is on the list and all of which were experiencing economic and political crises concurrent with the 2001 recession (Lowell, Bump, and Martin 2007).[5] Other visa classes also declined over this time period; new visas issued to tourists declined 27 percent between 1999 and 2002, and admissions for nationals in the "visa waiver" program declined 22 percent (U.S. Department of State 2008; U.S. Department of Homeland Security 2008).[6] Tourists and business travelers from the roughly thirty-six visa waiver countries need not apply for a visa; they can use their passports to enter the United States. In other words, the decline in tourism was at least commensurate for individuals subject to visa procedures as it was for individuals who were not subject to visa procedures, demonstrating that the decline is more likely attributable to something other than a change in procedures (Neiman and Swagel 2009). Economic factors are the more likely cause of the drop in visas issued.

International Competition

Traditionally, the United States has been the leader in attracting the largest number of the world's students, but the past decade has witnessed increasing international competition for students. Countries compete for students through student admission policies and procedures, retention policies to keep desirable students, outreach and marketing programs, and curriculum design. For example, France simplified its student visa procedures in 1998, and in the mid-1990s, the United Kingdom launched a promotional campaign to reach students in English-speaking countries (Institute of International Education 2010). France, Germany, Australia, and Canada have modified their laws to allow for an easier transition from student to worker (International Center for Migration Policy Development 2006). European countries are increasingly providing instruction in English, and are redesigning their curriculum to create a universal bachelor's and master's degree format.

Despite the competition, the United States has long had competitive policies. It does not have numerical caps and, compared to other countries, visa requirements have been straightforward. Although the U.S. government has not actively marketed U.S. institutions of higher education—the responsibility for higher education lies primarily with the states and private sector—the federal government is improving outreach.[7] In practice, the United States facilitates student retention; all foreign students may avail themselves of one year of practical training after graduation, and many graduate students transition to the temporary H-1B working visa, which includes 20,000 visas set aside for graduates in fields of science and engineering. Close to three-quarters of foreign doctoral students stay after completing their degree (Rosenzweig 2007; Lowell, Bump, and Martin 2007).[8] An index ranking various competitive aspects of student-admission policies for ten countries suggests that the United States ranks in the middle (Lowell, Bump, and Martin 2007).

Still, the U.S. share of the international student body fell by slightly more than 3 percentage points between 2000 and 2006 (OECD 2008). However, the U.S. share of worldwide foreign students had been in decline; in the 1980s, nearly four-tenths of all international students had enrolled in U.S. higher education, but the share declined to about one-third of international students in the mid-1990s. Thus, the post-2001 decline was not particularly sharp or unusual. Marginal gains in market share were distributed among many smaller competitors. Still, among English-speaking countries, the United States may have lost the greatest share of foreign students (Roberts 2006b). As figure 3-3 demonstrates, the U.S. foreign-student population fell from 583,000 to 573,000 between 2001 and 2003, a larger drop than the other English-speaking countries experienced in that time period (the U.S. share of foreign students in English-speaking countries fell from 53 to 50 percent). However, the loss of the U.S. share after 2001 was not sharp and appears to have been part of a longer trend. Indeed, as a group, the English-speaking countries lost a greater share of the global market between 1995 and 2000 than it has lost since (Lowell, Bump, and Martin 2007). It is clear that worldwide competition for international students is increasing, but 9/11 and changes to procedures that followed do not appear to have either caused or intensified this shift.

FIGURE 3-3
FOREIGN STUDENTS IN ENGLISH-SPEAKING COUNTRIES, 1997–2006

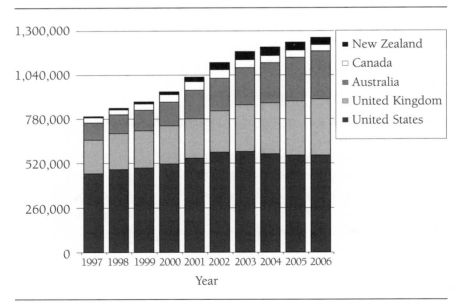

SOURCE: Veronica Lasanowski and Line Verbik, *International Student Mobility: Patterns and Trends* (London: Observatory on Borderless Higher Education, 2007).

At the same time, the number of international students, as well as the number of students enrolled in institutions of higher education, has been increasing steadily worldwide; over the past three decades the total number of international students has risen from 600,000 in 1975 to 2.9 million in 2006 (OECD 2006). Globally, the percentage of the college-age cohort enrolled in postsecondary education has grown from 19 percent in 2000 to 26 percent in 2007, with the most dramatic gains in upper-middle-income countries, which are the source of the largest number of international students. Today, there are some 151 million postsecondary students globally, indicating roughly a 53 percent increase since 2000 alone (Altbach, Reisberg, and Rumbley 2009). Thus, increasingly more students are enrolling in institutions of higher education, and the pool of students choosing to study abroad continues to grow. These numbers are projected to continue rising.

Econometric Evaluation of Student Migration

There are many theories about the causes of migration, and there is little agreement about which theory fits best, although the role economic incentives play in decisions to migrate dominates most empirical work (Massey et al. 1994). However, there has been less analysis of the destinations international students choose, although some research exists based on surveys and microdata that inquire into individual perceptions and choices (Kuptsch and Pang 2006; Yang 2003). Our econometric evaluation focuses on country-level analyses of student mobility.[9]

Rosenzweig (2007) examines two competing explanations for international student migration to the United States. He proposes that students choose to study abroad either to acquire skills that they could not acquire in their home countries or because high-skill employment is underrewarded at home. The first explanation posits that a shortage of institutions of higher education (or of quality institutions) is a driving force behind the choice to study abroad, while the alternative explanation is that opportunities for higher wages abroad drive student migration in much the same way as they drive other forms of migration. He conducts a cross-sectional econometric model of foreign students in the United States by country of birth and rejects the source country schooling shortage explanation. Instead, he finds that students from low-wage countries seek schooling in higher-wage countries as a means of augmenting their chances of obtaining a high-wage job in those countries. Increases in the number of students in the tertiary system in source countries actually generate a growing pool of potential international students—especially from low-income countries—and Rozenzweig finds it is associated with an increase in the number of students from source countries who pursue their studies abroad in higher-wage countries.

DeVoretz assumes a lagged demand function for student enrollment in Canadian higher education (2006). He proposes that students decide where to migrate based on the cost of college tuition. He predicts current enrollments of foreign students by country of origin with the following: one period of lagged enrollment, source-country income level, and exchange-rate-weighted tuition fees in Canada. He finds the estimated coefficients for lagged enrollment and source-country income level are positively correlated with the number of students choosing to study abroad in Canada, but he finds an inverse relationship for exchange-weighted Canadian tuition fees (indicating that fewer students will choose to study abroad in Canada as tuition increases). Naidoo (2007) analyzes time series data on international student migration to the United Kingdom and finds, like DeVoretz (2006), that the cost of tuition in the host country reduces migration and, like Rosenzweig (2007), that access to source-country educational opportunities increases student mobility.

While these models serve as useful starting points, none of them explicitly modeled the role of policy constraints or international competition for students. Thus, we estimate an econometric model in which the dependent variable is the log of student visa issuances, or *FV*, to represent the so-called F, or student, visa.[10] The sample includes data on students from 130 countries from 1999 through 2004. We estimate a pooled cross-sectional and time-series model of a measure of the student flow specified as follows:

$$
\begin{aligned}
lnFV_{j,t} = {} & \alpha_j + \alpha_1 lnGDPPC_{j,t-1} + \alpha_2 lnER_{j,t-1} + \alpha_3 lnGDPPC\,j,t_{-1} * lnER_{j,t-1} \\
& + \alpha_4 lnPOP_{j,t} + \alpha_5 lnRR_{j,t-1} + \alpha_6 lnTC_{j,t-1} + \alpha_7 lnACUN_{j,t-1} \\
& + \alpha_8 lnFGJ_{j,t-1} + \alpha_9 post911 + \varepsilon_{j,t}
\end{aligned}
$$

In the above specification, *j* denotes a student's home country and *t* denotes the year. The estimated parameters are α_1 through α_9. Like

DeVoretz (2006), we assume a lagged demand function, and all of the right-hand side variables are lagged by one year to avoid contemporaneous effects (except *lnPOP*, the log of population in the source country, and *post911*, which is a dummy variable equal to one for the years 2002–2004 and zero in all other years). Students also typically decide where to study and apply for visas at least one year prior to the academic year in which they migrate. We prefer the log-log specification typical of migration research and present the results of a fixed-effect model.[11]

The set of independent variables used in the regression analysis include *lnPOP*; *lnGDPPC*, the log of per-capita GDP (in purchasing-power parity terms with constant 2000 U.S. dollars); *lnER*, the log of the source-country enrollment ratio or students as a percentage of young people enrolled in institutions of higher education within the source country; *lnTC*, the log of four-year tuition costs at public colleges and universities (adjusted for real exchange rates in 2000 U.S. dollars); *lnRR*, the log of nonimmigrant visa refusal rates;[12] *lnACUN*, the log of foreign-student enrollments in other English-speaking countries (Australia, Canada, the United Kingdom, or New Zealand); *lnFGJ*, the log of foreign-student enrollment in one of the leading non-English-speaking countries (France, Germany, or Japan); and the dummy variable called *post911*. The variables *lnRR*, *lnTC*, *lnACUN*, *lnFGJ*, and *post911* are included in the regression to control for the effects of U.S. visa procedures, tuition costs, foreign-student enrollment patterns in competing countries, and the mobility of students before and after 9/11. Based on the earlier discussion in this chapter, we expected the estimated coefficients on these variables not to be positive.

In the aforementioned specification, we introduced an interaction between *lnGDPPC* and *lnER* that is intended to capture differences in applicants' incentive levels.[13] The variable *lnGDPPC* is expected to capture the effects both of the prospective foreign student's ability to pay to study abroad and the applicant's incentive to obtain a U.S. visa to get access to the U.S. labor market where the skill prices are higher. Similarly, *lnER* is intended to control for the source country's educational capacity and output. A lower *ER* in the source country implies an inadequate supply of institutions of higher education, a lower premium for higher education, or both. *ER* also acts as an indicator for the quality of the student visa applicant pool. There is a correlation of 0.74 between *lnGDPPC* and *lnER*; this suggests that applicants from relatively poorer countries, for which both *GDPPC* and *ER* are lower, have greater incentives to obtain student visas. For these applicants, the skill-price premiums and the value of access to better education can be expected to be higher than for applicants from relatively wealthier countries.

Table 3-1 provides the summary statistics for these variables, the data for which were collected from a variety of sources.[14] Table 3-2 shows the results for alternative specifications and includes *t*-statistics given in parentheses that are based on robust standard errors. Specification 1 includes the basic set of variables—*lnGDPPC, lnER, lnPOP, lnRR, lnTC, lnACUN,* and *lnFGJ*—while specification 2 adds the post-9/11 dummy variable to the first specification. Specification 3 adds the interaction term *lnGDPPC*lnER*, and specification 4 includes both the interaction term and the post-9/11 dummy. The signs on the estimated coefficients are consistent across the specifications, but magnitudes change notably when the interaction term, the post-9/11 dummy, or both are included.

With this model, we found that both per-capita GDP (*GDPPC*) and enrollment ratios (*ER*) are positively related to student flows, but neither is

TABLE 3-1

SUMMARY STATISTICS OF VARIABLES FOR THE PERIOD 1999–2004

Variables	Observations	Mean	Standard Deviation
$lnFV_{j,t-1}$	968	5.97	1.60
$lnGDPPC_{j,t-1}$	911	8.48	1.16
$lnPOP_{j,t}$	579	16.00	1.65
$lnER_{j,t-1}$	553	2.81	1.25
$lnRR_{j,t-1}$	897	−1.34	0.69
$lnTC_{j,t-1}$	952	8.17	0.32
$lnACUN_{j,t-1}$	765	6.21	1.84
$lnFGJ_{j,t-1}$	764	6.24	2.03

SOURCE: Authors' calculations including data from the following: U.S. Department of State, *Report of the Visa Office*, 2008, 110th Cong., 2d sess. (Washington, DC) available through www.travel.state.gov/visa/statistics/statistics_1476.html; World Bank, *World Development Indicators: Global Economy Series*, 11th ed. (Washington, DC: World Bank Publications, 2007); United Nations Educational, Scientific, and Cultural Organization (UNESCO), "Statistics Database: All Reports," United Nations, available at http://stats.uis.unesco.org/ReportFolders/reportFolders.aspx; and College Board, "Trends in College Pricing," *Trends in Higher Education Series*, 2009, last updated July 2, 2010, available at www.trends-collegeboard.com/college_pricing.

TABLE 3-2
FIXED-EFFECTS REGRESSION RESULTS: THE NATURAL LOG OF FOREIGN-STUDENT VISAS

Variables:	Specifications			
	1	2	3	4
$lnGDPPC_{j,t-1}$	0.055 (0.18)	0.469 (1.61)	1.206 (2.86)	1.278 (3.13)
$lnER_{j,t-1}$	0.011 (0.06)	0.156 (0.88)	3.060 (3.77)	2.475 (3.07)
$lnGDPPC_{j,t-1}$ $* logER\_1_{j,t-1}$	--	--	−0.365 (−4.14)	−0.281 (−3.16)
$lnPOP_{j,t-1}$	−1.731 (−1.51)	−0.805 (−0.71)	−2.567 (−2.40)	−1.622 (−1.48)
$lnRR_{j,t-1}$	−0.239 (−4.94)	−0.176 (−3.72)	−0.185 (−3.81)	−0.147 (−3.02)
$lnTC_{j,t-1}$	−0.287 (−2.19)	−0.150 (−1.35)	−0.299 (−2.62)	−0.185 (−1.83)
$lnACUN_{j,t-1}$	−0.130 (−1.79)	−0.051 (−0.69)	−0.141 (−1.99)	−0.074 (−1.03)
$lnFGJ_{j,t-1}$	−0.068 (−1.30)	−0.062 (−1.23)	−0.030 (−0.59)	−0.034 (−0.67)
post911 dummy	--	−0.227 (−5.90)	--	−0.184 (−4.83)
Constant	18.70 (1.97)	16.54 (0.89)	41.02 (2.48)	23.54 (1.39)
Number of Observations	506	506	506	506
R-Squared: Within	0.28	0.34	0.33	0.38
Overall	0.45	0.19	0.40	0.28

SOURCE: Authors' calculations.

statistically significant unless the interaction term is included in the regression. When the interaction term is added, *GDPPC, ER,* and their interaction term are significantly correlated with the student flow at better than the 0.01 level. The interaction term has a negative estimated coefficient as expected and as is consistent with Rosenzweig's findings (2007). Based on specification 4, the elasticity of the student flow with respect to per-capita income, computed at the sample mean, is 0.49 [= 1.28 + (−0.281 * 2.81)]. Similarly, the student flow elasticity vis-à-vis the enrollment ratio is 0.10 [= 2.48 + (−0.281 * 8.48)]. These estimates suggest that, on average, a 10 percent increase in per-capita income is followed by a 5 percent increase in student flow. However, when the source-country enrollment ratio increases by 10 percent, the student flow increases by only 1 percent.

These elasticities are notably different when computed for lower- as compared with higher-income countries. For India, the per-capita income and enrollment ratio elasticities are 0.61 and 0.29. In contrast, for the United Kingdom the corresponding figures are 0.13 and –0.38; this indicates that it would take a larger change in per-capita income or enrollment ratios to affect the number of students studying abroad from the United Kingdom than would be necessary to affect the number studying abroad from India. Together, the results are consistent with the expectation that students from poorer countries have a greater incentive to study abroad. The student flows from poorer countries with lower *GDPPC* or *ER* respond more positively to increases in income or a higher ratio of students enrolled in college. The incentives for students from poor countries to study abroad in the United States are high because the United States has both higher skill prices than they are likely to earn in their home countries and many quality institutions of higher education. These incentives are much weaker for students from more affluent countries. Increased enrollment ratios are associated with increased flows from lower-income countries, while students from high-income countries are less likely to go abroad as enrollment ratios increase. The interaction term accounts for the varying degrees of incentives among applicants from countries that range widely on the income scale.

As for the measure of policy or the impact of visa procedures, the negative association between student visas issued and rejection rates (*lnRR*) is significant at the 0.01 level in all regressions. Specification 4 showed that a 10 percent increase in visa refusal rates (*lnRR*) is associated with a 1.5 percent decrease in student inflows. This is roughly the same order of magnitude as the effect of tuition costs (*lnTC*), in which a 10 percent increase in tuition costs is associated with a 1.9 percent decrease in student inflows. However, the statistical significance of the estimated coefficient on *lnTC* is sensitive to the inclusion of the post-9/11 dummy in the regression; the dummy variable reduces the significance of *lnTC*.

The regression also indicates that there are competitive effects on student flows to the United States; the enrollments of students in competing English-speaking (*ACUN*) and non-English-speaking (*FGJ*) countries are negatively correlated with the student flow into the United States. However, the results are statistically significant only when the post-9/11 dummy variable is not included in the regression (specifications 1 and 3). The coefficients on *lnACUN* and *lnFGJ* are not significant and have small magnitudes when the post-9/11 dummy is included in the regressions (specifications 2 and 4). As expected, the dummy variable has a negative coefficient, and in specification 4, we found an 18 percent decrease in the student flow in 2002–2004 compared to 2000–2001. Finally, *lnPOP*, included primarily to scale for the relative number of student visas issued, has a negative coefficient and is generally statistically insignificant.

To summarize, these findings show that the major determinants of foreign-student flow into the United States are per-capita income, visa rejection rates, tuition costs, and domestic enrollments in source countries. Student flow is more responsive to increases in national per-capita income or the enrollment ratio when these levels are low, as in poorer or middle-income countries. Competition with other countries for international students reduces flows to the United States, but that does not appear to have been a cause of declining student numbers between 2001 and 2004. Higher rejection rates and tuition costs adversely affect the flow to about the same degree, indicating that visa difficulties are no more a deterrent to foreign-student migration to the United States than the high cost of college.

Conclusion

In this chapter, we argue that the procedural changes in U.S. visa policies following 9/11 had only a contributory impact on the downturn in foreign-student numbers. The recession of 2001 had a greater impact on the reduction; it reduced both the sources of income that enable students to afford to study abroad and the wages in the destination country, both of which are primary incentives to attract foreign students. Simultaneously, the cost of education increased at an accelerated pace at this juncture, a fact that is little appreciated by most observers. The cost of a college education has been and will increasingly be a marketing challenge for U.S. colleges and, indeed, for many countries competing for international students. There is every reason to seek continued improvement in visa procedures (International Visitors Office 2009), but continued assertions that U.S. policy restricts student migration—particularly policies set in place after 9/11—misstate the reasons for the decline in foreign-student numbers.

Concerns about a declining U.S. market share of international students conflate two issues. First, the U.S. share of the global market for students has long been in decline, and—even if it stabilizes in the near term—it is difficult to see how it could increase over the long run. Second, theory and available research on enrollments indicate that the pool of students seeking to study abroad will increase notably in the future. International higher education is projected to grow enormously—from 1.8 million international students in 2000 to 7.2 million in 2025 (Böhm et al. 2002). The United States likely will attract a growing number of international students. Other countries that actively compete for international students may attract some who might otherwise have chosen to study in the United States. It would be prudent to debate how the United States might attract the best students, especially as global trends demonstrate that it is unlikely the United States will regain its market share of international students, even while the actual number of foreign students enrolled in the United States increases.

This chapter does not address at least two issues that future research should examine. First, the formulations of many of those concerned about the post-9/11 decline in student numbers vacillate between explanations based on policy changes and those of "perception." The so-called newly implemented restrictive policies or visa procedures actually affected few students or had a very short-lived effect. Perhaps, then, potential applicants perceived widespread problems based on the prevalent anecdotes of students caught in visa limbo. Perhaps applicants, like many tourists, were deterred by the fear of further terrorist action or perceptions of an aggressively nationalistic and less-than-welcoming America. Unfortunately, theory or measures of perceptions, and their impact on how students choose where to study do not yet exist. Second, at the time of this writing, the world has entered another recession. But student visas declined by only 3 percent in 2008–2009, primarily because student visas from China, the student leader, increased a remarkable 47 percent. Other leading nations, such as India, Korea, and Saudi Arabia, have seen their visas decline by about 20 percent or commensurate with the earlier 2000–2001 decline. Yet, there has been no change in visa rejection rates and, one might surmise, that the off-putting perceptions created after 9/11 have dissipated. The impacts of this recession on foreign-student flows should be examined in more detail in the future.

Notes

1. Individuals admitted as refugees who were also students were removed from the student visa counts in the 1980s, but their numbers were too few to account for the observed decline, and the decline does not correspond with the timing of this removal.

2. The U.S. Department of State posts visa fees and consular visa processing times, but these data are not readily available over time. In practice, visa fees are generally the same for most regions, and in principle, refusal rates across nations should be highly correlated with the length of processing times (U.S. Department of State 2008).

3. These are "initial refusals," which refers to refusals that occur before an individual reapplies or an adjustment for subsequent approval of the application is made. The adjusted refusal rate mimics the trend in initial refusals, but tends to be 6–10 percentage points lower. Increases in rates of initial refusal do increase the time from application to final visa approval.

4. Student applicants in certain fields may be subject to review on the Technology Alert List.

5. Political shocks alone are estimated to lead to a 20 percent decrease in the number of nonimmigrant visas issued to citizens of affected countries by the United States (Krepps et al. 2005).

6. Data on admissions for visa waivers are unavailable for 2000 and 2001 (U.S. Department of Homeland Security 2008).

7. While not marketing per se, the U.S. government does provide extensive programs for potential students (see Schneider 2000).

8. One estimate suggests that 20 percent of foreign students adjust to permanent status (see Rosenzweig 2007). For estimates by degree type, see Lowell, Bump, and Martin (2007).

9. There are other, less well-known studies. One student paper applies simple ordinary least squares to a pooled, cross-sectional time series and finds a statistically significant correlation between source-country rates of Internet usage and income tax treaties with the United States, but not with per-capita GDP differentials. Yet another econometric estimation finds that per-capita GDP does matter for different measures of migrant flows, depending on if the migrants are students, visitors, or business travelers (Han 2005; Roberts 2006b).

10. The dependent variable includes both the F-1 principal and F-2 dependent visas, and includes both undergraduate and graduate students. Flow data that separate students by undergraduate or graduate status are not available.

11. A Hausman test rejected a random-effects model, although the results of the random- and fixed-effect estimators are similar.

12. The U.S. Department of State does not make national-level data on refusal rates for detailed visa classes publicly available. However, there is a high correlation between total nonimmigrant visa refusal rates and those for the foreign student (F)

visa. The total refusal rate may better capture students' perceptions when applying for visas, which may be based upon the experiences of the average visa applicant; this is more easily ascertained from the total visa refusal rates and is what we used in our model.

13. Rosenzweig (2007) measures per-country GDP both as ability to pay and as a skill-price measure available for only a cross-section of countries. He also includes several measures of source-country educational capacity, quality, and output, while we include only enrollment ratios. Regardless, he notes that per-capita income, while imperfect, captures skill-price differentials. In our final analysis, our findings replicate the essence of his more complete and nuanced specification, which supports the robustness of his general theoretical expectations.

14. The number of student visas issued (*FV*) and the refusal rates (*RR*) come from the U.S. Department of State (2008). The figures for per-capita GDP and source country population (*GDPPC* and *POP*) are obtained from the World Bank (2007). The source country enrollment ratio (*ER*) and the foreign student–enrollment data in competing nations (*ACUN* and *FGJ*) are obtained from the UNESCO database. The competing-enrollment measures are similar to the specifications of prior research on migration flows between countries, where increases (decreases) in flows to competitors decrease (increase) flows to the United States (Cobb-Clark and Connolly 1997). The data on four-year public college tuition (*TC*) comes from the College Board (2009) and are weighted by source country exchange rates for the U.S. dollar. In the UNESCO database, the enrollment data for Canada are missing for 2001 and 2003, and the data for Australia are missing for 2003. These missing values have been linearly interpolated or extrapolated.

References

Alden, E. 2008. *The Closing of the American Border: Terrorism, Immigration, and Security Since 9/11*. New York: Harper Collins.

Altbach, P. G., L. Reisberg, and L. E. Rumbley. 2009. Trends in Global Higher Education: Tracking an Academic Revolution; A Report Prepared for the UNESCO 2009 World Conference on Higher Education. Paris: United Nations Educational, Scientific, and Cultural Organization (UNESCO). Available at http://unesdoc.unesco.org/images/0018/001831/183168e.pdf.

American Electronics Association. 2005. *Losing the Competitive Advantage? The Challenge for Science and Technology in the United States*. Washington, DC: American Electronics Association.

Beine, M., F. Docquier, and H. Rapoport. 2009. On the Robustness of Brain Gain Estimates. Institute for the Study of Labor (IZA) Discussion Series no. 4293. Bonn, Germany.

Board of Education and Workforce, National Research Council. 2005. *Policy Implications of International Graduate Students and Postdoctoral Scholars in the United States*. Washington, DC: The National Academies Press. Available at www.nap.edu/catalog/11280.html.

Böhm, A., A. Davis, D. Meares, and D. Pearce. 2002. Global Student Mobility 2025: Forecasts of the Global Demand for International Higher Education. Australia: IDP Education Australia.

Bound, J., S. Turner, and P. Walsh. 2009. Internationalization of U.S. Doctorate Education. National Bureau of Economic Research (NBER) Working Paper 14792. Washington, DC. Available at www.nber.org/papers/w14792.

Bush, J. T., F. McLarty III, and E. Alden. 2009. *U.S. Immigration Policy*. Washington, DC: Council on Foreign Relations. Independent Task Force Report no. 63. Available at www.cfr.org/content/publications/attachments/Immigration_TFR63.pdf.

Cobb-Clark, D. A., and M. D. Connolly. 1997. The Worldwide Market for Skilled Migrants: Can Australia Compete? *International Migration Review* 31 (3): 670–93.

College Board. 2009. Trends in College Pricing. *Trends in Higher Education Series*. Available at www.trends-collegeboard.com/college_pricing.

Committee on Prospering in the Global Economy of the Twenty-first Century: An Agenda for American Science and Technology, National Academy of Sciences, National Academy of Engineering, Institute of Medicine. 2007. *Rising Above the Gathering Storm: Energizing and Employing America for a Brighter Economic Future*. Washington, DC: The National Academies Press. Available at www.nap.edu/catalog.php?record_id=11463.

Council of Graduate Schools (CGS). 2009. Findings from the 2009 CGS International Graduate Admissions Survey, Phase I: Applications. Washington, DC: CGS Research Report. Available at www.cgsnet.org/portals/0/pdf/R_IntlApps09_I.pdf.

DeVoretz, D. J. 2006. *The Education, Immigration and Emigration of Canada's Highly Skilled Workers in the 21st Century*. Washington, DC: Institute for the Study of International Migration, Georgetown University. Available at http://isim.georgetown. edu/Event%20Documents/Sloan%20Global%20Competition%20Meeting/ DevoretzCanada.pdf.

Doomerrik, J., R. Koslowski, J. Laurence, and R. Maxwell. 2009. *Transatlantic Academy Report on Immigration: No Shortcuts: Selective Migration and Integration*. Washington, DC: Transatlantic Academy. Available at www.gmfus.org/publications/ article.cfm?parent_type=P&id=600.

Han, M. 2005. International Students: Why Do They Choose the United States as a Study Abroad Destination? Paper presented at the annual meeting of the Midwest Political Science Association, Chicago.

Hanson, G. H., and A. Spilimbergo. 1999. Illegal Immigration, Border Enforcement, and Relative Wages: Evidence from Apprehensions at the U.S.-Mexico Border. *American Economic Review* 89 (December): 1337–57.

Hatton, T. J., and J. G. Williamson. 2003. What Fundamentals Drive World Migration? National Bureau of Economic Research Working Paper no. 9159, Cambridge, MA.

Institute of International Education (IIE). 2008. Open Doors 2008 Data Tables. New York: IIE. Available at: http://opendoors.iienetwork.org/?p=131530

———. 2010. Promotional Activities and Policies. In *Atlas of Student Mobility*. New York: IIE. Available at http://atlas.iienetwork.org/?p=85685.

International Center for Migration Policy Development. 2006. *Comparative Study on Policies toward Foreign Students: Study on Admission and Retention Policies toward Foreign Students in Industrialized Counties*. Vienna, Austria: International Center for Migration Policy Development.

International Visitors Office. 2009. Statement and Recommendations on Visa Problems Harming America's Scientific, Economic, and Security Interests. Board on International Scientific Organizations, The National Academies. Available through http://sites.nationalacademies.org/pga/biso/visas/index.htm.

Krepps, S., B. L. Lowell, G. Flores, and M. Rom. 2005. Consular Affairs Futures Study. Report by Change Navigators to the U.S. Department of State, Bureau of Consular Affairs, Washington, DC.

Kuptsch, C., and E. Pang, eds. 2006. *Competing for Global Talent*. Geneva: International Labor Organization.

Lasanowski, Veronica, and Line Verbik. 2007. *International Student Mobility: Patterns and Trends*. London: Observatory on Borderless Higher Education.

Lowell, B. L., M. Bump, and S. Martin. 2007. *Foreign Students Coming to America: The Impact of Policy, Procedures, and Economic Competition*. Washington, DC: Institute for the Study of International Migration, Georgetown University. Available at http://isim.georgetown.edu/Publications/SloanMaterials/Foreign%20Students%20Coming%20to%20America.pdf.

Massey, D. S., J. Arango, G. Hugo, A. Kouaouci, A. Pellegrino, and J. E. Taylor. 1994. An Evaluation of International Migration Theory: The North American Case. *Population and Development Review* 20 (4): 699–751.

Mayda, A. M. 2005. International Migration: A Panel Data Analysis of Economic and Non-economic Determinants. IZA. IZA Discussion Series no. 1590. Bonn, Germany.

Naidoo, V. 2007. Research on the Flow of International Students to UK Universities: Determinants and Implications. *Journal of Research in International Education* 6 (3): 287–307.

National Commission on Terrorist Attacks upon the United States. 2004. *9/11 and Terrorist Travel*. Washington, DC: Staff Report of the National Commission on Terrorist Attacks upon the United States. Available at www.9-11commission.gov/staff_statements/911_TerrTrav_Monograph.pdf.

Neiman, Brent, and Phillip Swagel. 2009. The Impact of Post-9/11 Visa Policies on Travel to the United States. *Journal of International Economics* 78 (1): 86–99.

New Zealand Ministry of Education. 2007. *Making a Choice about Where to Study: The Experiences of International Students in New Zealand; Report on the Results of the National Survey*. New Zealand: Ministry of Education.

Organisation for Economic Co-operation and Development (OECD). 2004. *Internationalization and Trade in Higher Education*. Paris: OECD Publishing.

———. 2006. Indicator C3: Student Mobility and Foreign Students in Tertiary Education. In *Education at a Glance 2006*. Paris: OECD Publishing. Available at www.oecd.org/dataoecd/46/0/37368660.xls.

———. 2008. *Education at a Glance 2008: OECD Indicators*. Paris: OECD Publishing. Available at www.oecd.org/dataoecd/23/46/41284038.pdf.

Orrenius, P. M. 2003. Do Amnesty Programs Reduce Undocumented Immigration? Evidence from IRCA. *Demography* 40 (3): 437–50.

Roberts, B. 2006a. Foreign Student Enrollments in the U.S. Since 9/11. Presentation to NAFSA: Association of Educators, Washington, DC. Available at www.nafsa3.org/conferences/regional2007/presentations/dhspres.pdf.

———. 2006b. The Impacts of 9/11 and Changes in Visa and Entry Policies and Procedures on Overseas Visitors to the U.S. Washington, DC: Department of Homeland Security, Private Sector Office.

Rosenzweig, M. R. 2007. Global Wage Differences and International Student Flows. *Brookings Trade Forum*: 57–86.

Schneider, M. 2000. Others' Open Doors: How Other Nations Attract International Students; Implications for U.S. Educational Exchange. Report for the Maxwell–Syracuse Washington International Relations Program. Syracuse, NY: Syracuse University.

Tierney, William G., and Vicente M. Lechuga. 2005. Academic Freedom in the 21st Century. *Thought & Action* (Fall): 7–22.

Todaro, R. M. 2001. APS News Survey Tracks Chinese Student Visa Problems. *American Physical Society* 10 (10). Available at www.aps.org/publications/apsnews/200111/visa.cfm.

U.S. Department of Homeland Security. 2008. *Yearbook of Immigration Statistics*. Washington, DC: U.S. Department of Homeland Security. Available through www.dhs.gov/ximgtn/statistics/publications/yearbook.shtm.

U.S. Department of State. 2008. *Report of the Visa Office*. Washington, DC: U.S. Department of State. Available through www.travel.state.gov/visa/statistics/statistics_1476.html.

United Nations Educational, Scientific, and Cultural Organization (UNESCO). Statistics Database: All Reports. New York: United Nations. Available at http://stats.uis.unesco.org/ReportFolders/reportFolders.aspx.

Varghese, N. V. 2008. Globalization of Higher Education and Cross-Border Student Mobility. UNESCO: International Institute for Education and Planning. Available at www.unesco.org/iiep/PDF/pubs/2008/Globalization_HE.pdf.

Verbik, L., and V. Lasanowski. 2007. International Student Mobility: Patterns and Trends. Report for the Observatory on Borderless Higher Education.

Walker, K. C. 2004. Creating a Virtual Border: The Manifest Destiny of U.S. Border Security. Paper presented at the American Immigration Lawyers Association (AILA) Midsouth Conference.

Wassem, R. E. 2003. Foreign Students in the United States: Policies and Legislation. Congressional Research Service.

World Bank. 2007. *World Development Indicators: Global Economy Series*. 11th ed. Washington, DC: World Bank Publications.

Yale-Loehr, S., D. Papademetriou, and B. Cooper. 2005. *Secure Borders, Open Doors: Visa Procedures in the Post–September 11 Era*. Washington, DC: Migration Policy Institute. Available at www.migrationpolicy.org/pubs/visa_report.pdf.

Yang, R. 2003. Globalization and Higher Education. *International Review of Higher Education* 49: 269–91.

PART III

The Adjustment of High-Skilled Immigrants

4

Educational Mismatch: Are High-Skilled Immigrants Really Working in High-Skilled Jobs, and What Price Do They Pay If They Are Not?

Barry R. Chiswick and Paul W. Miller

The United States is home to millions of immigrants. Its "golden door" has been open to many flows of immigrants, including "the wretched refuse of your teeming shore," as termed in Emma Lazarus's 1883 poem engraved on the base of the Statue of Liberty. In addition to these "huddled masses," however, from colonial times to the present, the United States has attracted many skilled immigrants.[1] High-skilled immigrants currently in the United States are the subject of this chapter.

Figure 4-1 displays the flow of legal permanent residents (LPRs) into the United States for fiscal years 1987–2007. These numbers reflect both new arrivals and adjustments of status among those already living in the United States. Permanent-residence status is primarily gained on the basis of a family relationship with a U.S. citizen or LPR, with permanent residency based

The authors thank Derby Voon for research assistance and Charles Beach and other participants at the American Enterprise Institute (AEI) conference, "High-Skilled Immigration in a Globalized Labor Market," held in Washington, D.C., April 22–23, 2009, as well as seminar participants at the University of Illinois at Chicago and the Australian National University, for helpful comments. Chiswick and Miller acknowledge research support from AEI, and Miller acknowledges financial assistance from the Australian Research Council.

FIGURE 4-1

**TOTAL LEGAL PERMANENT-RESIDENT VISAS AND EMPLOYMENT-PREFERENCE
VISAS ISSUED IN THE UNITED STATES, FISCAL YEARS 1987–2007**

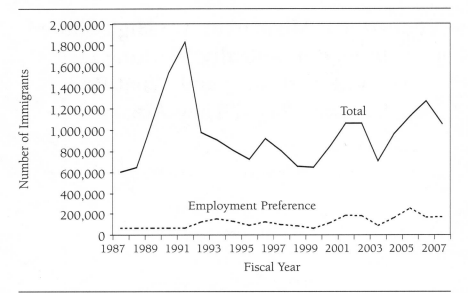

SOURCE: U.S. Department of Homeland Security (DHS), Office of Immigration Statistics, *2004 Yearbook of Immigration Statistics* (Washington, DC: DHS, 2006); and U.S. DHS, Office of Immigration Statistics, *2007 Yearbook of Immigration Statistics* (Washington, DC: DHS, 2008).
NOTE: The spike in permanent-resident visas from 1989 to 1992 is related to the granting of amnesty to nearly 3 million illegal migrants under the 1986 Immigration Reform and Control Act.

on skills (employment preferences) serving as a much smaller, but the second-largest, category of admissions (see table 4-1 for a breakdown of 2007 admissions). Figure 4-1 also provides information on the number of LPRs in the employment-preference categories.[2] The number of immigrants entering the United States in the employment-preference categories has increased considerably over the past two decades. In 1986, they numbered 56,617, or 9.4 percent of total immigration, while in response to 1990 legislation to increase the number of immigrants admitted based on employer preferences, they numbered 162,176 in 2007, or 15.4 percent of total immigration. However, in both years nearly half of immigrants in this category consisted of spouses and minor children of principal applicants.

TABLE 4-1
IMMIGRATION TO THE UNITED STATES BY TYPE OF VISA,
FISCAL YEAR 2007

Type of Visa	Immigrants (Thousands)	
Immediate Relatives of U.S. Citizens	494	} 688
Family-Sponsored Preferences	194	
Employment-Based (and Their Families)	162	
Diversity	42	
Refugees, Asylum Recipients, Parolees	138	
Other	20	
Total	**1,052**	

SOURCE: U.S. DHS, Office of Immigration Statistics, *2007 Yearbook of Immigration Statistics* (Washington, DC: DHS, September 2008).
NOTE: Detail may not add to total due to rounding.

Understanding how employment-preference immigrants perform in the U.S. labor market is important from the perspective of guiding the mix of immigrants, that is, whether relatively more low- or high-skilled immigrants should be granted entry to the United States. Unfortunately, visa category information is not available in the data sets—such as from the decennial censuses—that are otherwise most useful for labor-market analyses of immigrants in the United States. Therefore, this paper looks at all skilled foreign-born workers, as reported in the U.S. census, regardless of their visa status, including those on temporary work visas (such as H1-B visa recipients).

This chapter adopts perspectives from the overeducation and undereducation literature. This literature proposes that there is a "usual" education level for each occupation. Some workers will have this level of education, and will therefore be regarded as being matched to the typical educational requirements of their jobs. Other workers will have a higher level of education than that which is usual in their job. These workers with "surplus" years of schooling are viewed as being overeducated.[3] Still other workers will have a lower level of education than that which is usual in their job. Such workers are viewed as being undereducated. Chiswick and Miller (2008, 2009) show that, for analyses of the United States and Australia, this framework yields important insights into the international transferability of human capital for immigrant workers across all skill levels, but this chapter will focus on high-skilled immigrant workers.

This chapter will include a discussion of how a "mismatch" of education and occupation in the labor market is determined. While the factors that bring about this mismatch for the native born also apply for immigrants, two additional factors (skill transferability and selectivity in migration) also apply for immigrants. Following this, the chapter provides an overview of data on the education levels of the native- and foreign-born population. Next is a brief review of a selection of previous studies in the overeducation and undereducation literature.[4] The broad aim of this review is to highlight methodological issues pertinent to a study of high-skilled immigrants. The chapter then outlines the empirical framework adopted in this study and provides information on the data sources. The statistical analyses of the extent of the educational mismatch and the earnings consequences of these mismatches are then presented. The final section concludes with a summary and the policy implications of the findings.

Why Do Education Mismatches Occur?

Consider the typical or usual level of education in an occupation. Why would there be education mismatches, that is, individuals whose educational attainment differs from the norm for their occupation?

The usual level or norm is merely a measure of central tendency. Depending on the particular technology that they employ, or the educational attainment of the labor market from which they draw their labor supply, firms may have a different optimal level of education for their workers in a particular occupation compared to the occupation as a whole nationwide. Workers also differ by age, so there are cohort differences in when they received their formal schooling, when they joined the labor force, and the extent of their labor-market experience. Mismatches related to cohorts may arise if there has been an upgrading of educational requirements for new hires, but longer-term employees are retained because of their seniority or because their greater on-the-job training (labor-market experience) compensates for their falling behind the educational norms for new hires.

The mismatches here would be overeducated new hires and undereducated established workers compared to the average worker currently in place.

Workers clearly differ in characteristics that may be difficult, if not impossible, to measure in survey or census data, but which may be revealed in the labor market. These unmeasured characteristics include dimensions of worker and allocative (decision-making) ability, efficiency, ambition, aggressiveness, energy, job dedication, favorable and unfavorable personality traits, and so on. On the one hand, those with higher levels of desirable unmeasured abilities can attain a higher occupation level for the same amount of schooling, and thereby may appear to be undereducated. On the other hand, those who the market evaluates as being deficient in beneficial unmeasured traits are more likely to be relegated to occupations that are at a lower level compared to their schooling, and hence appear to be overeducated given their occupation.

The reasons just discussed for educational mismatches would apply equally to native-born and foreign-born workers. There are, however, immigrant-specific factors that may contribute to a greater mismatch of education and occupation among the foreign-born population in the labor market: the limited international transferability of skills and selectivity in migration.

For most immigrants to a destination, skills acquired in the country of origin are not perfectly transferable. These skills include information about how labor markets operate, as well as destination-language skills. There may be occupation-specific skills that are not readily transferable because of differences related to types of technology (such as English measures versus the metric system or legal systems based on English common law versus those based on the Napoleonic code). There may be differences in levels of technology because of differences in capital-to-labor ratios or relative-factor prices (for example, high-technology medicine in the United States versus low-technology medicine in the former Soviet Union and the least developed countries). Moreover, there may be barriers to entry in occupations in immigrants' destination countries that they trained for and practiced in their origin countries (examples include occupational licensing, union regulations, and governmental requirements, such as citizenship). In addition, cultural differences may make it difficult for immigrants in certain occupations to transfer their skills to the labor market in their destination country.[5]

Immigrants and those who assist their integration into the destination country's labor market frequently express concern about the nonrecognition of premigration skills, whether acquired in school or on the job. In some instances nonrecognition results from requirements for occupational licensing, but it may also arise when risk-averse employers and consumers do not know how to evaluate foreign credentials compared to credentials earned in the destination country.[6] Further, discrimination against immigrants can also reduce their ability to transfer their skills in whole or in part to their destination country.

A lower degree of transferability of skills from an immigrant's origin country to the destination leads to a greater occupational downgrade for the immigrant. This increases the likelihood that immigrants will appear to be overeducated for the occupations they ultimately hold in the destination country. Over time, immigrants who stay in the destination country generally invest in destination human capital, either by modifying (or increasing the transferability of) premigration skills, or by acquiring new skills altogether. Thus, immigrants' occupational levels improve, thereby diminishing the extent to which they are seen as overeducated.

Selectivity in immigration is the other immigrant-specific factor that can contribute to a mismatch in immigrant education and occupation. For several reasons, economic migrants tend to be favorably selected for labor-market success in their destination country (Chiswick 1999, 2008). Indeed, economic migrants have success in the destination country as their primary goal by definition (this relates to the supply of immigrants). Moreover, some immigrants are specifically granted visas because of their high levels of skill (relating to the demand for immigrants), although the relative importance of employment-based visas varies across destinations. The considerations that lead to self-selection for economic immigration and the considerations that lead employers to sponsor immigrants suggest that such immigrants are likely predisposed to be successful.

Other measured variables being equal, including educational attainment, these circumstances indicate that immigrants are more likely to have higher unmeasured dimensions of ability than others in their origin country who do not emigrate. If these unmeasured dimensions of ability are similarly distributed among the native-born population in the origin and destination countries, by implication the immigrants will also have, on average, a higher level of unmeasured dimensions of ability than the native-born population in the destination country. If the usual educational attainment in an occupation is based on the native-born population, a higher level of unmeasured ability would enable immigrants to attain a higher occupational level in the destination country than native-born workers with the same level of schooling might attain. Alternatively, such immigrants might gain employment in the same occupation as more highly educated natives. Immigrants in this situation would appear to be undereducated for their occupation level.

In summary, one would expect to observe workers in the labor market who appear to be over- or undereducated relative to the usual educational attainment for their occupation. Along with the factors relevant for the native-born population, immigrants face two additional factors that may lead to an education-occupation mismatch. Less-than-perfect international transferability of skill tends to result in overeducated immigrants, that is, immigrants who are more likely to be employed in occupations for which the usual schooling level is lower than the level they have attained. In contrast, the favorable selectivity of immigrants tends to lead to undereducated immigrants for their occupation, that is, immigrants who are more likely to be working in occupations in which the usual education level is higher than that which they have attained. The issue of skill transferability becomes more intense as skill levels increase, while the issue of selectivity becomes more intense as the ratio of out-of-pocket or direct costs of immigration relative to the opportunity cost of time increases, that is, the effects will be stronger for lower-skilled workers (Chiswick 1999, 2008; Chiswick and Miller 2008). As a result, in a study of high-skilled immigrants, it is to be expected that immigrants with an educational mismatch will tend to be overeducated.

Education Levels of the Native- and Foreign-Born Populations

Figure 4-2 presents information on the distribution of education levels of native- and foreign-born males twenty-five years old and older in 1999.[7] This figure shows that only around 14 percent of native-born males left school before completing high school, while 33 percent are classified as high school graduates, 18 percent attended college but did not receive a

FIGURE 4-2

**DISTRIBUTION OF EDUCATIONAL ATTAINMENT LEVELS
OF ADULT MALES BY NATIVITY, 1999**

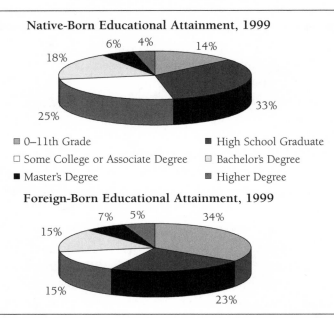

Native-Born Educational Attainment, 1999

6% 4% 14%
18%
33%
25%

▨ 0–11th Grade   ■ High School Graduate
☐ Some College or Associate Degree   ☐ Bachelor's Degree
■ Master's Degree   ▦ Higher Degree

Foreign-Born Educational Attainment, 1999

7% 5% 34%
15%
15%
23%

SOURCE: U.S. Bureau of Labor Statistics (BLS), *Current Population Survey,* 1999 (Washington, DC: BLS, 1999).
NOTES: "Adult" refers to ages twenty-five and older. The "higher degree" category includes those with degrees above the master's level, including professional degrees (such as M.D. or LLB) and doctorates (Ph.D.).

degree, 7 percent attained an associate's degree, 18 percent a bachelor's degree, 6 percent a master's degree, and 4 percent attained either a professional degree or doctorate.

The data for foreign-born males show a much lower mean and greater inequality in the distribution of schooling. A major difference occurs among those who left school very early. Only 14 percent of native-born males did not complete high school, but 34 percent of foreign-born males are in this category. This relatively high representation of those leaving school early is responsible for the mean level of education for the foreign born being nearly 1.5 years lower than the mean level of education for the native born (11.76 years of education for foreign-born males compared with 13.13 years for native-born males in 1999).

The foreign- and native-born populations are more similar in categories denoting higher levels of education. Among the foreign born, 15 percent have bachelor's degrees, compared with 18 percent of native-born males. Foreign-born males are slightly more likely to have attained degrees above a bachelor's than native-born males; 7 percent of the foreign-born population holds a master's degree, compared to 6 percent among the native-born population, and 5 percent of foreign-born males have attained either a professional degree or doctorate, compared to 4 percent of native-born males. Foreign-born males are more heavily represented at the lowest and—albeit to a smaller extent—the highest educational levels.

There are various ways to define the skilled-immigrant group that is the focus of this study: the group could include the approximately 28 percent of the population in each birthplace group (native or foreign) who have attained bachelor's degrees or higher, or the group could be more restrictive and consist only of those who have attained master's degrees or higher. The second option would include 12 percent of the immigrant population and 10 percent of the native-born population. The following analyses consider both definitions.[8]

Literature Review of the ORU Technique

The overeducation and undereducation literature has been used to examine the allocation of workers across the overeducated, undereducated, and correctly matched educational categories in the United States. This literature has also examined how educational mismatches affect earnings. The latter research has been based on a variant of the human-capital earnings function that has been termed the ORU specification (representing overeducation, required education, and undereducation). In this model, the dependent variable is the natural logarithm of earnings (lnY_i) and the variable for actual years of education is decomposed into three terms. This produces the following specification:

$$(1) \quad lnY_i = \alpha_0 + \alpha_1 \text{Over\_Educ}_i + \alpha_2 \text{Req\_Educ}_i + \alpha_3 \text{Under\_Educ}_i + \ldots + u_i$$

where   Over_Educ = years of surplus or over education,
        Req_Educ = the usual or reference years of education,
        Under_Educ = years of deficit or under education,

and the actual years of education equals Over_Educ + Req_Educ – Under_Educ. Note that for each individual, "Over_Educ" and "Under_Educ" cannot both be positive.[9] Either one or both must be zero. Equation (1) also contains other variables generally included in earnings functions, such as years of labor-market experience, marital status, location, veteran of the U.S. Armed Forces, and race/ethnicity, as well as variables specific to the foreign born, such as duration of residence in the United States and citizenship status.

All studies report a high incidence of educational mismatches in the U.S. labor market. In most studies, equation (1) is estimated on samples of all workers, though separate analyses are often undertaken for particular groups of interest. For example, Rumberger (1987) reported findings from estimations undertaken on separate samples of men and women. Duncan and Hoffman (1981) present results for four gender-race groups (white men, black men, white women, black women). Chiswick and Miller (2008) conduct separate analyses for foreign-born and native-born male workers and, among the foreign born, for country of origin.

Some analyses extend the disaggregation of the sample beyond that based on nativity, gender, or race to consider occupations (Rumberger 1987; Verdugo and Verdugo 1989). Rumberger (1987, 31), for example, argued that "we would expect the estimated return to required and surplus schooling to vary across occupations just as the estimated return to actual schooling varies across occupations." Rubb (2003, 54) explains that "the theory behind the occupational analysis is that some occupational groups may be better suited than others in using the surplus human capital of the over-educated workers." Rumberger's 1987 study was based on only five broad categories of occupations: (i) professional/managerial, (ii) support, (iii) craft, (iv) operative, and (v) service. Verdugo and Verdugo (1989) expanded the occupation-specific analyses to nine occupations. Other studies have focused only on particular skill segments of the labor force. Rubb (2003) and Duncan and Hoffman (1981), for example, studied the links between overeducation and earnings among workers with postcollege schooling.

In analyses of earnings, the return to the usual number of years of education for a particular occupation (α_2) is typically much higher than the return to actual years of education (β_1) (Hartog 2000). Years of education above those that are usual in a particular job are associated with a payoff that is much lower than the payoff for each year of education up to the point that is usual within an occupation ($\alpha_2 > \alpha_1$), whereas years of undereducation are associated with an earnings penalty compared to those correctly matched ($\alpha_2 > |\alpha_3|$). These earnings effects, however, have been shown to vary by nativity, occupation, and skill level.

Chiswick and Miller (2008) report that the payoff to a year of education (generally) in the 2000 U.S. population census was 10.6 percent for native-born males and only 5.2 percent for foreign-born males. That is, each additional year of schooling is expected to be associated with 10.6 percent higher earnings among the native born, but with only 5.2 percent higher earnings among the foreign born. The payoff to a year of education that is usual in a person's job did not differ by nativity: it was 15.4 percent for the native born and 15.3 percent for the foreign born. A year of surplus schooling was associated with a payoff of 5.6 percent for the native born and of 4.4 percent for the foreign born. In comparison, the earnings penalty associated with a year of undereducation was −6.7 percent for the native born and only −2.1 percent for the foreign born.

Vahey (2000) examined the incidence and returns to educational mismatch in Canada with a modification to the ORU model. Thus, the estimating equation was:

$$(2) \quad lnY_i = \gamma_0 + \gamma_1 \text{Over\_Educ}_i^A + \gamma_2 \text{Req\_Educ}_i^A + \gamma_3 \text{Under\_Educ}_i^A + \ldots + u_i$$

where the superscript "A" on the ORU variables simply indicates an alternative definition. In particular, Vahey (2000) defined Req_Educ_i^A as a vector of dichotomous variables for each usual level of education. Because the usual level of education was rarely more than one level from the attained level of education, in Vahey's empirical analysis a restricted specification was employed, where Over_Educ_i^A and Under_Educ_i^A comprised, for each usual level of schooling, single dichotomous variables for overeducation and undereducation regardless of the number of years.

The analyses of overeducation and undereducation have shown that knowledge of educational mismatch can enhance understanding of labor-market outcomes. The efforts to extend the analyses to consider variation across education levels and across occupations revealed that this extension can be useful, although the limitations of these earlier studies prevent strong conclusions from being drawn. The analyses presented below, based on the large Public Use Microdata Sample from the 2000 U.S. population census, overcome these limitations and demonstrate the considerable potential of a study disaggregated by occupation that uses more detailed information regarding the required level of school and schooling mismatches.

Measurement of Mismatches and Data

This section reviews the way the "required" or "usual" level of education is measured. It also presents a brief overview of the data used.

The method used to identify the "required" or "usual" level of education in this study is the realized-matches (RM) technique.[10] This is based on the actual educational attainments of workers in each occupation and, therefore, reflects the outcome of the labor-market matching process. Either the mean of educational attainments within each occupation (as in Verdugo and Verdugo 1989) or the modal educational attainment (as in Cohn and Khan 1995) may be used.

The analyses reported below are based on the 2000 U.S. population census 5 percent Public Use Microdata Sample and use the approximately five hundred occupations that are separately identified. This data set contains information on labor-market outcomes (earnings, occupation) and demographic characteristics (educational attainment, age, marital status, veteran of U.S. Armed Forces, English proficiency, location, and, among the foreign born, citizenship and duration of residence in the United States). While this data source covers the entire population, the analyses are based on twenty-five- to sixty-four-year-old men who worked in paid employment in 1999.[11] The analyses are restricted to those in nonmilitary occupations, as these are the most likely to respond to market forces. Separate analyses are conducted for native-born workers and for foreign-born workers. Both wage and salary earners and the self-employed are covered by the study. All foreign-born men and a 15 percent random sample of native-born men from the 5 percent sample meeting the sample restrictions are included in the analysis.

The modal level of education of native-born workers in the 2000 U.S. population census data is used to determine the usual level of education in each of the approximately five hundred occupations. The focus on native-born male workers is appropriate because the economic majority group sets the norm for all workers in the occupation.[12] This RM measure ranges from twelve years of schooling to the professional degree and doctorate categories (there are seven educational categories in total).

Statistical Analyses

The statistical analyses that follow have several main sections. The first contains a brief overview of the incidence of educational mismatch in the U.S. labor market. This is followed by a section that presents the analyses of the determinants of earnings for high-skilled workers: workers with a bachelor's degree or higher, and workers with a master's degree or higher. Next, the analyses of earnings for the skilled workers are conducted separately by major occupation. This permits assessment of whether some occupations are able to utilize any surplus educational attainments more effectively than others. That section is followed with the analysis of earnings, which is undertaken using the more flexible specification of the ORU model Vahey introduced (2000). This approach offers advantages for understanding whether the apparent inability of the labor market to effectively utilize surplus schooling depends on the usual level of schooling for a given occupation. The final section reports findings from an analysis of the effects of education—actual years, usual years, and surplus years—on earnings by duration of residence in the United States.

The Incidence of Skill Mismatch. Table 4-2 lists the percentage of correctly matched education and mismatched education in the U.S. labor market based on the modal education level for each individual's occupation by nativity, skill level, and occupation, using data on adult males from the 2000 U.S. population census. The data for the native born are in standard font (first row) and the data for the foreign born are in italics (second row) for each occupation. The first three columns of the table cover all educational attainments, while the final two columns are for the two definitions of high-skilled workers used in this study. When all workers are considered, information is presented on undereducation, correctly

TABLE 4-2

PERCENTAGE OF OVEREDUCATION, CORRECTLY MATCHED EDUCATION, AND UNDEREDUCATION BY NATIVITY, SKILL LEVEL, AND OCCUPATION, MALES AGES TWENTY-FIVE TO SIXTY-FOUR YEARS

| Occupation | All Education Levels | | | Bachelor's Degree + | Master's Degree + |
	Under-educated (i)	Correctly Matched (ii)	Over-educated (iii)	Over-educated (iv)	Over-educated (v)
All Occupations	26.3	40.2	33.4	50.3	69.7
	45.0	*26.0*	*29.1*	*62.5*	*79.0*
Management	32.3	36.1	31.5	45.2	86.7
	36.9	*28.1*	*35.0*	*57.8*	*96.5*
Business and Financial	23.9	45.2	30.9	35.3	100.0
Operations	*33.5*	*40.4*	*26.1*	*46.0*	*100.0*
Computer and Mathematical	22.3	40.2	37.5	37.8	97.5
Science	*46.0*	*38.6*	*15.4*	*55.5*	*99.2*
Architecture and Engineering	18.2	42.9	38.9	33.8	100.0
	41.1	*38.4*	*20.6*	*55.3*	*100.0*
Life, Physical, and Social Sciences	39.3	43.8	16.9	42.4	69.4
	41.4	*40.6*	*18.0*	*43.4*	*50.7*
Community and Social Services	17.6	38.7	43.7	24.0	42.8
	20.9	*33.2*	*45.9*	*29.6*	*51.0*
Legal	11.6	79.0	9.4	12.2	7.3
	23.7	*57.2*	*19.1*	*26.6*	*18.1*
Education, Training, and Library	46.0	41.1	12.9	48.8	80.4
	52.0	*32.9*	*15.1*	*55.2*	*71.6*
Arts, Design, Entertainment,	16.0	38.3	45.8	30.1	100.0
Sports, and Media	*22.2*	*30.2*	*47.5*	*43.3*	*100.0*
Health Care Practitioner and	14.5	62.5	23.0	19.6	20.4
Technical	*19.0*	*65.6*	*15.4*	*22.8*	*23.5*
Health Care Support	51.1	31.2	17.7	100.0	100.0
	51.7	*22.7*	*25.6*	*100.0*	*100.0*
Protective Service	34.3	26.0	39.7	84.4	100.0
	41.3	*25.2*	*33.5*	*91.6*	*100.0*
Food Preparation	39.5	34.3	26.2	100.0	100.0
	20.5	*20.8*	*58.7*	*100.0*	*100.0*
Building and Grounds Cleaning	31.4	44.2	24.5	100.0	100.0
and Maintenance	*15.7*	*19.6*	*64.7*	*100.0*	*100.0*
Personal Care and Service	44.2	32.3	23.5	78.4	100.0
	35.3	*25.4*	*39.3*	*91.4*	*100.0*
Sales and Related	43.5	29.5	27.1	63.8	100.0
	44.3	*21.7*	*34.0*	*81.2*	*100.0*
Office and Administrative Support	47.0	24.8	28.2	99.8	100.0
	45.3	*18.4*	*36.3*	*99.8*	*100.0*
Farming, Fishing, and Forestry	26.3	40.7	33.0	100.0	100.0
	5.1	*9.2*	*85.7*	*100.0*	*100.0*
Construction and Extraction	33.2	44.1	22.6	100.0	100.0
	17.1	*21.9*	*61.0*	*100.0*	*100.0*
Installation, Maintenance, and	33.6	40.6	25.8	100.0	100.0
Repair	*30.2*	*24.6*	*45.3*	*100.0*	*100.0*
Production	37.6	46.0	16.4	100.0	100.0
	25.9	*22.8*	*51.3*	*100.0*	*100.0*
Transportation and Material	30.1	47.7	22.2	78.4	100.0
Moving	*24.8*	*25.3*	*49.9*	*95.3*	*100.0*

SOURCE: U.S. Census Bureau, "Public Use Microdata Sample: 5 Percent Sample of the Population," in *2000 U.S. Census of Population and Housing* (Washington, DC, U.S. Census Bureau, 2005).

NOTE: For each occupation, the data in the first row are for the native born and the data in the second row (italicized) are for the foreign born. The numbers are based on the realized-matches procedure (mode).

matched education, and overeducation. When only high-skilled workers (defined as those having attained a bachelor's degree and higher or a master's degree and higher) are considered, however, undereducation is not a material issue, as very few workers are in this category, so only the incidence of overeducation is presented, with the balance of the workforce being considered correctly matched.

Across all occupations (see the first row of data in table 4-2) the rate of correctly matched education among the native born is around 40 percent, and the rates of undereducation and overeducation are 26 percent and 33 percent, respectively. The rate of being overeducated among the foreign born is similar to that of the native born (29 percent). The foreign born, however, are far more likely than the native born to be undereducated (45 percent compared to 26 percent) and are far less likely than the native born to be in the correctly matched group (26 percent compared to 40 percent).

The patterns in the incidence of educational match and mismatch across occupations are affected by two sets of factors. First, the usual level of education varies by occupation, from twelve years in some occupations (such as in sales and related) to a doctorate in other occupations (such as in the life, physical, and social sciences). Second, the proportion of highly educated workers varies across occupations. Hence, the mean actual years of education by occupational group in table 4-2 ranges from 12.19 years to 18.05 years among the native born, and from 9.24 years to 17.77 among the foreign born.[13]

In the fourth column of table 4-2, the analysis is restricted to workers with at least a bachelor's degree. Thus, by definition, these workers have a higher mean level of actual years of education than the sample of all workers. This tends to increase the percentage of overeducated workers.

The results in column iv of table 4-2 show that in approximately one-third of the occupational groups, all of the workers with at least a bachelor's degree are overeducated, regardless of nativity. The foreign born have a greater rate of overeducation than the native born in the remaining occupations. Furthermore, when the analysis focuses on the group with a master's degree or higher (see table 4-2, column v), all the workers are overeducated in over half of the occupational groups regardless of nativity. The incidences of overeducation are similar for both the native born and the foreign born in the remaining occupations, with the exception of the legal occupation group, where the rate of overeducation for the foreign born is only 18 percent and the rate for the native born is only 7 percent.

The incidence of educational mismatches can also be considered by duration in the United States, as is shown in table 4-3. Among high-skilled workers in the United States for ten or more years in 2000, the extent of overeducation declines with duration of residency. This suggests that with longer residencies in the U.S. labor market, immigrants are more likely to acquire the U.S.-specific skills, credentials, and reputation that permit more workers to get jobs in occupations commensurate with their educational attainment. Note, however, that the degree of overeducation is lower for those in the U.S. fewer than ten years in 2000 compared with those who have resided in the United States for between ten and nineteen years. The better occupational matching of the foreign born who came to the United States in the 1990s may reflect cohort differences arising from the 1990 Immigration Act. That legislation had two major effects on this issue. First, it increased the number of labor certification/employer-sponsored visas, and workers entering under these visas are more likely to be better matched than those entering under other visas, such as the family-based, diversity, or

TABLE 4-3

PERCENTAGE OF OVEREDUCATION, CORRECTLY MATCHED EDUCATION, AND UNDEREDUCATION FOR FOREIGN-BORN MALES AGES TWENTY-FIVE TO SIXTY-FOUR YEARS, BY DURATION OF U.S. RESIDENCY AND SKILL LEVEL

Duration of U.S. Residency (Years)	All Skill Levels			Bachelor's Degree +	Master's Degree +
	Under-educated (i)	Correctly Matched (ii)	Over-educated (iii)	Over-educated (iv)	Over-educated (v)
All Durations	45.0	26.0	29.1	62.5	79.0
0–9	42.6	28.2	30.2	62.7	80.0
10–19	48.5	24.0	27.5	67.1	83.7
20–29	46.5	25.3	28.1	59.4	75.5
30+	38.3	29.5	32.2	57.8	73.4

SOURCE: U.S. Census Bureau, "Public Use Microdata Sample: 5 Percent Sample of the Population," in *2000 U.S. Census of Population and Housing* (Washington, DC: U.S. Census Bureau, 2005).
NOTE: Numbers are based on the realized-matches procedure (mode).

refugee visas. Secondly, the act created the H1-B (temporary worker) visas for employer-sponsored high-skilled workers, for which, again, workers are better matched (there are fewer overeducated workers).

Thus, educational mismatch, especially for highly educated workers, is a major feature of the U.S. labor market. Its importance increases when the focus is on the most highly skilled workers. Indeed, in many occupations, all of the most highly educated workers are categorized as overeducated. This would be expected to have major implications for these workers' earnings. These implications are explored in the subsections that follow.

Analyses for High-Skilled Workers. Table 4-4 presents results from the estimation of the standard and ORU models of earnings determination on a sample restricted to workers with at least a bachelor's degree.

The payoff to actual years of education for skilled workers is 11.1 percent for the native born and 10.6 percent for the foreign born. These estimates are greater than those for the full sample of all male workers (of 10.3 and 5.3 percent, respectively), indicating a nonlinearity in the returns to education, particularly among the foreign born. At first glance this might suggest that the limited international transferability of formal schooling is less of an issue for high-skilled immigrants than for less-skilled immigrants. Chiswick and Miller (2008), however, present a decomposition of the lower payoff to schooling for the foreign born than for the native born into the components due to the international transferability of human-capital skills and due to selection in migration. They suggest that the latter factor, which is likely to be more prevalent among the less educated, is of far greater importance than the former factor. The finding in table 4-4, which excludes those with less than a bachelor's degree, appears to reinforce the findings from the Chiswick and Miller (2008) analyses.

The payoff to labor-market experience is higher in the analyses for the high-skilled group of workers than for all workers. It is 3.26 percent for native-born, skilled workers for each year of experience (evaluated at ten years) compared to 2.20 percent for all native-born workers. The payoff to preimmigration labor-market experience is 1.62 percent for foreign-born, skilled workers, compared to 0.86 percent for all foreign-born workers. Thus, there appear to be complementarities between formal education and labor-market experience, particularly among the foreign born. This suggests

TABLE 4-4

ESTIMATES OF STANDARD AND ORU MODELS OF EARNINGS FOR SKILLED
(BACHELOR'S OR HIGHER DEGREE) MALES AGES TWENTY-FIVE
TO SIXTY-FOUR YEARS, BY NATIVITY

Variable	Native Born		Foreign Born	
	Standard	ORU	Standard	ORU
Constant	4.073	4.131	4.669*	4.297
	(52.08)	(54.16)	(71.98)	(67.29)
Educational Attainment	**0.111**	(a)	**0.106**	(a)
	(42.49)		**(49.52)**	
Usual Level of Education	(a)	**0.122**	(a)	**0.140***
		(47.85)		**(64.45)**
Years of Overeducation	(a)	**0.020**	(a)	**0.019**
		(7.15)		**(8.34)**
Experience	0.057	0.059	0.031*	0.039*
	(48.12)	(50.65)	(25.67)	(32.55)
Experience Squared/100	−0.122	−0.124	−0.074*	−0.085*
	(39.64)	(41.38)	(24.61)	(29.17)
Log Weeks Worked	0.999	0.979	0.972	0.945
	(59.77)	(59.75)	(73.07)	(72.22)
Married	0.302	0.271	0.232*	0.215*
	(48.67)	(44.59)	(36.23)	(34.64)
South	−0.031	−0.034	−0.061*	−0.054*
	(5.43)	(6.01)	(9.86)	(9.12)
Metropolitan	0.333	0.308	0.147*	0.154*
	(36.82)	(34.82)	(8.28)	(8.96)
Veteran of U.S. Armed Forces	−0.056	−0.043	−0.128*	−0.106*
	(7.22)	(5.68)	(8.97)	(7.70)
Black	−0.188	−0.162	−0.296*	−0.262*
	(17.17)	(14.98)	(30.40)	(27.70)
English Very Well	−0.072	−0.064	−0.141*	−0.110*
	(5.37)	(4.79)	(18.76)	(14.98)
English Well	−0.068	−0.055	−0.403*	−0.304*
	(1.97)	(1.64)	(42.61)	(32.84)
English Not Well/Not at All	−0.109	−0.099	−0.690*	−0.492*
	(2.57)	(2.35)	(49.40)	(35.70)
Years Since Migration (YSM)	(a)	(a)	0.009	0.011
			(9.81)	(12.23)
YSM Squared/100	(a)	(a)	−0.005	−0.011
			(2.41)	(6.07)
Citizen	(a)	(a)	0.035	0.024
			(4.95)	(3.42)
Adjusted R^2	0.230	0.259	0.278	0.322
Sample Size	100,885	100,885	100,968	100,968

SOURCE: U.S. Census Bureau, "Public Use Microdata Sample: 5 Percent Sample of the Population," in *2000 U.S. Census of Population and Housing* (Washington, DC: U.S. Census Bureau, 2005).
NOTES: Heteroskedasticity-consistent t-statistics in parentheses; * indicates that the estimated coefficient for the foreign born is significantly different from that for the native born; (a) indicates the variable is not relevant or not entered into the estimating equation; coefficients of the education variables are in bold.

that with additional years of formal schooling, immigrants receive greater earnings for skills acquired on the job prior to immigration.

The earnings payoff to an additional year of living in the United States among high-skilled immigrants, holding total labor-market experience constant, is 0.80 percent, which is about the same as the payoff for all immigrants (0.82 percent).

Finally, the earnings penalties associated with limited English skills are greater when the focus is on skilled immigrants than when all immigrants are considered. For example, among immigrants, skilled workers who self-report that they speak English well have earnings 40 percent lower than the earnings of skilled immigrants who speak only English at home. When all immigrants are included in the analysis, this earnings penalty is only 25 percent. To put this another way, among immigrants there is evidence of a complementarity between English-language skills and formal education, with a greater earnings return to English proficiency among skilled immigrants. Among the native born, almost all of whom speak only English at home regardless of schooling level, the change in sample from all workers to skilled workers (bachelor's degree and above) is associated with only minor changes in the estimated coefficients of the English-language variables.

The coefficients on the ORU variables in table 4-4 differ by up to 4 percentage points compared with those in a regression for all male workers (compared with Chiswick and Miller 2008). Thus, the payoff to years of usual education, as measured by the RM procedure, falls by 2–3 percentage points when the focus is shifted from all workers to workers with at least a bachelor's degree, whereas the payoff to years of surplus schooling falls by up to 4 percentage points.[14]

Table 4-5 lists results for the more stringent definition of skilled workers, that is, of workers with a master's, professional, or doctorate degree. These findings show that the payoff to education is 11 percent for the native born and only 5.5 percent for the foreign born. This difference in the payoff to education is comparable to that reported from the analyses based on all workers, but contrasts with the findings for workers with a bachelor's degree or higher (table 4-4), where the payoffs for the native born and foreign born are about the same, at 11 percent. This difference may be due to the relatively high earnings among the native born with a professional degree—which involves fewer years of schooling than a doctorate—compared to the

TABLE 4-5

ESTIMATES OF STANDARD AND ORU MODELS OF EARNINGS FOR HIGHLY
SKILLED (MASTER'S OR HIGHER DEGREE) MALES AGES TWENTY-FIVE
TO SIXTY-FOUR YEARS, BY NATIVITY

Variable	Native Born		Foreign Born	
	Standard	ORU	Standard	ORU
Constant	3.775	3.695	5.663*	5.231*
	(26.57)	(26.72)	(49.87)	(46.52)
Educational Attainment	**0.110**	(a)	**0.055***	(a)
	(19.37)		**(13.43)**	
Usual Level of Education	(a)	**0.132**	(a)	**0.091***
		(23.67)		**(22.00)**
Years of Overeducation	(a)	**0.027**	(a)	**−0.018***
		(4.50)		**(4.20)**
Experience	0.069	0.069	0.034*	0.041*
	(31.39)	(32.16)	(18.51)	(22.75)
Experience Squared/100	−0.154	−0.153	−0.076*	−0.087*
	(27.66)	(28.14)	(16.62)	(19.51)
Log Weeks Worked	1.056	1.024	0.936*	0.909*
	(39.25)	(38.85)	(45.18)	(44.64)
Married	0.326	0.295	0.268*	0.245*
	(27.87)	(25.78)	(26.89)	(25.11)
South	−0.030	−0.033	−0.054	−0.049
	(2.97)	(3.27)	(5.93)	(5.53)
Metropolitan	0.336	0.331	0.097*	0.133*
	(20.66)	(21.06)	(3.71)	(5.28)
Veteran of U.S. Armed Forces	−0.020	0.000	−0.153*	−0.132*
	(1.49)	(0.03)	(5.91)	(5.28)
Black	−0.179	−0.143	−0.368*	−0.334*
	(7.81)	(6.39)	(24.02)	(22.59)
English Very Well	−0.072	−0.060	−0.09	−0.078
	(2.96)	(2.51)	(8.30)	(6.97)
English Well	−0.026	−0.011	−0.424*	−0.336*
	(0.44)	(0.19)	(29.36)	(23.54)
English Not Well/Not at All	−0.191	−0.021	−0.816*	−0.590*
	(2.00)	(2.17)	(35.27)	(25.38)
Years Since Migration (YSM)	(a)	(a)	0.016	0.016
			(11.51)	(12.21)
YSM Squared/100	(a)	(a)	−0.017	−0.021
			(6.22)	(7.92)
Citizen	(a)	(a)	0.068	0.053
			(6.08)	(4.86)
Adjusted R^2	0.221	0.251	0.269	0.307
Sample Size	36,572	36,572	47,539	47,539

SOURCE: U.S. Census Bureau, "Public Use Microdata Sample: 5 Percent Sample of the Population," in *2000 U.S. Census of Population and Housing* (Washington, DC: U.S. Census Bureau, 2005).
NOTES: Heteroskedasticity-consistent t-statistics in parentheses; * indicates that the estimated coefficient for the foreign born is significantly different from that for the native born; (a) indicates the variable is not relevant or not entered into the estimating equation; coefficients of the education variables are in bold.

earnings of those with a doctorate, and the increased numerical importance of workers with professional degrees when the more stringent definition of skilled workers is used.[15]

The payoff to a year of labor-market experience (evaluated at ten years) for native-born workers with a master's degree or higher is 3.82 percent, about 17 percent higher than the 3.26 percentage-point effect for native-born workers with at least a bachelor's degree. Among the foreign born, however, the payoffs to experience acquired in the country of origin and in the United States for the high-skilled group in table 4-5 are slightly higher than the payoffs established using the broader definition of skilled immigrants in table 4-4.[16] However, the earnings effects associated with very limited English-language skills are greater among immigrants with a master's degree or higher than were reported in table 4-4. This further emphasizes the complementarity between formal schooling and English-language proficiency in the immigrant workforce.

Analyses by Occupation. Do some occupations use surplus skills more effectively than elsewhere in the economy? This question can be addressed through the ORU model via a smaller gap between the payoffs to the years of education that are usual for a worker's occupation and to years of education that are considered surplus in the occupation.[17]

The coefficients on the education variables (actual years of education, usual years of education, and surplus years of education) for each skill-birthplace group are presented in appendix 4B. Sets of simple correlations between the estimated coefficients on the various education variables are presented in table 4-6 (bachelor's degree and above) and table 4-7 (master's degree and above). Shaded figures in the lower cells in each of these tables are for the foreign born, while the figures in the top, unshaded cells are for the native born. Correlations with the mean level of schooling in the occupation (computed by nativity) are also provided to illustrate how these payoffs vary with the educational level for the occupation.

Consider the findings for the foreign born with a bachelor's degree or higher (table 4-6). The payoff to actual years of education within the broad occupational categories ranges from less than zero and very small positive amounts in a number of occupations to 17.4 percent in the group for health care practitioners and technical occupations (see appendix table 4B-1).

TABLE 4-6

CORRELATION COEFFICIENTS AMONG PAYOFFS OF EDUCATION AND MEAN
LEVEL OF EDUCATION FROM ANALYSES DISAGGREGATED BY OCCUPATION
AND NATIVITY, SKILLED (BACHELOR'S DEGREE OR HIGHER)
MALES AGES TWENTY-FIVE TO SIXTY-FOUR YEARS

Foreign Born/ Native Born		Level of Education				
		Actual	Usual	Surplus	Gap	Mean
Level of Education	Actual	–	0.49*	0.18	0.24	0.84*
	Usual	0.52*	–	0.41	0.46*	0.19
	Surplus	0.52*	0.15	–	–0.63*	0.08
	Gap	0.19	0.85*	–0.40	–	0.08
	Mean	0.72*	0.11	0.31	–0.07	–

SOURCE: Appendix 4B.
NOTES: Table based on realized-matches procedure; shaded cells represent correlations for the foreign born. "Actual" represents the payoff to actual years of schooling; "usual" the payoff to usual years of schooling; "surplus" the payoff to years of surplus schooling; "gap" the difference between payoff to usual and surplus years of schooling; and "mean" the mean educational attainment of the occupation; * denotes coefficients significant at the 5 percent level.

Education is rewarded more highly in the more skilled occupations. Thus, there is a simple correlation coefficient of 0.72 between the payoff to actual years of education and the mean level of education (as a measure of over-all skill) in an occupation. The mean payoff to actual years of education for the twenty occupations included in this analysis is 7.3 percent, which is 3.3 percentage points lower than the 10.6 percent reported in the pooled (across all occupation groups) analyses in table 4-4.[18] This shows that about one-third of the payoff to schooling among skilled immigrants is due to interoccupational mobility across the major occupation groups included in the census data.

The payoffs to years of usual education within the broad occupational category are listed in the second column of appendix table 4B-1. There is one negative payoff to usual education—for the community and social services occupation group. This is due to the combination of relatively low earnings and a high usual level of education for the clergy. Apart from this anomaly, the payoff to usual education ranges from zero (arts, design, entertainment, sports, and media; personal care and services; and construction and extraction) to 25.6 percent (architecture and engineering) among those

TABLE 4-7

CORRELATION COEFFICIENTS AMONG PAYOFFS OF EDUCATION AND MEAN
LEVEL OF EDUCATION FROM ANALYSES DISAGGREGATED BY OCCUPATION
AND NATIVITY, HIGHLY SKILLED (MASTER'S DEGREE OR HIGHER)
MALES AGES TWENTY-FIVE TO SIXTY-FOUR YEARS

Foreign Born/ Native Born		Level of Education				
		Actual	Usual	Surplus	Gap	Mean
Level of Education	Actual	–	0.49*	0.77*	–0.12	0.73*
	Usual	0.54*	–	0.18	0.73*	0.47*
	Surplus	0.92*	0.46*	–	–0.54*	0.29
	Gap	–0.19	0.68*	–0.34	–	0.20
	Mean	0.59*	0.07	0.33	–0.20	–

SOURCE: Appendix 4B.
NOTES: Table based on realized-matches procedure; shaded cells represent correlations for the foreign born. "Actual" represents the payoff to actual years of schooling; "usual" the payoff to usual years of schooling; "surplus" the payoff to years of surplus schooling; "gap" the difference between payoff to usual and surplus years of schooling; and "mean" the mean educational attainment of the occupation; * denotes coefficients significant at the 5 percent level.

with a bachelor's degree or higher level of schooling. The payoff to usual education is positively correlated across occupations with the payoff to actual years of education (r = 0.52). However, there is no association between the payoff to usual education and the mean level of education in the occupation (r = 0.11). The mean payoff to usual years of education across the twenty occupations is 14.9 percent, which is of the same order of magnitude as the 14.0 percent reported in table 4-4. Within the sample analyzed, the usual education variable takes into account movements to occupations where the worker's schooling is at the usual level. The fact that there is little change in the payoffs to usual schooling when the major occupation groups in the census data are held constant suggests that the payoff to matching occurs mainly within the major occupation groups, rather than across occupations. Schooling may be used to qualify for a higher-status occupation, but there is a sorting/matching process within these occupations that is very important to the earnings-determination process.

The payoffs to years of overeducation range from zero (in eight occupations) to over 15 percent (in education, training and library, and health care support). The mean payoff to years of overeducation is 5.2 percent, which compares favorably with the 4.6 percent for the analyses across occupations in table 4-4.

The absence of a pattern to the ways the payoffs to years of surplus education and usual education change across occupations shows up clearly when the gap between these payoffs is linked to the mean level of schooling: the simple correlation coefficient is −0.07. That is, surplus schooling is not used effectively in high-skilled occupations, nor is it used effectively in less-skilled occupations.

Similar patterns are evident for the native born and for the high-skilled groups, and when the WSA procedure is used to construct the usual level of schooling for each occupation (Chiswick and Miller forthcoming, a). This reinforces the conclusion that there is minimal evidence that some sections of the economy are immune to the ineffective use of surplus schooling. Whether this conclusion carries across to all levels of schooling is considered in the next section.

Analyses by Level of Education. Vahey's theoretical estimating equation includes dichotomous variables for each level of overeducation and undereducation for a given level of usual education (2000). In other words, for a usual level of education of a bachelor's degree, for example, workers who hold a master's degree would be represented by one dichotomous overeducation variable, those who hold professional degrees by a separate dichotomous overeducation variable, and workers who hold a doctorate by a further separate dichotomous overeducation variable. In the same way, workers who only completed tenth grade or who only hold a high school diploma would be represented by particular dichotomous undereducation variables if they were working in occupations with a usual level of education of a bachelor's degree. In some instances, however, this flexible approach would result in very small samples in specific overeducation and undereducation groups. Indeed, for this reason Vahey considered only one variable for overeducation and one for undereducation at each usual level of education (2000).

In the current analysis, however, the maximum detail on the extent of overeducation is incorporated into the estimating equation. This follows from the aim of the section, which is to assess whether the difficulties in using surplus education are equally prevalent across all levels of education.

These analyses are undertaken only for the sample of skilled workers with at least a bachelor's degree.

Given the array of findings from this approach, a graphical presentation of the main results is provided. Figure 4-3 presents the relevant findings for the foreign born, and figure 4-4 provides comparable results for the native born using the realized-matches (RM) approach.

Figures 4-3 and 4-4 have the natural logarithm of earnings on the vertical axis and the usual level of education in the occupation on the horizontal axis.[19] Earnings by usual level of education profiles are presented for each of four actual levels of education: bachelor's degree, master's degree, professional qualifications, and doctorates. The first line to consider is the short line for workers with a bachelor's degree that is truncated where the usual level of education for an occupation is a bachelor's degree; it has the letters *A, B,* and *C* positioned on it.

FIGURE 4-3

**RESULTS FROM FLEXIBLE SPECIFICATION OF ORU MODEL IN EQUATION (2)
FOR FOREIGN BORN, BASED ON REALIZED-MATCHES PROCEDURE**

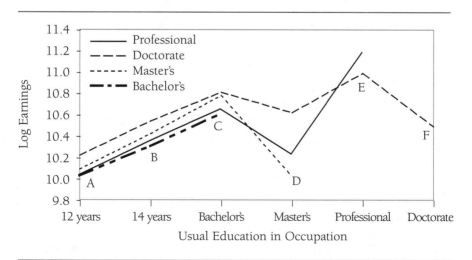

SOURCE: U.S. Census Bureau, "Public Use Microdata Sample: 5 Percent Sample of the Population," in *2000 U.S. Census of Population and Housing* (Washington, D.C.: U.S. Census Bureau, 2005).

FIGURE 4-4

RESULTS FROM FLEXIBLE SPECIFICATION OF ORU MODEL IN EQUATION (2)
FOR NATIVE BORN, BASED ON REALIZED-MATCHES PROCEDURE

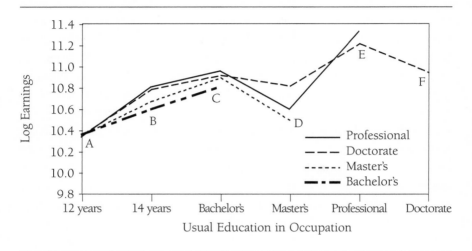

SOURCE: U.S. Census Bureau, "Public Use Microdata Sample: 5 Percent Sample of the Population," in *2000 U.S. Census of Population and Housing* (Washington, DC: U.S. Census Bureau, 2005).

If workers with a bachelor's degree are employed in an occupation where the usual level of education is a bachelor's degree, they will be correctly matched in terms of educational attainment. These workers are represented in figure 4-3 by the point C. If workers with a bachelor's degree are employed in an occupation where the usual level of education is twelve or fourteen years, they are overeducated for their occupation. Workers in these situations are represented in figure 4-3 by the points A and B, respectively. The highest earnings among workers with a bachelor's degree occur when these workers are correctly matched, that is, they are working in occupations in which the usual level of education is a bachelor's degree (point C). The overeducated workers earn considerably less than the correctly matched workers (21 percentage points lower earnings if working in an occupation where the usual level of schooling is fourteen years, at point B, and 45 percentage points less if working in an occupation where the usual level of schooling is twelve years, at point A). The fact that points A and B are lower than point C shows that among holders of bachelor's degrees, years of surplus education are not used as effectively in the labor market as are years of correctly matched education.

Now consider the earnings by usual level of education profile for individuals who possess a master's degree. This is the dotted line that is truncated at point D. Across the usual education levels of twelve years to a bachelor's degree, where workers with a master's degree would be overeducated, this profile is a little above the profile for workers who possess a bachelor's degree and is essentially parallel. There is thus some advantage to having a master's degree rather than a bachelor's degree if overeducated. Note, however, that the higher qualification does not greatly assist in overcoming the difficulties degree-qualified workers have in getting adequate reward for their schooling if they are working in an occupation for which they are classified as overeducated.

The foreign-born men with a master's degree who are correctly matched to the usual educational requirements of their job earn less than workers who have master's degrees and who work in jobs that require only a bachelor's degree. The master's degree appears to offer access to a particular set of occupations that are relatively poorly paid (schoolteachers and social workers, for example). This may explain why only 9 percent of the foreign-born workers with a master's degree are correctly matched in terms of levels of education.

Foreign-born workers with either professional qualifications or doctorates (the lines truncated at E and F, respectively) earn amounts similar to workers with either a bachelor's degree or a master's degree when working in occupations where the usual level of education is from twelve years of education to a bachelor's degree. Compared to when working in occupations where a bachelor's degree is usual, workers with either professional qualifications or doctorates tend to earn even less if they work in an occupation where a master's degree is usual. They earn more, however, than workers with a master's degree who work in an occupation where the usual level of education is a master's degree. These slightly higher earnings are the modest rewards to the surplus years of education.

Workers with a professional degree who are correctly matched to the usual educational requirements of their jobs have very high earnings (point E), whereas workers with a doctorate who are correctly matched tend to have much more modest salaries (point *F*). Figures 4-3 and 4-4 also demonstrate that those with doctorates working in occupations where the usual level of education is a professional qualification actually earn more than their counterparts who work in occupations where a doctorate is the usual level of education.[20] Again, this evidence shows that earnings follow the usual level of education in the occupation rather than the actual years of education for the individual. Workers' occupations govern their relative success in the labor market, not simply their years of education, although years of education, in part, influence the occupations that they can attain.

These analyses show that if a skilled worker works in an occupation that requires between twelve years of education and a bachelor's degree, surplus years of schooling are used ineffectively, and the extent of ineffectiveness is largely invariant to the actual level of schooling. In the small group of occupations with usual levels of schooling greater than a bachelor's degree, the pattern of earnings effects is irregular, but this pattern supports the view that earnings are more strongly related to the usual level of education for the job than to an individual's actual years of education.

Figure 4-4 shows information on the earnings rewards to overeducation and correctly matched education by the level of schooling for native-born, high-skilled workers. The earnings by usual level of education profiles for each of the levels of schooling (bachelor's, master's, professional, and doctorates) for the native born are largely the same as those discussed for the foreign born. Thus, the ineffective use of surplus years of education that occurs at each level is not a foreign-born phenomenon: it is a labor-market phenomenon.

Analysis of the Effect of Education by Duration of U.S. Residency. The analysis can be extended by asking whether the effect of education on earnings varies systematically with duration of residency in the United States. To answer this question, the education variables in the standard and ORU equations are interacted with the variables for duration of residency and duration-squared. These interaction terms are highly statistically significant.[21] Based on the regression results with these variable interactions, figures 4-5 and 4-6, respectively, plot the partial effects of education on earnings with respect to years since migration for immigrants with at least a bachelor's degree and at least a master's degree. The effects of education on earnings with respect to years since migration for educational attainment (standard analysis) and for

FIGURE 4-5

PARTIAL EFFECTS OF EDUCATION ON EARNINGS BY DURATION
OF U.S. RESIDENCY, SKILLED FOREIGN-BORN ADULT MALES

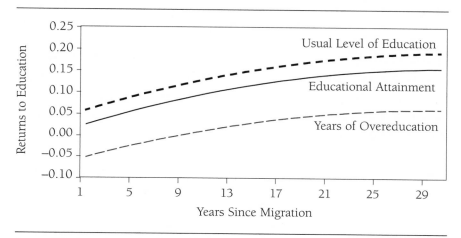

SOURCE: U.S. Census Bureau, "Public Use Microdata Sample: 5 Percent Sample of the Population," in *2000 U.S. Census of Population and Housing* (Washington, D.C.: U.S. Census Bureau, 2005).
NOTES: "Skilled" refers to bachelor's degree or higher. "Adult" refers to ages twenty-five to sixty-four years.

usual level and years of overeducation (ORU analysis) show that the partial effects increase, albeit at a decreasing rate, with duration of residency in the United States. That is, educational attainment has a greater positive effect on earnings the longer an individual's U.S. residency.

However, the partial effects are systematically higher for the usual level of education than for the respondent's actual level of schooling. Most dramatic is the consistently very low effect on earnings of years of overeducation across the range of years since migration. Indeed, the effect of overeducation on earnings is negative until about nine years of U.S. residency for those with at least a bachelor's degree and until about twenty years of U.S. residency for those with at least a master's degree.

Conclusion

This chapter is concerned with the consequences of a mismatch between educational attainment (measured by formal schooling) and employment

FIGURE 4-6

**PARTIAL EFFECTS OF EDUCATION ON EARNINGS BY DURATION
OF U.S. RESIDENCY, HIGHLY SKILLED FOREIGN-BORN ADULT MALES**

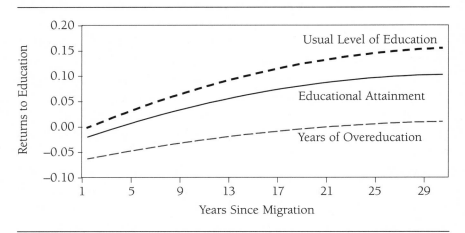

SOURCE: U.S. Census Bureau, "Public Use Microdata Sample: 5 Percent Sample of the Population," in *2000 U.S. Census of Population and Housing* (Washington, D.C.: U.S. Census Bureau, 2005).
NOTES: "Highly skilled" refers to master's degree or higher. "Adult" refers to ages twenty-five to sixty-four years.

among high-skilled, adult male immigrants in the United States and the extent to which such a mismatch affects earnings. The ORU education decomposition methodology is employed with mismatches identified based on a realized-matches approach (modal educational level in the occupation). The empirical analyses focus on the foreign born, but, for comparative purposes, parallel analyses are conducted for the native born. The empirical analyses are conducted using the public use microdata sample of 5 percent of the U.S. population from the 2000 U.S. population census. Skilled immigrants are defined as those with at least a bachelor's degree, and parallel analyses are conducted at a higher level for those with at least a master's degree.

While there has been a long history of high-skilled migration to the United States, the provisions of the 1990 Immigration Act increased the number of permanent and temporary visas to the United States for these workers. In 2007, of the nearly 1.1 million who became legal immigrants, 162,000 received a permanent-resident visa under an employment-based category; half of these were the spouses and minor children of the principal applicants.

Educational mismatches refer to the difference in the educational attainment of a worker and the usual or typical (modal) level of education of those working in a given occupation. These mismatches can result from several causes, including occupational-skill upgrading for younger cohorts of workers and unmeasured worker-productivity characteristics that may be positive or negative. Among immigrants, mismatches may also arise from the limited international transferability of skills and selectivity in migration, or they may be the result of labor-market discrimination against immigrants. Educational mismatches due to overeducation and undereducation are expected to occur among both native- and foreign-born workers.

Conducting an empirical analysis necessitates the identification of a required or usual level of education in each occupation. An RM approach was used, which refers to what actually occurs in the labor market as reflected by the modal level of education in each of the approximately five hundred occupations identified in the 2000 U.S. census.

Over all educational levels among adult men, there are greater mismatches among immigrants than among the native born. Among all immigrants, only 26 percent were correctly matched (compared to 40 percent for the native born), with 45 percent undereducated and 29 percent overeducated (in contrast to 26 percent and 33 percent, respectively, for the native born). Among high-skilled workers, however, 63 percent of immigrants with a bachelor's degree or higher were overeducated for their occupations (compared to 50 percent of the native born), while among those with a master's degree or higher, fully 79 percent of immigrants are considered overeducated (70 percent of the native born). Nearly all of the rest were correctly matched; that is, their own education was equal to that of the modal education in their occupation. Except for the immigrants who arrived in the 1990s, the extent of correct matching of education and occupation increases as duration of U.S. residency increases. Thus, among the highly educated, particularly among immigrants, there is a high degree of "surplus" education. But is this surplus education wasted?

When the analysis is limited to those with a bachelor's degree or higher, earnings among both the foreign and native born increase by about 11 percent per year of schooling. When years of education is divided into years of usual (modal) education in the worker's occupation and years of overeducation, the effect on earnings of usual education is about 13 percent for both nativity groups, whereas the effect of years of overeducation is about 2 percent per surplus year for both groups. Thus, whereas the return to years of required or usual schooling is high, the returns to education in excess of what is needed for one's occupation are extremely low.

When the analysis is limited to those who have attained a master's degree or higher, the educational coefficients are less stable but tell a similar story: workers receive high returns to years of usual education and extremely low returns (even negative returns among immigrants) for years of overeducation.

When separate analyses are conducted by broad occupational categories, similar patterns emerge. Such analyses generally show a high return to years of usual education and very little or no returns to years of surplus education. When analyses are performed by educational level, the most striking feature is that perhaps the group with the greatest number of years in school (those who receive a doctorate) tends to have relatively low earnings compared to the group of individuals who attained a professional degree. Among high-skilled immigrants, the return to surplus education is actually negative in the first ten to twenty years of U.S. residency, after which the returns become positive but remain very small.

The very low return to years of overeducation indicates that, among the highly educated, educational attainments beyond what is required for the occupation in which one works are not productive. This is true for native- as well as foreign-born workers. This means earnings are influenced more by the educational norms in a particular occupation than by an individual's educational level.

The private and social losses in economic welfare are substantial for all workers (whether native or foreign born) who are not employed in the higher-level occupations that might make better use of their educational credentials. This has implications for immigration and absorption policy. It suggests that, in general, employment-based immigrant visas are more likely to attract high-skilled immigrants who will be working in jobs better matched to their educational attainment than is the case for family or refugee visa recipients. An employer-sponsored, targeted-employment approach might result in better educational matches than one that does not require an employment sponsor. Even a points system for rationing visas, as used in Canada and Australia, might be improved by adding a set of points for prearranged employment or for having a particular set of skills in high demand.[22] Proactive efforts to facilitate the adjustment of high-skilled, new immigrants in the labor market might be most productive. These could include specific programs for English-language training, obtaining a U.S. certification or occupational license, or even learning how to navigate the job-search process in the United States for particular occupations.

The analyses reported above focus on high-skilled male immigrants and are based on a single cross-section of data. They demonstrate that including demand-side considerations (such as the usual level of education in the occupation) in addition to the usual supply-side factors (such as the actual educational attainment of workers) has considerable merit. This research could be extended in a number of ways, including by undertaking separate analyses for high-skilled females, conducting analyses of low- and medium-skilled workers, and using data from earlier censuses in synthetic cohort models. Disaggregating the analysis by age at migration could permit a study of differences in the effects on income of schooling acquired in the United States and schooling acquired abroad. Conducting separate analyses for each of the major foreign-born groups in the United States and relating the estimates of the RM specification to characteristics of the immigrants' countries of origin, such as the internationally standardized scores from the Programme for International Student Assessment (PISA), may provide a means of determining how the quality of schooling acquired abroad influences the estimated effects of surplus schooling.[23] A study of the sensitivity of the estimates to the specification of the empirical model (such as more extensive controls for U.S. region of residence, race, as well as interaction effects between the more important regressors) might also be considered.

Appendix 4A
Definitions of Variables

DEPENDENT AND EXPLANATORY VARIABLES USED IN THE STATISTICAL ANALYSES

Dependent Variables	
Income in 1999	Natural logarithm of earnings in 1999 (where earnings are defined as gross earnings from all sources).

Explanatory Variables	
Years of Education	This variable records the total years of full-time equivalent education. It has been constructed from the U.S. census data on educational attainment by assigning the following values to the census categories: completed less than fifth grade (2 years); completed fifth or sixth grade (5.5); completed seventh or eighth grade (7.5); completed ninth grade (9); completed tenth grade (10); completed eleventh grade (11); completed twelfth grade, no diploma (11.5); completed high school (12); attended college for less than one year (12.5); attended college for more than one year or completed college (14); completed bachelor's degree (16); completed master's degree (17.5); completed professional degree (18.5); completed doctorate (20). Further discussion of these years-of-schooling equivalents is presented in the text. Note: (a) As with other census data, the values for educational attainment are self-reported responses. While academic degrees may have required different years of schooling for immigrants educated in some countries of origin, U.S. values are used in the analysis. (b) Sensitivity tests were performed using eighteen, twenty, and twenty-one years of schooling for the master's, professional, and doctorate degrees, respectively. The findings are essentially invariant with respect to this alternative set of years of schooling. Vocational and technical training for a specific trade that does not require an advanced degree beyond the bachelor's is excluded from the category of professional degrees.
Usual Level of Education	This variable records the typical years of education. It is constructed using the modal level of education of the native-born workers in the respondent's occupation of employment based on the realized-matches procedure.

TABLE 4A-1 (cont.)
DEPENDENT AND EXPLANATORY VARIABLES USED IN THE STATISTICAL ANALYSES

Explanatory Variables

Years of Overeducation	The overeducation variable equals the difference between a worker's actual years of education and the years of education required for the worker's job where the number is positive. Otherwise, it is set equal to zero.
Logarithm of Weeks Worked in 1999	This is the natural logarithm of the number of weeks an individual worked in 1999.
Experience	Potential labor-market experience is computed as age minus years of education minus 6.
Location	The two location variables record residence in a metropolitan area or in one of the southern states. The latter includes Alabama, Arkansas, Delaware, District of Columbia, Florida, Georgia, Kentucky, Louisiana, Maryland, Mississippi, Missouri, North Carolina, Oklahoma, South Carolina, Tennessee, Texas, Virginia, and West Virginia.
Marital Status	This is a dichotomous variable set equal to one for individuals who are married (and whose spouse is present in the household) and set equal to zero for all other marital states.
Veteran	This is a dichotomous variable set equal to one for someone who has served in the U.S. Armed Forces and set equal to zero otherwise.
Race	This is a dichotomous variable that distinguishes between individuals who are black and all other races.
English-Language Proficiency	Three dichotomous variables (speaks English very well, well, and not well or not at all) are used to record respondents' English-language proficiency.
Years Since Migration	This is computed from the year a foreign-born person came to the United States to stay.
Citizenship	This is a dichotomous variable set equal to one for foreign-born workers who are U.S. citizens.

SOURCE: U.S. Census Bureau, "Public Use Microdata Sample," in *2000 U.S. Census of Population and Housing* (Washington, DC: U.S. Census Bureau, 2005). The statistical analyses relied on the 5 percent sample of the population from the U.S. census microdata file for the foreign born and a 15 percent random sample of the 5 percent sample for the native born.

NOTE: Population is defined as native-born and foreign-born employed men, ages twenty-five to sixty-four years.

TABLE 4A-2

MEANS AND STANDARD DEVIATIONS OF VARIABLES IN EARNINGS
EQUATION FOR SKILLED (BACHELOR'S DEGREE OR HIGHER) MALES
AGES TWENTY-FIVE TO SIXTY-FOUR YEARS, BY NATIVITY

Variable	Native Born	Foreign Born
Log Income	10.800 (0.98)	10.650 (1.03)
Educational Attainment	16.744 (1.10)	17.046 (1.29)
Usual Level of Education	15.335 (1.93)	15.121 (2.10)
Years of Overeducation	1.447 (1.72)	1.960 (1.93)
Experience	20.008 (10.07)	18.332 (9.94)
Experience Squared	501.808 (426.05)	434.95 (410.70)
Log Weeks Worked	3.855 (0.34)	3.812 (0.40)
Married	0.704 (0.46)	0.695 (0.46)
South	0.330 (0.47)	0.272 (0.45)
Metropolitan	0.890 (0.31)	0.971 (0.17)
Veteran of U.S. Armed Forces	0.192 (0.39)	0.045 (0.21)
Black	0.053 (0.22)	0.076 (0.27)
English Very Well	0.046 (0.21)	0.537 (0.50)
English Well	0.005 (0.07)	0.196 (0.40)
English Not Well/Not at All	0.004 (0.06)	0.060 (0.24)
Years Since Migration (YSM)	N/A	16.683 (11.82)
YSM Squared	N/A	418.13 (526.92)
Citizen	N/A	0.514 (0.50)
Sample Size	100,885	100,968

SOURCE: Authors' calculations based on U.S. Census Bureau, "Public Use Microdata Sample: 5 Percent Sample of the Population," in 2000 U.S. Census of Population and Housing (Washington, DC: U.S. Census Bureau, 2005).

Appendix 4B
Regression Analyses of Effects of Education on Earnings

TABLE 4B-1

SELECTED ESTIMATES FROM STANDARD AND ORU MODELS OF
EARNINGS BY OCCUPATION, SKILLED (BACHELOR'S DEGREE OR HIGHER),
FOREIGN-BORN MALES AGES TWENTY-FIVE TO SIXTY-FOUR YEARS

Occupation	Educational Attainment	Usual Education	Over-education	Mean of Education	Sample Size
Management	0.078 (11.93)	0.175 (21.56)	0.050 (7.64)	16.914	15,175
Business and Financial Operations	0.099 (8.81)	0.149 (7.15)	0.098 (8.69)	16.762	7,171
Computer and Mathematical Science	0.038 (6.47)	0.146 (13.27)	0.028 (4.76)	16.925	11,360
Architecture and Engineering	0.074 (14.32)	0.256 (21.21)	0.064 (12.27)	16.992	9,231
Life, Physical, and Social Sciences	0.054 (7.07)	0.039 (4.92)	0.047 (5.17)	18.464	3,133
Community and Social Services	0.004 (0.40)	−0.129 (6.66)	0.020 (1.45)	17.200	2,097
Legal	0.132 (5.78)	0.173 (6.82)	0.079 (2.08)	18.095	1,360
Education, Training, and Library	0.157 (28.57)	0.140 (13.07)	0.169 (22.53)	18.095	6,769
Arts, Design, Entertainment, Sports, and Media	0.031 (1.62)	0.047 (1.51)	0.031 (1.63)	16.724	3,071
Health Care Practitioner and Technical	0.174 (22.92)	0.224 (30.99)	0.016 (1.52)	18.023	9,384
Health Care Support	0.156 (5.14)	0.209 (3.63)	0.152 (4.99)	16.978	495
Protective Service	0.016 (0.56)	0.159 (5.28)	0.002 (0.06)	16.515	1,088
Food Preparation	−0.011 (0.61)	0.109 (3.45)	−0.014 (0.75)	16.549	1,901
Personal Care and Service	0.004 (0.12)	0.064 (1.78)	0.001 (0.05)	16.541	730
Sales and Related	0.051 (4.42)	0.155 (12.19)	0.045 (3.96)	16.545	9,578
Office and Administrative Support	0.053 (5.06)	0.172 (11.81)	0.053 (4.99)	16.546	5,506
Construction and Extraction	−0.010 (0.57)	−0.005 (0.14)	−0.010 (0.57)	16.622	2,413
Installation, Maintenance, and Repair	0.034 (1.82)	0.062 (2.34)	0.036 (1.93)	16.524	2,230
Production	0.069 (5.57)	0.092 (2.07)	0.069 (5.55)	16.583	3,824
Transportation and Material Moving	−0.005 (0.32)	0.130 (5.95)	−0.005 (0.34)	16.583	3,123

NOTE: Heteroskedasticity-consistent t-statistics in parentheses.

TABLE 4B-2

SELECTED ESTIMATES FROM STANDARD AND ORU MODELS OF
EARNINGS BY OCCUPATION, SKILLED (BACHELOR'S DEGREE OR HIGHER),
NATIVE-BORN MALES AGES TWENTY-FIVE TO SIXTY-FOUR YEARS

Occupation	Educational Attainment	Usual Education	Over-education	Mean of Education	Sample Size
Management	0.065 (9.27)	0.133 (16.51)	0.017 (2.34)	16.627	19,193
Business and Financial Operations	0.080 (6.69)	0.157 (9.40)	0.077 (6.42)	16.486	9,722
Computer and Mathematical Science	0.058 (5.67)	0.132 (9.23)	0.045 (4.41)	16.461	5,182
Architecture and Engineering	0.044 (4.94)	0.233 (15.06)	0.378 (4.22)	16.497	6,060
Life, Physical, and Social Sciences	0.087 (9.57)	0.080 (8.50)	0.093 (8.64)	17.469	2,398
Community and Social Services	0.061 (6.43)	−0.043 (3.10)	0.068 (4.96)	17.061	3,439
Legal	0.155 (7.92)	0.148 (6.40)	0.020 (0.57)	18.312	4,498
Education, Training, and Library	0.100 (21.71)	0.071 (7.50)	0.098 (16.03)	17.295	9,878
Arts, Design, Entertainment, Sports, and Media	−0.029 (1.12)	0.008 (0.19)	−0.030 (1.16)	16.438	3,635
Health Care Practitioner and Technical	0.230 (25.71)	0.263 (30.56)	0.081 (5.95)	17.898	6,299
Health Care Support	0.233 (3.90)	0.073 (0.76)	0.228 (3.87)	16.776	226
Protective Service	0.007 (0.34)	0.115 (4.64)	0.012 (0.58)	16.269	2,499
Food Preparation	−0.018 (0.46)	0.121 (2.35)	−0.013 (0.34)	16.279	731
Personal Care and Service	0.074 (1.63)	0.083 (1.71)	0.074 (1.63)	16.423	742
Sales and Related	0.024 (1.49)	0.127 (7.80)	0.022 (1.36)	16.287	11,704
Office and Administrative Support	0.048 (3.19)	0.160 (9.08)	0.041 (2.74)	16.349	5,299
Construction and Extraction	0.013 (0.57)	−0.021 (0.34)	0.012 (0.53)	16.316	2,183
Installation, Maintenance, and Repair	−0.050 (1.43)	−0.073 (1.90)	−0.049 (1.42)	16.268	1,439
Production	0.023 (0.97)	−0.079 (0.63)	0.024 (1.01)	16.341	2,307
Transportation and Material Moving	−0.008 (0.28)	0.178 (6.64)	−0.012 (0.47)	16.299	2,406

NOTE: Heteroskedasticity-consistent t-statistics in parentheses.

TABLE 4B-3

SELECTED ESTIMATES FROM STANDARD AND ORU MODELS OF
EARNINGS BY OCCUPATION, HIGHLY SKILLED (MASTER'S DEGREE OR HIGHER),
FOREIGN-BORN MALES AGES TWENTY-FIVE TO SIXTY-FOUR YEARS

Occupation	Educational Attainment	Usual Education	Over-education	Mean of Education	Sample Size
Management	0.033 (2.63)	0.149 (8.90)	0.026 (2.09)	18.010	6,883
Business and Financial Operations	0.022 (0.81)	0.142 (3.16)	0.020 (0.75)	17.881	2,912
Computer and Mathematical Science	−0.012 (1.16)	0.079 (4.37)	−0.020 (1.80)	17.866	5,677
Architecture and Engineering	0.056 (6.14)	0.276 (9.79)	0.055 (6.07)	18.037	4,478
Life, Physical, and Social Sciences	0.044 (3.61)	0.005 (0.34)	0.019 (1.26)	19.122	2,461
Community and Social Services	−0.008 (0.44)	−0.156 (4.81)	0.002 (0.13)	18.064	1,242
Legal	0.093 (2.04)	0.153 (2.85)	0.068 (1.20)	18.547	1,115
Education, Training, and Library	0.209 (25.22)	0.207 (14.20)	0.209 (22.02)	18.777	5,065
Arts, Design, Entertainment, Sports, and Media	−0.010 (0.26)	0.064 (0.99)	−0.011 (0.28)	17.942	1,150
Health Care Practitioner and Technical	0.029 (1.42)	0.156 (7.63)	−0.051 (2.44)	18.605	7,310
Health Care Support	0.089 (1.24)	0.127 (1.44)	0.091 (1.28)	18.419	201
Protective Service	−0.104 (1.42)	0.116 (1.57)	−0.110 (1.64)	17.968	284
Food Preparation	0.011 (0.21)	0.196 (2.88)	0.004 (0.08)	18.067	487
Personal Care and Service	0.034 (0.50)	0.085 (1.16)	0.038 (0.57)	18.150	184
Sales and Related	−0.028 (1.01)	0.106 (3.61)	−0.016 (0.60)	17.867	2,807
Office and Administrative Support	0.032 (1.20)	0.182 (5.17)	0.052 (1.95)	17.971	1,517
Construction and Extraction	−0.125 (2.33)	−0.223 (2.66)	−0.129 (2.38)	18.016	751
Installation, Maintenance, and Repair	−0.073 (1.42)	−0.040 (0.62)	−0.070 (1.36)	17.938	611
Production	0.059 (1.98)	0.008 (0.10)	0.061 (2.06)	18.026	1,089
Transportation and Material Moving	0.076 (1.85)	0.281 (6.70)	0.073 (2.13)	17.980	911

NOTE: Heteroskedasticity-consistent t-statistics in parentheses.

TABLE 4B-4

SELECTED ESTIMATES FROM STANDARD AND ORU MODELS OF EARNINGS
BY OCCUPATION, HIGHLY SKILLED (MASTER'S DEGREE OR HIGHER),
NATIVE-BORN MALES AGES TWENTY-FIVE TO SIXTY-FOUR YEARS

Occupation	Educational Attainment	Usual Education	Over-education	Mean of Education	Sample Size
Management	0.003 (0.19)	0.059 (3.24)	−0.001 (0.04)	17.810	6,680
Business and Financial Operations	−0.020 (0.60)	0.072 (1.41)	−0.021 (0.61)	17.737	2,735
Computer and Mathematical Science	0.018 (0.75)	0.054 (1.79)	0.012 (0.52)	17.806	1,337
Architecture and Engineering	−0.008 (0.34)	0.155 (3.76)	−0.006 (0.25)	17.761	1,691
Life, Physical, and Social Sciences	0.096 (6.16)	0.093 (6.04)	0.107 (5.98)	18.588	1,328
Community and Social Services	0.013 (0.74)	−0.068 (2.81)	0.022 (1.22)	17.890	1,976
Legal	0.058 (1.47)	0.093 (2.20)	−0.018 (0.43)	18.546	4,100
Education, Training, and Library	0.110 (15.16)	0.087 (7.84)	0.125 (13.62)	18.165	5,770
Arts, Design, Entertainment, Sports, and Media	−0.109 (1.54)	−0.188 (1.92)	−0.111 (1.57)	17.808	902
Health Care Practitioner and Technical	0.123 (4.26)	0.205 (7.27)	0.011 (0.37)	18.541	4,714
Health Care Support	0.451 (2.61)	−0.130 (0.59)	0.365 (2.32)	18.241	78
Protective Service	−0.001 (0.02)	0.074 (0.98)	−0.007 (0.11)	17.696	397
Food Preparation	−0.278 (2.62)	−0.200 (1.35)	−0.272 (2.56)	17.926	102
Personal Care and Service	0.010 (0.08)	0.046 (0.34)	0.023 (0.18)	17.846	174
Sales and Related	−0.071 (1.39)	0.094 (1.80)	−0.043 (0.87)	17.714	1,964
Office and Administrative Support	−0.009 (0.23)	0.106 (2.23)	−0.002 (0.05)	17.791	1,034
Construction and Extraction	0.127 (2.27)	−0.021 (0.07)	0.125 (2.18)	17.884	371
Installation, Maintenance, and Repair	−0.134 (1.42)	−0.085 (0.79)	−0.136 (1.43)	17.826	208
Production	0.028 (0.42)	0.127 (1.50)	0.023 (0.35)	17.834	414
Transportation and Material Moving	−0.130 (1.50)	0.112 (1.28)	−0.062 (0.75)	17.744	414

SOURCE FOR ALL APPENDIX 4B DATA: U.S. Census Bureau, "Public Use Microdata Sample: 5 Percent Sample of the Population," in 2000 U.S. Census of Population and Housing (Washington, DC: U.S. Census Bureau, 2005).

NOTE: Heteroskedasticity-consistent t-statistics in parentheses.

Notes

1. For a study of high-skilled immigrants to the United States in the nineteenth and early twentieth centuries, see chapter 1.

2. The employment-preference categories include: (i) priority workers; (ii) professionals with advanced degrees or aliens with exceptional ability; (iii) skilled workers, professionals without advanced degrees, and needed unskilled workers; (iv) special immigrants, such as religious workers; and (v) employment-creation immigrants (that is, investors). The data include the immediate family members (spouse and minor children) of the principal applicant as recipients of employment visas. Family members typically constitute about one-half of the category.

3. In the immigration literature this is frequently referred to as the nonrecognition of foreign educational credentials.

4. For a more robust review, see Chiswick and Miller (2008).

5. For example, Remennick (2008) found that primary- and secondary-school teachers from the former Soviet Union who immigrated to Israel generally could not make the adjustment from the rigid, highly disciplined, highly structured Soviet classroom to the informal, flexible, less-structured Israeli classroom. These teachers may have been able to overcome differences in subject matter or language issues, but the school and classroom cultural gap was too great for their teaching skills to be transferable.

6. The issue of the nonrecognition of the skills of immigrant physicians in the United States and Canada is the theme of chapters 5 and 6 of this volume. For a study of the adjustment of high-skilled immigrants in Israel, see chapter 8.

7. See Appendix 4A for definitions of the various educational categories. Sensitivity tests were performed for alternate measures of years of schooling for those with master's, professional, and doctorate degrees as their highest level of schooling. The findings are essentially invariant with respect to these alternative values.

8. See chapter 1 for a discussion of why the definition of skilled immigration is time and place specific.

9. The standard equation, $lnY_i = \beta_0 + \beta_1 \text{Actual Educ}_i + \ldots + \upsilon_i$, forces $\alpha_1 = \alpha_2 = |\alpha_3|$. As this condition does not hold, the ORU specification results in a higher R-squared and $\alpha_2 > \beta_1$.

10. Two other options are the worker self-assessment (WSA) and the job analyst techniques, where the latter is based on experts' "objective" evaluations. For a comparative analysis of the WSA and RM techniques, see the methodological analysis in Chiswick and Miller (forthcoming, a). That analysis shows a strong correlation between the WSA and RM data series in which the simple correlation coefficient between these measures is around 0.8 for all skill-nativity groups considered in that study. Under each of the three assessment methods, the "typical" or "required" level of education is related to the technology employed, the relative factor prices, and the educational distribution of the population under study. There is no fixed or unique required level of education in an occupation across either time or space.

11. Conventionally, a sixty-four-year upper threshold has been used to minimize any selection bias associated with retirement from the paid labor force. Using a lower threshold of fifty-four years has no material effect on the regression estimates presented in tables 4-4 and 4-5.

12. Chiswick and Miller (2008) report that tests of robustness with respect to alternative definitions of the population for defining the modal education showed virtually no substantive differences.

13. These numbers are based on imputed years of schooling where a bachelor's degree is assumed to require 16 years, a master's degree 17.5 years, a professional degree 18.5 years, and a doctorate 20 years.

14. Chiswick and Miller (2008) report estimated effects of the required level of education on earnings of 0.154 for all native-born workers and 0.153 for all foreign-born workers. Their estimates of the effects of surplus years of schooling on earnings were 0.056 for the native born and 0.044 for the foreign born.

15. The mean earnings in 1999 for bachelor's, master's, professional, and doctorate degrees are $72,067; $88,168; $111,730; and $82,521, respectively, for the adult, male, native-born population, and $65,163; $78,393; $92,011; and $78,650, respectively, for the adult, male, foreign-born population. Especially for the native born, earnings are very high for those with a professional degree.

16. The payoff to origin-country labor-market experience (evaluated at ten years) is 1.88 percent in the table 4-5 estimates for foreign-born workers, compared to 1.62 percent in the table 4-4 estimates. The payoff to labor-market experience (evaluated at ten years) acquired in the United States is 1.26 percent in the table 4-5 results, compared to 0.80 in the table 4-4 results.

17. There are twenty-two major nonmilitary occupations listed in the 2000 U.S. population census data. Due to the absence of variation in the usual level of schooling within two of these occupations, the analyses in this subsection are performed on twenty occupations.

18. All means in this section are weighted by the number of workers in the occupation.

19. In this presentation, doctorates are ranked above professional qualifications based on the typical years of formal schooling. If postqualification training, such as residencies for physicians, is considered formal schooling rather than on-the-job training, professional qualifications might be ranked above doctorates. This alternative ranking would reduce or remove the anomaly associated with the comparison of points E and F in the figures.

20. To ascertain if the relatively poor earnings outcome for doctorates was simply linked to either low salaries in the education sector or misreporting of weeks worked in that sector, a dichotomous variable for employment in the education industry was included in the model. This variable was associated with coefficients of −0.154 among the native born, and −0.192 among the foreign born. This change in the specification was associated with a 4 (native born) to 8 (foreign born) percentage points

improvement in the *ceteris paribus* earnings of workers holding doctorates compared to workers who hold bachelor's degrees, but there is little change in the relative standing of workers with professional qualifications and doctorates.

21. Regression equations for this analysis are available from the authors upon request.

22. The points test used in Australia at present, for example, allocates points for "specific employment," defined as employment in an occupation listed as a government-determined "skilled occupation" for at least three of the four years immediately preceding application for a visa. Further points are allocated for "occupation in demand (and job offer)," for which visa applicants earn points if they have been offered a job in an occupation listed as a government-determined "migration occupation in demand."

23. For a study of the effect of school quality in the country of origin on the payoff to schooling for immigrants in the United States that uses PISA scores to index school quality, see Chiswick and Miller (forthcoming, b).

References

Chiswick, B. R. 1999. Are Immigrants Favorably Self-Selected? *American Economic Review* 89 (2): 181–85.

———. 2008. Are Immigrants Favorably Self-Selected? An Economic Analysis. In *Migration Theory: Talking across Disciplines,* ed. C. B. Brettell and J. F. Hollifield. 2nd ed., 63–82. New York: Routledge.

Chiswick, B. R., and P. W. Miller. 2008. Why Is the Payoff to Schooling Smaller for Immigrants? *Labour Economics* 15 (6): 1317–40.

———. 2009. The International Transferability of Immigrants' Human Capital Skills. *Economics of Education Review* 28 (2): 162–69.

———. Forthcoming, a. Does the Choice of Reference Levels of Education in the ORU Earnings Equation Matter? *Economics of Education Review.*

———. Forthcoming, b. The Effects of School Quality in the Origin on the Payoff to Schooling for Immigrants. In *Culture and Migration (Frontiers of Economics and Globalization),* ed. G. Epstein and I. Gang. Bingley, UK: Emerald Publishers.

Cohn, E., and S. P. Khan. 1995. The Wage Effects of Overschooling Revisited. *Labour Economics* 2: 67–76.

Duncan, G. J., and S. D. Hoffman. 1981. The Incidence and Wage Effects of Overeducation. *Economics of Education Review* 1 (1): 75–86.

Hartog, J. 2000. Over-Education and Earnings: Where Are We, Where Should We Go? *Economics of Education Review* 19 (2): 131–47.

Remennick, L. 2008. Survival of the Fittest: Russian Immigrant Teachers in Israeli Schools. Paper presented at the Conference on Understanding Contemporary Migration: Challenges to Society, Kibbutz Tsuba, Israel.

Rubb, S. 2003. Post-College Schooling, Overeducation, and Hourly Earnings in the United States. *Education Economics* 11 (1): 53–72.

Rumberger, R. W. 1987. The Impact of Surplus Schooling on Productivity and Earnings. *Journal of Human Resources* 22 (1): 24–49.

U.S. Census Bureau. 2005. Public Use Microdata Sample: 5 Percent Sample of the Population. In *2000 U.S. Census of Population and Housing.*

U.S. Department of Homeland Security. 2006. *2004 Yearbook of Immigration Statistics.*

———. 2008. *2007 Yearbook of Immigration Statistics.*

U.S. Department of Labor. Bureau of Labor Statistics. 1999. *Current Population Survey.*

Vahey, S. P. 2000. The Great Canadian Training Robbery: Evidence on the Returns to Educational Mismatch. *Economics of Education Review* 19: 219–27.

Verdugo, R. R., and N. T. Verdugo. 1989. The Impact of Surplus Schooling on Earnings: Some Additional Findings. *The Journal of Human Resources* 26 (4): 629–43.

5

Physician Migration to the United States and Canada: Criteria for Admission

Linda G. Lesky

International medical graduates (IMGs) are physicians who complete medical school outside of the United States or Canada. They constitute nearly one-quarter of the physician workforce in both countries (Akl et al. 2007; Pong and Pitblado 2005). Besides immigration hurdles, IMGs face a complex set of education and certifying requirements before they can be licensed to practice medicine in either country. Many similarities exist between U.S. and Canadian requirements for IMG entrance into the profession, but there are also significant differences. This chapter outlines the requirements in both countries to help elucidate the complex process facing IMGs who choose to pursue medical practice in the United States or Canada.

Medical Education in the United States and Canada

Basic medical education in the United States and Canada entails a four-year graduate program after receipt of a bachelor's degree. Additional postgraduate residency training in a specialty discipline is required to be eligible for licensure and board certification. This period of residency training, which lasts from two to ten years, constitutes graduate medical education (GME). In both the United States and Canada, GME is publicly funded and, to varying degrees, government regulated. The training in most disciplines is hospital-based, and residents are a vital component of the workforce in teaching hospitals. In the United States, hospitals determine the specialty composition of their residency positions, but the total number of positions has been capped at 1998 levels since enactment of the 1997 Balanced Budget Amendment. In Canada, provincial ministries of health determine both the number and composition of residency positions. In both countries, the number of first-year residency positions exceeds the number of graduating medical students (by approximately 25 percent in the United States and 12 percent in Canada).

Although graduating medical students in both countries choose the specialty they wish to pursue and the particular residency programs that interest them, a country-based centralized matching process ("the match") is used to assign students to residency positions (Canadian Resident Matching; National Resident Match). The match was created to set a uniform date of appointment for positions in GME and to establish a venue for matching applicants' and programs' preferences for each other. During their fourth year of medical school, students apply to residency programs and, if invited, visit programs for interviews. At the conclusion of this so-called recruitment season, students rank programs in order of preference. Residency programs generate a similar list ranking the students interviewed. The ranking lists are submitted to a centralized agency, and students receive notification of their assignment in mid-March of each year. The decision of the match is binding on both students and residency programs.

In Canada, this process is coordinated by the Canadian Residency Matching Service (CaRMS; Canadian Resident Matching). The corresponding agency in the United States is the National Resident Match Program (NRMP; National Resident Match). Since U.S. and Canadian medical schools are accredited by the same organization, they are deemed equivalent, and there is reciprocity for residency training. Canadian and U.S. medical students can apply to programs in both countries, although the licensing examinations required to enter the match are different and not interchangeable.

The Application Process for International Medical Graduates

Physicians with foreign medical training face substantial obstacles when attempting to migrate to either the United States or Canada. Although medical school outside of the United States or Canada is accepted toward licensure in both countries, GME generally is not. With few exceptions, GME must be completed in the United States or Canada to enter the profession in either country. Students who attend medical school outside of the United States or Canada and apply for residency training apply as IMGs. The IMG classification is based upon the medical school attended, not citizenship. A U.S. citizen who completes medical school outside of the United States or Canada is considered an IMG, whereas a non-U.S. citizen who completes medical school in the United States or Canada would not be considered an IMG. IMGs apply and compete for residency positions through the same matching process as U.S. and Canadian medical students.

The educational and examination requirements for IMGs to enter GME are similar in the United States and Canada. Although there are minor variations in requirements across provinces, all Canadian provinces require documentation of graduation from a medical school listed in the International Medical Education Directory (IMED), successful completion of the Medical Council of Canada Evaluating Examination, and completion of a test of English-language proficiency (Canadian Resident Matching). Medical schools listed in IMED are those that are recognized by the appropriate agencies (generally, the Ministry of Health) in their respective countries. A listing in IMED does not provide any information regarding the quality of the education, nor does it imply any quality assurance by an accrediting agency or the host country.

IMGs applying for residency in the United States require certification from the Educational Commission for Foreign Medical Graduates (ECFMG a). The ECFMG is a nonprofit organization that certifies IMGs' readiness to enter residency training in the United States. Certification includes verification of medical education credentials from a school listed in IMED and the successful completion of steps one and two (Basic Sciences and Clinical Sciences, respectively) of the U.S. Medical Licensing Examination (USMLE). Step two consists of two components: a computer-based clinical-knowledge examination available through testing centers around the world and a clinical- and communication-skills component that utilizes standardized patients and is administered only at five evaluation centers in the United States. Once IMGs are certified by the ECFMG and have had at least one interview, they are eligible to submit a rank list to the NRMP.

Unlike the educational and examination requirements, the United States and Canada have substantially different immigration requirements for the entry of foreign-born IMGs into the residency match. These differences have implications for the number of foreign-born IMGs residing in the country and the number who ultimately enter the profession. In Canada, an IMG must be a permanent resident or Canadian citizen to apply for a GME position. IMGs generally enter Canada on a skilled-worker visa, which is awarded based on points granted for education, work experience, age, language proficiency, and adaptability (Citizenship and Immigration Canada). Foreign-trained physicians generally have little difficulty accruing enough points to meet the immigration requirements, but the skilled-worker visa does not require an employer sponsor. As a result, IMGs enter Canada without a prearranged residency position and begin applying for a spot only after arriving.

In contrast, foreign-born IMGs who seek entry into U.S. residency programs may do so as naturalized citizens, permanent residents, or with an appropriate temporary visa. Since immigration policy in the United States favors family reunification, the only option for many IMGs is a temporary visa, either an H1-B temporary-professional-worker visa or the J-1 exchange-visitor visa. Both visas require an employer sponsor. In the case of IMGs seeking to enter residency training, this means IMGs must have proof of acceptance into an accredited GME program before a visa will be issued. The advantage of the H1-B visa is that recipients are eligible to apply for permanent-resident status. However, not all residency programs sponsor the more expensive H-1B visas. In contrast, the J-1 visa is sponsored by the ECFMG and broadly accepted by residency programs, but it is valid only while the IMG is in the residency program. Following the completion of training, J-1 visa holders are required to return to their country of origin for at least two years. The two-year home rule can be waived by working in a state or federally designated health-professional-shortage area for three years, at which point the visa is converted to an H-1B. The number of J-1 waivers allowed and granted has varied over time, but most J-1 visa holders secure a waiver position and ultimately establish practice in the United States (U.S. General Accounting Office 1996).

A final obstacle to entry is the cost of the application and interview process. The computerized knowledge tests cost approximately $700 each, and the USMLE clinical-skills examination adds an additional $1,200 (ECFMG b). Taking the clinical-skills examination requires IMGs to travel to the United States, as does interviewing for residency positions. Economic constraints impeded many competitive IMGs from applying (Leon et al. 2007).

International Medical Graduates in "the Match"

Although the number of residency positions in the United States and Canada exceeds the number of graduating medical students in each country, positions available to IMGs are competitive. In order to enter the match, IMGs must meet the educational and immigration requirements discussed above and be invited for at least one interview. Canada runs two iterations of the match (Canadian Resident Matching). In the first iteration, eligible IMGs participate in a separate track for a small number of designated positions (approximately two hundred in 2007), 80 percent of which were in family medicine (Canadian Resident Matching Service 2007). The second iteration is offered for positions and applicants who were not matched in the first iteration and is a single track for both Canadian graduates and IMGs.

In the United States, there is a single match track and the number of IMGs who match into a specialty or into a specific residency program is related to the competitiveness of the specialty and the specific program among U.S. medical graduates. For example, in 2007, less than 10 percent of positions in orthopedic surgery, vascular surgery, and otolaryngology were filled by IMGs (National Resident Match 2007). In contrast, IMGs filled over 50 percent of family-medicine residency positions.

The 2007 results illustrate arduousness of the process and the competitiveness of the match for IMGs. In 2007 ECFMG completed 25,123 registrations for step one of the USMLE (ECFMG 2007). This represents the number of foreign medical graduates beginning the process of seeking a residency position in the United States. In that same year, ECFMG issued only 10,172 certificates. A total of 21,845 first-year residency positions were available in the U.S. match, and 9,986 IMGs participated (National Resident Match 2007). Forty-five percent (4,527) of IMG participants matched into a position. The prospects for success are worse for IMGs entering the match in Canada. In 2007, 1,486 IMGs entered the match and competed for a total of 2,449 first-year residency positions (Canadian Resident Matching Service 2007). Including both the first and second iterations of the match, only 298 (20 percent) matched into a spot.

Implications and Future Trends

As previously stated, the Canadian model for accepting IMGs into GME requires applicants to be permanent residents or citizens before applying. The skilled-worker visa, which allows entry for most high-skilled professionals, does not require an employer sponsor. This has attracted many who ultimately do not succeed at obtaining a residency position, achieving licensure, and entering medical practice. Although the exact number of unlicensed IMGs in Canada is unknown, estimates range from two to four thousand in Ontario alone (Crutcher et al. 2003). To put these numbers in perspective, the Ontario Physician Human Resources Data Centre reports that the province had just over twenty-four thousand physicians in active practice in 2009. The population-to-physician ratio for family medicine ranged from 709 to 1 in Toronto and 1,536 to 1 in the rural underserved areas of the province.

The backlog of foreign graduates and the worsening physician shortages in Canada have prompted greater consideration of ways to accelerate the integration of IMGs into Canadian medical practice (Dauphinee 2006). A provisional license is available to IMGs who can demonstrate recent practice experience (Audas, Ross, and Vardy 2005). IMGs with a provisional medical license represent less than 5 percent of the physician workforce but provide care to the most remote and medically underserved regions of the country. In addition, the program allows provinces to fill positions that Canadian medical graduates rarely consider. The majority of these positions are in Saskatchewan and in Newfoundland and Labrador. Under the requirements for a provisional license, IMGs undergo a skills assessment and brief training program (Nasmith 2000). If successful, individuals are offered four to six months of additional training before being eligible for a provisional license. The physician bears the costs of the assessment and training. After a three- to five-year period of monitored practice, the physician is eligible for a permanent license.

A second program, implemented in Ontario in 2004, is also available to those who can document recent practice experience. The Practice Ready Assessment Program offers a six-month assessment in a supervised university-based clinical setting to approximately two hundred IMGs per year (Ontario Ministry). The program determines a physician's need for further training or confirms readiness to sit for licensure examinations and, if successful, to enter directly into practice with a permanent license. Finally, IMGs have filled over 50 percent of the positions available for a pilot project, also in Ontario, evaluating the role of physician assistants in health care settings (Magnus 2008).

Unlike in Canada, many IMGs enter the United States with a temporary visa that requires a confirmed residency position prior to being issued. The exact number of IMGs entering training as citizens, permanent residents, or visa holders is not known. However, one recent study suggests that the composition of IMGs entering the United States is changing. Using data from the New York State Survey of Residents Completing Training, Richards, Chou, and Lo Sasso (2009) disaggregated IMGs in New York State by citizenship and immigration status for the period from 1998 to 2007. New York has the largest percentage of IMGs in residency training. A striking trend in their data is the nearly 40 percent decline in non-U.S. citizen IMGs, from 42 percent in 1998 to 26 percent in 2007. The subgroup that experienced the greatest decline was the group of IMGs with J-1 visas, which fell from 41.5 percent of all IMGs in 1999 to 13 percent in 2007. In contrast, naturalized U.S. citizen IMGs grew from 14 percent to 28 percent, native-born U.S. citizen IMGs from 6 percent to nearly 15 percent, and H-1 temporary visa holders rose from 8 percent to 22 percent during the same time period. The ECFMG has also reported that an increasing number of U.S. IMGs is being certified for residency training and that there is a higher match rate for U.S. IMGs compared to foreign-born IMGs, despite U.S. IMGs' poorer performance on certification examinations (Boulet et al. 2006).

The reasons behind these shifts are unclear. There is speculation that immigration policy changes after 9/11 raised concerns about both fewer training visas and delays in visa processing. (For more on how immigration changes after 9/11 may have affected student admissions to the United States generally, see chapter 3 of this volume.) ECFMG statistics from 2003 estimated that 18 percent of J-1 physicians in their first year of sponsorship arrived 31 days or more after their start date (Leon et al. 2007). Training programs that are dependent upon a full cohort of residents to meet clinical demands are uniquely sensitive to these delays and may be more inclined to choose applicants who do not require a visa to enter the country.

If these trends hold, they have important implications. First, fewer foreign-born physicians will have the opportunity to immigrate to the United States. Second, those who do continue to pursue residency training in the United States will look for means of entering the country other than via temporary visas. This could create a circumstance similar to that in Canada wherein large numbers of foreign-trained physicians are restricted from entering practice. Finally, the decline in J-1 visa holders will reduce the number of physicians with an obligation to work in health-professional-shortage areas. Studies already show that growth in the physician workforce in health-professional-shortage areas lags far behind the overall growth in the physician workforce (Hart et al. 2007).

Both the United States and Canada are dependent upon IMGs to meet physician-workforce needs in both training sites and practice settings. Both countries also report ongoing physician shortages, and, at least in the short run, will continue to look to foreign-trained physicians to fill the gap. Despite the obstacles, large numbers of foreign-born IMGs seek entry into the United States and Canada to obtain excellent medical training and better living conditions. Regardless of immigration status, those who succeed rarely return to their countries of origin. The fate of those who do not succeed is poorly understood. Additional research is needed to determine how many return to their country of origin to pursue a medical career, retrain to pursue another career, or remain underemployed.

References

Akl, E. A., R. Mustafa, F. Bdair, and H. J. Schunemann. 2007. The United States Physician Workforce and International Medical Graduates: Trends and Characteristics. *Journal of General Internal Medicine* 22: 264–68.

Audas, R., A. Ross, and D. Vardy. 2005. The Use of Provisionally Licensed International Medical Graduates in Canada. *Canadian Medical Association Journal* 173: 1315–16.

Boulet, J. R., D. B. Swanson, R. A. Cooper, J. J. Norcini, and D. W. McKinley. 2006. Comparison of Characteristics and Examination Performances of U.S. and non-U.S. Citizen International Medical Graduates Who Sought Educational Commission for Foreign Medical Graduates Certification: 1995–2004. *Academic Medicine* 81: S116–19.

Canadian Resident Matching Service (CaRMS). Website. Available at www.carms.ca.

———. 2007. Operations: Reports and Statistics; R1 Match Results. Available at www.carms.ca/eng/operations_R1reports_07_e.shtml.

Citizenship and Immigration Canada. Immigrating to Canada: Skilled Workers and Professionals. Website. Available at www.cic.gc.ca/english/immigrate/skilled/index.asp.

Crutcher, R. A., S. R. Banner, O. Szafran, and M. Watanabe. 2003. Characteristics of International Medical Graduates Who Applied to the CaRMS 2002 Match. *Canadian Medical Association Journal* 168: 1119–23.

Dauphinee, W. D. 2006. The Circle Game: Understanding Physician Migration Patterns within Canada. *Academic Medicine* 81: S49–54.

Educational Commission for Foreign Medical Graduates (ECFMG) (a). Website. Available at www.ecfmg.org.

——— (b). Set Fees. ECFMG website. Available at www.ecfmg.org/fees.html.

———. 2007. *Annual Report.* Philadelphia, PA: ECFMG.

Hart, L. G., S. M. Skillman, M. Fordyce, M. Thompson, A. Hagopian, and T. R. Konrad. 2007. International Medical Graduate Physicians in the United States: Changes since 1981. *Health Affairs* 26: 1159–69.

Leon, L. R. Jr., H. Ojeda, J. I. Mills Sr., C. R. Leon, S. B. Psalms, and H. V. Villar. 2007. The Journey of a Foreign-Trained Physician to a United States Residency: Controversies Surrounding the Impact of This Migration to the United States. *Journal of the American College of Surgeons* 204: 486–94.

Magnus, B. 2008. Foreign-Trained Doctors Dominate Pilot Project. *Canadian Medical Association* Journal 178: 1411.

Nasmith, L. 2000. License Requirements for International Medical Graduates: Should National Standards Be Adopted? *Canadian Medical Association Journal* 162: 795–96.

National Resident Match Program (NRMP). Website. Available at www.nrmp.org.

———. 2007. *Results and Data: 2007 Main Residency Match.* Washington, DC: NRMP. Available at www.nrmp.org/data/resultsanddata2007.pdf.

Ontario Ministry of Health and Long-Term Care. Health Care Professionals: International Medical Graduates; Practice Ready Assessment. Available at www.health. gov.on.ca/english/providers/project/img/img_mn.html.

Ontario Physician Human Resources Data Centre. Website. Available at www. ophrdc.org/Home.aspx.

Pong, R. W., and J. R. Pitblado. 2005. International Medical Graduates. In *Geographic Distribution of Physicians in Canada: Beyond How Many and Where*, 26–28. Ottawa: Canadian Institute for Health Information.

Richards, M. R., C. F. Chou, and A. T. Lo Sasso. 2009. Importing Medicine: A Look at Citizenship and Immigration Status for Graduating Residents in New York State from 1998 to 2007. *Medical Care Research and Review* 66 (4): 472–85.

U.S. General Accounting Office. 1996. *Foreign Physicians Exchange Visitor Program Becoming Major Route to Practicing in the U.S. Underserved Areas.* Report GAI/HEHS-97-26, Washington, DC.

6

Earnings, Occupations, and Schooling Decisions of Immigrants with Medical Degrees: Evidence for Canada and the United States

*James Ted McDonald, Casey Warman,
and Christopher Worswick*

In countries like Canada and the United States, immigration policy has a significant impact on the supply of workers in different occupations. While considerable research has been conducted on the overall performance of different groups of immigrants arriving in each of these two countries, considerably less research has been carried out at the occupation level in which unique challenges may exist in terms of the successful integration of immigrants into employment suitable for their skills and qualifications. The medical profession is an important example of an occupation in which significant hurdles often must be overcome before an immigrant with a foreign medical degree receives permission to work as a physician.

The nature of medical training varies across countries, and this lack of standardization means that many immigrants may come to either the United States or Canada and then be disappointed to learn that they are not considered qualified to work as a physician. In both countries, holders of medical degrees from other countries must go through an expensive and time-consuming process of examinations, medical residencies in Canadian or U.S. hospitals, and licensing procedures before they are licensed to practice medicine. Given these costs as well as the costs associated with leaving their home country, immigrants may choose instead to accept alternative employment rather than enter a medical program to obtain the credentials necessary to work as a physician. Furthermore, delays in licensing can result in significant differences in physician earnings if, for example, immigrant physicians are delayed in establishing a practice or are more likely to accept employment as physicians in lower-paying sectors or regions of the country.

In this paper, we investigate the earnings outcomes of immigrants employed as physicians in both Canada and the United States. Since we are able to identify immigrants with medical degrees who are not employed as physicians in the Canadian census data, we investigate the occupational outcomes of immigrants with medical degrees in Canada in order to identify which group of immigrants with medical degrees is most likely to be employed in alternative occupations. Finally, we analyze the postmigration schooling decisions of immigrants with medical degrees, both those employed as physicians (for the case of Canada and the United States) and for all immigrants with medical degrees irrespective of whether they are employed as physicians (only for the case of Canada). The goal of this part of the analysis is to identify whether immigrants with medical degrees are returning to school after arrival in the United States or Canada to upgrade either their skills or their credentials.

A number of studies have analyzed the labor-market outcomes of immigrants with medical degrees for both the United States and Canada. A study that is particularly relevant for our analysis is Boyd and Schellenberg (2007), which analyzed data from the 2001 Canadian census and investigated the extent to which internationally educated physicians and engineers are not employed in their chosen professions, relative to Canadian-educated physicians and engineers. The foreign-born doctor's birthplace is the most important determinant of the probability of working as a doctor. Boyd and Schellenberg find underemployment to be most common for foreign-trained immigrant doctors born in Southeast Asia and East Asia, while those from Eastern Europe and South Asian countries are the most likely immigrants to be employed as doctors in Canada.

Another study that is also relevant is that of Szafran et al. (2005), who carried out a small-scale survey of the educational levels of individuals who received their educational training outside of Canada but subsequently applied to the Canadian Resident Matching Service for postgraduate training.

Immigrants within this group were more likely to cite the presence of barriers to training and licensing barriers to practice as having been important.

Grant and Oertel (1997) argue that a long queue exists of foreign-trained physicians seeking entry into Canada, representing an important source of medical human capital. However, they make the case that barriers have been set up by the provincial medical licensing boards that are similar to a protective tariff, and which limit the country's access to a lower-cost supply of physician's services.

In a recent paper, Phillips and others (2007) examine administrative data from the American Medical Association, the Canadian Medical Association, and other sources to document the extent to which Canadian-educated physicians are working in the United States and U.S.-educated physicians are working in Canada. They find that while only 408 U.S.-educated physicians were working in direct patient care in Canada in 2004, 8,162 Canadian-educated physicians were working in direct patient care in the United States in 2006, and close to 70 percent of these physicians were specialists. Canadian-educated specialists in the United States represent 19 percent of the Canadian specialist workforce, while Canadian-educated primary-care physicians in the United States represent 8 percent of the Canadian general-practitioner workforce. Overall, one in nine Canadian-educated physicians are practicing in the United States; after excluding U.S.-born physicians educated in Canada, still one in twelve are practicing in the United States. They conclude that physician emigration to the United States is in fact an important contributing factor to the shortage of physicians in Canada.

A significant body of U.S. literature exists on physicians' remuneration (see, for example, Bashaw and Heywood 2001). However, there appears to be a dearth of literature explicitly about the labor-market outcomes of foreign-born physicians in the United States. An exception is a report by the U.S. Government Accountability Office (2006). The report provides statistics on use of visas for foreign physicians intended to alleviate physician shortages in the United States.

This study contributes to the existing literature by presenting new econometric results on the success of immigrants with medical degrees at having their credentials recognized and remunerated in Canada and the United States. This chapter describes policy differences between Canada and the United States in terms of how these differences may affect the earnings and probability of immigrants with medical degrees working as physicians. Next, this chapter describes the U.S. census microdata files. The sample restrictions are outlined and a number of key summary statistics are presented. The results of the Logit and ordinary least squares (OLS) regression estimation are presented and interpreted in a following section of this chapter. Finally, the chapter concludes with a discussion of ongoing and future work by the authors.

Relevant Policy Differences between Canada and the United States

Before comparing the labor-market outcomes of immigrants with medical degrees in Canada and the United States, it is important to have an understanding of the relevant policy environments in each country. Three main types of policies are relevant to this question. First, public policies toward access to health services and health insurance differ considerably between the two countries. In the United States, provision is mixed between a large private health care system augmented by some government provision. Medical insurance is primarily provided through the private sector with an important role of provision of medical services managed through the Medicare system for individuals over the age of sixty-five. In contrast, Canadian health care is primarily provided through government-run hospitals and physician payment schemes. Health insurance is universal, and limits are placed on the ability of physicians to determine their own compensation or bill in excess of the government-regulated fees-for-service system. However, it is important to note that variation exists across provinces since health care is under provincial jurisdiction under the Canadian constitution. Transfers from the federal government to the provinces to help pay for health care are at least partly conditional on the provinces' following the same set of core principles (as stipulated by the Canadian Health Act) in the delivery of health care. However, across the provinces there are differences along at least some dimensions in the way in which these services are provided.

A large literature exists that compares the health outcomes of Canadians and Americans in order to try to identify the effects of the different systems of health care provision. Lasser, Himmelstein, and Woolhandler (2006) compare the health status, access to care, and use of medical services in the

United States and Canada using data from the joint Canada-U.S. Survey of Health. U.S. respondents (compared with Canadians) are found to be less likely to have a regular doctor, more likely to have unmet health needs, and more likely to forgo needed medicines. Both countries are found to have disparities based on race, income, and immigrant status but these were more extreme in the U.S. case. The authors conclude that residents of the United States are less able to access care than are Canadians and that the universal coverage available in Canada appears to reduce most disparities in access to care.

A second relevant policy dimension relates to the recognition of foreign medical training. In chapter 5 of this volume, Lesky comprehensively reviews the expensive, time-consuming, and complex processes required for foreign-trained medical professionals to work as physicians in both Canada and the United States (see also McMahon 2004; Boyd and Schellenberg 2007). In both countries, there is strong evidence that these administrative hurdles make it difficult for individuals with foreign medical training to receive licenses to practice as physicians. Shafqat and Zaidi (2005) argue that the large-scale influx of foreign medical graduates into Western developed countries has been present for decades. However, they argue that the processes of both having foreign educational credentials recognized and finding employment as physicians have become much more difficult in countries like the United States and Canada. McMahon (2004) describes the situation in the United States with regard to the reliance on foreign-trained physicians. International medical graduates are reported to account for one-quarter of the physicians in the United States, which represents an increase of 160 percent since 1975. McMahon argues that there is an ever-increasing dependence on international medical graduates on the part of the U.S. health care industry.

In spite of this, many urban and rural communities continue to have shortages of physicians. Micka, Leeb, and Wodchisc (2000) study U.S. administrative data to see whether international medical graduates (IMGs) are more likely than U.S. medical graduates (USMGs) to be found in medically underserved areas or areas with higher need. They find that consistently more states have IMGs who are disproportionately represented in underserved areas than is the case for USMGs. They also find that IMGs are more likely to be found in states with a high number of physicians relative to USMGs. Statistics are presented on the number of foreign-trained doctors in the United States and the number of IMG residents. The former group grew dramatically over the period 1950 through 1996, and at a much faster rate than did the latter group. Micka, Leeb, and Wodchisc report that in 1996, 23.4 percent of the active postresident physician workforce was foreign trained. They conclude that the majority of IMGs (as is the case for USMGs) have located in nonneedy counties. See Benarroch and Grant (2004), and Dostie and Leger (2009) for related research on the internal migration of physicians in Canada.

The key immigration-policy difference for our analysis relates to the different selection processes in Canada and the United States related to the admission of skilled immigrants. Many foreign-born individuals wishing to work as physicians in the United States would enter the country on H1-B "professional worker" visas, and these visas require the applicant to have (i) already passed step three of the United States Medical Licensing Examination, (ii) an offer of a training position already in place, and (iii) a temporary state medical license already. In contrast, the Canadian immigrant-selection (points) system for skilled workers and professionals does not place the same professional requirements on applicants wishing to immigrate to Canada. While significant barriers exist to acquiring a medical license for individuals with foreign medical degrees, individuals with medical degrees and good language ability in either English or French stand a good chance of satisfying the points requirements for admission based mainly on their high level of formal education. Even if their educational credentials do not allow them to work as physicians in Canada, the system is designed to admit the person based on the high level of human capital that the applicant is deemed to possess.

The Data and Estimation Sample

The data used in the estimation come from the 2001 Canadian census confidential master file and the 2000 United States public-use 5 percent file. The Canadian data were accessed through the University of New Brunswick Research Data Centre and are drawn from the 20 percent file. The age range in the analysis of both the Canadian and the U.S. data is restricted to individuals age twenty-nine to sixty-five. One strength of the Canadian census data is that the field of study is available as well as the level of education attained, allowing us to identify with some precision those individuals who have obtained a medical degree.

While the U.S. census data permit much larger sample sizes, there are no data on field of study, so medical degree holders cannot be identified separately from other higher-degree holders. Although most people working as physicians in the United States report a professional degree as their highest degree (86.6 percent of the native-born and 85.8 percent of the foreign-born physicians), another 8.3 and 10.5 percent of the native-born and the foreign-born physicians, respectively, report a doctorate degree as their highest degree. Of course, it is possible that someone who reports a doctorate as their highest degree may also have a professional degree. The remaining 4 percent of the native- and foreign-born physicians had either a master's or bachelor's degree as their highest degree.[1] Although people with a bachelor's degree may be currently working as a physician while completing their medical degree, only 7.6 percent of people with bachelor's as their highest degree reported being currently in school.

We restrict the Canadian sample to include only individuals who have at least a medical degree (regardless of occupation), while we restrict the U.S. sample to include only individuals employed as physicians or medical specialists. Using the Canadian data, we can estimate the determinants of working as a physician, being a student, and the level of earnings conditional on having a medical degree. For the United States, we can estimate the determinants of being a student and the level of earnings conditional on working as a physician. For comparative purposes, we also carry out a parallel analysis using the Canadian census data on the subsample of individuals employed as medical doctors.

In both the Canadian and the U.S. analyses, immigrants who arrived in either country at age twenty-nine or older are assumed to have received their medical degree outside of the receiving country. Immigrants who arrived in their new country at the age of eighteen or younger are assumed to have received their medical degree at a university in the receiving country. The remaining group of immigrants, those who arrived between the ages of eighteen and twenty-nine, are referred to as the "M.D. degree indeterminate" group, since it is unclear whether these individual immigrants are likely to have received their training within the receiving country. Boyd and

Schellenberg (2007) use a similar approach. Unfortunately, individuals who study in the United States or Canada, return to their home countries (as would be required on a J-class visa in the United States), and then migrate to the United States or Canada will be classified as having obtained their medical credentials in another country.

In addition, it is possible to identify temporary residents in the 2001 Canadian census. These individuals are typically in Canada on either temporary work permits or temporary student visas.[2] As part of the analysis, the population of individuals within Canada who have a medical degree is divided into three groups: (i) the Canadian born, (ii) immigrants, and (iii) temporary residents. Since the census data do not contain the year of entry into Canada for temporary residents, we are unable to distinguish between temporary residents who received their medical training in Canada and temporary residents who received their medical training outside of Canada.

Table 6-1 contains percentages of labor-force status, occupation, and student status for the sample of individuals in the 2001 Canadian census who hold a medical degree. There is generally a high rate of employment as a physician for those individuals who received their medical degrees in Canada; it is 87.7 percent for the Canadian born and 85.8 percent for the foreign born. Canadian-born individuals with Canadian medical degrees[3] have a very low unemployment rate (0.5 percent) and a very low rate of nonparticipation in the labor force (3.8 percent). Foreign-born individuals with Canadian medical degrees have somewhat higher rates of unemployment (1.1 percent) and of nonparticipation (4.8 percent).

However, these statistics change considerably once the focus is placed on the foreign born with foreign medical degrees. For example, the rate of employment as a physician falls to 42.0 percent for all foreign born, 25.4 percent for permanent residents, and 51.3 percent for naturalized Canadians. The unemployment rate and nonparticipation rate are 13.9 percent and 28.9 percent, respectively, for permanent residents. This is strong preliminary evidence that difficulties with recognition of international medical degrees have a significant impact on the ability to work as a doctor in Canada for the foreign born with international medical degrees.

The statistics for the "M.D. degree indeterminate" group generally fall between the statistics of the individuals with medical degrees obtained in Canada and those with international medical degrees. For example, 68.3

TABLE 6-1

PERCENTAGE OF CANADIAN RESIDENTS HOLDING MEDICAL DEGREES BY OCCUPATION, IMMIGRANT STATUS, AND LOCATION OF MEDICAL TRAINING, ADULTS AGES TWENTY-NINE TO SIXTY-FIVE YEARS

| | Location of Medical Training | | | | | | | | |
| | In Canada | | Outside Canada | | | Location Uncertain | | | |
Immigrant Status	All Foreign Born	All Native Born	All Foreign Born	Permanent Residents	Naturalized Canadians	All Foreign Born	Permanent Residents	Naturalized Canadians	Temporary Residents
Current Occupation									
Specialist M.D.	27.7	31.5	14.5	8.5	17.8	20.3	12.3	21.8	21.7
General Practitioner	58.1	56.2	27.5	16.9	33.5	48.0	24.8	52.5	33.5
Total: All M.D.	85.8	87.7	42.0	25.4	51.3	68.3	37.1	74.3	55.2
Other Health-Related Occupations	3.1	2.5	6.9	7.2	6.7	6.1	10.8	5.2	4.0
Manager/Professional	6.2	6.5	18.6	20.3	17.7	11.2	14.3	10.6	16.1
Trades/Services	1.6	1.4	14.8	20.7	11.5	6.6	16.7	4.6	4.1
No Occupation Stated	3.4	2.0	17.7	26.3	12.8	7.9	21.1	5.4	20.7
Labor-Force Status									
Unemployed	1.1	0.5	7.7	13.9	4.2	3.7	8.6	2.7	4.6
Not in Labor Force	4.8	3.8	19.6	28.9	14.3	9.7	24.6	6.9	27.9
Student Status									
Full-Time Student	8.3	6.3	7.1	12.0	4.3	7.2	16.1	5.5	30.1
Part-Time Student	4.2	3.0	6.9	9.9	5.2	4.0	5.7	3.7	4.9

SOURCE: Authors' calculations based on Statistics Canada, "2001 Canadian Census: 20 Percent Master File," accessed through the CRISP-UNB Research Data Centre at the University of New Brunswick–Fredericton, Canada.

NOTE: Imputed information based on age at arrival in Canada: individuals age twenty-nine years or older upon arrival in Canada are classified as having obtained their medical training outside of Canada and individuals age eighteen years or under upon arrival are classified as having obtained their medical training in Canada; for individuals who arrived in Canada when they were between ages nineteen and twenty-eight years, the location where they obtained their medical training is classified as uncertain.

percent of the individuals in this group are employed as physicians. This number decreases to 37.1 percent for the permanent residents within the M.D. degree indeterminate group. The equivalent statistics for naturalized Canadians and temporary residents are 74.3 percent and 55.2 percent.[4]

Within the M.D. degree indeterminate group, the unemployment rate for permanent residents is 8.6 percent and the rate of nonparticipation is 24.6 percent. For naturalized Canadians, the unemployment and nonparticipation rates are generally closer to those of the Canadian born, though important differences remain. For temporary residents, the unemployment and nonparticipation rates are close to those of the permanent residents for whom the location of training is uncertain, at 4.6 percent and 27.9 percent, respectively.

Temporary residents' high rate of nonparticipation is driven by the high likelihood that a temporary resident is either a full- or part-time student, at 30.1 percent and 4.9 percent, respectively. Permanent residents whose medical training occurred outside of Canada also are relatively likely to be students; 12 percent are full-time students and 9.9 percent are part-time students. Similar results are found for permanent residents in the M.D. degree indeterminate group.

In table 6-2, the regional distribution of individuals with medical degrees is presented by immigrant status. In the upper panel, the table is based on the Canadian data and includes individuals with medical degrees who are not working as medical doctors by immigrant status. When immigrants and the Canadian born are compared, we see that immigrants with medical degrees are more likely to reside in Ontario and in British Columbia relative to native-born medical degree holders, regardless of whether or not the individuals are practicing as physicians. In terms of the distribution across Canada's major cities, immigrant medical degree holders are more concentrated than nonimmigrant medical degree holders in Toronto and Vancouver, two Canadian cities with large concentrations of immigrants. It is worth noting that immigrant medical degree holders who are not practicing as physicians are especially concentrated in Toronto (40.7 percent), suggesting that immigrants may seek out immigrant communities for support when their medical credentials are not recognized or that they prefer to live closer to their immigrant communities rather than reside in locations for which there may be better labor-market opportunities.

TABLE 6-2

DISTRIBUTION OF IMMIGRANTS AND NONIMMIGRANTS WITH MEDICAL DEGREES
BY LOCATION, ADULTS AGES TWENTY-NINE TO SIXTY-FIVE YEARS (PERCENTAGES)

Canada

	Total Population with Medical Degrees	Working as Medical Doctor		Not Working as Medical Doctor	
		Foreign Born	Native Born	Foreign Born	Native Born
Region[a]					
Atlantic	7.6	6.9	7.8	2.7	6.8
Quebec	24.1	12.6	32.0	14.3	31.5
Ontario	38.0	45.4	33.2	56.5	34.7
Prairies	3.7	7.6	5.4	3.9	5.1
Alberta	9.9	10.8	9.0	7.6	8.0
British Columbia	13.0	16.7	12.7	15.0	13.9
City[b]					
Toronto	15.6	25.0	12.9	40.7	15.8
Montreal	11.4	10.2	16.0	12.9	15.2
Vancouver	6.6	11.1	6.9	13.1	9.0

United States

	Total Population with Medical Degrees	Working as Medical Doctor	
		Foreign Born	Native Born
Region			
New England	4.9	5.8	6.9
Mid-Atlantic	14.1	24.9	15.7
East North Central	16.0	15.4	14.4
West North Central	6.8	4.0	6.9
South Atlantic	18.4	18.2	19.1
East South Central	6.0	2.8	5.5
West South Central	11.2	9.1	9.8
Mountain	6.5	2.8	6.5
Pacific	16.0	16.9	15.2
City[c]			
New York	6.4	16.5	6.9
Los Angeles	4.3	7.0	3.5
Chicago	3.1	5.6	3.1
Philadelphia	1.8	2.1	2.8
Boston	1.5	2.8	2.5
Washington, D.C.	1.8	2.8	2.2
San Francisco	1.8	2.1	2.0

SOURCES: Statistics Canada, "2001 Canadian Census: 20 Percent Master File," accessed through the CRISP-UNB Research Data Centre at the University of New Brunswick–Fredericton, Canada; and Steven Ruggles et al., "Integrated Public-Use Microdata Series: Version 4.0 (Machine-Readable Database)," from *2000 U.S. Census* (Minneapolis, MN: Minnesota Population Center, 2008).

NOTES: a. Canadian territories are not reported; thus the general population numbers do not add to 100 percent. b. Statistics are for the Statistics Canada Census Metropolitan Area. c. Statistics are for Metropolitan Area.

In the lower panel of table 6-2, equivalent statistics are presented based on the U.S. census data for individuals currently employed as physicians in the United States. As is the case for Canada, considerable variation exists across the U.S. regions for both the native born and the foreign born. In contrast to the Canadian case, the immigrant and U.S.-born differences in the distributions are small with the exception of the Mid-Atlantic region, where immigrant doctors are more concentrated relative to U.S.-born doctors. Greater differences between foreign- and U.S.-born doctors are present in the distributions across the major cities. Relatively more foreign-born doctors are present in New York (16.5 percent), Los Angeles (7.0 percent), and Chicago (5.6 percent) than U.S.-born doctors (6.9, 3.5, and 3.1 percent, respectively). As with immigrants generally, a greater preference on the part of immigrant physicians to reside in larger urban areas with more-established immigrant communities is an additional obstacle to the successful attraction and retention of immigrant doctors in more rural areas. In addition, this regional variation indicates the importance of using multivariate models when comparing outcomes of immigrants and the native born, since it is important to control for these regional and urban/rural differences so they do not hide other important differences in employment and investment behavior of immigrants with medical degrees working as foreign doctors. Finally, the comparison of the foreign born with medical degrees in Canada who are and are not employed as physicians provides compelling preliminary evidence that significant challenges are present in the Canadian case in terms of finding employment as physicians for these individuals.

While finding employment as a physician is clearly a key part of the economic assimilation of the foreign born with medical degrees, the earnings of these individuals are also an important indicator of their overall success. In table 6-3, sample statistics related to earned income and hours of work are presented by immigrant status for individuals employed as physicians in Canada and the United States.[5] In Canada, immigrants working as doctors earn approximately $10,000 less than Canadian-born individuals working as doctors.[6] Although immigrant doctors in the United States earn more than immigrant doctors in Canada, the gap between earnings for U.S.-born and immigrant doctors is larger; mean earned income for foreign-born doctors in the United States is $141,273, compared to $161,037 for U.S.-born doctors. The median values of earned income show similar overall patterns,

TABLE 6-3

**EARNINGS AND HOURS WORKED, IMMIGRANTS AND NONIMMIGRANTS
WORKING AS PHYSICIANS OR WITH MEDICAL DEGREES, AGES
TWENTY-NINE TO SIXTY-FIVE YEARS, CANADA AND UNITED STATES**

	Canada				United States	
	Not Working as Medical Doctor		Working as Medical Doctor		Working as Medical Doctor	
	Foreign Born	Native Born	Foreign Born	Native Born	Foreign Born	Native Born
Earned Income						
Average	$39,495	$98,152	$130,785	$140,907	$141,384	$161,329
Median	$19,421	$71,211	$103,574	$116,521	$100,000	$123,000
Hours of Work						
Average	39.5	44.7	50.7	49.1	52.6	53.9
Median	40	45	50	50	50	52

SOURCES: Authors' calculations based on Statistics Canada, "2001 Canadian Census: 20 Percent Master File," accessed through the CRISP-UNB Research Data Centre at the University of New Brunswick–Fredericton, Canada; and Steven Ruggles et al., "Integrated Public-Use Microdata Series: Version 4.0 (Machine-Readable Database)," from *2000 U.S. Census* (Minneapolis, MN: Minnesota Population Center, 2008).

NOTES: Earned income includes wages and salaries, as well as self-employment income, converted into constant 1999 U.S. dollars. The samples are restricted to individuals with positive earnings during the year.

but in each case, the median is roughly $40,000 less than the relevant mean in the United States and around $25,000 less in Canada. Earnings may differ because of age and years in practice, location of practice, hours of work, and related factors, but the difference in earnings might also indicate difficulties immigrant doctors have in establishing and growing their practices. Disentangling possible causes will be taken up in the econometric analysis, but we cannot control for possible quality differences in terms of training between foreign- and domestic-trained doctors that may influence earning and employment outcomes or other factors that may impact economic integration, such as domestic language ability that could be influenced by where medical training was obtained.

Table 6-4 presents a number of characteristics about immigrants with medical degrees in Canada (whether working or not working as physicians) and immigrants working as physicians in the United States. For Canada, there is a fairly even distribution across source-country regions, but with

TABLE 6-4

CHARACTERISTICS OF IMMIGRANTS WITH MEDICAL DEGREES, AGES
TWENTY-NINE TO SIXTY-FIVE YEARS, CANADA AND UNITED STATES

| | Canada, Foreign Born | | | United States, Foreign Born | |
| | All | Working as Medical | Not Working as Medical | | Working as Medical |
Characteristics	IMGs	Doctor	Doctor	Characteristics	Doctor
Percent by Region of Birth				**Percent by Region of Birth**	
United States	4.4	5.7	2.7	Canada	4.0
UK/Aus/NZ	13.0	19.0	5.1	UK/Aus/NZ	3.6
Western Europe	6.3	8.2	3.8	Western Europe	6.1
Eastern Europe	12.9	9.2	17.8	Eastern Europe	5.8
South Africa	4.8	7.6	1.1	South Africa	0.8
Rest of Africa	9.8	10.1	9.5	Rest of Africa	6.1
Western Asia/Mideast	7.3	5.3	10.0	Western Asia/Mideast	7.2
South Asia	12.4	11.2	14.0	South Asia	25.4
East Asia, developed	7.6	8.5	6.4	East Asia, developed	9.2
East Asia, less developed	12.7	7.2	19.9	East Asia, less developed	8.2
Philippines	2.4	1.4	3.8	Philippines	8.4
Central/South America	3.6	3.3	4.1	Central/South America	9.0
Caribbean	2.7	3.2	1.9	Caribbean	6.0
Percent by Immigration Status				**Percent by Immigration Status**	
Canadian citizen	69.2	80.4	54.2	Naturalized citizen	64.4
Permanent resident	30.8	12.4	38.0	Not a citizen	35.6
Temporary resident	7.4	7.2	7.8		
Percent by Period of Arrival				**Percent by Period of Arrival**	
1997–2001	19.2	5.9	37.1	1997–2001	8.0
1992–1996	16.1	9.3	25.2	1992–1996	15.4
1987–1991	11.7	10.4	13.4	1987–1991	13.3
1982–1986	8.5	10.6	5.6	1982–1986	10.6
1977–1981	8.0	10.4	4.9	1977–1981	12.6
1972–1976	14.5	21.2	5.6	1972–1976	15.3
1967–1971	12.3	18.0	4.6	1967–1971	13.0
1962–1966	4.2	6.3	1.4	1962–1966	6.8
Pre-1961	5.5	8.0	2.2	Pre-1961	5.0
Average Age at Arrival				**Average Age at Arrival**	
Years	28.4	23.9	34.4	Years	24.9
				Percent by Location of Medical Education	
Percent by Location of Medical Education					
Not in Canada	56.9	41.6	77.4	Not in United States	29.7
In Canada	23.0	34.5	7.7	In United States	20.8
Uncertain	20.1	23.9	14.9	Uncertain	49.5

SOURCES: Authors' calculations based on Statistics Canada, "2001 Canadian Census: 20 Percent Master File," accessed through the CRISP-UNB Research Data Centre at the University of New Brunswick–Fredericton, Canada; and Steven Ruggles et al., "Integrated Public-Use Microdata Series: Version 4.0 (Machine-Readable Database)," from *2000 U.S. Census* (Minneapolis, MN: Minnesota Population Center, 2008).

NOTES: Year of arrival is not available for Canadian temporary residents. For the United States, the immigration status "not a citizen" includes both landed immigrants (permanent residents) and temporary residents.

larger differences across regions based on whether individuals are working as physicians. As the table shows, while 4.4 percent of immigrants to Canada who have medical degrees are from the United States, U.S.-born medical graduates make up 5.7 percent of immigrants working as doctors but only 2.7 percent of those who are not working as doctors. An even larger discrepancy can be seen for immigrants from the United Kingdom, Australia, and New Zealand; they constitute 13 percent of immigrants with medical degrees and 19 percent of immigrants with medical degrees who are working as doctors, but only 5.1 percent of immigrants with medical degrees who are not working as doctors. Similarly, immigrants from South Africa, Western Europe, and the developed countries of East Asia are relatively more likely to be working as doctors. In contrast, especially high percentages of immigrants with medical degrees who are not working as doctors were born in Eastern Europe, Western Asia and the Middle East, and less-developed countries in East Asia.

Table 6-4 also shows that permanent residents with medical degrees have especially high rates of not working as doctors relative to the rate of permanent residents who are working as doctors. In addition, there is a clear relationship between the period in which an immigrant arrived in Canada and the likelihood that an immigrant is working as a doctor. For example, although 19.2 percent of immigrants with medical degrees arrived in the period 1997–2001, only 5.9 percent of immigrants who are working as doctors arrived in this period; 37.1 percent of immigrants with medical degrees not working as doctors arrived during this period. In contrast, 21.2 percent of immigrants with medical degrees who are working as doctors arrived between 1972 and 1976, while only 5.6 percent of the immigrants with medical degrees who arrived during that period are not working as doctors. Earlier arrivals have been in Canada longer and are more likely to have overcome any obstacles to the recognition of their medical credentials. Earlier arrivals in Canada are also more likely to have arrived at younger ages and to have obtained their medical training in Canada. There is a strong relationship between working as a doctor and having received one's medical training in Canada: 77.4 percent of immigrants with medical degrees who are not working as doctors received their medical training outside Canada.

For immigrants working as physicians in the United States, the last column in table 6-4 indicates that fully one-quarter (25.3 percent) of immigrant physicians are from South Asia. Also in contrast to the figures for Canada, immigrant physicians in the United States are more likely to be recent arrivals, though immigrants to Canada who are not working as physicians are heavily skewed toward recent arrivals. This may, in part, reflect the fact that skilled immigrants to the United States are more likely to be admitted with occupation-based visas as opposed to immigrants to Canada, who are granted entry based on a points system that gives credit for higher education even if an individual's credentials may not be recognized in Canada.

The final set of descriptive statistics that we consider in this section relate to the industry in which individuals holding medical degrees are employed. Industry of employment is likely to be an important determinant of earnings, even for the subset of individuals who report working as physicians. For example, physicians working in the emergency rooms of public hospitals are likely to earn less than physicians in private practice. There is also interest in ascertaining the extent to which physicians may be working in research positions or hospital administration rather than in the direct provision of medical care to patients. For M.D. holders who are not working as physicians, there is interest in identifying whether they are working in other health-related industries or in industries unrelated to the practice of medicine. The top two panels of table 6-5 present a breakdown by industry of individuals working as physicians in the United States and Canada, respectively. In the United States, a little more than 50 percent of U.S.-born physicians work in physician's offices, while in Canada, 64 percent of Canadian-born physicians work in physician's offices. Among physicians working in the United States, the biggest difference is between noncitizens (permanent and temporary residents) and citizens (whether born in the United States or abroad): fewer than 30 percent of noncitizens work in physician's offices. Similarly, in Canada the main difference is between temporary residents and others (Canadian-born and immigrants who are permanent residents or citizens); 46 percent of temporary residents in Canada work in physician's offices. The number of physicians working in other industries is relatively small in both countries, regardless of immigrant status.

The bottom panel of table 6-5 presents the industry distribution of medical-degree holders in Canada who are not working as physicians. For both immigrants and the Canadian-born, the two largest categories are industries outside of the health, education, and government sectors and no

TABLE 6-5

INDUSTRY OF EMPLOYMENT BY OCCUPATION, IMMIGRANT STATUS,
AND LOCATION OF MEDICAL TRAINING, ADULTS AGES TWENTY-NINE
TO SIXTY-FIVE YEARS (PERCENTAGES)

	United States, Working as Medical Doctor				
Immigrant Status	**U.S.-Born**		**Citizens**		**Noncitizens**
Location of Medical Training	United States	Not United States	Uncertain	United States	Uncertain
Physician's Office	52.4	48.4	52.2	45.1	29.7
Hospital	35.1	39.9	37.9	45.3	59.0
Outpatient Clinic	4.4	6.2	4.0	3.9	3.9
Other Health Industry	2.3	1.7	1.8	1.9	1.9
University/College	2.3	0.9	1.6	1.7	2.6
Other Industry	3.5	3.0	2.5	2.1	3.0

	Canada, Working as Medical Doctor				
Immigrant Status	**Canadian Born**	**Permanent Residents, Citizens**			**Temporary Residents**
Location of Medical Training	Canada	Not Canada	Uncertain	Canada	Uncertain
Physician's Office	64.0	61.9	71.9	67.1	46.0
Hospital	30.7	33.4	24.8	29.3	50.8
Outpatient Clinic	3.1	2.4	2.0	2.1	*
Other Health Industry	1.2	1.5	*	*	*
Other Industry	1.1	0.8	*	*	*

	Canada, Not Working as Medical Doctor				
Immigrant Status	**Canadian Born**	**Permanent Residents, Citizens**			**Temporary Residents**
Location of Medical Training	Canada	Not Canada	Uncertain	Canada	Uncertain
Physician's Office	9.3	4.3	6.6	10.3	*
Hospital	16.3	9.6	14.0	*	13.1
Other Health Industry	12.0	9.5	10.1	13.4	*
University/College	13.5	8.3	8.3	15.3	16.1
Government	3.9	1.8	2.8	*	*
Other Industry	48.5	36.1	33.3	27.0	22.0
No Industry Reported	16.5	30.4	24.9	23.8	46.1

SOURCES: Authors' calculations based on Statistics Canada, "2001 Canadian Census: 20 Percent Master File," accessed through the CRISP-UNB Research Data Centre at the University of New Brunswick–Fredericton, Canada; and Steven Ruggles et al., "Integrated Public-Use Microdata Series: Version 4.0 (Machine-Readable Database)," from *2000 U.S. Census* (Minneapolis, MN: Minnesota Population Center, 2008).

NOTES: * denotes data that have been suppressed due to confidentiality restrictions.

industry reported. Close to 50 percent of temporary residents report no industry at all. As well, temporary residents with medical degrees who are not working as doctors are more likely than permanent residents or citizens to report working in universities or colleges (16 percent).

Estimation Results

The next stage of the analysis involves estimating multivariate models to explore the underlying relationships between immigrant status, source country, period of arrival, and place of medical training and the following: (i) whether an immigrant is working as a physician, (ii) whether an immigrant is currently either a full- or part-time student, and (iii) the log earnings of individuals with medical degrees. The main goal of the econometric analysis is to identify and disentangle possible explanations for what might explain the patterns outlined above. The fact that in Canada significant numbers of immigrants with medical degrees are not working as physicians is of great concern for policymakers, given the ongoing shortages of medical professionals in many areas of the country. While we do not directly observe whether the nonrecognition of medical credentials obtained outside of Canada is driving this result, considering the relative importance of demographic and geographic factors will yield useful insights into this issue. Furthermore, while our U.S. data are restricted to practicing physicians only, we can still investigate the importance of immigration-system parameters to the underutilization of medical training by comparing both the incidence of training and earnings patterns of immigrant and nonimmigrant medical degree holders between Canada and the United States. For example, if recently arrived immigrant physicians are more likely to need further education and training to work as physicians in Canada than in the United States, it might indicate that the U.S. immigration system is more successful in attracting and selecting immigrant physicians whose qualifications are such that they are able to begin practice as fully licensed physicians more quickly than immigrant physicians entering Canada.

Table 6-6 presents the results from the Logit estimation of whether the person is employed as a physician and whether the person is currently a student, based on the Canadian census data. The first column contains

TABLE 6-6

LOGIT ESTIMATION OF DETERMINANTS OF WORKING AS A MEDICAL DOCTOR AND BEING A STUDENT, INDIVIDUALS IN CANADA HOLDING A MEDICAL DEGREE, AGES TWENTY-NINE TO SIXTY-FIVE YEARS

	Indicator for Working as Medical Doctor			Indicator for Being a Student		
	Odds Ratio	95 Percent Confidence Interval		Odds Ratio	95 Percent Confidence Interval	
Foreign Born (FB)	0.779	0.450	1.348	**2.187**	1.191	4.015
FB–Perm. Res. (PR)	0.759	0.573	1.005	1.013	0.689	1.490
Temp. Res. (TR)	**0.242**	0.145	0.404	**2.949**	1.674	5.193
Female	0.873	0.735	1.036	**1.240**	1.029	1.495
Female*FB	**0.710**	0.555	.909	0.850	0.619	1.168
Female*FB-PR	1.001	0.695	1.441	0.909	0.596	1.387
Female*TR	**0.441**	0.264	0.739	0.629	0.352	1.124
Arrival Period						
1997–2001	**0.120**	0.081	0.175	0.931	0.552	1.570
1992–96	**0.205**	0.151	0.279	0.808	0.514	1.270
1987–91	**0.424**	0.312	0.575	0.656	0.412	1.043
1982–86	1.000	--	--	1.000	--	--
1977–81	1.106	0.765	1.599	0.618	0.373	1.023
1972–76	**1.888**	1.334	2.672	**0.471**	0.284	0.781
1967–71	**1.942**	1.336	2.822	**0.464**	0.269	0.802
1962–66	**2.136**	1.205	3.786	**0.112**	0.026	0.485
Pre-1961	1.347	0.811	2.237	0.959	0.466	1.972
Region of Birth						
United States	1.000	--	--	1.000	--	--
UK/Aus/NZ	1.503	0.967	2.336	0.767	0.448	1.313
W. Europe	1.127	0.688	1.845	0.740	0.419	1.307
E. Europe	0.849	0.536	1.345	1.192	0.695	2.044
South Africa	**6.890**	3.518	13.49	0.632	0.321	1.245
Rest of Africa	0.945	0.598	1.493	1.179	0.688	2.021
Philippines	**0.408**	0.225	0.738	0.521	0.228	1.194
W. Asia/M.E.	0.862	0.532	1.396	1.337	0.764	2.341
South Asia	0.909	0.579	1.428	0.738	0.428	1.273
E. Asia–dev.	1.281	0.777	2.110	**0.450**	0.239	0.845
E. Asia–less dev.	**0.540**	0.344	0.848	1.114	0.657	1.890
C./S. America	0.627	0.366	1.075	1.490	0.799	2.777
Caribbean	0.694	0.380	1.267	0.893	0.378	2.108
Education						
Canada	1.000	--	--	1.000	--	--
Not Canada	0.746	0.548	1.016	1.487	0.994	2.225
Uncertain	0.885	0.660	1.187	0.900	0.587	1.380
Lang. Other Than Mother Tongue	.999	.819	1.218	0.963	0.760	1.222
Language at Home	**0.510**	0.429	0.606	1.141	0.901	1.444
	N=13,049	~R²=0.279		N=13,049	~R²=0.206	

SOURCE: Statistics Canada, "2001 Canadian Census: 20 Percent Master File," accessed through the CRISP-UNB Research Data Centre at the University of New Brunswick–Fredericton, Canada.
NOTES: Regressions also included controls for age, age squared, city, region of residence, and urban/rural status. Numbers in bold font indicate that the odds ratios are significantly different from one at the 5-percent level of significance.

estimates of odds ratios[7] and confidence intervals for the Logit estimation of the likelihood that an individual who holds a medical degree is working as a physician. Neither the estimate of the odds ratio for the immigrant-indicator variable nor the estimate of the odds ratio for the interaction of the immigrant indicator (FB) with the permanent residence dummy variable (PR) is statistically significant.[8] Temporary residents (TR) with medical degrees are less likely to be working as physicians than the Canadian-born residents with medical degrees, and this effect is even more pronounced for female temporary residents. The interaction of the female indicator variable with FB-PR indicates that female permanent residents with medical degrees are less likely to be employed as physicians than are female Canadians with medical degrees.

As suggested by the data described in the previous section, a strong relationship is found in the Logit model between the period in which an immigrant arrived and the likelihood that an immigrant is working as a physician, with immigrants from the more recent arrival groups being much less likely to be working as physicians (odds ratio of 0.12 for the 1997–2001 group) compared to earlier arrival cohorts (odds ratio of 2.136 for the 1962–66 cohort). The results indicate that in Canada, recent immigrants are experiencing substantial delays before they are licensed to practice.[9] Furthermore, the fact that even after many years in Canada immigrant medical degree holders are less likely to be working as physicians suggests that some of these individuals are opting for other employment rather than going through the process of becoming licensed (which might even require the completion of another medical degree).

After controlling for period of arrival and other variables, we also find important differences in the likelihood of working as a physician in Canada by region of origin. Immigrants with medical degrees who were born in South Africa are more likely to be employed as physicians than are U.S.-born medical degree holders (the reference category in the regression model), while those from the Philippines and other developing countries in East Asia are less likely to be employed as physicians than are medical degree holders who were born in the United States. It is also notable that with other controls included, the location where individuals obtained their medical degrees does not have a significant effect on the likelihood that they will practice medicine in Canada.

Using the information in the Canadian census data on both mother tongue and language spoken at home, we include controls in the regression for immigrants whose mother tongue was neither English nor French (Other) and whose usual language spoken at home was neither English nor French. The mother tongue variable is not significant; however, the language spoken at home control is significant, indicating that individuals who speak a language other than English or French at home are less likely to be working as medical doctors in Canada than those who do speak English or French at home. This effect should be interpreted with caution since the decision to speak a language other than English at home is endogenous and could be capturing the effects of unobserved heterogeneity.[10]

In the second set of results in table 6-6, odds ratios from the Logit estimation are presented for a model of whether the individual with a medical degree is currently a student. Not surprisingly, immigrants with medical degrees are more likely to be students than the Canadian born. Similarly, temporary residents with medical degrees are also more likely to be students. A number of the coefficients on the year of arrival controls are not statistically significant, but several of them indicate that immigrants who arrived in Canada between 1962 and 1976 were significantly less likely to attend school in the survey year than are the default group, the 1982–86 arrival cohort. The coefficients on the source-country controls are generally not individually significant, though the East Asian developed countries are an exception and have an implied lower probability of attending school in the survey year.

Since we can identify the occupation of medical-degree holders in Canada who are not working as physicians, it is possible to estimate the determinants of the particular occupational group in which an individual is working. We specify five categories of occupation: (i) physician, (ii) other high-skilled occupations (including high-skilled occupations in the health industry, such as medical administrators), (iii) moderate-skilled occupations, (iv) lower-skilled occupations and all trades, and (v) people who do not report any occupation, who are unemployed, or who are out of the labor force. In table 6-7, we report the estimated relative-risk (RR) ratios from a multinomial Logit estimation with physicians as the reference category. Although the definition of RR ratios is somewhat different from the definition of odds ratios, interpretation is similar in that an RR greater than one

TABLE 6-7

OCCUPATION SKILL LEVEL FOR INDIVIDUALS IN CANADA WHO POSSESS
MEDICAL DEGREES, MULTINOMIAL LOGIT RELATIVE-RISK RATIOS

Reference Category: Physician/Specialist	Other High-Skilled Occupations		Moderate-Skilled Occupations		Lower-Skilled Occupations and Trades		No Occupation, Unemployed, Not in Labor Force	
	Relative Risk	P-value	Relative Risk	P-value	Relative Risk	P-value	Relative Risk	P-value
Foreign Born (FB)	0.95	0.90	1.18	0.63	1.27	0.83	1.11	0.80
FB–Perm. Res. (PR)	1.10	0.69	1.29	0.17	1.20	0.46	1.41	0.07
Temp. Resident (TR)	5.22	0.00	4.07	0.00	1.10	0.90	6.41	0.00
Female	0.58	0.00	1.44	0.01	1.58	0.06	1.61	0.00
Female*FB	2.23	0.00	1.07	0.72	0.70	0.24	1.40	0.07
Female*FB-PR	1.05	0.90	0.99	0.97	1.28	0.39	1.79	0.01
Female*TR	1.29	0.67	0.87	0.73	2.16	0.25	2.76	0.00
Arrival Period								
1997–2001	7.83	0.00	7.48	0.00	9.15	0.00	16.54	0.00
1992–96	5.90	0.00	3.35	0.00	4.51	0.00	6.63	0.00
1987–91	3.84	0.00	2.24	0.00	1.46	0.18	2.39	0.00
1982–86	1.00	--	1.00	--	1.00	--	1.00	--
1977–81	1.32	0.49	0.92	0.76	0.75	0.43	0.84	0.54
1972–76	1.25	0.53	0.52	0.01	0.28	0.00	0.39	0.00
1967–71	1.70	0.16	0.55	0.03	0.16	0.00	0.44	0.00
1962–66	0.79	0.71	0.68	0.31	0.11	0.05	0.61	0.20
Pre-1961	1.96	0.18	0.45	0.04	0.08	0.02	1.09	0.82
Region of Birth								
United States	1.00	--	1.00	--	1.00	--	1.00	--
UK/Aus/NZ	0.37	0.00	1.07	0.80	0.79	0.76	0.73	0.37
W. Europe	0.51	0.07	1.49	0.19	1.41	0.66	0.79	0.55
E. Europe	0.48	0.03	1.75	0.06	3.25	0.12	1.69	0.13
South Africa	0.11	0.00	0.20	0.00	0.05	0.01	0.17	0.00
Rest of Africa	0.37	0.01	1.09	0.77	1.75	0.46	2.24	0.02
Philippines	0.36	0.10	3.79	0.00	11.27	0.00	2.79	0.02
W. Asia/M.E.	0.33	0.01	1.15	0.68	3.33	0.12	2.23	0.03
South Asia	0.37	0.00	1.09	0.77	2.52	0.23	1.90	0.07
E. Asia–dev.	0.40	0.02	1.10	0.77	0.84	0.83	1.31	0.47
E. Asia–less dev.	1.04	0.89	2.91	0.00	3.11	0.14	1.54	0.22
C./S. America	0.53	0.16	2.59	0.01	4.50	0.06	1.98	0.08
Caribbean	0.42	0.11	1.73	0.22	3.11	0.20	1.91	0.13
Education								
Canada	1.00	--	1.00	--	1.00	--	1.00	--
Not Canada	1.80	0.06	1.12	0.62	1.91	0.10	1.13	0.59
Uncertain	1.60	0.11	1.00	0.99	1.28	0.53	0.78	0.26
Language Other Than Mother Tongue	0.95	0.77	1.00	0.97	1.24	0.27	0.87	0.36
Home Language	1.68	0.00	1.57	0.00	2.21	0.00	2.32	0.00
	N=13,049		~R^2=0.219					

SOURCE: Authors' calculations based on Statistics Canada, "2001 Canadian Census: 20 Percent Master File," accessed through the CRISP-UNB Research Data Centre at the University of New Brunswick–Fredericton, Canada.

NOTES: Regressions also included controls for age, age squared, city, region of residence, and urban/rural status. Numbers in bold font indicate that the odds ratios are significantly different from one at the 5 percent level of significance.

means a greater likelihood of working in that occupational category than working as a physician. Temporary residents are more likely than Canadian-born individuals to be in most of the other occupation groups and less likely to be working as physicians. Women are more likely to be not working, and the estimated effect is even larger for temporary and permanent residents.

Recent arrivals are relatively more likely to be working in other occupational groups and not to be working at all than are nonimmigrants, and while this is also true for earlier arrivals, the magnitude of the difference is smaller. Thus, at least some recent immigrants with medical degrees who do not work as physicians are working in other relatively highly paid occupations. Immigrants from most regions are less likely to be working in another highly skilled occupation in Canada than immigrants from the United States. Medical-degree holders from the Philippines in particular are more likely to be working in lower-skilled occupations or not working. Finally, individuals who normally speak a language other than English or French at home are more likely to be working in every broad occupation group other than as a physician.

In table 6-8, we limit both Canadian and U.S. samples to currently practicing physicians and present estimates from Logit models of the likelihood that physicians are also students. This type of educational investment could represent time spent as an intern or resident, something that is required of almost all individuals with medical training outside of Canada before they can be licensed to practice in Canada. The first column results for Canada are generally similar to those found in the second set of results in table 6-6. This indicates that immigrants (and temporary residents) with medical degrees are more likely to be attending school than those born in Canada who hold medical degrees. This is true whether or not an individual is employed as a physician. For earlier arrival cohorts of immigrants, evidence suggests this effect may not be present. In contrast, the estimates in the second set of results of table 6-8 do not indicate the same pattern for immigrants in the United States. The coefficient on the immigrant indicator variable is not statistically significant. Also, the coefficients on the year of arrival variables are not significant. In fact, the U.S. model generally has poor explanatory power, indicating that postmigration education patterns may not differ appreciably for immigrants from U.S.-born doctors' education patterns.

TABLE 6-8

LOGIT ESTIMATION OF DETERMINANTS OF BEING A STUDENT,
INDIVIDUALS EMPLOYED AS MEDICAL DOCTORS

	Canadian Data			U.S. Data		
	Odds Ratio	95 Percent Confidence Interval		Odds Ratio	95 Percent Confidence Interval	
Foreign Born (FB)	**2.658**	1.303	5.421	0.803	0.359	1.799
FB–Perm. Resident (PR)	1.092	0.618	1.932	--	--	--
Temp. Resident (TR)	**2.300**	1.143	4.629	--	--	--
Noncitizen	--	--	--	0.993	0.691	1.425
Female	1.123	0.907	1.390	**0.808**	0.669	0.976
Female*FB	0.825	0.536	1.270	**1.713**	1.215	2.415
Female*FB-PR	0.859	0.368	2.004	--	--	--
Female*TR	0.852	0.341	2.126	--	--	--
Female*Noncitizen	--	--	--	0.848	0.541	1.329
Arrival Period						
1997–2001	0.599	0.268	1.338	1.691	0.990	2.888
1992–96	0.714	0.373	1.366	0.998	0.605	1.645
1987–91	0.645	0.349	1.194	1.099	0.679	1.777
1982–86	1.000	--	--	1.000	--	--
1977–81	0.652	0.353	1.203	0.998	0.632	1.577
1972–76	**0.470**	0.261	0.849	1.100	0.713	1.697
1967–71	**0.489**	0.261	0.917	0.830	0.506	1.363
1962–66	**0.141**	0.032	0.631	1.154	0.627	2.125
Pre-1961	1.190	0.513	2.762	1.157	0.588	2.277
Region of Birth						
U.S./Canada	1.000	--	--	1.000	--	--
UK/Aus/NZ	0.609	0.328	1.130	1.744	0.803	3.788
W. Europe	0.759	0.389	1.479	1.251	0.614	2.547
E. Europe	0.799	0.374	1.709	0.530	0.234	1.199
South Africa	0.688	0.326	1.452	1.739	0.519	5.824
Rest of Africa	1.014	0.523	1.968	0.706	0.320	1.556
Philippines	0.238	0.050	1.122	1.231	0.610	2.486
W. Asia/M.E.	1.354	0.642	2.856	0.750	0.357	1.579
South Asia	0.678	0.341	1.345	0.620	0.319	1.202
E. Asia-dev.	**0.324**	0.148	0.709	1.062	0.515	2.188
E. Asia-less dev.	0.509	0.238	1.086	1.299	0.653	2.587
C./S. America	0.984	0.420	2.306	1.207	0.609	2.392
Caribbean	0.495	0.126	1.949	1.738	0.827	3.653
Education						
Receiving Country	1.000	--	--	1.000	--	--
Not Rec. Country	1.573	0.947	2.611	1.205	0.787	1.845
Uncertain	1.319	0.774	2.25	1.349	0.940	1.936
Language Other Than Mother Tongue	0.936	0.701	1.25	1.000	--	--
Language at Home	1.062	0.743	1.518	**1.582**	1.291	1.940
	N=9,640	~R²=0.224		N=31,027	~R²=0.044	

SOURCES: Statistics Canada, "2001 Canadian Census: 20 Percent Master File," accessed through the CRISP-UNB Research Data Centre at the University of New Brunswick–Fredericton, Canada; and Steven Ruggles et al., "Integrated Public-Use Microdata Series: Version 4.0 (Machine-Readable Database)," from *2000 U.S. Census* (Minneapolis, MN: Minnesota Population Center, 2008).
NOTES: Regressions also included controls for age, age squared, city, region of residence, and urban/rural status. Numbers in bold font indicate that the odds ratios are significantly different from one at the 5 percent level of significance.

This difference between U.S. and Canadian postmigration schooling patterns may possibly be explained by the different selection processes for skilled immigrants in each country. In Canada, relatively few immigrants enter the country with prearranged employment. Instead, skilled immigrants with no family connections to Canadians typically enter Canada under the points system, meaning they are more likely to be accepted if they have characteristics that are associated with greater labor-market success. Internationally trained physicians applying to enter Canada are likely to be admitted because their extended time spent in school means they are more likely to have a high number of points. However, these immigrants face protracted administrative and educational hurdles before they can be licensed to practice medicine, including the requirement that they complete a residency in a Canadian teaching hospital. Therefore, postmigration investments in education are likely required for these immigrants to work as physicians. Immigrants entering the United States with medical degrees are much more likely to have prearranged employment, and while medical residency requirements still must be met in most cases, the accreditation process may be more streamlined and timely. Alternatively, differences in student status between the United States and Canada may be due to systematic differences in how individuals interpret and respond to the relevant question about student status. Unfortunately, we are unable to verify our hypothesis that differences in the immigration systems between Canada and the United States lead to a greater requirement for postmigration medical training with the data available, since the stage of education (for example, intern, resident, or fellow) is not reported in either the Canadian or U.S. census data files.

A comparison of the earnings of physicians in the United States and Canada is instructive not only because it can yield insights into the potential impact of the immigration system on the labor-market outcomes of immigrant physicians, but also more broadly because differences in earnings between the two countries may be an important factor in the subsequent migration decisions of both immigrant and nonimmigrant physicians. Table 6-9 contains regression results from log-earnings regressions estimated using the 2001 Canadian census data and the 2000 U.S. census data. In all regressions, we restrict the sample to include only those individuals who report positive income (including from wages, salaries, and self-employment). The

TABLE 6-9

ORDINARY LEAST SQUARES REGRESSION: ESTIMATES OF DETERMINANTS
OF LOG EARNINGS, INDIVIDUALS HOLDING A MEDICAL DEGREE,
AGES TWENTY-NINE TO SIXTY-FIVE YEARS

	Canada, Any Occupation		Canada, Employed as Medical Doctor		United States, Employed as Medical Doctor	
	Coef.	P-value	Coef.	P-value	Coef.	P-value
Foreign Born (FB)	0.003	0.975	−0.079	0.385	**0.228**	0.001
FB–Perm. Res. (PR)	−0.066	0.291	−0.010	0.892	--	--
Temp. Resident (TR)	**−0.788**	0.000	**−0.812**	0.000	--	--
Noncitizen	--	--	--	--	**−0.102**	0.006
Female	**−0.377**	0.000	**−0.350**	0.000	**−0.453**	0.000
Female*FB	−0.006	0.890	0.008	0.877	0.060	0.094
Female*FB–PR	−0.054	0.517	0.001	0.997	--	--
Female*TR	**0.382**	0.004	**0.415**	0.010	--	--
Female*Noncitizen	--	--	--	--	−0.008	0.878
Arrival Period						
1997–2001	**−1.096**	0.000	**−0.473**	0.000	**−0.710**	0.000
1992–96	**−0.636**	0.000	**−0.214**	0.018	**−0.306**	0.000
1987–91	**−0.246**	0.001	−0.054	0.492	**−0.097**	0.046
1982–86	--	--	--	--	--	--
1977–81	**0.157**	0.036	**0.139**	0.065	0.033	0.483
1972–76	**0.261**	0.000	**0.193**	0.007	**0.120**	0.006
1967–71	**0.156**	0.038	0.100	0.191	**0.216**	0.000
1962–66	**0.332**	0.000	**0.273**	0.002	0.074	0.210
Pre-1961	0.158	0.088	0.098	0.297	**0.159**	0.021
Region of Birth						
U.S./U.S./Canada	0.000	--	0.000	--	0.000	--
UK/Aus/NZ	−0.068	0.318	−0.032	0.630	−0.137	0.065
W. Europe	−0.048	0.552	−0.034	0.664	**−0.295**	0.000
E. Europe	**−0.290**	0.000	−0.053	0.536	**−0.367**	0.000
South Africa	**0.441**	0.000	**0.267**	0.003	−0.094	0.435
Rest of Africa	**−0.281**	0.001	**−0.193**	0.022	**−0.368**	0.000
Philippines	**−0.549**	0.000	−0.163	0.364	**−0.281**	0.000
W. Asia/M.E.	**−0.356**	0.000	−0.095	0.372	**−0.163**	0.016
South Asia	**−0.196**	0.015	−0.008	0.923	**−0.217**	0.000
E. Asia–dev.	−0.142	0.113	−0.085	0.363	**−0.280**	0.000
E. Asia–less dev.	**−0.322**	0.000	−0.127	0.184	**−0.416**	0.000
C./S. America	**−0.326**	0.001	−0.115	0.275	**−0.330**	0.000
Caribbean	**−0.419**	0.000	**−0.360**	0.005	**−0.425**	0.000
Education						
In Host Country	--	--	--	--	--	--
Not Host Country	−0.102	0.080	−0.057	0.345	0.010	0.824
Uncertain	−0.026	0.617	−0.071	0.178	0.063	0.085
Language Other Than Mother Tongue	−0.023	0.530	−0.001	0.991	--	--
Language at Home	**−0.341**	0.000	**−0.182**	0.000	**−0.090**	0.000
	N=11,678	aR²=0.315	N=9,411	aR²=0.173	N=30,007	aR²=0.19

SOURCES: Statistics Canada, "2001 Canadian Census: 20 Percent Master File," accessed through the CRISP-UNB Research Data Centre at the University of New Brunswick–Fredericton, Canada; and Steven Ruggles et al., "Integrated Public-Use Microdata Series: Version 4.0 (Machine-Readable Database)," from *2000 U.S. Census* (Minneapolis, MN: Minnesota Population Center, 2008).

NOTES: Regressions also included controls for age, age squared, city, region of residence, and urban/rural status. Log earnings include all annual earnings from wages and salaries as well as self-employment income. The sample is restricted to individuals with positive annual earnings. Numbers in bold font indicate that the odds ratios are significantly different from one at the 5 percent level of significance.

first set of regression results is based on the specification of the right-hand side control variables used in the Logit estimation described in table 6-6, that is, the estimation is over the entire sample of individuals who have a medical degree. The second and third sets of results in table 6-9 correspond to the same specification but apply to a sample limited to individuals working as physicians in Canada and the United States, respectively.

For the determinants of earnings across all medical-degree holders, we see that neither the coefficients on FB nor those on its interaction with PR are significant. Temporary residents have much lower earnings than those born in Canada. Period of arrival is strongly related to earnings, and immigrants arriving in the 1997–2001 period have much lower earnings (66 percent lower) than those in the default category (the 1982–86 cohort), and the 1962–66 arrival group has roughly 39 percent higher earnings than the default group.[11]

The coefficients on the region of birth variables reveal that immigrants with medical degrees born in South Africa have higher earnings than those in the default group (born in the United States). Immigrants from all other regions have lower log earnings than U.S. immigrants, although the estimated difference for the United Kingdom, Australia, and New Zealand group, the Western Europe group, and the developed countries in East Asia group are not significantly lower. Among regions with significantly lower earnings, variation is substantial, ranging from 18 to 42 percent lower than earnings for otherwise comparable U.S. immigrants. Neither the controls for education outside of Canada nor the controls for mother tongue being neither English nor French is individually significant. However, the group in which neither English nor French is spoken at home did have significant results that indicated that immigrants in this group have 29 percent lower earnings on average than immigrants who do speak English or French at home.

The second and third sets of results in table 6-9 give the determinants of earnings for Canadian and U.S. physicians respectively. Earnings differences between Canadian-born physicians and immigrant physicians are substantially smaller than what the model estimated for immigrant and Canadian-born individuals with medical degrees, although they are still significantly different from zero. Similarly, differences in earnings across region of origin among physicians are also of smaller magnitude, and most are not significantly different from zero. For the U.S. results, immigrant physicians in the United States who arrived in the default category time period (1982–86) have an earnings advantage of 25.6 percent relative to those born in the United States. However, a strong pattern in the arrival period coefficients is present: the three more recent arrival cohorts have significantly lower earnings than the default arrival group, and the earliest arrival cohorts typically have significantly higher earnings. This overall pattern is similar to what was found for immigrant physicians in Canada, but the most recent cohort in the U.S. analysis has a greater initial disadvantage relative to earlier cohorts. In contrast to the Canadian results, source-country variation seems large: immigrant doctors from countries other than Canada; the United Kingdom, Australia, and New Zealand; and South Africa have significantly lower earnings than the Canadian default group. Among the groups with significantly lower earnings, differences range from around 13 percent lower for the Western Asia and Middle East group to 35 percent lower for the Caribbean group.

With detailed controls for region of birth and period of arrival already included, the location of an immigrant's medical education again does not appear to have any additional effect on earnings for physicians in either country. In contrast, controls for language spoken at home suggest that in both Canada and the United States, when English (or French in Canada) is not the usual language spoken at home, physician earnings are 16.6 percent lower in Canada and 8.7 percent lower in the United States, all else being held equal.

Since barriers to credential recognition likely delay the time at which immigrants who hold M.D.s enter the workforce as physicians, those individuals may also elect to delay any decision to reduce work hours or to retire. Among working physicians, a higher likelihood that older immigrants will be working full time than the likelihood for native-born physicians of the same age may explain the positive wage differential of the earlier arrival cohorts. However, restricting the sample to working physicians ages twenty-nine to fifty-five has little effect on the arrival period results in either country. The only exception is that the earnings of immigrant physicians who arrived in the United States prior to 1961 are even larger. When examined by country of origin, the estimated earnings differences in the United States results are marginally more negative.

The earnings differences may also be explained by the industry distribution of physicians between immigrants and nonimmigrants as illustrated in table 6-5. For example, if physicians working in private practice earn more on average than salaried physicians working in public hospitals, and it is immigrant physicians who are more likely to be working in hospitals (because of preferences, less experience, or perhaps because of systemic difficulties in establishing private practice), then after accounting for differences in industry of employment there should no longer be an earnings gap between immigrant and nonimmigrant doctors. However, while including a set of industry dummy variables in the earnings regressions for both Canada and the United States improves the overall fit of the models and yields coefficient estimates for these variables that are highly significant, the estimated arrival period effects and country of origin effects remain almost identical to what is reported in table 6-9. Thus, many immigrant physicians earn less than otherwise comparable nonimmigrant physicians within particular employment settings.

Table 6-10 presents the final set of regression results on the determinants of earnings among medical-degree holders who are not working as physicians, with other occupations grouped as they were for the previous regressions. In contrast to what was observed in table 6-9, there are no significant differences in the earnings of immigrants in other highly skilled occupations compared to Canadian-born medical-degree holders by period of arrival or by region of origin. Earnings are significantly lower for temporary residents and for individuals whose medical degrees were not obtained in Canada. For immigrants with medical degrees who are working in moderately skilled occupations, recent immigrants have significantly lower earnings, but the difference goes to zero for people arriving prior to 1992. This regression also shows significantly lower earnings for individuals from most regions of origin compared to U.S.-born immigrants in these jobs. In the final column of results, we see that all classes of immigrants working in lower-skilled jobs and trades actually earn substantially more than nonimmigrants. However, this earnings gap is more or less entirely negated for immigrants from regions of birth other than the United States.

Conclusion

Given the shortages of physicians in many areas of Canada and the United States, particularly in rural areas, the substantial number of immigrants with

TABLE 6-10

ORDINARY LEAST SQUARES REGRESSION: ESTIMATES OF DETERMINANTS OF LOG EARNINGS, INDIVIDUALS IN CANADA HOLDING A MEDICAL DEGREE BUT NOT EMPLOYED AS PHYSICIANS, AGES TWENTY-NINE TO SIXTY-FIVE YEARS, BY BROAD OCCUPATIONAL GROUP

	Other High-Skilled Occupations		Moderate-Skilled Occupations		Lower-Skilled Occupations and Trades	
	Coef.	P-value	Coef.	P-value	Coef.	P-value
Foreign Born (FB)	−0.11	0.78	−0.40	0.24	**2.45**	**0.00**
FB–Perm. Res. (PR)	0.23	0.18	−0.11	0.47	−0.19	0.37
Temp. Resident (TR)	**−0.97**	**0.00**	−0.48	0.10	**2.30**	**0.00**
Female	**−0.31**	**0.02**	**−0.64**	**0.00**	0.00	1.00
Female*FB	0.07	0.72	**0.58**	**0.00**	−0.31	0.29
Female*FB–PR	−0.35	0.22	−0.16	0.34	0.04	0.85
Female*TR	0.18	0.63	0.52	0.09	0.23	0.69
Arrival Period						
1997–2001	−0.35	0.31	**−0.55**	**0.02**	**−0.71**	**0.00**
1992–96	−0.07	0.83	**−0.46**	**0.02**	**−0.47**	**0.02**
1987–91	0.16	0.62	−0.20	0.28	−0.29	0.17
1982–86	0.00	--	0.00	--	0.00	--
1977–81	0.50	0.16	0.21	0.33	0.38	0.17
1972–76	0.30	0.40	0.46	0.07	**0.68**	**0.01**
1967–71	0.46	0.23	0.47	0.06	−0.39	0.68
1962–66	0.40	0.41	0.42	0.29	**1.29**	**0.01**
Pre-1961	−0.16	0.72	0.65	0.06	0.85	0.11
Region of Birth						
United States	0.00	--	0.00	--	0.00	--
UK/Aus/NZ	0.14	0.61	−0.31	0.25	**−1.94**	**0.00**
W. Europe	0.41	0.16	−0.34	0.29	**−2.85**	**0.00**
E. Europe	−0.29	0.34	**−0.79**	**0.01**	**−2.51**	**0.00**
South Africa	0.30	0.33	0.35	0.40	**−1.60**	**0.04**
Rest of Africa	−0.52	0.08	**−0.61**	**0.04**	**−2.73**	**0.00**
Philippines	−0.26	0.40	**−0.87**	**0.00**	**−2.51**	**0.00**
W. Asia/M.E.	−0.57	0.20	**−0.90**	**0.01**	**−2.85**	**0.00**
South Asia	−0.49	0.20	**−0.93**	**0.00**	**−2.87**	**0.00**
E. Asia–dev.	−0.27	0.43	−0.54	0.08	**−2.67**	**0.00**
E. Asia–less dev.	−0.38	0.19	**−0.68**	**0.01**	**−2.63**	**0.00**
C./S. America	0.12	0.72	**−0.78**	**0.01**	**−2.57**	**0.00**
Caribbean	0.48	0.12	**−1.09**	**0.00**	**−2.55**	**0.00**
Education						
In Canada	0.00	--	0.00	--	0.00	--
Not in Canada	**−0.60**	**0.03**	0.20	0.35	0.42	0.29
Uncertain	−0.15	0.55	0.22	0.24	0.29	0.43
Language Other Than Mother Tongue	0.02	0.90	0.05	0.70	−0.36	0.14
Language at Home	0.51	0.14	0.15	0.48	−0.01	0.98
	N=572	aR²=0.403	N=950	aR²=0.413	N=443	aR²=0.443

SOURCE: Statistics Canada, "2001 Canadian Census: 20 Percent Master File," accessed through the CRISP-UNB Research Data Centre at the University of New Brunswick–Fredericton, Canada.

NOTES: Regressions also included controls for age, age squared, city, region of residence, and urban/rural status. Log earnings include all annual earnings from wages and salaries as well as self-employment income. The sample is restricted to individuals with positive annual earnings. Numbers in bold font indicate that the odds ratios are significantly different from one at the 5-percent level of significance.

medical degrees who are not employed as physicians is a cause for concern. Significant financial and administrative barriers, combined with the relatively low number of residencies available to immigrant doctors, either significantly delay the point at which an immigrant doctor can become licensed to practice medicine or result in the individual seeking employment outside of the medical profession. The Canadian points system for the selection of immigrants in the skilled workers and professionals class of immigrants may contribute to this occupational mismatch by recognizing the value of a foreign medical degree in terms of immigration without taking into account individuals' actual ability or qualifications to practice medicine in Canada. It would also be expected that institutional delays in physician licensing would lead immigrant medical degree holders to be more likely to be students and to earn less than otherwise comparable nonimmigrant physicians, and this is in fact what we observe. Interestingly, however, we also observe earnings differences between immigrant and nonimmigrant physicians in the United States that are of comparable magnitude to those observed in Canada even though the immigration and licensing systems are substantially different. In both countries, significant earnings disadvantages are present for more recent arrivals and for physicians from many regions outside of the United States and Canada. Such differences may imply a certain degree of underemployment of immigrant physicians compared to their nonimmigrant peers. An interesting question for future research is whether earnings gaps between immigrant and nonimmigrant physicians narrow significantly with additional time in the host country. While the pattern in the arrival period effects suggests convergence, longitudinal data on the earnings of particular physicians over time are required in order to confirm this pattern.

A number of limitations should be mentioned. First, the analysis relies on data in the Canadian and U.S. census files that are entirely self-reported. Aside from errors in reported educational qualifications, occupation, and earnings, these data may also include differences related to how respondents evaluate student status with regard to physicians working as interns or medical residents. The fact that we have employed only a single census file for each country means we cannot distinguish the effects of additional time in the United States or Canada on immigrants' training, occupation, and earnings from cohort effects. We cannot control for potential quality differences in the medical training between foreign and domestically trained doctors. We also have not considered the potentially important issue of the subsequent emigration from the United States or Canada of immigrants who originally went to Canada or the United States, although census questions on migration patterns will allow us to gain some insights about the extent of physician movement between the two countries. Finally, we have not controlled for the fact that certain variables, such as the language normally spoken at home, are potentially endogenous. Thus, the causality of the relationship between language and the various outcomes examined should not be inferred.

Notes

1. A small number of people in the U.S. sample report working as physicians but state that they have less than a bachelor's degree. While this may be due to reporting errors, it is possible for medical students to enter medical school without completing a bachelor's degree. In any event, omitting these observations has no effect on the results.

2. The sample of temporary residents in the Canadian census also includes refugee claimants and a small number of minister's permit holders.

3. In the analysis of both the Canadian and U.S. census data, it is assumed that education of the native-born population is obtained in their country of birth.

4. Permanent residents typically have fewer years of residence in Canada than naturalized Canadians, given that immigrants cannot immediately apply for citizenship and will be more likely to choose Canadian citizenship the longer they have lived in Canada.

5. For both the Canadian and the U.S. data, an individual's earned income is defined as the sum of earnings from wages, salaries, and self-employment. This is to ensure that earnings from medical work that may be taken as self-employment are not excluded.

6. Earned income is in constant 1999 U.S. dollars.

7. An odds ratio is a commonly used format for the presentation of results from discrete outcome Logit models. The odds ratio is interpreted as the odds of an event occurring if a certain condition is true (such as being an immigrant) divided by the odds of the event occurring if a certain condition is not true. An odds ratio that is greater than one means that the condition is associated with a greater likelihood of the event occurring, while an odds ratio less than one means a lower likelihood of the event occurring.

8. The odds ratio for the "foreign born" variable (FB) can be thought of as identifying the separate effect of naturalized citizens since the interaction of FB and the permanent resident variable (FB-PR) identifies the other possible immigrant group. Note that FB equals zero for temporary residents (TR=1). Since year of arrival is not available for temporary residents in the Canadian census data, immigrant controls for period of arrival and location of medical education apply to permanent residents and citizens only, while temporary residence status is modeled simply as an intercept shift captured by the TR variable.

9. It should be noted that it is not possible to distinguish arrival cohort differences from the effects of duration in Canada using a single cross-sectional data set. Thus, the cause of these differences could arise from a dynamic pattern of immigrants being more likely to transition to working as physicians with more time in Canada, or they could be caused by differences across immigrant arrival cohorts that result in recent arrival groups being less likely to be employed as physicians relative to the earlier arrival groups (differences that may or may not change over time).

10. We also used Logit models to estimate whether individuals are likely to be medical specialists, conditional on being medical doctors. However, we found that very few variables were statistically significant other than the province of residence controls, so we decided not to include these results.

11. The earning differentials are calculated as $e^{\beta} - 1$.

References

Bashaw, D. J., and J. S. Heywood. 2001. The Gender Earnings Gap for U.S. Physicians: Has Equality Been Achieved? *Labour* 15 (3): 371–91.

Benarroch, M., and H. Grant. 2004. The Interprovincial Migration of Canadian Physicians: Does Income Matter? *Applied Economics* 36: 2335–45.

Boyd, M., and G. Schellenberg. 2007. Re-accreditation and the Occupations of Immigrant Doctors and Engineers. *Canadian Social Trends*. Statistics Canada. Catalogue no. 11-008.

Dostie, B., and P. T. Leger. 2009. Self-Selection in Migration and Returns to Unobservable Skills. *Journal of Population Economics* 22 (4): 1005–24.

Grant, Hugh and R. R. Oertel. 1997. The Supply and Migration of Canadian Physicians, 1970–1995: Why We Should Learn to Love an Immigrant Doctor. *Canadian Journal of Regional Sciences* 20: 157–68.

Lasser, K. E., D. U. Himmelstein, and S. Woolhandler. 2006. Access to Care, Health Status, and Health Disparities in the United States and Canada: Results of a Cross-National Population-Based Survey. *American Journal of Public Health* 96 (July): 1300–1307.

McMahon, G. T. 2004. Coming to America: International Medical Graduates in the United States. *The New England Journal of Medicine* 350 (24): 2435–37.

Micka, S. S., S. D. Leeb, and W. P. Wodchisc. 2000. Variations in Geographical Distribution of Foreign and Domestically Trained Physicians in the United States: "Safety Nets" or "Surplus Exacerbation"? *Social Science and Medicine* 50: 185–202

Phillips, R. Jr., S. Petterson, G. Freyer Jr., and W. Rosser. 2007. The Canadian Contribution to the U.S. Physician Workforce. *Canadian Medical Association Journal* 176 (8): 1083–87.

Ruggles, S., M. Sobek, T. Alexander, C. A. Fitch, R. Goeken, P. K. Hall, M. King, and C. Ronnander. 2008. Integrated Public-Use Microdata Series: Version 4.0 (Machine-Readable Database). Minneapolis, MN: Minnesota Population Center.

Shafqat, S., and A. K. M. Zaidi. 2005. Unwanted Foreign Doctors: What Is Not Being Said about the Brain Drain. *Journal of the Royal Society of Medicine* 98: 492–93.

Statistics Canada. 2001. Canadian Census: 20 Percent Master File. Accessed through the CRISP-UNB Research Data Centre at the University of New Brunswick–Fredericton, Canada.

Szafran, O., R. A. Crutcher, S. R. Banner, and M. Watanabe. 2005. Canadian and Immigrant International Medical Graduates. *Canadian Family Physician* 15: 1243–49.

U.S. Government Accountability Office. 2006. *Foreign Physicians: Data on Use of J-1 Visa Waivers Needed to Better Address Physician Shortages.*

PART IV

High-Skilled Immigrants: Impact and Policy

9

High-Skilled Immigration Policy in Europe

Martin Kahanec and Klaus F. Zimmermann

Europe has always been a crossroads of cultures and an intersection of countless immigration trajectories. In the postwar period, especially since the 1960s, immigration from Southern Europe, Africa, Asia, former colonies, and other parts of the world has been rising in Western Europe. The yoke of Communist regimes staunched immigration flows in Eastern Europe until the fall of the Berlin Wall, after which the difficulties of transformation move many Eastern Europeans westward (see figures 9-1 and 9-2). In effect, noncitizen and foreign-born populations today constitute significant shares of the population in most of the old member states of the European Union today, with freedom and economic convergence, some immigration into the new member states from Central and Eastern Europe can be assumed (see table 9-1).

Both high-skilled low-skilled workers can be found among these immigrants. While in a number of member states (and also on aggregate in the

The authors thank René Böheim, Ana Rute Cardoso, Barry R. Chiswick, Corrado Giulietti, Inna Fernández-Huertas, Benjamin Elsner, Christer Gerdes, Zaiko Kanaiaci, Karin/Mayr, Janet Oriepa, Dean Pohlman, Uli Sauer, Marcel Skersly, Jean Tatsi, Anna Iriondo Jacur, Petros Petrossian, Erkel Mumenye, Alan Winters, and the participants of the ASE conference in Washington, D.C., for helpful comments. The views expressed are the authors' alone and do not necessarily correspond to those of the Institute for the Study of Labor.

7

High-Skilled Immigration: The Link to Public Expenditure and Private Investments

Volker Grossmann and David Stadelmann

In the last decades, high-skilled workers have become increasingly mobile across countries. For instance, the number of tertiary-educated immigrants living in Organisation for Economic Co-operation and Development (OECD) countries increased from 12.5 million in 1990 to 20.4 million in 2000 (Docquier and Marfouk 2006). About half of them immigrated to the United States. The United States in particular attracts key workers with the potential to enhance productivity (through both formal and informal research and development [R&D] activities) such as scientists, engineers, and other highly trained professionals. In 2004, about 12 percent of individuals holding doctorates in the United States were foreign citizens and about 26 percent were foreign born (Auriol 2007). In addition to the United States, the main beneficiaries of international high-skilled migration in the past decades were Canada, Australia, Luxembourg, and Switzerland. Luxembourg has traditionally been an immigration country for high-skilled German and French citizens. After institutional changes that facilitated

---

The authors are grateful to participants at the conference on "High-Skilled Immigration in a Globalized Labor Market" organized by the American Enterprise Institute on April 22–23, 2009, for the valuable discussion. In particular, the authors are indebted to the discussant of this chapter, Ira N. Gang, and to the scientific organizer of the conference, Barry R. Chiswick, for many insightful comments and suggestions.

mobility of labor between Switzerland and the European Union (EU), Switzerland became the main destination country for German emigrants (formerly it had been the United States). The bulk of these immigrants are at least tertiary-educated (in contrast to relatively low-skilled Italian migrants to Switzerland three decades ago).

These observations fit well with cross-country evidence suggesting that language proximity, learning capability, and the wage level for skilled workers are important determinants that foster high-skilled immigration (for recent contributions, see Beine, Docquier, and Ozden 2009; Grogger and Hanson 2010).[1] One may ask, however, if countries like the United States, Canada, and Switzerland will continue to be the most attractive places for internationally mobile, high-skilled workers in the future. The answer to this question depends largely on the evolution of income opportunities in these economies for high-qualified migrants relative to the income opportunities in other countries. These income opportunities depend on previous high-skilled immigration and its consequences for economic growth.

This chapter attempts to shed light on the channels through which immigration of high-skilled individuals affects average income in an economy in the longer run. We argue that both private and public investment may be stimulated when more high-skilled workers immigrate.[2] We first provide theoretical considerations about the impact of higher (net) immigration on incentives for governments to invest in education and infrastructure (such as roads, railways, and electricity) as well as for private investors to contribute to the accumulation of physical capital.[3] We then provide empirical evidence on the relationship between immigration of tertiary-educated workers on the one hand and various forms of public expenditure and private productive spending on the other hand. The empirical analysis employs a recent international dataset on high-skilled migration into OECD countries (Docquier and Marfouk 2006; Docquier, Lowell, and Marfouk 2007). We focus on OECD countries to reduce potential biases from omitted variables that generally plague cross-country studies. OECD countries have comparable institutions, and the OECD headquarters provides data on internationally comparable measures in member countries of public expenditures, capital stocks, and private investments.

That public spending reacts to higher immigration of skilled labor in a productivity-enhancing way presumes that governments care about aggregate income. In light of the theoretical arguments discussed in the coming section, our evidence suggests that this holds true on average within the OECD. Public spending on infrastructure and education is, by and large, positively associated with the number of high-skilled immigrants (net of emigrants) as a fraction of skilled residents, whereas public spending on social purposes and more consumptive matters does not seem to be related to high-skilled immigration. We also find evidence in favor of the hypothesis that high-skilled immigration raises the return to physical capital. Our empirical analysis suggests that higher (net) immigration of tertiary-educated, working-age individuals is positively related to an increase in a country's capital stock.

The literature on high-skilled immigration has been growing quickly in recent years. Traditionally, the literature on international labor mobility of high-qualified labor focused on consequences of emigration (brain drain) on source countries (see, for example, Bhagwati and Hamada 1974). Recent literature suggests that effects can be beneficial for poor source countries due to increased educational incentives that are triggered by enhanced possibilities to emigrate (see, for example, Mountford 1997; Beine, Docquier, and Rapoport 2001, 2008).[4] Our focus in the empirical analysis is on OECD countries in which such mechanism is unlikely to hold. Moreover, we primarily take the perspective of a destination country like the United States.

Our contribution complements, from an international perspective, the findings by Cohen-Goldner and Weiss (chapter 8 of this volume), who analyze implications of the dramatic high-skilled immigration waves in Israel. In line with our international evidence, they argue that public investments increased in the aftermath of high-skilled immigration. The authors also report a gradual transition from blue-collar occupations to white-collar occupations. The transition was associated with an increase in wages for the high skilled and a moderate increase for the low skilled. In a similar vein, Eckstein and Weiss (2002) argue that the large immigration waves from the former Soviet Union to Israel stimulated economic growth: gross domestic product (GDP) per capita, private consumption per capita, the capital stock per capita, and the capital-labor ratio have risen over most of the considered period.

Our empirical analysis on the relationship between migration and public provision of goods is also related to the contribution of Usher (1977) and more recent work of Grossmann and Stadelmann (2009). Usher (1977) argues that as migrants move from one country to another they abandon their share of public property, such as schools and roads, in the origin country and acquire a share of public property in th destination. Migrants might thereby confer benefits on the origin and costs un the destination. However, he does not analyze the potential response of governments to migration. Grossmann and Stadelmann (2009) develop a theoretical framework with increasing returns to scale that suggests that higher immigration raises the marginal benefit for domestic workers of investment in public infrastructure. The next section provides the essence of that paper and extends the considerations to private investment.

We shall stress that our analysis focuses on immigration of tertiary-educated workers rather than on student immigration. By contrast, Lowell and Khadka (chapter 3 of this volume) argue that international students may also be an important source of supply of future high-qualified workers in Western countries. They show that the number of foreign students in the United States declined for several years in the wake of 9/11 but later returned to previous levels.

Theoretical Considerations

We start out with some theoretical considerations regarding the relationship between high-skilled immigration, public investments, and the private stock of physical capital. The key hypothesis we derive is that immigration of high-skilled workers increases the marginal product of both the private and the public capital input. To develop theoretical hypotheses that are tested empirically in the next section, suppose an economy's GDP is generated according to the following aggregate production function (of a homogenous final good) that is increasing in all of its arguments:

(1) $Y = F(X, G, \mathbf{Z})$;

where X denotes a composite intermediate input of producer goods, G is the level of productive public spending, and $\mathbf{Z}$ is a vector of other inputs. Such other inputs could be land or different types of labor, for example. The

composite intermediate input is produced according to the following production function:

$$(2) \qquad X = \sum_{i=1}^{n} (A_i)^{1-\alpha} (x_i)^{\alpha},$$

$0 < \alpha < 1$, where x_i and A_i denote quantity and quality of producer good $i =$
$1, 2, \ldots n$, respectively.

Suppose that one unit of physical capital in the economy can be transformed into one unit of each producer good. Due to a decreasing marginal
product of each single producer good, output of the composite input X is
enhanced when the number of producer goods (n) increases, holding constant the total capital input $K \equiv \sum_i x_i$.[5] To see this, suppose that there is a
symmetric case for which all producer goods are in the same quality and
quantity, that is, $A_i = A$ and $x_i = x = K/n$ for all i. In this case, according to
(1) and (2), output can be written as

$$(3) \qquad Y = F(K^{\alpha} \cdot (A \cdot n)^{1-\alpha}, G, \mathbf{Z}) \equiv \tilde{F}(K, B, G, \mathbf{Z}),$$

where $B \equiv A \cdot n$. Now suppose high-skilled immigration raises either the
quality of producer goods, A, or the number of intermediate-good firms, n.
For example, high-skilled immigrants may be allocated to R&D activity and
thereby affect the quality of producer goods. The number of intermediate-
good firms may be raised when high-skilled immigrants become entrepreneurs. In both cases, an increase in high-skilled immigration raises total
output (that is, GDP), by increasing B (that is, $\tilde{F}_B > 0$).[6]

More importantly, it also raises the return to private physical capital, $\tilde{F}_K$;
formally, according to (3), we have $\tilde{F}_{KB} > 0$. Thus, we would expect that an
increase in high-skilled immigration is positively related to the private capital stock. In addition, if an increase in productive government expenditure,
G, raises the return to the composite input (that is, if F_X is increasing in G),
then $\tilde{F}_{GB} > 0$. More intuitively, if the capital input X and productive government spending are complementary factors, and the government cares
about GDP, the government should raise the stock of productive public
capital when more high-skilled workers immigrate. To the extent that the
stock of public capital (G) and public investment are positively related (this
is the case, for instance, in a steady state with constant depreciation), this

leads to the hypothesis that high-skilled immigration is positively related to public investment.

Empirical Analysis

This section presents evidence that supports the hypotheses derived from the outlined theoretical framework. We first focus on the data and the estimation strategy before turning to results.

Data and Estimation Strategy: High-Skilled Immigration. The first challenge is to find a measure for the net immigration rate of high-skilled individuals for OECD countries. As Dumont and Lemaître (2005) point out, quality and comparability of international data on migration have barely kept pace with the increased interest of economists and policymakers in international migration of high-skilled workers. Docquier and Marfouk (2006) have recently established a comparable dataset of (gross) emigration stocks and rates by educational attainment for the years 1990 and 2000. The census in OECD countries includes a question on the country of birth of persons enumerated, as well as on their nationality. Using this information, it is possible to provide a more detailed, comparable, and reliable picture of immigrant populations within OECD countries. This picture reflects the cumulative effect of movements of high-skilled individuals within and to the OECD area over the past decades. The authors count as immigrants all foreign-born individuals who are at least twenty-five years old and live in an OECD country, and we classify them by educational attainment and country of origin. Although only immigration into OECD countries is captured, the dataset accounts for approximately 90 percent of tertiary-educated migrants in the world, as most immigrants migrate to OECD member countries.[7]

By extending this dataset, Docquier, Lowell, and Marfouk (2007) provide bilateral immigration stocks of tertiary-educated individuals in OECD countries. Denote by M_{ij} the number of tertiary-educated emigrants from country i living in OECD country j. Furthermore, let Ψ be the set of all 195 countries in the dataset and Ω be the set of OECD countries. Then the *net high-skilled immigration stock* in OECD country $j \in \Omega$, *MigStock$_j$*, is given by the total number of immigrants in j minus the total number of emigrants from j:

(4)
$$MigStock_{j\cdot} \equiv \sum_{i \in \Psi} M_{ij} - \sum_{i \in \Omega} M_{ji}.$$

Denoting the number of tertiary-educated residents in country j by S_j, we construct the *net high-skilled immigration rate, Mig_j*, as $Mig_j \equiv MigStock_j / S_j$.

In the empirical analysis we regress different measures of public expenditure, the private capital stock, and private investment in the year 2000 on the net high-skilled immigration rate (Mig) and other controls (discussed below) in the year 2000. To deal with the problem of reverse causality, we also use the lagged immigration rate, in 1990, as an instrument for the contemporaneous immigration rate (in 2000). Moreover, to address the concern of omitted-variable bias, we present first-difference estimates, regressing the change of our dependent variables between 2000 and 1990 on the change in Mig between 2000 and 1990. This nets out all omitted factors that are constant over time.

Dependent Variables. The main data source for dependent variables is the OECD Economic Outlook for various years. The OECD Economic Outlook is a twice-yearly publication with economic forecasts and analyses for the OECD member states. It provides a set of consistent macroeconomic data that are used in science and for policy analysis. The data serve as inputs into our macroeconometric analysis.[8]

Table 7-1 defines the variables used in the regression tables and provides summary statistics. The list of countries in the dataset is given in table 7-2.

The data source provides the physical capital stock (K) as one important dependent variable in our analysis; it is the sum of the written past investments in assets that are still in use. Regarding private investment, we use measures for gross investment (I); net investment ($I - \delta K$), which is calculated by assuming a depreciation rate (δ) of 5 percent; and the subcategories of (gross) investment in transport, housing, and manufacturing.

We also use several government-expenditure categories as dependent variables. Our preferred measure for productive public spending is the OECD measure of government gross fixed-capital formation. This includes acquisitions of new tangible assets (such as machinery and equipment, transport equipment, construction) and new intangible assets (such as computer software) when used for more than one year. It excludes acquisitions of land, mineral deposits, timber tracts, and so forth, as well as outlays that

TABLE 7-1

DATA DESCRIPTION AND SOURCES

Variable	Description and Source	N	Mean	Standard Deviation
Mig	Net high-skilled immigration rate. Construction on the basis of data from Docquier, Lowell, and Marfouk (2007).	30	−0.01243	0.10923
DeltaMig	Mig in 2000 minus Mig in 1990.	30	0.02455	0.04885
TotalPubExp	Log of total public expenditure per capita. OECD General Government Accounts Database and Economic Outlook.	26	9.183	0.50098
DeltaTotalPubExp	Exp in 2000 minus Exp in 1990.	22	0.2782	0.21289
GovInv	Log of government gross fixed-capital formation per capita. OECD Economic Outlook Database.	22	6.506	0.57332
DeltaGovInv	GovInv in 2000 minus GovInv in 1990.	22	0.1478	0.20903
ExpEdu	Log of public expenditure per capita for education. OECD General Government Accounts Database and Economic Outlook.	25	7.201	0.40681
DeltaExpEdu	ExpEdu in 2000 minus ExpEdu in 1990.	22	0.3254	0.32131
ExpSocial	Log of social expenditure per capita. OECD General Government Accounts Database and Economic Outlook.	25	8.092	0.63589
DeltaExpSocial	ExpSocial in 2000 minus ExpSocial in 1990.	22	0.3382	0.15898
ExpHealth	Log of public-health expenditure per capita. OECD General Government Accounts Database and Economic Outlook.	25	7.207	0.48506
DeltaExpHealth	ExpHealth in 2000 minus ExpHealth in 1990.	22	0.402	0.20673
ExpEco	Log of public expenditure per capita for economic affairs. OECD General Government Accounts Database and Economic Outlook.	25	6.949	0.39381
DeltaExpEco	ExpEco in 2000 minus ExpEco in 1990.	22	0.06894	0.33444
CapitalStock	Log of the private capital stock per capita. OECD General Government Accounts Database and Economic Outlook.	22	11.18	0.25154
DeltaCapitalStock	CapitalStock in 2000 minus CapitalStock in 1990.	22	0.1542	0.063
GrossInv	Log of private gross investment per capita. OECD General Government Accounts Database and Economic Outlook.	30	8.495	0.39461
DeltaGrossInv	GrossInv in 2000 minus GrossInv in 1990.	29	0.2844	0.20502
NetInv	Log of private net investment per capita. Calculated from GrossInv and CapitalStock with a depreciation rate of 5 percent.	22	7.871	0.26153
DeltaNetInv	NetInv in 2000 minus NetInv in 1990.	22	0.6817	0.57236
InvMetal	Log of investment in metal and machinery per capita. OECD Economic Outlook Database.	27	7.317	0.32412
DeltaInvMetal	InvMetal in 2000 minus InvMetal in 1990.	21	0.4604	0.3361
InvTransport	Log of investment in transportation per capita. OECD Economic Outlook Database.	27	6.273	0.40877

TABLE 7-1 (cont.)
DATA DESCRIPTION AND SOURCES

Variable	Description and Source	N	Mean	Standard Deviation
DeltaInvTransport	InvTransport in 2000 minus InvTransport in 1990.	21	0.2795	0.29335
InvHousing	Log of investment in housing per capita. OECD Economic Outlook Database.	27	7.04	0.59506
DeltaInvHousing	InvHousing in 2000 minus InvHousing in 1990.	23	0.06273	0.37433
Pop	Log population midyear estimate. OECD Population and Labor Force Statistics Database.	30	9.617	1.55114
Pop16–	Population under sixteen years as share of total population. OECD Population and Labor Force Statistics Database.	30	21.32	5.27227
Pop65+	Population over sixty-five years as share of total population. OECD Population and Labor Force Statistics Database.	30	13.79	3.39122
Regulation	Index of Regulation. From the Heritage Foundation's Index of Economic Freedom.	30	75	9.09718
DeltaPop	Pop in 2000 minus Pop in 1990.	30	1.075	0.06834
DeltaGDP	Log real GDP in 2000 minus log real GDP in 1990. Penn World Tables 6.2.	30	1.243	0.17745

SOURCE: Authors' calculations and compilations.
NOTES: The range, mean, and standard deviations are based on the respective number of observations. All statistics for levels of the variables are for the year 2000.

are primarily for military purposes. We also consider total government expenditure, public-education expenditure, social expenditure, public-health expenditure, and public expenditure for economic affairs. The latter four categories typically account for more than 70 percent of total government spending in OECD countries. The latter three categories are, however, not necessarily capturing the type of public expenditures that can best be considered investments as opposed to consumptive spending.[9] We would, therefore, not expect that a higher net high-skilled immigration rate has a significant impact on those spending categories (and, therefore, not expect a robust effect on total government spending), whereas our theoretical considerations suggest that there is a positive effect on government gross fixed-capital formation and, possibly, on public-education spending.

Other Controls. Apart from our main variable of interest, Mig, several controls are included in the regression analysis. First, we include (log) population size in order to account for possible economies of scale associated with

TABLE 7-2
COUNTRIES INCLUDED IN EMPIRICAL ANALYSIS

Australia	Hungary	Norway
Austria	Iceland	Poland
Belgium	Ireland	Portugal
Canada	Italy	Slovak Republic
Czech Republic	Japan	Spain
Denmark	Korea	Sweden
Finland	Luxembourg	Switzerland
France	Mexico	Turkey
Germany	Netherlands	United Kingdom
Greece	New Zealand	United States

public goods. If anything, population size should thus be negatively related to public expenditure per capita. It may also affect private investment. According to endogenous growth theory, larger-scale economies typically lead to higher GDPs and capital stocks per capita ("weak-scale effects") or affect the growth rate of these variables ("strong-scale effects").[10] Moreover, to account for the age structure of a country, we include both the fraction of a country's population under the age of sixteen and over the age of sixty-five as control variables. In the regressions that relate changes of high-skilled immigration over time to changes in private investment or public spending, we control for changes in (log) population size (approximately equal to the population growth rate). To account for possible business-cycle phenomena, we also include the change in (log) GDP per capita in those estimations.

Finally, we control for government regulation. The employed quantitative measure is provided by the Heritage Foundation (2000). It reflects the ability to start, operate, and close a business and also attempts to reflect efficiency of the government procedures in these matters in general. It is based on factors such as the number of procedures to complete in order to start and close a business, the costs involved, the minimum capital requirements, and so forth. The measure may be related, therefore, to private investment. We also include the regulation measure as a control when public expenditure of some kind is the dependent variable. Countries that have more government intervention may also be characterized by higher public spending, possibly due to the citizens' attitude toward the role of the government in general or historical factors that affect the size of government.

Results: Correlations. Figures 7-1 and 7-2 provide a first glance at the evidence on the relationship of the net high-skilled immigration rate to public spending and private capital, respectively. We plot levels against levels (for the year 2000) in the left-hand side panels and changes (between 1990 and 2000) against changes in the right-hand side panels.

According to figure 7-1, the correlation between the level of high-skilled immigration and the level of (log) total government spending per capita is significant. However, significance disappears once omitted factors that are constant over time are netted out by looking at first difference estimations (though the correlation is still positive). By contrast, a higher change in net immigration of high-skilled individuals is significantly related to a higher (approximate) growth rate of both per-capita public investment (gross government fixed-capital formation) and public-education spending per capita. Correlation coefficients are almost 50 percent. These results are consistent with the aforementioned hypothesis that high-skilled immigration, by enhancing productivity of various sectors in the economy, raises an economy's return to public investment. By contrast, and as expected, social expenditure and public spending on economic affairs are not significantly related to high-skilled immigration.

Looking at countries individually, Ireland had the largest net inflow of high-skilled workers in the OECD between 1990 and 2000 and it increased public expenditure substantially in this time period (particularly on education). The United Kingdom fits into the picture in a similar way. Countries like Mexico and Portugal, which experienced substantial brain drain along with large public spending cuts on investment and education, are on the other end of the spectrum. Germany and Japan are countries below the regression line, but they are nevertheless consistent with the general picture. Experiencing only a modest net inflow of high-skilled workers between 1990 and 2000, neither country increased productive public spending in that time period. That the change in public investment was lower than average, given their inflow of high-skilled workers from abroad, may be understandable in view of the severe structural problems these countries experienced in the 1990s (reflected, *inter alia*, by significant increases in the unemployment

FIGURE 7-1

**CORRELATIONS BETWEEN NET HIGH-SKILLED IMMIGRATION
AND GOVERNMENT EXPENDITURES**

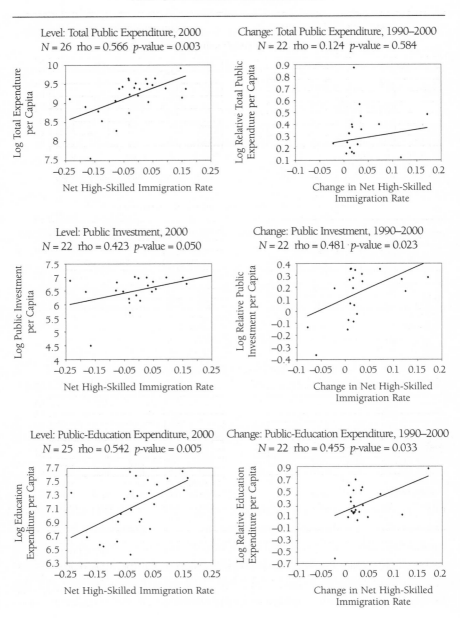

FIGURE 7-1 (cont.)

**CORRELATIONS BETWEEN NET HIGH-SKILLED IMMIGRATION
AND GOVERNMENT EXPENDITURES**

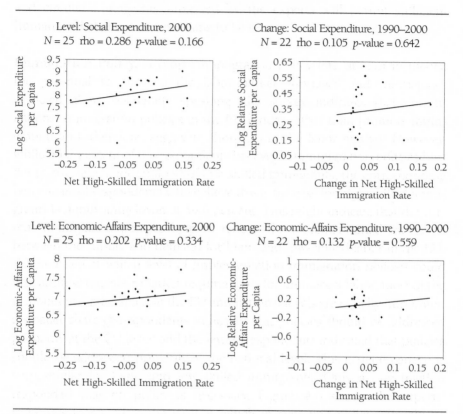

Level: Social Expenditure, 2000
$N = 25$ rho = 0.286 p-value = 0.166

Change: Social Expenditure, 1990–2000
$N = 22$ rho = 0.105 p-value = 0.642

Level: Economic-Affairs Expenditure, 2000
$N = 25$ rho = 0.202 p-value = 0.334

Change: Economic-Affairs Expenditure, 1990–2000
$N = 22$ rho = 0.132 p-value = 0.559

SOURCES: Authors' calculations. Expenditure measures for 1990 and 2000 are from the Organisation for Economic Co-operation and Development (OECD) General Government Accounts Database and Economic Outlook.

NOTES: rho represents the correlation coefficient. The p-value results from a test of the significance of the correlation.

rate). Japan barely recovered from the stock market crash that took place at the end of the 1980s (together with the bust of a property price bubble that the current global financial and economic crisis parallels). Germany had to adjust to reunification. Both countries increased public spending substantially around 1990 in order to provide "Keynesian" stimulus, but did not increase public spending anymore in the aftermath.

FIGURE 7-2

CORRELATIONS BETWEEN NET HIGH-SKILLED IMMIGRATION AND CAPITAL STOCK AND INVESTMENTS

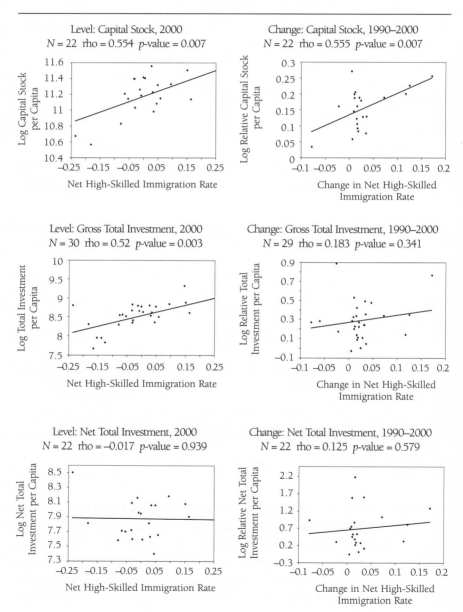

FIGURE 7-2 (cont.)

CORRELATIONS BETWEEN NET HIGH-SKILLED IMMIGRATION AND CAPITAL STOCK AND INVESTMENTS

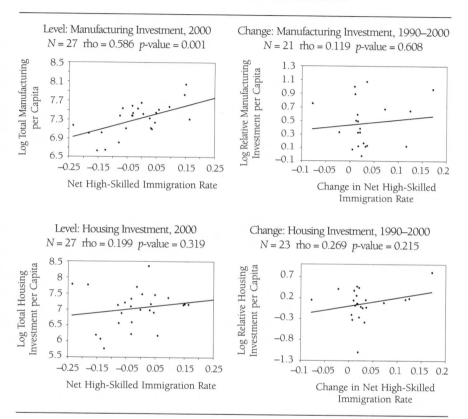

SOURCES: Authors' calculations. Expenditure measures for 1990 and 2000 are from the Organisation for Economic Co-operation and Development (OECD) General Government Accounts Database and Economic Outlook.

NOTES: rho represents the correlation coefficient. The *p*-value results from a test of the significance of the correlation.

Figure 7-2 deals with private productive expenditure per capita. According to the aforementioned theoretical considerations, the stock of high-skilled immigration (as a fraction of high-skilled residents) is positively related to the return to private capital. Therefore, we would expect the high-skilled immigration rate and private capital stock to have a positive association. Similarly, we would expect an increase in the net high-skilled immigration rate over time to be positively related to an increase in the physical capital stock (netting out omitted, time-invariant factors). Both predictions are consistent with the evidence. Even plotting changes against changes (see the first right-hand side panel in figure 7-2) gives us a correlation coefficient of about 56 percent, which is statistically significantly different from zero below the 1 percent level. The capital stock per capita increased in Ireland, the main destination country in the period 1990–2000, by about 25 percent. Capital stock per capita increased by about 20 percent in the United Kingdom, Austria, and Iceland, all of which attracted high-skilled immigrants on a larger scale over this time period. By contrast, New Zealand experienced a net brain drain between 1990 and 2000, and it had the least change in capital stock among countries in the data set.

What figure 7-2 also shows, however, is that changes in the stock of high-skilled immigration (as a fraction of skilled residents) are not significantly related to changes in private investment per capita, neither to total (gross or net) investment nor to subcategories of (gross) private investment. If that were the case, then an increase in high-skilled immigration would lead to an acceleration of the increase in the physical capital stock. This is not suggested by the theoretical framework we presented previously. In the left-hand side panels we show a significant relationship to the net high-skilled immigration rate to both gross investment and manufacturing investment. However, significance disappears in the right-hand side panels. This indicates that there are omitted factors that drive the positive relationship of levels to levels.

Regression Analysis. Next, we present our regression results. These largely confirm the insights from the correlations in figures 7-1 and 7-2. We also present information on the quantitative effects of high-skilled immigration on public and private spending and on the role of additional covariates.

Table 7-3 looks at relationships similar to those presented in figure 7-1. It confirms that total public expenditure per capita is not significantly affected by high-skilled immigration once other factors are accounted for.[11] It is positively related to the extent of government regulation and negatively related to the fraction of the population under the age of sixteen.

By contrast, high-skilled immigration fosters both public gross fixed-capital formation and public education. When accounting for possible

TABLE 7-3

EFFECT OF NET HIGH-SKILLED IMMIGRATION RATES ON GOVERNMENT EXPENDITURES

Dependent Variable	Regression (1)	Regression (2)	IV Regression (3)	Regression (4)	Regression (5)	IV Regression (6)	Regression (7)	Regression (8)	IV Regression (9)
	TotalPubExp			GovInv			ExpEdu		
(Intercept)	9.2380*** (0.0723)	9.2366*** (0.6949)	9.3643*** (0.7362)	6.5090*** (0.1068)	10.2986*** (2.6415)	10.6961*** (2.5391)	7.2320*** (0.0627)	6.1479*** (1.1816)	6.4262*** (1.3952)
Mig	2.8200*** (1.0056)	0.4672 (0.6507)	0.1186 (0.6605)	2.1590* (1.3304)	1.4109* (0.9305)	0.7482* (0.4870)	2.2510*** (0.7819)	2.0760*** (0.5114)	1.5820*** (0.8138)
Pop		-0.0466* (0.0271)	-0.0424 (0.0313)		-0.1100* (0.0721)	-0.1034 (0.0765)		-0.0569*** (0.0243)	-0.0591*** (0.0278)
Pop16-		-0.0376*** (0.0151)	-0.0439*** (0.0157)		-0.0732 (0.0575)	-0.0886 (0.0586)		-0.0012 (0.0285)	-0.0113 (0.0366)
Pop65+		0.0272 (0.0221)	0.0203 (0.0243)		-0.0633 (0.0681)	-0.0787 (0.0625)		-0.0014 (0.0284)	-0.0103 (0.0335)
Regulation		0.0110*** (0.0020)	0.0117*** (0.0022)		-0.0042 (0.0129)	-0.0032 (0.0138)		0.0222*** (0.0050)	0.0231*** (0.0060)
Adj. R-squared	0.292	0.815	0.809	0.138	0.188	0.136	0.263	0.522	0.410
N	26	26	26	22	22	22	25	25	25
F-Value, first stage			40.470			32.580			34.430

(continued)

TABLE 7-3 (cont.)

EFFECT OF NET HIGH-SKILLED IMMIGRATION RATES ON GOVERNMENT EXPENDITURES

Dependent Variable	ExpSocial			ExpHealth			ExpEco		
	Regression (10)	Regression (11)	IV Regression (12)	Regression (13)	Regression (14)	IV Regression (15)	Regression (16)	Regression (17)	IV Regression (18)
(Intercept)	8.1180*** (0.1211)	6.0463*** (2.4371)	6.2814*** (2.5874)	7.2350*** (0.0815)	3.8284*** (1.4061)	3.8322** (2.2092)	6.9600*** (0.0786)	7.6590*** (1.6067)	7.8565*** (1.7035)
Mig	1.8560* (1.1269)	0.5620 (0.9901)	0.2633 (1.0404)	2.0480*** (0.9321)	0.6677 (0.7445)	0.9783 (1.0912)	0.8104 (0.9846)	0.8900 (0.7656)	0.5975 (0.8176)
Pop		-0.0946*** (0.0401)	-0.0945*** (0.0402)		-0.0076 (0.0422)	-0.0578 (0.0469)		-0.1204*** (0.0453)	-0.1210*** (0.0472)
Pop16–		-0.0484 (0.0494)	-0.0566 (0.0554)		0.0437 (0.0354)	0.0113 (0.0558)		0.0053 (0.0300)	-0.0017 (0.0404)
Pop65+		0.1462*** (0.0660)	0.1394** (0.0710)		0.0854*** (0.0405)	0.1058** (0.0513)		0.0027 (0.0262)	-0.0032 (0.0286)
Regulation		0.0234*** (0.0087)	0.0237*** (0.0088)		0.0183*** (0.0034)	0.0287*** (0.0100)		0.0041 (0.0084)	0.0045 (0.0087)
Adj. R-squared	0.042	0.552	0.547	0.135	0.574	0.318	0.061	0.134	0.108
N	25	25	25	25	25	25	25	25	25
F-Value, first stage			34.430			34.430			34.430

SOURCE: Authors' calculations.

NOTES: Robust clustered standard errors in parentheses. *** indicates a significance level below 5 percent; ** indicates significance level between 5 and 10 percent; * indicates significance level between 10 and 15 percent. In IV regressions, the instrument is the lagged net high-skilled immigration rate of the year 1990 (Mig1990).

endogeneity, the instrumental variable (IV) estimates are lower than the ordinary least squares (OLS) coefficients. This result suggests that the relationships in figure 7-1 partly reflect reverse causality. However, the IV estimates are significantly different from zero. Importantly, they point to quantitative important effects. For instance, according to column six of table 7-3, an increase of one standard deviation in the net high-skilled immigration rate (*Mig*) raises government gross fixed-capital formation per capita (*GovInv*) by about 8.2 percent (0.11, the standard deviation from table 7-1 for *Mig*, times 0.75, the coefficient for the combination of *Mig* and *GovInv*). A similar increase in high-skilled immigration increases public-education expenditure per capita (*ExpEdu*) by about 17.2 percent (column seven, 0.11 times 1.58). Population size has a negative effect on public-education expenditure, which points to some economies of scale in publicly financed human-capital formation.

Public expenditure on social matters, health, and economic affairs are not significantly related to high-skilled immigration once we control for population variables and the extent of government regulation. Both the extent of regulation and the fraction of older persons are positively related to social spending and to health spending per capita.

Table 7-4 presents regressions of changes in the different public-expenditure categories on changes in high-skilled migration over the time period 1990–2000. It shows that once the change in (log) GDP per capita (*DeltaGDP*) is accounted for (capturing business-cycle effects), coefficients for the variable of interest drop.[12] However, the effect on our preferred public-investment measure (*DeltaGovInv*) remains positive and highly significant (see columns four to six of table 7-4). It is also quantitatively important: an increase in *DeltaMig* by one standard deviation raises the growth rate of public investment per capita (*DeltaGovInv*) by about 5.7 percentage points (0.05 times 1.15). IV estimates for the variables *DeltaExpEdu, DeltaExpSocial, DeltaExpHealth,* and *DeltaExpEco* are insignificant.

We now turn to table 7-5, which contains the results from regressions of the private capital stock per capita and measures of private investment per capita on the net high-skilled immigration rate. Again, the IV estimates suggest smaller effects than OLS coefficients. But in line with the insights from figure 7-2, the coefficient of interest (*CapitalStock*) in the IV estimate of column three remains positive and significant. This is not only consistent

TABLE 7-4
EFFECT OF CHANGES IN NET HIGH-SKILLED IMMIGRATION RATES ON CHANGES IN GOVERNMENT EXPENDITURES

Dependent Variable	Regression (1)	Regression (2)	Regression (3)	Regression (4)	Regression (5)	Regression (6)	Regression (7)	Regression (8)	Regression (9)
	DeltaTotalPubExp			DeltaGovInv			DeltaExpEdu		
(Intercept)	0.2575*** (0.0495)	0.0349 (1.0277)	-0.4026 (0.4004)	0.0995*** (0.0473)	1.1545*** (0.5054)	0.8836 (0.6198)	0.2098*** (0.0915)	-0.3647 (1.1870)	-0.7217 (0.6507)
DeltaMig	0.6387 (0.7522)	0.6428 (0.7352)	-1.6901** (0.8680)	1.8176*** (0.6688)	1.6010*** (0.5312)	1.1536*** (0.5471)	3.5534** (1.7572)	3.5638** (1.7160)	1.6603 (2.2554)
DeltaPop		0.2084 (0.9772)	-0.4809 (0.3509)		-0.9673*** (0.4569)	-1.0452*** (0.4588)		0.5378 (1.1120)	-0.0246 (0.8002)
DeltaGDP			0.9917*** (0.2357)			0.2929 (0.2084)			0.8092*** (0.3404)
Adj. R-squared	0.034	0.084	0.493	0.193	0.243	0.255	0.168	0.136	0.275
N	22	22	22	22	22	22	22	22	22

TABLE 7-4 (cont.)

EFFECT OF CHANGES IN NET HIGH-SKILLED IMMIGRATION RATES ON CHANGES IN GOVERNMENT EXPENDITURES

Dependent Variable	Regression (10)	Regression (11)	Regression (12)	Regression (13)	Regression (14)	Regression (15)	Regression (16)	Regression (17)	Regression (18)
	DeltaExpSocial			DeltaExpHealth			DeltaExpEco		
(Intercept)	0.3250***	0.3166	0.1755	0.3513***	0.3875	-0.0421	0.0341	-1.1180	-1.5274
	(0.0364)	(0.5146)	(0.3764)	(0.0477)	(0.9320)	(0.3327)	(0.0797)	(1.8260)	(1.3078)
DeltaMig	0.4058	0.4059	-0.3466	1.5557*	1.5551*	0.7361	1.0707	1.0920	-1.0921
	(0.5840)	(0.5830)	(0.7799)	(1.0010)	(1.0010)	(0.5919)	(2.0320)	(1.9520)	(1.8187)
DeltaPop		0.0078	-0.2145		-0.0339	-0.7108***		1.0780	0.4332
		(0.4851)	(0.3155)		(0.8852)	(0.3200)		(1.7180)	(1.1383)
DeltaGDP			0.3199**			0.9740***			0.9283*
			(0.1833)			(0.1329)			(0.5877)
Adj. R-squared	0.038	0.093	0.035	0.051	0.059	0.597	0.032	0.040	0.129
N	22	22	22	22	22	22	22	22	22

SOURCE: Authors' calculations.

NOTES: Robust clustered standard errors in parentheses. *** indicates a significance level below 5 percent; ** indicates significance level between 5 and 10 percent; * indicates significance level between 10 and 15 percent.

TABLE 7-5

EFFECT OF NET HIGH-SKILLED IMMIGRATION RATES ON CAPITAL STOCK AND INVESTMENTS

Dependent Variable	Regression (1)	Regression (2)	IV Regression (3)	Regression (4)	Regression (5)	IV Regression (6)	Regression (7)	Regression (8)	IV Regression (9)
	CapitalStock			*GrossInv*			*NetInv*		
(Intercept)	11.1690***	13.9532***	14.5136***	8.5180***	9.6234***	10.0668***	7.8714***	9.5159***	10.3773***
	(0.0440)	(0.9737)	(1.0768)	(0.0584)	(1.1602)	(0.9881)	(0.0569)	(1.2137)	(1.2140)
Mtg	1.3150***	0.8460**	0.4643**	1.8800***	0.9146*	0.3147	-0.0427	0.2606	0.9271
	(0.5316)	(0.3913)	(0.2284)	(0.6744)	(0.5410)	(0.7050)	(0.7170)	(0.4708)	(1.5883)
Pop		-0.0198	-0.0105		-0.0432*	-0.0377		0.0174	0.0272
		(0.0284)	(0.0295)		(0.0287)	(0.0322)		(0.0265)	(0.0273)
Pop16-		-0.0762***	-0.0858***		-0.0511**	-0.0658***		0.0126	-0.0098
		(0.0178)	(0.0203)		(0.0222)	(0.0180)		(0.0250)	(0.0296)
Pop65+		-0.0641***	-0.0866***		-0.0243	-0.0415*		-0.0787**	-0.1096***
		(0.0299)	(0.0343)		(0.0334)	(0.0269)		(0.0403)	(0.0356)
Regulation		-0.0018	-0.0033		0.0096*	0.0103*		-0.0114***	-0.0121***
		(0.0036)	(0.0035)		(0.0064)	(0.0066)		(0.0045)	(0.0043)
Adj. R-squared	0.272	0.424	0.348	0.245	0.566	0.516	0.050	0.087	
N	22	22	22	30	30	30	22	22	22
F-Value, first stage			32.580			38.260			32.580

TABLE 7-5 (cont.)

EFFECT OF NET HIGH-SKILLED IMMIGRATION RATES ON CAPITAL STOCK AND INVESTMENTS

Dependent Variable	Regression (10)	Regression (11)	IV Regression (12)	Regression (13)	Regression (14)	IV Regression (15)	Regression (16)	Regression (17)	IV Regression (18)
	InvMetal			InvTransport			InvHousing		
(Intercept)	7.3280*** (0.0500)	9.5887*** (1.1264)	10.0625*** (1.0270)	6.2830*** (0.0705)	9.1216*** (1.5798)	9.5534*** (1.4322)	7.0470*** (0.1060)	6.8622*** (2.3236)	7.5376*** (2.2035)
Mig	1.7060*** (0.5549)	1.0471*** (0.4592)	0.3539 (0.4729)	1.3910* (0.8711)	0.7852 (0.6688)	0.1760 (0.8993)	1.0660 (1.0990)	0.6518 (1.0049)	-0.2245 (1.1622)
Pop		-0.0228 (0.0301)	-0.0182 (0.0338)		-0.0934** (0.0408)	-0.0894** (0.0432)		-0.0740 (0.0656)	-0.0685 (0.0669)
Pop16–		-0.0703*** (0.0257)	-0.0908*** (0.0260)		-0.0673** (0.0339)	-0.0855*** (0.0297)		-0.0205 (0.0548)	-0.0473 (0.0547)
Pop65+		-0.0511* (0.0300)	-0.0690*** (0.0270)		-0.0636*** (0.0275)	-0.0796*** (0.0247)		0.0222 (0.0564)	-0.0022 (0.0555)
Regulation		0.0015 (0.0055)	0.0034 (0.0068)		0.0042 (0.0073)	0.0058 (0.0078)		0.0129 (0.0132)	0.0150 (0.0143)
Adj. R-squared	0.317	0.368	0.270	0.109	0.213	0.176	0.043	0.072	0.083
N	27	27	27	27	27	27	27	27	27
F-Value, first stage			36.110			36.110			36.110

SOURCE: Authors' calculations.

NOTES: Robust clustered standard errors in parentheses. *** indicates a significance level below 5 percent; ** indicates significance level between 5 and 10 percent; * indicates significance level between 10 and 15 percent. In IV regressions the instrument is the lagged net high-skilled immigration rate of the year 1990 (Mig1990).

with a positive association between high-skilled immigration and the physical capital stock but also points to a causal effect, as we hypothesized. The estimate suggests that an increase in the immigration rate (*Mig*) by one standard deviation raises the per-capita capital stock (*CapitalStock*) by 5.1 percent (0.11 times 0.46). Also in line with the insights from figure 7-2, however, there is no robust association of high-skilled immigration with investment once we control for additional factors in IV estimates (see variables *NetInv, InvMetal, InvTransport,* and *InvHousing*).

It is interesting to look at the other covariates as well. Government regulation seems primarily to affect total net investment, but not gross-investment measures or the stock of capital. Moreover, population structure seems to matter much more than population size. The evidence suggests that the fraction of the population aged between seventeen and sixty-four years (roughly working age) is positively related to private productive spending per capita. There is no evidence on a scale effect, however, to match the effect postulated by endogenous growth theory; in the few cases where (log) population size enters significantly, the coefficient is negative rather than positive.

Finally, the results in table 7-6 allow us to discuss the robustness of the positive effect of an increase in high-skilled immigration on the capital stock. According to column three of table 7-6, regressing changes in the (log) capital stock (*DeltaCapitalStock*) on changes in high-skilled immigration (*DeltaMig*) over time leads to a positive and significant coefficient of interest. It suggests that an increase in *DeltaMig* by one standard deviation raises the growth rate of *DeltaCapitalStock* by about 3.5 percentage points (0.05 times 0.69). Again, this is a rather large effect. As expected from the previous results, however, an increase in *DeltaMig* has no robust effect on changes of our private-investment measures. We shall remark that these are sometimes highly positively related to the growth rate of GDP per capita (*DeltaGDP*), particularly to the growth rate of total net investment per capita (*DeltaNetInv*), and may well reflect reverse causality. However, in our preferred specification, the regression in column three, *DeltaGDP* does not enter significantly.

Conclusion

In this chapter we analyzed the relationship of high-skilled immigration to both public expenditure and productive private spending from an

TABLE 7-6

EFFECT OF CHANGES IN NET HIGH-SKILLED IMMIGRATION RATES ON CHANGES IN CAPITAL STOCK AND INVESTMENTS

Dependent Variable	Regression (1)	Regression (2)	Regression (3)	Regression (4)	Regression (5)	Regression (6)	Regression (7)	Regression (8)	Regression (9)
	DeltaCapitalStock			DeltaGrossInv			DeltaNetInv		
(Intercept)	0.1336***	0.0666	0.0731	0.2646***	0.8687	0.3303	0.6395***	0.7270	-1.4968
	(0.0139)	(0.1420)	(0.1717)	(0.0452)	(0.6186)	(0.5287)	(0.1366)	(2.3080)	(1.7837)
DeltaMig	0.6746***	0.6809***	0.6916***	0.7647	0.6665	0.1253	1.3798	1.3716	2.3051
	(0.1301)	(0.1379)	(0.1649)	(0.9991)	(1.0714)	(0.7646)	(1.6355)	(1.6560)	(1.9902)
DeltaPop		0.0622	0.0634		-0.5587	-0.7901**		-0.0812	-0.5016
		(0.1261)	(0.1215)		(0.5466)	(0.4549)		(2.1360)	(1.6494)
DeltaGDP			-0.0066			0.6453***			2.2547***
			(0.0575)			(0.2712)			(0.7455)
Adj. R-squared	0.274	0.240	0.198	0.022	0.036	0.247	0.034	0.088	0.151
N	22	22	22	29	29	29	22	22	22

TABLE 7-6 (cont.)

EFFECT OF CHANGES IN NET HIGH-SKILLED IMMIGRATION RATES ON CHANGES IN CAPITAL STOCK AND INVESTMENTS

Dependent Variable	Regression (10)	Regression (11)	Regression (12)	Regression (13)	Regression (14)	Regression (15)	Regression (16)	Regression (17)	Regression (18)
	DeltaInvMetal			DeltaInvTransport			DeltaInvHousing		
(Intercept)	0.4354***	0.3374	-0.2809	0.2548***	2.0950***	1.4049**	0.0008	-0.1350	-0.4809
	(0.0848)	(1.5990)	(1.2866)	(0.0749)	(0.7738)	(0.7422)	(0.0910)	(1.0271)	(1.1671)
DeltaMig	0.7599	0.7718	-0.4050	0.7539	0.5300	-0.7837	1.9909	2.0060	1.2771
	(1.4557)	(1.4340)	(1.3373)	(1.3916)	(1.4549)	(0.8387)	(1.4381)	(1.4594)	(1.1581)
DeltaPop		0.0902	-0.2055		-1.6940***	-2.0241***		0.1253	-0.0709
		(1.4960)	(1.2108)		(0.6801)	(0.5396)		(0.9037)	(0.7949)
DeltaGDP			0.7648**			0.8538***			0.4580
			(0.4022)			(0.3263)			(0.4688)
Adj. R-squared	0.038	0.095	0.073	0.033	0.060	0.278	0.028	0.020	0.030
N	21	21	21	21	21	21	23	23	23

SOURCE: Authors' calculations.
NOTES: Robust clustered standard errors in parentheses. *** indicates a significance level below 5 percent; ** indicates significance level between 5 and 10 percent; * indicates significance level between 10 and 15 percent.

international perspective. The presented evidence suggests that, on average, governments of OECD countries respond to inflows and outflows of skilled labor by adjusting public investment in infrastructure and education. Raising net high-skilled immigration has a positive and quantitatively important impact on productive public expenditure. Our theoretical considerations suggest that governments that care about GDP should indeed follow that route. On average, governments in the OECD seem, in this sense, to respond rationally to high-skilled immigration. Other public spending, like on health, social matters, and consumption, however, seem to be unrelated to high-skilled migration. We also find evidence that an increase in high-skilled immigration raises the return to private-capital investment. Changes in the net high-skilled immigration rate over time are positively related to changes in the physical capital stock per capita of a country.

However, more work needs to be done to identify the exact types of private investments that are stimulated by high-skilled immigration. Moreover, future research should be concerned with the effects of high-skilled immigration on the composition of public-investment spending. Our work may be seen as a starting point for this important topic.

Notes

1. Migration policy is another factor, of course. Kahanec and Zimmermann (chapter 9 of this volume) provide survey evidence from a questionnaire addressed to labor-market experts from the Institute for the Study of Labor (an international network of labor economists located in Bonn, Germany) on the need of European countries to attract more skilled immigrants. They state that, according to expert opinion, current EU policies are not likely to help reduce labor shortages.

2. Reasons for higher immigration may be manifold, but they are exogenous for our considerations. For instance, immigration may rise in response to a decline in mobility costs triggered by international labor–market integration when a country possesses favorable characteristics like high (initial) income, widespread knowledge of language, past immigration that creates social-network effects for potential immigrants, and so forth.

3. In national accounting, education expenditure is classified as consumption rather than investment. We will nevertheless refer to public-education expenditure as government investment, as it potentially raises production capacity in a manner similar to the effects of private investment in physical capital.

4. The basic idea of this so called brain-gain literature is that in very poor countries uncertainty about migration possibilities may induce individuals to invest in their education. Under certain circumstances the additional number of individuals that get educated can exceed the number of individuals that actually emigrate.

5. This feature, implied by (2), may be interpreted as capturing specialization gains and is borrowed from both new growth theory and trade theory.

6. Subscripts on functions denote partial derivatives.

7. Notable exceptions are migration flows to South Africa and the Gulf States.

8. The OECD employs measures from National Accounts, which are estimated by national statistical offices using their underlying local data based on OECD methodology and assumptions for comparability. The methodology used is the System of National Accounts 1993 (SNA 1993).

9. Expenditure on economic affairs, for instance, includes some kinds of consumptive spending. Social expenditure is mainly redistributive. Health spending is, in part, both consumptive and redistributive.

10. For instance, see Jones (2005) and Grossmann (2009) for recent discussions.

11. The level of statistical significance is determined on the basis of robust standard errors in all regressions.

12. The coefficient is even negative and significant for total public expenditure.

References

Auriol, L. 2007. Labour Market Characteristics and International Mobility of Doctorate Holders: Results for Seven Countries. Organisation for Economic Co-operation and Development (OECD) STI Working Paper 2007/2, OECD, Paris.

Beine, M., F. Docquier, and C. Ozden. 2009. Diasporas. *Journal of Development Economics*. Available online: doi:10.1016/j.jdeveco.2009.11.004.

Beine, M., F. Docquier, and H. Rapoport. 2001. Brain Drain and Economic Growth: Theory and Evidence. *Journal of Development Economics* 64: 275–89.

————. 2008. Brain Drain and Human Capital Formation in Developing Countries: Winners and Losers. *Economic Journal* 118: 631–52.

Bhagwati, J. N., and K. Hamada. 1974. The Brain Drain, International Integration of Markets for Professionals and Unemployment. *Journal of Development Economics* 1: 19–42.

Cohen-Goldner, S., and Y. Weiss. 2010. High-Skilled Russian Immigrants in the Israeli Labor Market: Adjustment and Impact. In *High-Skilled Immigration in a Global Labor Market,* ed. B. R. Chiswick, ch. 8. Washington, DC: AEI Press.

Docquier, F., and A. Marfouk. 2006. International Migration by Educational Attainment, 1990–2000, Release 1.1. In *International Migration, Remittances, and Development,* ed. C. Ozden and M. Schiff, 151–99. New York: Palgrave Macmillan.

Docquier, F., B. L. Lowell, and A. Marfouk. 2007. A Gendered Assessment of the Brain Drain. Institute for the Study of Labor (IZA) Discussion Paper no. 3235, Bonn, Germany.

Dumont, J. C., and G. Lemaître. 2005. Counting Immigrants and Expatriates in OECD Countries: A New Perspective. OECD Social Employment and Migration Working Papers no. 25, OECD, Paris.

Eckstein, Z., and Y. Weiss. 2002. The Integration of Immigrants from the Former Soviet Union in the Israeli Labor Market. In *The Israeli Economy, 1985–1998: From Government Intervention to Market Economics, Essays in Memory of Prof. Michael Bruno,* ed. A. Ben-Bassat, 349–78. Cambridge, MA: MIT Press.

Grogger, J., and G. H. Hanson. 2010. Income Maximization and the Selection and Sorting of International Migrants. *Journal of Development Economics*. Available online: doi:10.1016/j.jdeveco.2010.06.003.

Grossmann, V., 2009. Entrepreneurial Innovation and Economic Growth. *Journal of Macroeconomics* 31: 602–13.

Grossmann, V., and D. Stadelmann. 2009. Does High-Skilled Migration Affect Publicly Financed Investments? University of Fribourg, mimeo.

Heritage Foundation. 2000. *Index of Economic Freedom.* Washington, DC: Heritage Foundation. Available at www.heritage.org/index.

Heston, A., R. Summers, and B. Aten. 2006. Penn World Table Version 6.2, Center for International Comparisons of Production, Income and Prices at the University of Pennsylvania. Available through http://pwt.econ.upenn.edu.

Jones, C. I. 2005. Growth and Ideas. In *Handbook of Economic Growth,* ed. P. Aghion and S. Durlauf, chapter 16. Amsterdam: North-Holland.

Kahanec, M., and K. F. Zimmermann. 2010. High-Skilled Immigration Policy in Europe. In *High-Skilled Immigration in a Global Labor Market,* ed. B. R. Chiswick, ch. 9. Washington, DC: AEI Press.

Lowell, B. L., and P. Khadka. 2010. Trends in Foreign-Student Admissions to the United States: Policy and Comparative Effects. In *High-Skilled Immigration in a Global Labor Market,* ed. B. R. Chiswick, ch. 3. Washington, DC: AEI Press.

Mountford, A. 1997. Can a Brain Drain Be Good for Growth in the Source Economy? *Journal of Development Economics* 53: 287–303.

OECD. (various years). OECD Economic Outlook, Paris.

———. General Government Accounts Database and Population and Labor Force Statistics Database.

United Nations Statistics Division. System of National Accounts 1993. Available through http://unstats.un.org/unsd/sna1993/tocLev8.asp?L1=18&L2=1.

Usher, D. 1977. Public Property and the Effects of Migration upon Other Residents of the Migrants' Countries of Origin and Destination. *Journal of Political Economy* 85: 1001–20.

8

High-Skilled Russian Immigrants in the Israeli Labor Market: Adjustment and Impact

Sarit Cohen-Goldner and Yoram Weiss

This chapter summarizes the accumulated evidence on the integration of immigrants who arrived in Israel during the 1990s from the former Soviet Union (FSU). The mass emigration of Jews from the FSU to Israel started toward the end of 1989 after an unexpected policy change relaxed many of the emigration restrictions on FSU Jews. This sudden change, which was exogenous to labor-market conditions in Israel, precipitated one of the largest immigration inflows in Israel's history. The fact that FSU Jews did not have the option to migrate to Israel before 1989 plays a major role in our analysis because it allows us to treat the shock their arrival caused as exogenous.

The two main features of this wave are its extraordinary magnitude relative to the native population (almost 1 million immigrants over a decade versus a 1989 Israeli population of about 4.6 million [Statistical Abstract of Israel 2009]) and the immigrants' exceptionally high level of education. Those who arrived through January 1992 possessed an average of 14.5 years of schooling, and 68 percent of men and 78 percent of women had held academic and

The authors thank Eric Gould for sharing his data. The authors also thank the participants of the American Enterprise Institute conference, "High-Skilled Immigration in a Globalized Labor Market" held in Washington, D.C., in April 2009 for their helpful comments. Tali Larom provided excellent research assistance.

managerial positions before immigrating. In contrast, 69 percent of male native Israelis worked in blue-collar occupations in 1991.

The mismatch between the occupational distribution of immigrants and the local labor-market distribution of jobs created an interesting dilemma for both the immigrants and Israeli policymakers. The Israeli government tried to aid immigrants' integration by providing them a package of benefits that included a free Hebrew language course (called Ulpan) and made them eligible to participate in government-sponsored vocational-training courses. Nonetheless, the government intervened only minimally in the immigrants' occupational choices in the labor market. Ex post facto, the mismatch between immigrants' occupational distribution and the local labor market played a major role in mitigating the adverse effect on natives, since it slowed immigrants' integration into the labor market. Gradually, immigrants adapted to the Israeli labor market and became closer substitutes for Israeli workers with similar schooling and work experience. The high level of imported human capital of these immigrants and the sheer number of immigrants provide a unique opportunity to study how high-skilled immigrants became integrated in the labor market, their occupational mobility, and their impact on the native Israeli population.

The data we present in this chapter are based on several panels and cross-sectional data sets collected in Israel. The general patterns that characterize the labor-market integration of FSU immigrants are quite similar in all of the data sources that we use, and the patterns of male immigrants resemble those of female immigrants. These patterns consist of a sharp decline in the unemployment rate of immigrants accompanied by an increase during the first two to four years in a new country in the share of immigrants employed in blue-collar occupations. After a longer duration in the new country, we see that immigrants gradually move from blue-collar to white-collar occupations, and their occupations correspond more closely with immigrants' original occupations in the FSU. This process of occupational upgrading is associated with a rise in the average wage and in the variability of wages immigrants receive in Israel. The latter feature reflects gradual sorting wherein most immigrants—irrespective of their imported skills—initially worked in simple, low-wage, blue-collar jobs (for example, as cleaners, gas-station workers, cashiers, or security guards) and later found higher-wage white-collar jobs that were better suited for their education and experience.[1]

The chapter proceeds as follows: we provide details on the integration of immigrants into the Israeli labor market and we present estimates on return and out-migration among FSU immigrants and some background on noneconomic issues related to integrating FSU immigrants. Following these, we turn to the macroeconomic implications of the fact that immigrants gradually climbed the occupational scale, and finish with our conclusion.

Employment, Occupation, and Wages

We use three sources of data to describe the integration patterns of FSU immigrants during their first two decades in Israel. The first source is based on panel data that were collected from three retrospective employment surveys conducted in 1992, 1995, and 2001–2002, among immigrants who arrived as part of the initial wave, 1989–92 (hereafter referred to as the Brookdale surveys).[2] The original 1992 employment survey consists of immigrants ages twenty-five to sixty-five who resided in thirty-one different locations in Israel at the time of the first survey.[3] We used these three surveys to construct a panel of 502 female immigrants and 419 male immigrants between twenty-five and fifty-five years old at arrival and who have actively searched for a job in Israel since arriving.

In addition to the representative Brookdale surveys, the Brookdale Institute conducted a retrospective survey during 1995 among 824 men and 608 women who arrived from the FSU during 1989–94 and reported that they had an engineering diploma upon entering Israel. About 750 of these immigrants were also interviewed in 2001–2002 (hereafter referred to as the engineers' survey).[4] The final source is the national annual labor-force surveys, 1990–2007 (LFS), which are conducted by the Israeli Central Bureau of Statistics. The LFS are large, cross-sectional, annual surveys.

Using data from the Brookdale surveys, figure 8-1 shows the share of male immigrants to Israel in each of four possible labor-market states: employed in white-collar occupations, employed in blue-collar occupations, participating in government-sponsored vocational training, and unemployed (which also includes those for whom employment status is unknown), over the number of quarters the immigrants have been in Israel. The figure shows that these immigrants entered the labor market

FIGURE 8-1
**SHARE OF MALE IMMIGRANTS TO ISRAEL BY LABOR-MARKET STATE
OVER QUARTERS SINCE ARRIVAL, PANEL DATA**

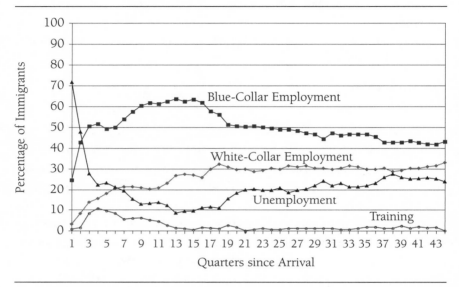

SOURCE: Brookdale surveys, conducted by the American Jewish Joint Distribution Committee (JDC)–Brookdale Institute of Gerontology and Human Development, Jerusalem, Israel, and by the Public Opinion Research of Israel survey company (PORI).
NOTE: The measure for training includes immigrants' first training only. The measure for unemployment includes respondents for whom occupations are unknown in the data set.

quickly. After one year in Israel, 22 percent of these immigrants were unemployed; by the end of two and a half years in Israel, immigrant unemployment had declined to 8 percent. In later years, however, we find a rise in unemployment, especially among older and less-educated immigrants, as we demonstrate below.

The majority of male immigrants were initially employed in blue-collar jobs. The share of immigrants employed in blue-collar jobs reached a peak of about 60 percent after two and one-half years, and started to decline after four years in Israel as immigrants moved to white-collar jobs. Figure 8-2, which presents the same information about labor-market states but for female immigrants, demonstrates that the employment trends of men and women are quite similar. The main difference between men and women is

FIGURE 8-2

SHARE OF FEMALE IMMIGRANTS TO ISRAEL BY LABOR-MARKET STATE
OVER QUARTERS SINCE ARRIVAL, PANEL DATA

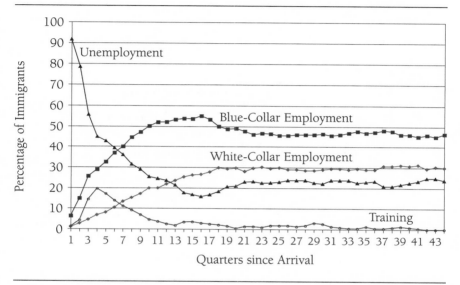

SOURCE: Brookdale surveys, conducted by the American Jewish Joint Distribution Committee (JDC)–Brookdale Institute of Gerontology and Human Development, Jerusalem, Israel, and by the Public Opinion Research of Israel survey company (PORI).
NOTE: The measure for training includes immigrants' first training only. The measure for unemployment includes respondents for whom occupations are unknown in the data set.

that unemployment declined faster for men, and women initially acquired more training.[5]

It should be noted, however, that these panel data suffer from substantive attrition. For men, the number of observations declines from 419 immigrants during their first quarter in Israel to 137 after forty quarters, and the number of observations of women declines from 502 during their first quarter to 183 after forty quarters. It is, therefore, important to compare the panel data from the Brookfield surveys to the labor-state breakdown described in the LFS. The LFS provides a good aggregate description of the labor-force distribution by occupation, industry, years since arrival, gender, and age. Figures 8-3 and 8-4 present the patterns we obtain from the cross-sectional LFS conducted 1990–2007 for male and female immigrants,

FIGURE 8-3

SHARE OF MALE IMMIGRANTS TO ISRAEL BY LABOR-MARKET STATE OVER
YEARS SINCE ARRIVAL, 1989–92 COHORTS, REPEATED CROSS-SECTION DATA

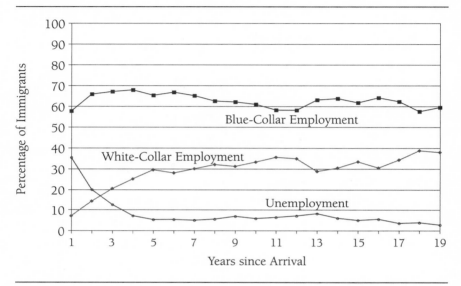

SOURCE: Labor Force Survey, conducted by the Central Bureau of Statistics and provided by the Israel
Social Science Data Center (ISDC) at the Hebrew University of Jerusalem.
NOTE: The figure displays immigrants born between the years 1944 and 1967 who immigrated to
Israel from the former Soviet Union between 1989 and 1992.

respectively, who arrived in Israel between 1989 and 1992. Because the LFS
do not include data on immigrants' participation in training programs, we
distinguish here only between three states: employment in white-collar jobs,
employment in blue-collar jobs, and unemployment.

According to the LFS, unemployment for immigrants from the fifth year
on is much lower than in the Brookdale surveys (near 10 percent versus 20
percent for both men and women). There are some differences in the definition of unemployment presented in the Brookdale surveys and the LFS.
The Brookdale panel data show only whether an immigrant was actively
searching for a job from the date of arrival. In the LFS, however, only individuals who actively searched for a job in the week prior to the survey are
considered participants in the labor force. Therefore, we excluded only

FIGURE 8-4

SHARE OF FEMALE IMMIGRANTS TO ISRAEL BY LABOR-MARKET STATE OVER
YEARS SINCE ARRIVAL, 1989–92 COHORTS, REPEATED CROSS-SECTION DATA

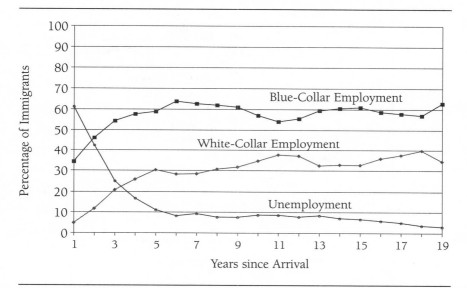

SOURCE: Labor Force Survey, conducted by the Central Bureau of Statistics and provided by the Israel
Social Science Data Center (ISDC) at the Hebrew University of Jerusalem.
NOTE: The figure displays immigrants born between the years 1944 and 1967 who immigrated to
Israel from the former Soviet Union betweem 1989 and 1992.

those immigrants who had not looked for a job since their arrival in Israel
from figures 8-1 and 8-2. It is likely, however, that some immigrants did not
search continuously since arrival, so, while we treated them in the panel
data as unemployed, they actually should have been considered as outside
the labor force.

Overall, the patterns observed from the Brookdale survey data are quite
similar to those observed from the LFS. In both data samples, men initially
found jobs more quickly than women, while in the long run the pattern of
integration for female immigrants is quite similar to that for male immigrants. The gradual transition from blue- to white-collar jobs is also found
in both samples and for both men and women with the distinction that the
LFS data show this trend persisting throughout the first decade immigrants
are in Israel, while in the Brookdale surveys the trend appears to stop after

FIGURE 8-5

UNEMPLOYMENT RATE OF MALE IMMIGRANTS TO ISRAEL AGES
TWENTY-FIVE TO FORTY YEARS UPON ARRIVAL OVER QUARTERS SINCE ARRIVAL

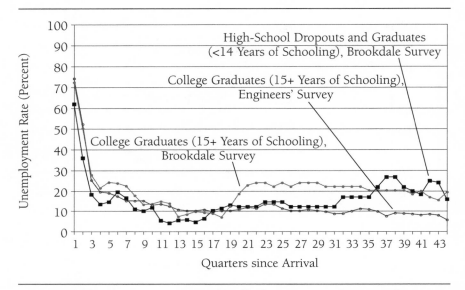

SOURCE: Brookdale and engineers' surveys, conducted by the American Jewish Joint Distribution Committee (JDC)–Brookdale Institute of Gerontology and Human Development, Jerusalem, Israel, and by the Public Opinion Research of Israel survey company (PORI).

five years in Israel. The long-run integration patterns obtained from the LFS suggest that even after nineteen years in Israel, the majority of FSU immigrants are still employed in blue-collar jobs and unemployment drops to less than 3 percent among both males and females. Thus, the LFS patterns depicted for long-run integration are quite similar to the LFS patterns for short-run integration.

In figures 8-5 and 8-6, we compare the share of unemployment among male immigrants with different levels of schooling and age at arrival (those ages twenty-five to forty upon arrival are presented in figure 8-5, while figure 8-6 presents the same information for those ages forty-one to fifty-five upon arrival). We distinguish two levels of schooling: those with zero to fourteen years of schooling, and those with fifteen or more years of education. All of the shares we present are based on the

FIGURE 8-6

UNEMPLOYMENT RATE OF MALE IMMIGRANTS TO ISRAEL AGES FORTY-ONE
TO FIFTY-FIVE YEARS UPON ARRIVAL OVER QUARTERS SINCE ARRIVAL

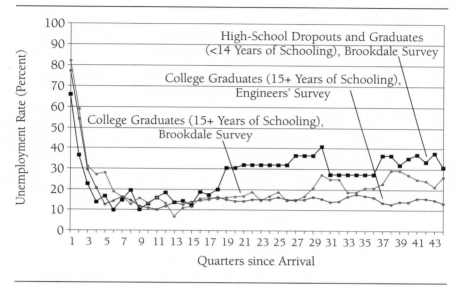

SOURCE: Brookdale and engineers' surveys, conducted by the American Jewish Joint Distribution Committee (JDC)–Brookdale Institute of Gerontology and Human Development, Jerusalem, Israel, and by the Public Opinion Research of Israel survey company (PORI).

Brookdale surveys; for immigrants who are college graduates, we also present the share of white-collar workers from the engineers' survey. The corresponding figures for females are presented in figure 8-7 for female immigrants who were between the ages of twenty-five and forty at arrival and in figure 8-8 for female immigrants who were between the ages of forty-one and fifty-five at arrival.

As seen in these figures, differences in unemployment are more pronounced according to age at arrival in Israel than according to years of schooling. In particular, older immigrants are more likely to be unemployed (about 30 percent after ten years in Israel for males and females who were forty-one to fifty-five years old upon arrival versus approximately 20 percent for males and females who were twenty-five to forty years old upon arrival).

FIGURE 8-7

UNEMPLOYMENT RATE OF FEMALE IMMIGRANTS TO ISRAEL AGES
TWENTY-FIVE TO FORTY YEARS UPON ARRIVAL OVER QUARTERS SINCE ARRIVAL

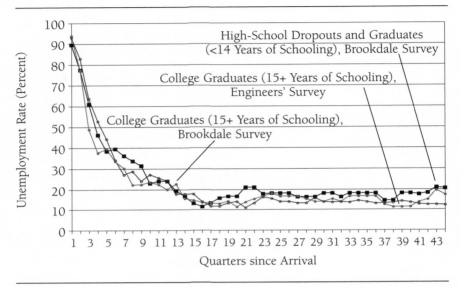

SOURCE: Brookdale and engineers' surveys, conducted by the American Jewish Joint Distribution Committee (JDC)–Brookdale Institute of Gerontology and Human Development, Jerusalem, Israel, and by the Public Opinion Research of Israel survey company (PORI).

Figures 8-9 and 8-10 present the share of workers in white-collar jobs for males ages twenty-five to forty upon arrival and males ages forty-one to fifty-five upon arrival, respectively. The corresponding figures for females are presented in figures 8-11 (ages twenty-five to forty upon arrival) and 8-12 (ages forty-one to fifty-five upon arrival).

Figure 8-9 shows that the share of white-collar workers among immigrants with zero to fourteen years of schooling ranges between 6 and 20 percent and does not have a monotonic trend over time. Among college graduates, however, the share of white-collar workers increases with time spent in Israel; most of the increase occurs during the first five years. Approximately 60 percent of male immigrants who are college graduates hold white-collar jobs after five years in Israel, and this percentage remains essentially unchanged over the next five years. The share of white-collar

FIGURE 8-8

UNEMPLOYMENT RATE OF FEMALE IMMIGRANTS TO ISRAEL AGES FORTY-ONE
TO FIFTY-FIVE YEARS UPON ARRIVAL OVER QUARTERS SINCE ARRIVAL

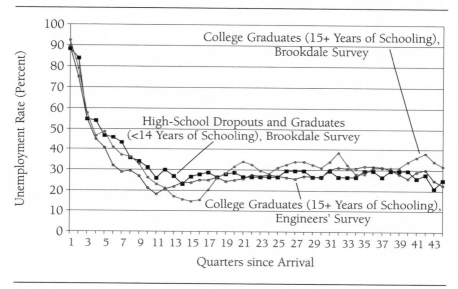

SOURCE: Brookdale and engineers' surveys, conducted by the American Jewish Joint Distribution Committee (JDC)–Brookdale Institute of Gerontology and Human Development, Jerusalem, Israel, and by the Public Opinion Research of Israel survey company (PORI).

workers among male engineers, provided they have fifteen or more years of schooling, is eventually 15 percent higher than the share of white-collar workers among the general population of male immigrants. A comparison between figures 8-9 and 8-10 demonstrates that the share of white-collar workers among male college graduates (fifteen or more years of schooling) is almost the same for the two age groups, but a significantly lower percentage of male engineers who arrived when they were older are in white-collar occupations compared to the percentage for male engineers who arrived when they were younger.

For females, we observe similar trends, but in this case, the difference between immigrants within the same schooling group who arrived when they were younger and those who arrived when they were older is more pronounced. After five years in Israel, the share of white-collar workers

FIGURE 8-9

PERCENTAGE OF WORKING IMMIGRANTS TO ISRAEL IN WHITE-COLLAR JOBS BY YEARS OF SCHOOLING, MALES AGES TWENTY-FIVE TO FORTY YEARS UPON ARRIVAL OVER QUARTERS SINCE ARRIVAL

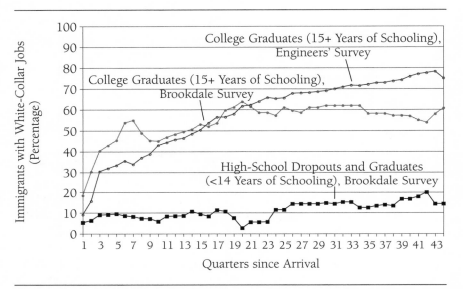

SOURCE: Brookdale and engineers' surveys, conducted by the American Jewish Joint Distribution Committee (JDC)–Brookdale Institute of Gerontology and Human Development, Jerusalem, Israel, and by the Public Opinion Research of Israel survey company (PORI).

NOTE: Percentage is out of the total number of working immigrants in each quarter.

among female college graduates whose age at arrival was between twenty-five and forty is about 1.8 times higher than the share among female college graduates whose age at arrival was between forty-one and fifty-five. In addition, after ten years in Israel, the share of white-collar workers among female engineers with fifteen or more years of schooling whose ages at arrival were between twenty-five and forty is substantially higher than the share among the general population of FSU female immigrants in the same age and schooling categories (75 percent versus 60 percent, respectively). Among female immigrants who were in the older age group upon arrival, the share of female engineers in white-collar jobs is similar to the share of white-collar occupations among the general population of female college graduates. In

FIGURE 8-10

PERCENTAGE OF WORKING IMMIGRANTS TO ISRAEL IN WHITE-COLLAR JOBS BY YEARS OF SCHOOLING, MALES AGES FORTY-ONE TO FIFTY-FIVE YEARS UPON ARRIVAL OVER QUARTERS SINCE ARRIVAL

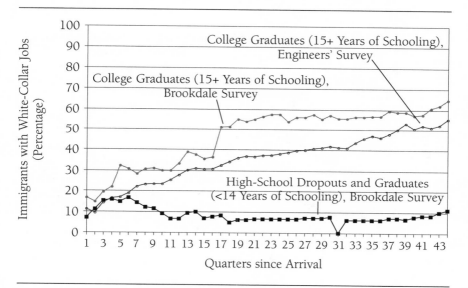

SOURCE: Brookdale and engineers' surveys, conducted by the American Jewish Joint Distribution Committee (JDC)–Brookdale Institute of Gerontology and Human Development, Jerusalem, Israel, and by the Public Opinion Research of Israel survey company (PORI).

NOTE: Percentage is out of the total number of working immigrants in each quarter.

general, female engineers are less likely to have white-collar jobs than male engineers in the same age group.

It should be noted that the imported human capital of female FSU immigrants is very similar to that of male immigrants. On average, female immigrants have the same amount of education as male immigrants, and the share of female immigrants who were employed in the FSU in white-collar jobs is almost identical to that of males. Thus, the poorer adjustment of female immigrants, in terms of the quality of employment (that is, occupation), cannot be attributed to gender differences in the occupational structure in the FSU. In addition, a greater share of female immigrants participated in the Israeli government–sponsored vocational-training

FIGURE 8-11

PERCENTAGE OF WORKING IMMIGRANTS TO ISRAEL IN WHITE-COLLAR
JOBS BY YEARS OF SCHOOLING, FEMALES AGES TWENTY-FIVE TO FORTY
YEARS UPON ARRIVAL OVER QUARTERS SINCE ARRIVAL

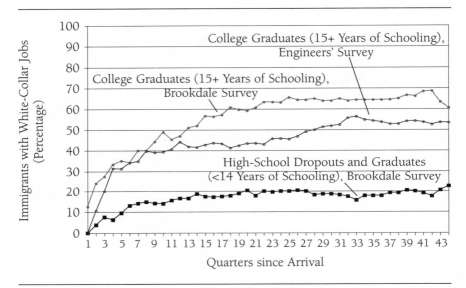

SOURCE: Brookdale and engineers' surveys, conducted by the American Jewish Joint Distribution Committee (JDC)–Brookdale Institute of Gerontology and Human Development, Jerusalem, Israel, and by
the Public Opinion Research of Israel survey company (PORI).
NOTE: Percentage is out of the total number of working immigrants in each quarter.

programs than male immigrants. Thus, there is also no evidence for the so-
called family-investment model among FSU immigrants, in which the wife
is expected to work in the destination country in order to finance the
investment of her husband in local human capital and therefore forgoes her
own investment.[6]

The general pattern that we observe from the panel and the cross-
sectional data implies that FSU immigrants entered the Israeli labor force
quickly and were willing to accept jobs in blue-collar, low-wage occupations. Following this initial phase is a second phase in which the highly educated immigrants upgrade their positions over time by finding better jobs in
white-collar occupations. This second phase is a slow and gradual process.

FIGURE 8-12

PERCENTAGE OF WORKING IMMIGRANTS TO ISRAEL IN WHITE-COLLAR JOBS BY YEARS OF SCHOOLING, FEMALES AGES FORTY-ONE TO FIFTY-FIVE YEARS UPON ARRIVAL OVER QUARTERS SINCE ARRIVAL

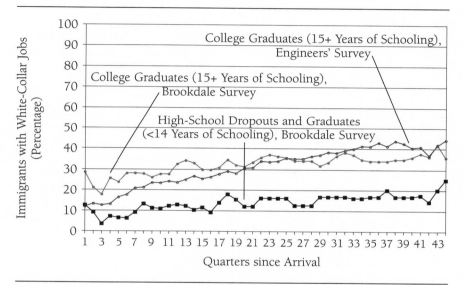

SOURCE: Brookdale and engineers' surveys, conducted by the American Jewish Joint Distribution Committee (JDC)–Brookdale Institute of Gerontology and Human Development, Jerusalem, Israel, and by the Public Opinion Research of Israel survey company (PORI).
NOTE: Percentage is out of the total number of working immigrants in each quarter.

We should mention that immigrants' initially low wages reflect this process; immigrants initially earn about half of the wages of comparable natives, but this is followed by a sharp increase in wages as immigrants spend more time in Israel. This gradual process is also consistent with the surprising finding that the adverse effect of the mass migration from the FSU on native Israelis was only temporary and minor.[7] Chiswick and Miller (chapter 4 of this volume) also find a mismatch between educational attainment and occupation among male immigrants to the United States. Similar to the patterns we observe for FSU immigrants to Israel, Chiswick and Miller find that, with the exception of immigrants in the 1990s, the extent of overeducation declines with duration in the United States, as high-skilled immigrants obtain jobs commensurate with their educational level.

FIGURE 8-13

LOG HOURLY WAGES BY YEARS OF SCHOOLING OVER TIME, NATIVE AND IMMIGRANT MALES AGES TWENTY-FIVE TO FORTY YEARS IN 1990–91

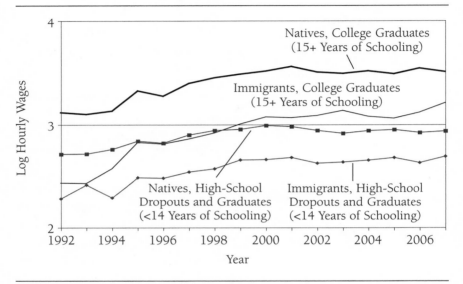

SOURCE: Income Survey, conducted by the Central Bureau of Statistics and provided by the Israel Social Science Data Center (ISDC) at the Hebrew University of Jerusalem.
NOTES: Immigrants are those who immigrated to Israel from the former Soviet Union, 1990–91. Natives include those born in Israel and those who immigrated to Israel prior to or during 1989. Wages are expressed in constant 1992 prices. The figure displays individuals born between the years 1950 and 1966, who were between twenty-five and forty years old in 1990–91.

We now turn to present the wage patterns of FSU immigrants associated with the occupational-transition process described above. Upon arrival, when most of the immigrants work in low-wage, low-skill jobs, we observe low average wages for immigrants and a low variability of wages across immigrants with different levels of schooling and experience acquired in the FSU. However, as immigrants' time spent in Israel increases, the subsequent process of occupational upgrading is associated with increases in both the average wage and the variability of wages. The basic reason for these two outcomes is that eventually immigrants are matched with jobs that suit their imported skills.

Figures 8-13 and 8-14 present the log hourly wage profiles from 1992 to 2007 for male and female immigrants, respectively, who arrived between

FIGURE 8-14

LOG HOURLY WAGES BY YEARS OF SCHOOLING OVER TIME, NATIVE AND IMMIGRANT FEMALES AGES TWENTY-FIVE TO FORTY YEARS IN 1990–91

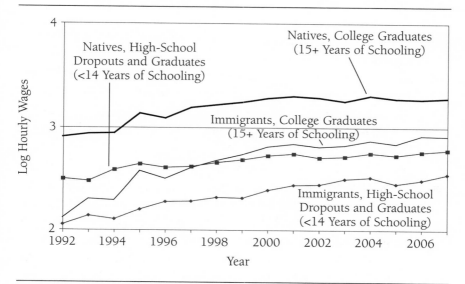

SOURCE: Income Survey, conducted by the Central Bureau of Statistics and provided by the Israel Social Science Data Center (ISDC) at the Hebrew University of Jerusalem.

NOTES: Immigrants are those who immigrated to Israel from the former Soviet Union, 1990–91. Natives include those born in Israel and those who immigrated to Israel prior to or during 1989. Wages are expressed in constant 1992 prices. The figure displays individuals born between the years 1950 and 1966, who were between twenty-five and forty years old in 1990–91.

1990 and 1991 and were between ages twenty-five and forty years upon arrival compared to the log hourly wage profiles for comparable Israeli workers who were between twenty-five and forty years old in 1990–91. The data are divided into two schooling groups: zero to fourteen and fifteen or more years of schooling.

As the figures show, wages for both female and male immigrants who arrived 1990–91 grew quickly in the initial years after arrival. This growth is more pronounced among the highly educated male and female immigrants; their wage growth also exceeds the wage growth of educated Israeli natives. For less-educated immigrants, wage growth is moderate and more similar to that of natives who did not graduate from college. These patterns continue until about 2001, after which time the wages of natives and immigrants stabilize along with the occupational profile for immigrants (see figures 8-3 and 8-4). The data show that after seventeen years in Israel, immigrants' wages still fall short of those of comparable natives: they are short by about 30 percent for highly educated men and women and by about 25 percent for less-educated men and women.[8]

Figures 8-15 and 8-16 present the variance of the log hourly wages of males and females, respectively, who arrived between 1990 and 1991 and were between twenty-five and forty years old upon arrival compared to the log hourly wage profiles for comparable Israeli workers between twenty-five and forty years old in 1990–91. Again, the data are divided into two schooling groups: zero to fourteen and fifteen or more years of schooling. These figures show that the variation of immigrants' log hourly wages grows with education and that for immigrants with fifteen or more years of schooling, it increases with time spent in Israel. As the figures show, the wage variability rises among highly educated immigrants by more than among highly educated Israelis and by substantially more than among less-educated immigrants. In particular, the variation in log hourly wages among native Israelis is almost independent from years of schooling, while the variance increases with years of schooling for immigrants. Finally, the variability among educated male immigrants converges to that among educated native Israeli males, while the variation of log hourly wages for educated female immigrants exceeds the variability of log hourly wages for comparable native females. Eckstein and Weiss (2004) report a similar finding of convergence in the residual log hourly wage distributions for male immigrants and native Israelis.

The observed wage patterns for immigrants suggest that inequality among immigrants increased due to both price and quantity effects. The price effect reflects the increase in the return to imported education and experience for FSU immigrants as time spent in Israel increased, while the quantity effect reflects the growing heterogeneity among immigrants with respect to their investment in local skills. In this manner, immigrants contributed to the overall rise in wage inequality in Israel.

The occupational downgrading immigrants experienced implies a loss for society and the immigrants. Weiss, Sauer, and Gotlibovski (2003) formulate and estimate a dynamic discrete-choice model to provide a deeper

FIGURE 8-15

VARIANCE OF LOG HOURLY WAGES BY YEARS OF SCHOOLING
OVER TIME, NATIVE AND IMMIGRANT MALES AGES TWENTY-FIVE
TO FORTY YEARS IN 1990–91

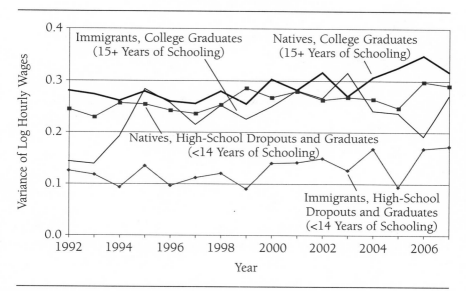

SOURCE: Income Survey, conducted by the Central Bureau of Statistics and provided by the Israel Social Science Data Center (ISDC) at the Hebrew University of Jerusalem.
NOTES: Immigrants are those who immigrated to Israel from the former Soviet Union, 1990–91. Natives include those born in Israel and those who immigrated to Israel prior to or during 1989. Wages are expressed in constant 1992 prices. The figure displays individuals born between the years 1950 and 1966, who were between twenty-five and forty years old in 1990–91.

analysis of the potential expected lifetime-earning loss for immigrants due to the potential that their imported skills will only partially adjust to the new country. The model is able to fit the main phenomena of immigrants' occupational and employment transitions. It finds that immigrants can expect lifetime earnings to fall short of the lifetime earnings of comparable Israelis by 57 percent, in which 14 percent reflects frictions associated with unemployment and job-distribution mismatches and 43 percent reflects the gradual adaptation of imported schooling and experience to the local labor market. The gap between immigrants and natives in terms of present value is larger than in terms of wages after twenty years, which reflects the loss in wages during the early phase of the integration process.

FIGURE 8-16

VARIANCE OF LOG HOURLY WAGES BY YEARS OF SCHOOLING
OVER TIME, NATIVE AND IMMIGRANT FEMALES AGES TWENTY-FIVE
TO FORTY YEARS IN 1990–91

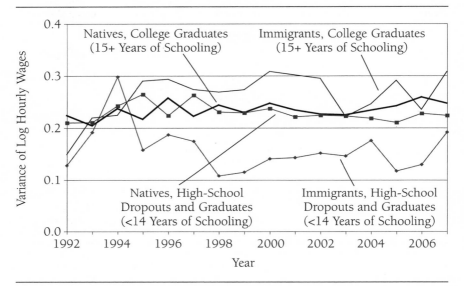

SOURCE: Income Survey, conducted by the Central Bureau of Statistics and provided by the Israel Social Science Data Center (ISDC) at the Hebrew University of Jerusalem.
NOTES: Immigrants are those who immigrated to Israel from the former Soviet Union, 1990–91. Natives include those born in Israel and those who immigrated to Israel prior to or during 1989. Wages are expressed in constant 1992 prices. The figure displays individuals born between the years 1950 and 1966, who were between twenty-five and forty years old in 1990–91.

Return Migration and Out-Migration

Immigration from the FSU in the initial wave (1989–91) occurred suddenly, and immigrants' arrival in Israel was exogenous to Israel's economic conditions. At the time, emigrants from the FSU had limited options to move immediately and in mass to other countries; as Israel was the only country without any visa restrictions or eligibility constraints for welfare payments, it received a large number of these emigrants. It is, therefore, interesting to examine whether Israel served as a temporary or long-term destination for these immigrants. Table 8-1 presents the survival rates as of 2004 of FSU immigrants who arrived during 1990–91, and who were in Israel in 1995

TABLE 8-1

SURVIVAL RATES AS OF 2004 OF FSU IMMIGRANTS WHO ARRIVED
IN ISRAEL, 1990–91, AND WHO WERE IN ISRAEL IN 1995

Age at Arrival (Years)	High School Dropouts	High School Graduates	College Graduates	Advanced Academic Degree Holders
		Males		
16–25	93.68% (0.71%)	91.72% (0.68%)	89.97% (1.54%)	88.14% (2.11%)
26–35	96.08% (0.65%)	93.82% (0.72%)	94.37% (1.02%)	91.88% (0.68%)
36–45	97.98% (0.44%)	96.98% (0.53%)	96.54% (0.73%)	96.2% (0.44%)
		Females		
16–25	94.38% (0.75%)	93.43% (0.61%)	91.03% (1.25%)	88.78% (1.56%)
26–35	95.93% (0.66%)	95.93% (0.51%)	95.33% (0.77%)	93.45% (0.56%)
36–45	97.83% (0.47%)	98.00% (0.37%)	97.47% (0.53%)	97.06% (0.36%)

SOURCE: Calculations of Eric Gould. For data descriptions see E. D. Gould and O. Moav, "When is 'Too Much' Inequality Not Enough? The Selection of Israeli Emigrants," 2008, available at http://ssrn.com/abstract=1146123.
NOTES: Survivors are defined as immigrants who were in Israel in 1995 and had not left the country for a full year or more as of 2004. Standard errors are in parentheses.

(survivors are defined as immigrants who had not left the country for a full year or more as of 2004). These figures are based on the data used by Gould and Moav (2008). We present the survival rates for males (the upper panel of the table) and females (the lower panel) by years of schooling and age at arrival (sixteen to forty-five years old).

The survival rates are very high and, conditional on age at arrival and schooling, very similar for both genders. However, the table suggests that immigrants who arrived when they were younger were more likely to leave the country than those who arrived in the older age ranges, and that within the age groups sixteen to twenty-five years and twenty-six to thirty-five years, immigrants with higher levels of education were more likely to emigrate from Israel than other immigrants. For example, the 93.7 percent of male immigrants who dropped out of high school and were sixteen to

TABLE 8-2
AVERAGE YEARS OF SCHOOLING OF FSU IMMIGRANTS WHO ARRIVED
IN 1990–91, BY THOSE REMAINING IN ISRAEL AS OF 2004 AND THOSE
WHO HAD EMIGRATED FROM ISRAEL AS OF 2004

Age at Arrival	Remaining	Emigrated	Remaining	Emigrated
	Males		Females	
16–25	12.26 (0.04)	12.71 (0.14)	12.75 (0.04)	13.40 (0.15)
26–35	13.77 (0.05)	14.44 (0.15)	13.94 (0.04)	14.32 (0.15)
36–45	14.04 (0.05)	14.53 (0.27)	14.14 (0.04)	14.43 (0.22)

SOURCE: Calculations of Eric Gould. For data descriptions see E. D. Gould and O. Moav, "When is 'Too Much' Inequality Not Enough? The Selection of Israeli Emigrants," 2008, available at http://ssrn.com/abstract=1146123.
NOTES: Remaining indicates immigrants who were is Israel in 1995 and had not left the country for a full year or more as of 2004. Standard errors are in parentheses.

twenty-five years old upon arrival in Israel remained in Israel until 2004, while only 88.1 percent of immigrants who arrived at that age level and hold advanced academic degrees remained in Israel until 2004. Immigrants aged twenty-six to thirty-five years upon arrival have survival rates of 96.1 percent and 91.9 percent for high school dropouts and advanced degree holders, respectively. The observation that, within age groups, those who do leave tend to be more educated is confirmed in table 8-2, which presents the average years of schooling for those who stay and for those who emigrate by age group. The emigrants have between 0.3 and 0.67 more years of schooling than those who remain, and these differences are statistically significant for the age groups sixteen to twenty-five years and twenty-six to thirty-five years for both males and females. Thus, the share of white-collar workers after ten years in Israel that we present in figures 8-5, 8-6, 8-7, and 8-8 underestimate the true share of white-collar occupations among immigrants who arrived between 1989 and 1992. In addition, this pattern of return migration mitigates the rise in the variance of the wages for immigrants who remain in Israel.

The differences in emigration rates are consistent with the idea that highly educated individuals receive a higher wage gain from moving abroad than less educated individuals. There are noneconomic considerations related to the general satisfaction of life in Israel, however, including

TABLE 8-3

CONCENTRATION OF FSU IMMIGRANTS WHO ARRIVED 1989–2000,
BY LOCALITY, 2000

Locality	Number of FSU Immigrants in Locality	Total Population of Locality	FSU Immigrant Percentage of Population
Jerusalem	32,234	717,637	4.49%
Tel-Aviv-Jaffa	41,792	437,556	9.55%
Haifa	61,556	299,524	20.55%
Rishon l'Zion	34,192	215,474	15.87%
Ashdod	55,090	187,568	29.37%
Holon	26,644	185,952	14.33%
Beer-Sheva	49,029	184,936	26.51%
Natanya	37,667	183,267	20.55%
Petach Tikva	32,153	181,948	17.67%
Bat-Yam	40,422	160,643	25.16%
Bnei-Brak	6,518	143,491	4.54%
Ramat-Gan	11,445	141,713	8.08%
Ashkelon	31,277	107,826	29.01%
Rechovot	14,561	106,182	13.71%
Herzelia	6,654	93,980	7.08%
Kfar-Sava	7,974	81,399	9.80%
Haddera	19,537	78,326	24.94%
Lod	15,983	72,004	22.20%
Kiryat-Gat	15,113	51,610	29.28%
Nazareth Ilit	21,685	50,951	42.56%

SOURCE: Population Registry, Ministry of the Interior.

considerations such as social status, quality of education, and culture. These considerations are probably more important for the highly educated than for less-educated individuals. In addition, FSU immigrants tend to live in enclaves such that, in some middle-size cities (Ashdod and Nazareth Ilit, for example), their share of the total population in the locality reached 30–40 percent in 2000 (see table 8-3). This concentration and the total number of FSU immigrants enabled them to maintain their language and culture (including the availability of newspapers, television, and theaters in Russian), easily create social networks, and feel more at home.[9] It should be noted that immigrants initially settled in large cities and only later moved to the enclaves across the country, trading job opportunities for lower housing costs and better social amenities (Bucshinsky and Gotlibovski 2008). In this regard, the policy of the Israeli government that allowed immigrants a free choice of location contributed to the overall high survival rate of immigrants in Israel.

The sociologist Larissa Remennik (2005) studied some of the noneconomic integration issues of FSU immigrants extensively. Among other things, she found that women had fewer concerns about a loss of occupational status in Israel than men. These findings are consistent with the relatively higher survival rates among highly educated women in prime age groups upon arrival, presented above.[10]

Macroeconomic Aspects of Immigration

We now turn to summarize the aggregate time-series evidence of the link between immigration, economic growth, employment, and wages. The common belief is that the increase in labor supply leads to a decline in natives' wages and in GDP per capita and to a rise in unemployment, all of which would negatively affect the native population, at least in the short run. However, there is a debate in the literature concerning the magnitude of these effects (see Borjas 2003; Card 2001). Israel provides an interesting case study for exploring the correlation between population growth and economic growth since it was built on large waves of immigrants, most of which were exogenous.

Table 8-4 extends some of the early work in Ben-Porath (1986) and shows that gross national product (GNP) per capita has increased in every period, including periods for which the population growth rate was especially high. A positive correlation between immigration and GNP per capita, consumption per capita, and capital growth was present in the earlier immigration waves to Israel (as indicated by Ben-Porath 1986) and persisted during the immigration wave to Israel from the FSU in the 1990s (Eckstein and Weiss 2002). We shall focus here primarily on how immigration from the FSU during the 1990s affected the wages and employment of native Israelis.

Several papers have analyzed how this immigration wave affected natives' labor-market outcomes. All of these papers found that despite the

TABLE 8-4
ANNUAL GROWTH RATES OF POPULATION, PRODUCTION,
AND CAPITAL, ISRAEL, 1922–2001

Year	Population	GNP	GNP per Capita	Capital Stock	Consumption per Capita	Immigration Rate
1922–1932	8.0%	17.6%	7.8%	13.7%		8.2%
1932–1947	8.4%	11.2%	0.3%	9.8%		6.4%
1947–1950	31.9%	11.2%	0.3%	9.8%		19.8%
1950–1951	20.0%	29.7%	10.0%			13.2%
1951–1964	4.0%	9.1%	4.9%	12.3%	12.8%	2.2%
1964–1972	3.0%	8.9%	5.5%	8.4%	8.7%	1.3%
1972–1982	2.1%	3.2%	0.8%	6.7%	6.1%	0.0%
1982–1989	1.4%	3.6%	1.9%	3.2%	2.5%	0.5%
1982–1986	1.4%	3.3%	1.7%	3.4%	2.4%	0.5%
1986–1989	1.4%	4.0%	2.3%	2.9%	2.7%	0.6%
1989–1997	2.9%	5.4%	2.2%	5.5%	3.2%	2.6%
1989–1993	3.8%	5.7%	1.9%	3.6%	2.7%	3.6%
1993–1997	2.1%	5.0%	2.4%	7.4%	3.8%	2.1%
1993–2001	1.9%	4.2%	1.7%	7.0%	2.3%	1.7%
1995–2001	1.7%	3.1%	0.6%	7.0%	1.2%	1.6%
1997–2001	1.7%	2.7%	0.3%	6.5%	0.9%	1.6%
1989–2001	2.5%	4.8%	1.8%	5.9%	2.5%	2.2%

SOURCE: Z. Eckstein and Y. Weiss, "The Integration of Immigrants from the Former Soviet Union in the Israeli Labor Market," in *The Israeli Economy, 1985–1998: From Government Intervention to Market Economics, Essays in Memory of Professor Michael Bruno,* ed. Avi Ben-Bassat (Cambridge, MA, Massachusetts Institute of Technology Press, 2002), 349–77.
NOTE: Blank cells indicate missing data.

extraordinary size of the influx of immigrants and the high level of skills that characterized them, these immigrants had only a slight and transitory effect on native workers. For example, Friedberg (2001) found that the relative growth rate in wages of native Israelis in occupations that absorbed large numbers of FSU immigrants fell from 1989 to 1994. However, since the occupational choices of immigrants in Israel are endogenous, Friedberg uses the occupational distribution of FSU Jews prior to immigration as an instrumental variable for the current occupational choice in Israel and finds little evidence of occupational wage pressures on native Israelis.

Gandal, Hanson, and Slaughter (2004) examined two possible open-economy mechanisms through which the increase in labor supply caused by the arrival of FSU immigrants was absorbed: the adoption of global skill-biased technological change, and changes in the mix of traded goods produced in Israel. They argue that an increase in the rate of skill-biased technological change swamped any negative effect the FSU immigrants may have had on the skill premium in Israel.

Cohen-Goldner and Paserman (2004) used repeated cross-sectional LFS data to estimate the impact of FSU immigrants on natives' employment and wages in a segmented labor market for which segments are defined by various combinations of occupation and skills. Controlling for the selection of immigrants into different labor-market segments, they find that immigration had a short-run adverse impact on the wages of both men and women that died out five to seven years after the immigration wave. Furthermore, they find that most of the adverse effect in the short run comes from the effect of immigrants on low-skilled, blue-collar native workers. These findings are consistent with the notion that immigrants are close substitutes to low-skilled natives in the short run and depress their wages, but the effect is diffused in the longer run as the labor market adjusts.

Overall, the aforementioned papers found that the adverse effect of FSU immigrants on the labor-market outcomes of native Israelis was relatively small and transitory, while the immigrants experienced positive wage growth during that period. We explain the small initial affect on natives' wages and employment first by the fact that it took time for immigrants to find higher level jobs that better corresponded to their occupations in their country of origin and, second, by the combination of capital flows into Israel and the entry of workers such that the effective capital-labor ratio remained almost constant during the initial wave. Hence, under a standard, constant return to scale aggregate production function, a constant capital-labor ratio would imply constant wages.

Figure 8-17 presents data on the actual and adjusted capital-labor ratio in Israel during the period 1990–2000. As expected, the unadjusted capital-labor ratio in Israel declined during 1990–1994. However, the standard measure of the capital-to-labor ratio implicitly assumes that immigrants are perfect substitutes for natives in production, which contrasts with the observation that in the short run immigrants earned sufficiently lower wages than comparable natives (see figures 8-13 and 8-14). Thus, the capital-labor ratio, as it is usually measured, underestimates the "true" capital-labor ratio. To account for these potential differences between natives and immigrants, we compute the adjusted capital-labor ratio. Here, we measure labor in

FIGURE 8-17
**ADJUSTED AND UNADJUSTED CAPITAL-TO-LABOR RATIO
IN ISRAEL, 1990–2000**

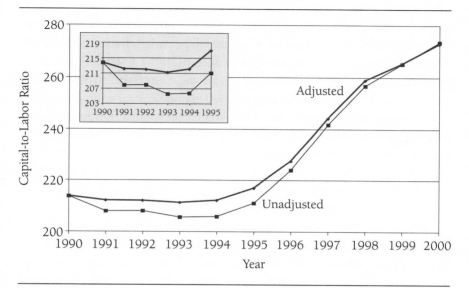

SOURCE: Z. Eckstein and Y. Weiss, "The Integration of Immigrants from the Former Soviet Union in the Israeli Labor Market," in *The Israeli Economy, 1985–1998: From Government Intervention to Market Economics, Essays in Memory of Professor Michael Bruno,* ed. Avi Ben-Bassat (Cambridge, MA: Massachusetts Institute of Technology Press, 2002), 349–77.
NOTE: Both ratios assume no immigrants to Israel in 1990.

efficiency units, assuming that relative wages of immigrants at different points in time (measured by their length of stay in Israel) reflect relative productivity. Making this adjustment, we see that the adjusted capital-labor ratio declined only slightly during 1990–93 and has subsequently risen.[11]

With constant returns to scale for technology and competitive conditions, a constant adjusted capital-labor ratio implies that growth in inputs has no effect on wages. The only sources for growth in average wages are changes in quality—which reflect shifts in the composition of the labor force toward more productive workers—and growth in total-factor productivity. Among immigrants, we find that there was a 20 percent increase in quality during the period 1990–1995, compared with only a 2 percent increase among native Israelis. In this respect, the aggregate data, when properly interpreted, are consistent with a stable average wage for native workers and a rising average wage for immigrants. As seen in figure 8-17, the adjusted and unadjusted capital-labor ratios are almost identical by 1999. This convergence reflects the increased quality of immigrants who came to Israel in the early 1990s and the declining number of new immigrants from the mid-1990s. In addition, it provides evidence about the massive investment in capital during the influx of FSU immigrants to Israel. Unfortunately, we do not have detailed data regarding the composition of investment (in other words, we cannot compare local and foreign investment or private and public investment), but there is evidence that the government invested heavily in Israel (mainly in housing) in the early 1990s and that foreign investment also increased during the early- to mid-1990s.[12]

Conclusion

This chapter provided a descriptive summary of the Israeli experience in absorbing a large wave of high-skilled immigrants that arrived in Israel during the early 1990s from the FSU. These high-skilled immigrants found jobs in Israel rather quickly, but they experienced a substantial occupational downgrading upon their arrival and earned significantly less than otherwise comparable Israeli natives.[13] In this regard, the immigrants were unable to transfer their imported skills to their new country immediately. With time spent in Israel, some of the more educated and younger immigrants were able to find jobs that better matched their skills, and they experienced growth in wages. However, this process was slow and gradual and took place mainly during the first years after arrival. After a decade in Israel, we do not see any substantial changes in the labor-market integration of immigrants. The relatively long process of adjustment for highly educated workers reflects three basic characteristics of the 1989–90 immigration wave:

1. The immigrants did not prepare themselves for the Israeli labor market while in the FSU and had to make substantial occupational adjustments upon arrival in Israel.

2. Although highly educated, immigrants from the FSU were quite heterogeneous in terms of their quality of schooling, work experience, and exposure to modern Western technology. Thus, Israeli employers were uncertain and often prejudiced about immigrants' skills.

3. The size of the immigration wave, combined with its unexpected nature, dictated a relatively complex process of matching skills with occupations in the labor market.

The flip side of the gradual matching process was that, despite their high level of schooling, immigrants from the FSU had little effect on the wages or employment of native Israeli workers. Initially, these immigrants competed with less-educated Israeli workers and foreign workers, the supply of whom is relatively elastic. By the time the immigrants entered skilled jobs, the capital stock increased, mainly due to foreign investment, so we also find minor effects on wages and employment of educated native Israelis. The new investment caused expansion of the new industries, especially high-tech and medical services, which absorbed many of the immigrants.[14]

Another lesson is that although the integration process was slow, educated immigrants from the FSU were quite successful in entering the labor market and climbing the occupational ladder. This dispels some initial prejudices concerning poor work habits or the inferiority of their medical and technical education and work experience, as compared to Israelis. In fact, immigrants from the FSU responded to economic incentives in Israel and displayed high participation rates in the labor force and adapted well to work with unfamiliar advanced technologies.

Notes

1. White-collar occupations include academic, managerial, technical, and other similar occupations (codes 000–299 in the 1972 occupation classification of the Israel Central Bureau of Statistics). All other occupations are classified as blue-collar occupations.

2. The first two surveys were conducted by the American Jewish Joint Distribution Committee (JDC)–Brookdale Institute of Gerontology and Human Development, Jerusalem, Israel. The 2001–2002 survey was conducted by the Public Opinion Research of Israel survey company (PORI) under the supervision of Sarit Cohen-Goldner and Zvi Eckstein.

3. Of the 1,200 immigrants surveyed in 1992, 910 were surveyed again in 1995, and 521 were surveyed again in 2001–2002. About 413 immigrants were observed in all three successive surveys.

4. The first engineers' survey was conducted by the JDC–Brookdale Institute of Gerontology and Human Development, Jerusalem, Israel, while the 2001–2002 survey was conducted by PORI under the supervision of Sarit Cohen-Goldner and Zvi Eckstein.

5. About 30 percent of the male immigrants and 40 percent of the female immigrants in the Brookdale surveys had participated in a government-sponsored training program. Most of them participated in training during their first year in Israel. Cohen-Goldner and Eckstein (2008 and 2010) studied the employment and training-participation decisions of male and female immigrants in a discrete-choice dynamic-model framework. They find that female immigrants benefit more from training than male immigrants and that training accelerates the probability for both males and females of receiving job offers in white-collar occupations.

6. Cohen-Goldner, Gotlibovski, and Kahana (2009) test the family-investment hypothesis among FSU immigrants to Israel and reject it.

7. Weak effects of immigration on the wages of natives have also been found in the United States (see Altonji and Card 1991; Card 1990). In some professions, such as medicine, collective wage bargaining yielded substantial wage hikes for natives, despite the sharp increase in labor supply (see Sussman and Zakai 1998).

8. These gaps are somewhat larger than those predicted by Eckstein and Weiss (2002; 2004) for years outside our sample. As they did not have data on the immigrants who arrived in Israel during 1990–91 after twenty years in Israel, they used predicted occupational outcomes based on immigrants who arrived from the FSU in the 1970s and 1980s. In retrospect, we see that occupational achievements of the immigrants who came in the 1990–91 wave fall short of the achievements of those who arrived earlier. This discrepancy may reflect differences in the number of immigrants in each time period or differential time effects for immigrants and native Israeli workers.

9. Kheimets and Epstein (2001) report that most Russians believe their language and cultural heritage are superior to the Hebrew-based Israeli culture and see no reason for shunning their established cultural identity. They also find that knowledge of English is crucial for successful social and economic integration of immigrant scientists.

10. According to Remennick (2005), "Women proved to be more ready than men to trade their higher occupational status for pragmatic benefits of employment and some financial security. Driven by their responsibility for the family, women were ready at the outset to undergo occupational change in any direction that would bring a steady income. By converting to white-, pink-, or blue-collar occupations demanded on the Israeli marker, these women revealed flexibility, ability to learn rapidly, and successful social networking with their new milieu. . . . Additional social benefits women get from their greater economic activity during initial resettlement years include faster improvement of their Hebrew skills and broadening circles of informal communication with both co-ethnics and Hebrew speakers."

11. The quality adjustment of the labor aggregate is described in Eckstein and Weiss (2002). Following Jorgenson and Griliches (1967), they assume that at each level of schooling, the difference in quality between immigrants and natives is represented by the differences in their wages. Therefore, they estimate a wage regression for immigrants in order to capture the growth in their wages over time in Israel according to skill levels, and they use the estimated wage profiles to create an adjusted measure of labor input (aggregated over skill levels).

12. Grossmann and Stadelmann (chapter 7 of this volume) develop a theoretical model with human-capital externalities that predicts that countries that face inflows of skilled labor increase their public investment. Their empirical evidence for this link is based on an instrumental variable approach using data for countries that are members of the Organisation for Economic Co-operation and Development.

13. The downgrading of immigrants is not unique to the Israeli case study and was also found in Britain (Dustmann, Frattini, and Preston 2008).

14. See Cohen-Goldner (2006) for discussion on immigrants in high-tech industries and Kugler and Sauer (2005) for detailed analysis on immigrant physicians.

References

Altonji, J. G., and D. Card. 1991. The Effects of Immigration on the Labor Market Outcomes of Less-Skilled Natives. In *Immigration, Trade and Labor,* ed. J. M. Abowd and R. B. Freeman. Chicago: University of Chicago Press.

Ben-Porath, Y. 1986. The Entwined Growth of Population and Product, 1922–1982. In *The Israeli Economy: Maturing through Crisis,* ed. Y. Ben-Porath. Cambridge, MA: Harvard University Press.

Borjas, G. J. 2003. The Labor Demand Curve *Is* Downward Sloping: Reexamining the Impact of Immigration on the Labor Market. *Quarterly Journal of Economics* 118 (3): 1335–74.

Brookdale Surveys. American Jewish Joint Distribution Committee (JDC)–Brookdale Institute of Gerontology and Human Development, Jerusalem, Israel, and Public Opinion Research of Israel survey company (PORI).

Buchinsky, M., and M. Gotlibovski. 2008. Residential Location, Work Location, and Labor Market Outcomes of Immigrants in Israel. Working paper.

Card, D. 1990. The Impact of the Mariel Boatlift on the Miami Labor Market. *Industrial and Labor Relations Review* 43 (1): 245–57.

———. 2001. Immigrant Inflows, Native Outflows, and the Local Labor Market Impacts of Higher Immigration. *Journal of Labor Economics* 19 (1): 22–64.

Chiswick, B. R., and P. W. Miller. 2010. Educational Mismatch: Are High-Skilled Immigrants Really Working in High-Skilled Jobs, and What Price Do They Pay if They Are Not? In *High-Skilled Immigration in a Global Labor Market,* ed. B. R. Chiswick, ch. 4. Washington, DC: AEI Press.

Cohen-Goldner, S. 2006. Immigrants in the Israeli Hi-Tech Industry: Comparison to Natives and the Effect of Training. *Research in Labor Economics* 24: 265–92.

Cohen-Goldner, S., and Z. Eckstein. 2008. Labor Mobility of Immigrants: Training, Experience, Language and Opportunities. *International Economic Review* 49 (3): 837–72.

———. 2010. Estimating the Return to Training and Occupational Experience: The Case of Female Immigrants. *Journal of Econometrics* 156 (1): 86–105.

Cohen-Goldner, S., M. Gotlibovski, and N. Kahana. 2009. A Reevaluation of the Role of Family in Immigrants' Labor Market Activity: Evidence from a Comparison of Single and Married Immigrants. Discussion Paper no. 4185, Institute for the Study of Labor (IZA), Bonn, Germany.

Cohen-Goldner, S., and M. D. Paserman. 2004. The Dynamic Impact of Immigration on Natives' Labour Market Outcomes: Evidence from Israel. Discussion Paper no. 4640, Center for Economic and Policy Research, Washington, DC.

Dustmann, C., T. Frattini, and I. Preston. 2008. The Effect of Immigration along the Distribution of Wages. Center for Research and Analysis of Migration. Discussion Paper no. 03/08, Department of Economics, University College London.

Eckstein, Z., and Y. Weiss. 2002. The Integration of Immigrants from the Former Soviet Union in the Israeli Labor Market. In *The Israeli Economy, 1985–1998: From*

Government Intervention to Market Economics, Essays in Memory of Prof. Michael Bruno, ed. A. Ben-Bassat, 349–77. Cambridge, MA: MIT Press.

———. 2004. On the Wage Growth of Immigrants: Israel 1990–2000. *Journal of the European Economic Association* 2 (4): 665–95.

Engineers' Survey. American Jewish Joint Distribution Committee (JDC)–Brookdale Institute of Gerontology and Human Development, Jerusalem, Israel, and Public Opinion Research of Israel survey company (PORI).

Friedberg, R. 2001. The Impact of Mass Migration on the Israeli Labor Market. *Quarterly Journal of Economics* 116: 1373–1408.

Gandal, N., G. H. Hanson, and M. J. Slaughter. 2004. Technology, Trade and Adjustment to Immigration in Israel. *European Economic Review* 48 (2): 403–28.

Gould, E. D., and O. Moav. 2008. When Is "Too Much" Inequality Not Enough? The Selection of Israeli Emigrants. Available at http://ssrn.com/abstract=1146123.

Grossmann, V., and D. Stadelmann. 2010. High-Skilled Immigration: The Link to Public Expenditure and Private Investments. In *High-Skilled Immigration in a Global Labor Market,* ed. B. R. Chiswick, ch. 7. Washington, DC: AEI Press.

Income Survey. Central Bureau of Statistics. Provided by the Israel Social Science Data Center (ISDC), Hebrew University of Jerusalem.

Jorgenson, D., and Z. Griliches. 1967. The Explanation of Productivity Change. *Review of Economic Studies* 34: 249–83.

Kheimets, N., and A. Epstein. 2001. English as a Central Component of Success in the Professional and Social Integration of Immigrant Scientists in Israel. *Language in Society* 30 (2): 187–215.

Kugler, A., and R. M. Sauer. 2005. Doctors without Borders: The Returns to an Occupational License for Soviet Immigrant Physicians in Israel. *Journal of Labor Economics* 23 (3): 437–66.

Labor-Force Survey. Central Bureau of Statistics. Provided by the Israel Social Science Data Center (ISDC), Hebrew University of Jerusalem.

Remennick, L. 2005. Immigration, Gender, and Psychosocial Adjustment: A Study of 150 Immigrant Couples in Israel. *Sex Roles* 53 (11–12): 847–63.

Statistical Abstract of Israel. 2009. Israel Central Bureau of Statistics, no. 60.

Sussman, Z., and D. Zakai. 1998. The Mass Immigration of Physicians and the Steep Rise in Wages of Veterans in Israel: A Paradox? *Economic Quarterly* 45: 28–63 (in Hebrew).

Weiss, Y., R. M. Sauer, and M. Gotlibovski. 2003. Immigration, Search, and Loss of Skill. *Journal of Labor Economics* 21 (3): 557–91.

9

High-Skilled Immigration
Policy in Europe

Martin Kahanec and Klaus F. Zimmermann

Europe has always been a crossroads of cultures and an intersection of countless immigration trajectories. In the postwar period, especially since the 1960s, immigration from Southern Europe, Africa, Asia, former colonies, and other parts of the world has been rising in Western Europe. The yoke of Communist regimes staunched immigration flows in Eastern Europe until the fall of the Berlin Wall, after which the difficulties of transformation drove many Eastern Europeans westward (see figures 9-1 and 9-2). In effect, noncitizen and foreign-born populations today constitute significant shares of the population in most of the old member states of the European Union (EU) and, with freedom and economic convergence, some immigration into the new member states from Central and Eastern Europe can be observed (see table 9-1).[1]

Both high- and low-skilled workers can be found among these immigrants. While in a number of member states (and also on aggregate in the

The authors thank René Böheim, Ana Rute Cardoso, Barry R. Chiswick, Carmel U. Chiswick, Jesus Fernandez-Huertas, Tommaso Frattini, Christer Gerdes, Zoltán Kántor, Karin Mayr, Javier Ortega, Panu Poutvaara, Ulf Rinne, Álmos M. Telegdy, Judit Tóth, Anna Triandafyllidou, Panos Tsakloglou, Eskil Wadensjö, Aslan Zorlu, and the participants of the AEI conference in Washington, D.C., for helpful comments. The views expressed are the authors' alone and do not necessarily correspond to those of the Institute for the Study of Labor.

FIGURE 9-1

NET IMMIGRATION TO **EU15, EU10,** AND **EU2** COUNTRIES, **1960–2005**

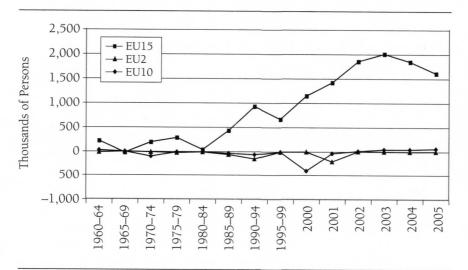

SOURCES: Eurostat, *Population Statistics* (Luxembourg: Office for Official Publications of the European Communities, 2006); and Eurostat, *Europe in Figures: Eurostat Yearbook* (Luxembourg: Office for Official Publications of the European Communities, 2008).

NOTES: Net migration is estimated as the difference between total population growth and natural increase and includes adjustments and corrections. For the periods 1960–64, 1965–69, and so forth through 1995–99, annual averages are reported. For Cyprus, starting from 1975 the numbers account for only the government-controlled area. Corrections due to the census are present for 2000–2001.

EU25 and EU10) the evidence shows that the percentage of individuals with tertiary education is highest among immigrants in several major destination countries—including France, Germany, and the Netherlands—immigrants are, on average, less educated than natives (see table 9-2). For the group of non-EU immigrants, the picture is similar: the share of high-skilled individuals in this group is somewhat lower than for immigrants in general, but it is still higher than among natives on aggregate in both the EU15 and EU25.[2]

The fact that Europe's labor markets need more skilled workers has been documented by a number of authors (see Zimmermann et al. 2007; Bauer and Kunze 2004). Looming demographic developments, such as aging populations, stalled economic growth, cash-strapped social-security systems, and the dearth of innovation potential and of skilled workforces, highlight

FIGURE 9-2

NET IMMIGRATION RATES IN SELECTED EU15 COUNTRIES, 1991–2006

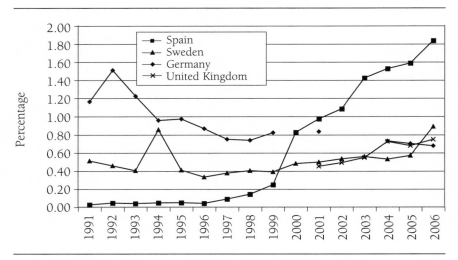

SOURCE: Eurostat, Online Database for Population and Social Conditions, Population, International Migration and Asylum, International Migration Flows, last updated July 4, 2010, available through http://epp.eurostat.ec.europa.eu/portal/page/portal/eurostat/home.

NOTE: Net immigration rates are calculated as a percentage of the receiving country's population.

the importance of the new dynamics skilled immigration can bring about (Zimmermann 2009). Indeed, empirical evidence suggests that the effects of economic immigration on European economies are rather more positive than negative, and the case is even stronger for skilled immigrants (Zimmermann 2005; Kahanec and Zimmermann 2009b; Kahanec, Zaiceva, and Zimmermann 2010). In particular, skilled immigrants seem, *inter alia,* to attenuate inequality, to increase growth potential and competitiveness, and, to the extent that high- and low-skilled labor are complementary, to boost productivity and employment of low-skilled workers, with all of the accompanying positive effects on social-security systems (Kahanec and Zimmermann 2008, 2009a; Bonin et al. 2008). Hence, with the ever-growing globalization of production processes and international mobility of production factors and the resulting global competition for human capital and skills, proper management of high-skilled immigration is of key importance for Europe.

TABLE 9-1

PROPORTION OF FOREIGN-BORN AND FOREIGN CITIZENS IN
EUROPEAN UNION (EU) COUNTRIES BY REGION OF ORIGIN

	Foreign-Born		Foreign Citizens	
	Other EU	Non-EU	Other EU	Non-EU
EU15:				
Austria	6.7	8.7	4.1	5.0
Belgium	6.8	6.7	6.4	2.6
Denmark	2.0	4.6	2.9^2	2.4
Finland	1.4	1.8	0.7	1.0
France	3.4	7.8	2.3	3.3
Germany	n.a.	n.a.	3.1	2.8
Greece	1.7	5.9	1.3	4.8
Ireland	8.8^1	3.4^1	5.4^1	2.6^1
Italy^2	2.2	5.3	1.3	3.8
Luxembourg	37.9	8.6	41.2	5.6
Netherlands	2.8	9.1	1.7	1.9
Portugal	1.8	5.7	0.6	2.8
Spain	4.5	10.0	3.9	8.3
Sweden	5.5	10.0	2.5	2.7
United Kingdom	3.5	8.8	2.6	4.3
EU12:				
Bulgaria	n.a.	n.a.	$(0.1)^4$	(0.1)
Cyprus	8.1	11.0	8.1	6.5
Czech Republic	1.3	0.6	0.4	0.4
Estonia	0.6^4	13.6	0.7	16.8
Hungary	1.3	0.4	0.5	0.2
Latvia	1.1^4	9.6	n.a.	0.7^3
Lithuania	$(0.3)^4$	3.8	n.a.	(0.6)
Malta	1.7^5	3.0	1.2	1.8
Poland	0.2	0.3	(0.1)	0.1
Romania	n.a.	$(0.1)^1$	0.1^2	0.1
Slovakia	0.6^4	(0.1)	(0.2)	$(0.1)^1$
Slovenia	$(0.7)^5$	4.6	$(0.2)^4$	(0.2)

SOURCE: H. W. Bonin et al., 2008, *Geographic Mobility in the European Union: Optimising Its Economic and Social Benefits,* Institute for the Study of Labor (IZA) Research Report no. 19, Bonn, Germany.
NOTES: In percent of total population, by domicile, 2006. "Other EU" and "Non-EU" refer to the EU27 as region of reference; "n.a." denotes not available. Share of active working-age residents is reported. Data in parentheses are as in Bonin and others (2008) and lack reliability due to small sample size. 1. Data are from 2005. 2. Data are from 2004. 3. The number for non-EU citizens is suspiciously low, and similarly low numbers are reported in the 2005 Labor Force Survey. This may arise because noncitizens were grouped together with nationals as in Eurostat (2006, 65). 4. Residents of EU10 and EU2 only. 5. Residents of EU15 only.

TABLE 9-2

EDUCATIONAL ATTAINMENT OF NATIVES AND IMMIGRANTS (PERCENTAGES) IN EU MEMBER STATES, 2005

	AT	BE	CY	CZ	DK	EE	FI	FR	DE	EL	HU	IE	IT
Natives													
High	13.18	25.95	20.72	9.49	26.75	22.16	26.32	19.53	20.18	13.28	11.11	20.85	8.43
Medium	27.82	39.68	43.02	20.60	28.63	27.79	33.53	42.81	25.14	54.95	38.87	45.73	60.44
Low	59.00	34.37	36.27	69.90	44.62	50.05	40.16	37.65	54.68	31.77	50.02	33.41	31.13
Immigrants													
High	14.18	22.94	32.54	12.39	33.86	33.04	21.80	18.06	17.36	13.72	22.09	39.79	11.72
Medium	39.46	49.46	35.67	34.14	27.89	16.74	33.74	57.47	41.73	47.74	29.38	26.58	49.80
Low	46.36	27.59	31.78	53.47	38.25	50.22	44.46	24.47	40.91	38.54	48.53	33.64	38.48
Non-EU immigrants													
High	9.82	22.28	27.13	22.60	30.41	32.71	18.18	19.64	–	11.71	20.69	–	–
Medium	48.87	49.76	39.45	26.37	33.76	16.59	41.99	55.00	–	52.39	29.58	–	–
Low	41.31	27.96	33.42	51.03	35.82	50.70	39.83	25.37	–	35.90	49.73	–	–

	LV	LT	LU	NL	PL	PT	SK	SI	ES	SE	UK	EU15	EU25
Natives													
High	16.35	17.86	15.44	26.13	11.93	7.72	10.62	15.69	20.58	24.73	26.30	19.06	17.33
Medium	30.45	30.53	32.92	33.18	30.11	80.83	26.92	27.30	62.33	21.78	13.97	42.86	41.03
Low	53.20	51.61	51.64	40.69	57.96	11.45	62.46	57.00	17.09	53.49	59.73	38.09	41.64
Immigrants													
High	24.13	24.94	27.51	23.28	11.86	18.83	19.31	13.68	21.33	28.50	27.70	22.44	21.94
Medium	19.50	19.82	39.93	31.69	51.62	54.72	24.14	32.23	46.76	23.86	18.45	38.45	38.32
Low	56.36	55.23	32.56	45.03	36.52	26.45	56.55	54.09	31.92	47.64	53.85	39.11	39.74
Non-EU immigrants													
High	24.40	25.00	31.31	21.65	12.30	17.34	17.65	13.21	18.73	26.66	28.22	21.53	20.65
Medium	17.06	18.87	28.84	35.62	52.58	56.55	31.37	33.37	49.02	27.89	19.72	39.80	39.76
Low	58.53	56.13	39.85	42.73	35.12	26.11	50.98	53.42	32.25	45.46	52.06	38.68	39.58

SOURCE: Authors' calculations based on data from the EU labor-force survey for civilians over fourteen years of age.

Box 9-1

NOTES TO TABLE 9-2 AND COUNTRY CODES FOR
TABLES 9-2 AND 9-4 AND FIGURES 9-3 AND 9-4

Percentages of individuals over fourteen years of age with high, medium, and low educational attainment. The values for the EU cover all twenty-five member states of the EU in 2005, except for Malta, for which no data are available. *Immigrants* denotes people who were not born in the country in which they live. *Non-EU immigrants* are those immigrants who were born in a non-EU country. *Natives* are those born to mothers residing in the respective country.

High level of education includes International Standard Classification of Education (ISCED) 5 and 6 levels. ISCED 5 denotes first-stage tertiary programs with an educational content more advanced than those offered by secondary levels. They do not lead to the award of an advanced research qualification and must have a cumulative duration of at least two years. ISCED 6 denotes second-stage tertiary education leading to an advanced research qualification and requiring an original research contribution in the form of a thesis or dissertation. Medium level of education includes ISCED 3 and 4 levels, which denote education that typically begins at the end of full-time compulsory education and involves higher qualification and specialization than the ISCED 2 level. ISCED 3–level education is often designed to provide direct access to ISCED 5. ISCED 4 serves to broaden the knowledge achieved in ISCED 3 but is not regarded as tertiary. Low level of education includes ISCED 0, 1, and 2 levels. These include preprimary, primary, and lower secondary or second-stage of primary education. The end of ISCED 2 often coincides with the end of compulsory schooling, where it exists. For further details, see UNESCO (1997).

Country codes are as follows: AT – Austria, BE – Belgium, BG – Bulgaria, CY – Cyprus, CZ – Czech Republic, DK – Denmark, EE – Estonia, FI – Finland, FR – France, DE – Germany, EL – Greece, HU – Hungary, IE – Ireland, IT – Italy, LV – Latvia, LT – Lithuania, LU – Luxembourg, MT – Malta, NL – Netherlands, PL – Poland, PT – Portugal, RO – Romania, SK – Slovakia, SI – Slovenia, ES – Spain, SE – Sweden, UK – United Kingdom

And still, the European public discourse is unclear about whether immigrants are a blessing or a curse. This ambivalence is reflected in—and is probably itself a reflection of—the incoherent policy response to the challenges immigration brings. European countries differ in their traditions of handling immigration, but the lack of an effective immigration policy is widely shared. Thus, managing international immigration flows remains one of the most significant challenges in Europe. In particular, any policy to attract high-skilled immigrants is still in its infancy.

Therefore, we study high-skilled immigration policies in Europe in this chapter. We start by reviewing what we know about the main postwar immigration trends. Next, we introduce and analyze unique data from the Institute for the Study of Labor (IZA) Expert Survey on High-Skilled Labor Immigration in the EU (ESHSLI).[3] We gauge experts' opinions about the demand for high- and low-skilled immigrants and contrast them with expected immigrant inflows and the perceptions of various native groups and institutions. Finally, we describe and evaluate the current immigration policies and propose prospective policy approaches.

European Migration and Immigration Policies in Historical Perspective

Modern European immigration, and immigration policy, can be divided into four distinct phases (Zimmermann 2005). The first dates back to the period shortly after World War II, during which large numbers of people displaced by the war returned to their homes or found new ones. Additional inflows of immigrants in this phase followed the process of decolonization. The initial period of postwar adjustment was followed by the second phase and characterized by the strong economic recovery in the 1960s and early 1970s, which created labor shortages in many European labor markets. The need for workers prompted several Western European countries to open their borders to immigration or even actively recruit migrant workers, generally targeting unskilled temporary immigrants from Southern Europe. Such "guest-worker" programs were halted circa 1973, however, when the oil shocks throttled the European economy and European governments feared additional immigrants would further strain social-security systems and increase unemployment. A third phase ensued, characterized by restrained immigration based primarily on family ties and humanitarian concerns.

The fourth phase of European immigration commenced with the fall of the Berlin Wall, an event that triggered significant inflows of economic immigrants from Eastern to Western Europe. The conflicts in the Balkans and other parts of the world provided further impetus for European immigration; they funneled significant flows of refugees and asylum seekers from the affected regions mainly to Western Europe. While some countries, such as Germany, adopted more restrictive policies toward these immigrants, flows of humanitarian immigrants remained large.

The most recent developments include the EU's eastern enlargements of 2004 and 2007, resulting in a gradual removal of the barriers to immigrants from the new member states as well as ongoing economic and financial turmoil that sparked protectionist rhetoric.[4] Another development that deserves mentioning is that the convergence between the traditional European cores and peripheries has transformed several formerly emigrant countries, such as Ireland and Spain, into immigrant destinations over the past decade. In fact, even some of the new member states are attracting nonnegligible numbers of immigrants.

European Policy Challenges: Institute for the Study of Labor Expert Opinion Survey

Before turning to the analysis of current European policies regarding high-skilled immigration, it is useful to identify the main contemporary and upcoming policy issues in Europe. To this end, we employ unique data from the ESHSLI conducted in March 2009 among all IZA research fellows, policy fellows, and research affiliates based in Europe. The objective of ESHSLI was to measure experts' perceptions about the EU's economic need for immigrants and about the size of future immigrant inflows, as well as to determine their opinions about European immigration policies with a special focus on high-skilled immigration.[5] A total of 545 fellows were sent a personalized e-mail invitation asking them to take the survey, and a reminder e-mail three days after receiving the initial invitation. This strategy resulted in the following turnout: 282 invitees clicked the personalized link to the questionnaire provided in the e-mail and 234 answered at least the first question (182 answered the last question). The highest numbers of respondents were from Germany and the United Kingdom; the largest numbers of fellows and affiliates were from these two countries as well (see figure 9-3). The response rates were between 30 and 60 percent of survey recipients for most countries (see figure 9-4).

The Need for Immigrant Labor. In the wake of the ongoing financial and economic turmoil, we first examined the perceptions of the experts surveyed regarding the effects these developments may have on the long-term demand for labor immigrants in the EU. Remarkably, 82.5 percent of respondents reported that their evaluation of the need for immigrant labor has not changed, which indicates that the crisis is not expected to systematically

FIGURE 9-3

NUMBER OF RESPONDENTS TO THE INSTITUTE FOR THE STUDY
OF LABOR (IZA) EXPERT SURVEY ON HIGH-SKILLED LABOR IMMIGRATION
IN THE EU BY COUNTRY, 2009

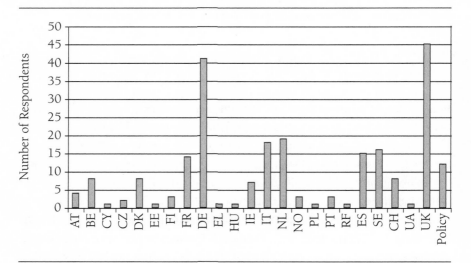

SOURCE: Authors' calculations based on the IZA Expert Survey on High-Skilled Labor Immigration in the EU (ESHSLI 2009).
NOTES: Number of respondents measures IZA research and policy fellows and research affiliates who responded to the survey by country. See box 9-1 on page 269 for country abbreviations.

FIGURE 9-4

RESPONSE RATES TO THE IZA EXPERT SURVEY ON HIGH-SKILLED LABOR IMMIGRATION IN THE EU BY COUNTRY, 2009

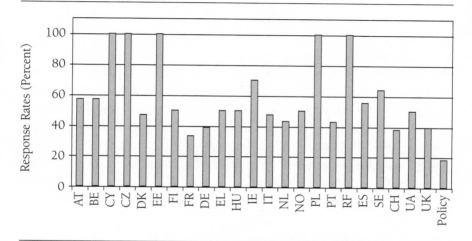

SOURCE: Authors' calculations based on the IZA Expert Survey on High-Skilled Labor Immigration in the EU (ESHSLI 2009).
NOTES: Response rates calculated from the populations of all IZA research and policy fellows and research affiliates from a given country. See box 9-1 on page 269 for country abbreviations.

change conditions in European labor markets. In particular, 87.3 percent of respondents indicate that the EU needs, economically speaking, at least as many immigrants as it has now, and 56.6 percent claim that the EU needs more or many more immigrants. There is less conviction regarding whether the EU needs low-skilled immigration (the corresponding figures are 58.1 and 25.8 percent). However, a massive 96.1 percent of respondents claim that the EU needs at least as many high-skilled immigrants as it has now, and 81.2 percent of them believe that the EU needs more or many more high-skilled immigrants compared to the current situation.

It is also informative to compare the answers of those who responded that the crisis will affect the long-term demand for immigrant labor to the answers of those who predicted no such effect. This comparison indirectly illuminates the effect of the crisis on the demand for low- and high-skilled labor. The results generally indicate that the crisis will have negative effects on the demand for immigrants. As the difference in the expected demand for high-

and low-skilled labor between the respondents who expect the crisis to have some effect on the demand for immigrants and those who do not expect such effects is smaller for high-skilled immigration, the long-term demand for high-skilled labor seems to be somewhat more robust to the crisis (see table 9-3).

The Supply of Immigrant Labor. According to the surveyed experts, the EU has a clear economic need for immigrants, especially high-skilled immigrants. What are the experts' expectations about the supply of immigrant labor given current immigration policies? The survey data show that 78.6 percent of the respondents expect some or significant net inflows of low-skilled immigrants in the coming five to twenty years, but only 58.3 percent think the same about high-skilled immigration. Recalling that 25.8 (81.2) percent of the respondents indicated that the EU needs more or many more low-skilled (high-skilled) immigrants, these results indicate that the experts expect to see a surplus of low-skilled and a shortage of high-skilled immigrant labor.

Will the ongoing crisis help to reduce this skill mismatch, or will it exacerbate it? According to the survey, 64.7 (15.2) percent of respondents believe the crisis will hinder or strongly hinder (promote or strongly promote) low-skilled immigration over the coming five years. In contrast, only 37.6 (19.5) percent believe the same about high-skilled immigration. This finding indicates that the crisis may help to alleviate the skill mismatch in the market for immigrant labor over the short run.

Another interesting question concerns the nature of immigrant inflows: what is going to be the distribution of immigrant inflows regarding permanent, temporary, and circular immigration? This aspect determines whether immigrants settle in their host countries forever (permanent); return to their countries of origin or move to another country after some period of time (temporary); or migrate along circular immigration trajectories going back and forth between two or more countries, following employment and career opportunities (circular). This is also correlated with immigrants' behavior and adjustment in their host countries.

Permanent migrants are more likely to invest in country-specific human capital and to assimilate; temporary migrants are more likely to work in jobs below the level for which they are qualified and to work longer hours than comparable peers, and circular immigration constitutes specific immigrants who closely follow demand and supply conditions in their target labor markets.

TABLE 9-3

SURVEYED EXPERTS' RESPONSES REGARDING EXPECTED EFFECTS
OF THE ONGOING CRISIS ON THE NEED FOR HIGH- AND
LOW-SKILLED IMMIGRATION IN THE EU, 2009

			Has the current economic and financial crisis changed your evaluation of the long-term demand for labor migrants in the EU?		
			Of those that responded "yes"	Of those that responded "no"	Difference
Please indicate whether the EU, economically speaking, needs more or fewer immigrants of the following categories of labor migrants in the long term:	"About the same number," "more," or "many more"	High-skilled immigrants	85.37	98.40	13.03
		Low-skilled immigrants	43.90	61.17	17.27
	"More" or "many more"	High-skilled immigrants	70.73	83.51	12.78
		Low-skilled immigrants	14.63	28.19	13.56

SOURCE: Authors' calculations from the IZA Expert Survey on High-Skilled Labor Immigration in the EU (ESHSLI 2009).

NOTES: 84.5 percent of respondents reported that their evaluation of the long-term demand for immigrant labor had not changed in connection to the current economic and financial crisis; 15.5 percent reported the opposite. Numbers given correspond to the percentage of experts offering each response. 1 = The remainder up to 100% in the first two columns with results corresponds to those experts responding "fewer" or "far fewer or none." 2 = The remainder up to 100 percent in the first two columns with results corresponds to those experts responding "about the same number," "fewer" or "far fewer or none."

The experts surveyed expect that, over the coming five to twenty years, permanent immigration will dominate among low-skilled immigrants, followed by temporary and then circular immigration. However, the surveyed experts believe temporary and permanent migrants will constitute similarly large shares of the high-skilled immigrant population (see figure 9-5, A–C). This indicates that the share of temporary immigration will be higher among high-skilled than low-skilled immigrants. We find a similar result for circular immigration as well, although the difference here is less pronounced. These findings highlight the importance of properly designed absorption policies that would enable otherwise temporary and circular high-skilled immigrants to use their human capital in jobs corresponding to their skill

FIGURE 9-5

SURVEYED EXPERTS' RESPONSES REGARDING THE NATURE
OF IMMIGRANT INFLOWS IN THE EU, 2009

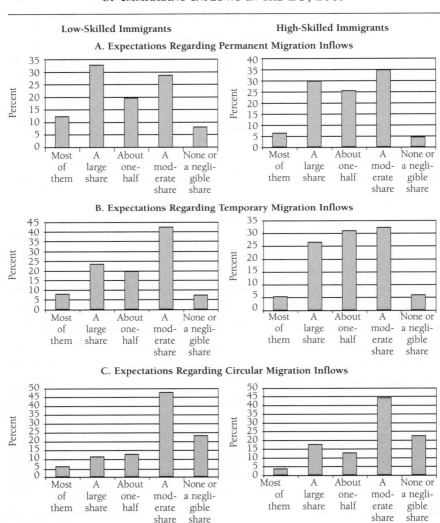

SOURCE: Authors' calculations based on the IZA Expert Survey on High-Skilled Labor Immigration in the EU (ESHSLI 2009).

NOTES: Responses are to the following prompt: "For these categories of labor migrants (high- and low-skilled), please indicate the expected distribution of migration inflows into the EU among the listed types (permanent, temporary, circular) in the coming 5 to 20 years, given the current immigration policies." Graph shows percentage of experts offering each response.

levels. In addition, the shares of temporary and circular immigrants in the expected immigrant flows will be decisive for circulating human capital between source and destination countries. Whether the flows of temporary and circular immigrants projected by the experts will permit sufficient human-capital circulation remains to be seen.

Immigration Policy. A proper immigration policy has, at least in theory, the potential to alleviate the labor-market shortages and mismatches depicted above. Generally speaking, the survey indicates that current national immigration policies in the EU hinder rather than promote immigration and, therefore, aggravate shortages in the labor market. However, while 65.2 percent of the respondents believe that immigration policies hinder or strongly hinder inflows of low-skilled immigrants, the corresponding percentage of respondents who believe this is the case for high-skilled immigrants is significantly lower at 39.6 percent. This might indicate that the current immigration policies help to reduce the aforementioned mismatch between the supply and demand for high- and low-skilled labor in the EU. When asked at which level of implementation immigration policies could best address the labor-market requirements for immigrant labor, most of the respondents indicated that the EU and national levels are equally important; a smaller share of respondents indicated that policies should be addressed primarily at the EU level; and the fewest respondents indicated that policies should be addressed primarily at the national level. This general pattern is very similar for high- and low-skilled immigrants. Only a tiny fraction responded that no policy is necessary. Figure 9-6 shows the experts' responses in regard to the level at which immigration policies should be governed for high-skilled immigrants.

Figure 9-7 indicates that respondents believe two policy approaches would address the economic needs of the EU most efficiently: job-dependent immigration (that is, allowing the labor market to select immigrants according to its needs), and positive selection based on skills or education (for example, through a points system giving preference to immigrants with a university degree or a professional qualification). Other responses given by more than 10 percent of experts surveyed include selection based on language, on immigrants' need (refugees and asylum seekers), and on the existence of family ties, as well as to simply open the borders.

FIGURE 9-6

SURVEYED EXPERTS' RESPONSES REGARDING THE LEVEL AT WHICH
IMMIGRATION POLICIES SHOULD BE IMPLEMENTED IN THE EU, 2009

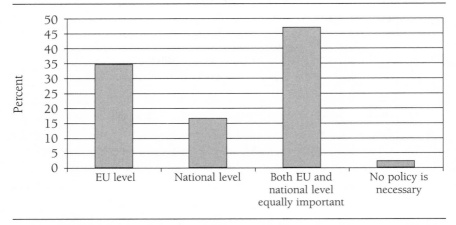

SOURCE: Authors' calculations based on the IZA Expert Survey on High-Skilled Labor Immigration in the EU (ESHSLI 2009).
NOTES: Responses are to the following prompt: "Please indicate the level of implementation at which you believe immigration policies would most efficiently address the economic needs of the EU; for high-skilled immigrants." Graph shows percentage of experts offering each response.

Perceptions. The survey also asked the experts to indicate how they believed the following five native groups or institutions perceive high- and low-skilled immigration: (i) the general public; (ii) national governments; (iii) the European Commission; (iv) trade unions, works councils, and other employee associations; and (v) employers and employer associations. The results, presented in figure 9-8, A–E, show that the surveyed experts believe the general public and trade unions, works councils, and other employee associations are particularly skeptical about the need for further low-skilled immigration; they believe national governments and the European Commission are nearly as skeptical. The experts believe that only employers and employer associations favor inflows of low-skilled immigrants. Across the board, high-skilled immigrants are significantly more welcome than their low-skilled counterparts. In fact, the experts surveyed believe that all native groups and institutions—except trade unions, works councils, and other employee associations—lean toward favoring an increase in the number of high-skilled immigrants.

FIGURE 9-7

SURVEYED EXPERTS' RESPONSES REGARDING THE TYPES OF POLICY
APPROACHES THAT SHOULD BE IMPLEMENTED IN THE EU, 2009

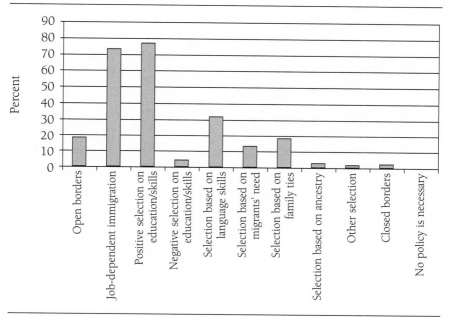

SOURCE: Authors' calculations based on the IZA Expert Survey on High-Skilled Labor Immigration in the EU (ESHSLI 2009).
NOTES: Responses are to the following prompt: "From the following list, please select up to three types of immigration policies you believe would most efficiently address the economic needs of the EU." Graph shows percentage of experts offering each response.

In this context, it is also crucial to look at what the survey reveals about what experts believe immigrants perceive about the attractiveness of a number of European countries, the EU as a whole, and Europe's main competitors in the global market for immigrants. The survey asked the experts to rate immigrants' perceptions of several destination countries; the experts rated the countries on a scale of one to ten, where a one indicates the least attractive destination for immigrants and ten represents the most attractive destination. The results, depicted in figure 9-9, show that, with the possible exception of the United Kingdom, both high- and low-skilled immigrants most likely see the considered European destinations as less attractive than

FIGURE 9-8

SURVEYED EXPERTS' RESPONSES REGARDING PERCEIVED ATTITUDES OF NATIVE GROUPS TOWARD IMMIGRATION, BY SKILL LEVEL, 2009

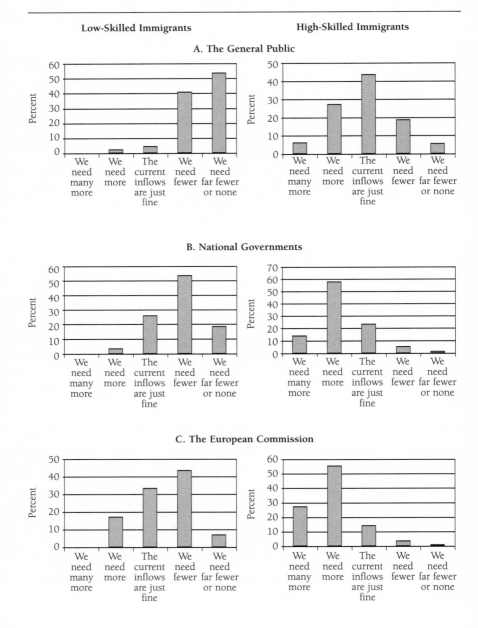

FIGURE 9-8 (cont.)

SURVEYED EXPERTS' RESPONSES REGARDING PERCEIVED ATTITUDES
OF NATIVE GROUPS TOWARD IMMIGRATION, BY SKILL LEVEL, 2009

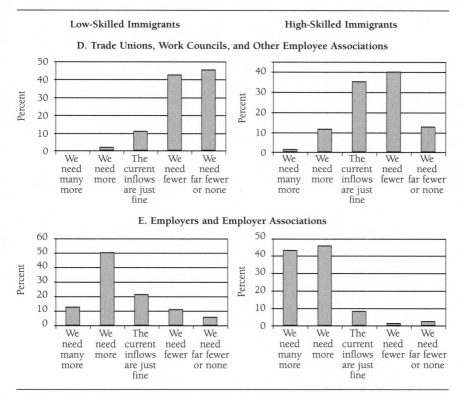

SOURCE: Authors' calculations based on the IZA Expert Survey on High-Skilled Labor Immigration in the EU (ESHSLI 2009).
NOTES: Responses are to the following prompt: "Please indicate which of the following you believe best describes the general perception the following native groups and institutions (the general public; national governments; the European Commission; trade unions, work councils, and other employee associations; and employers and employer associations) have about the immigration of these categories of labor migrants." Graph shows percentage of experts offering each response.

the United States, Canada, or Australia. In the context of the aforementioned skill mismatch, this is a key issue the EU should address if it hopes to entice more immigrants in a competitive global market. A close look at the balance of a country's attractiveness for high- and low-skilled immigrants, as depicted in figure 9-10, demonstrates that Spain and (to a lesser

FIGURE 9-9

SURVEYED EXPERTS' RESPONSES REGARDING LOW- AND HIGH-SKILLED MIGRANTS' PERCEPTIONS ABOUT DESTINATION COUNTRIES, 2009

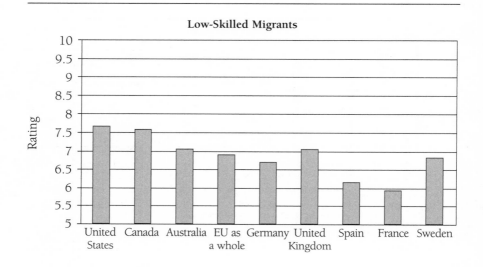

Low-Skilled Migrants

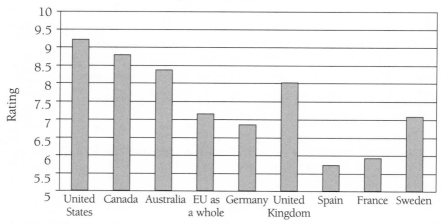

High-Skilled Migrants

SOURCE: Authors' calculations based on the IZA Expert Survey on High-Skilled Labor Immigration in the EU (ESHSLI 2009).

NOTES: Responses are to the following prompt: "Please rate the perception of the following categories of labor migrants (low- and high-skilled) about the destination countries listed below (1: least attractive, 10: most attractive)." Graph shows the average rating for each country.

FIGURE 9-10

**BALANCE OF LOW- AND HIGH-SKILLED MIGRANTS' PERCEPTIONS
BASED ON SURVEYED EXPERTS' RESPONSES**

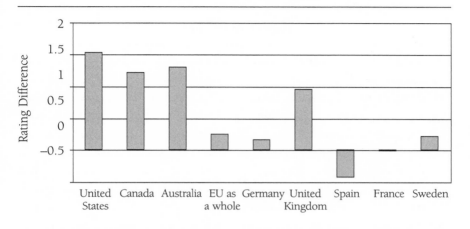

SOURCE: Authors' calculations based on the IZA Expert Survey on High-Skilled Labor Immigration in the EU (ESHSLI 2009).
NOTES: The balance in perceptions is calculated as the difference between the high- and low-skilled migrants' perception ratings. Refer to figure 9-9 for low- and high-skilled migrants' perceptions.

extent) France seem to be more attractive destinations for low-skilled immigrants than high-skilled immigrants. Again, only the United Kingdom is close to Europe's main global competitors in the attractiveness rating prescribed by the experts surveyed.

Current Approaches to High-Skilled Immigration in Europe

What has Europe done to address the labor-market mismatches revealed by the expert opinion survey analyzed above? Looking at the four phases of postwar European immigration explained earlier in this chapter, we see that Europe has not had a consistent policy for managing high-skilled immigration. One reason for this has been the prevalent perception of a "fortress Europe" among not only the general public and policymakers but also potential immigrants. Immigration is not seen as an opportunity to increase Europe's global competitiveness and alleviate its demographic problems; rather, it is perceived as a threat to the stability of Europe's labor markets and welfare systems. At best, immigration is seen as a humanitarian issue or a way to resolve particular temporary shortages in the labor market.

Only recently has Europe started to realize the potential benefits properly managed immigration might have for its internal and external challenges. Europe is also now beginning to recognize that it is not in a position to play the role of an almighty gatekeeper tending flocks of high-skilled (or any) immigrants; instead, it needs to attract immigrants actively. Besides instituting policies to target native populations in particular EU member states, Europe addresses the issue of labor-market shortages with two broad approaches. The first approach involves free mobility of labor between EU member states, which can increase the allocative efficiency of European labor markets and channel emigrants to the countries for which their skills will be most productive. The second broad approach concerns inflows of emigrants from countries outside the EU.[6]

The policy of free internal mobility coupled with the recent EU enlargements has indeed increased the immigration potential in Europe, including the potential for high-skilled immigration. While this has been manifested in an increase in the flows of immigrants from Eastern to Western Europe and signs indicate that these flows have contributed to increased efficiency in European labor markets (European Commission 2009b; Kahanec, Zaiceva, and Zimmermann 2010), the effectiveness of this policy approach has several limitations. First, some member states' transitional arrangements restricting free mobility from newer EU countries have distorted postenlargement immigration flows.[7] A few countries that opened their borders early received unexpectedly high inflows (Ireland and the United Kingdom, for example), while countries that applied strict transitional measures (such as Germany and Austria) often pushed immigrants to seek innovative modes of entry and discouraged those who had competitive alternatives. For example, while receiving significant immigrant inflows, Germany attracted relatively older and lower-skilled immigrants than other old EU member states that had opened their borders to the new EU states earlier (Brenke, Yuksel, and Zimmermann 2010).

Second, in comparison with U.S. citizens' propensity to move from state to state, Europeans generally exhibit a lower propensity to move from one

European country to another, even when faced with economic opportunities for moving.[8] Third, despite the policy of free internal mobility, immigrants—especially high-skilled immigrants, who are typically very mobile and often will live in one country and work in another—face burdensome administrative barriers to migrating. These include complicated and lengthy administrative procedures for transferring social-security benefits and health insurance.[9] In addition, tax systems are often excessively complex, do not allow for or limit tax deductibles from other member states, and sometimes involve implicit double taxation.[10] Not even the business world is free of frictions inhibiting the free movement of workers. For example, cross-border workers—those living in one member state and working in another—may not be able to access mortgage financing: banks in the country where they live may not recognize income from abroad or may discount it heavily, and banks in the country where they work may not finance housing abroad. Access to credit may be further complicated by the typically temporary nature of the employment contracts of mobile workers. Fourth, language barriers and practical difficulties involving the recognition of professional qualifications often lead to the down-skilling of well-qualified immigrants.[11] Fifth, emigration has already generated a number of bottlenecks and skill shortages in new member states in the short run, thus increasing the need for non-EU nationals in the affected skill groups and occupations (Kaczmarczyk, Mioduszewska, and Zilicz 2010).

Although still applying some transitional arrangements, several countries have opened special channels for high-skilled immigrants from the new EU member states. In Germany, for example, federal legislators passed a new law regulating labor migration (*Arbeitsmigrationssteuerungsgesetz*), which became effective January 1, 2009. This law includes provisions for free mobility and labor-market access for high-skilled citizens of the new EU member states and their family members. In particular, workers who hold a university degree, or a comparable certificate, and their family members do not need the consent of Germany's Federal Employment Agency to obtain a work permit. Additionally, German immigrants from the new member states who have a qualification recognized in Germany do not need a work permit to begin an apprenticeship.

Although EU enlargement and the ensuing migration flows have, to some extent, been embraced as a remedy for sclerotic labor markets and skill shortages, this is much less true when it comes to the immigration of non-EU nationals. Yet, non-EU immigrants constitute the bulk of the immigrant population in most European countries (Kahanec, Zaiceva, and Zimmermann 2010). Non-EU immigrants generally need a residence or settlement permit as well as a work permit to gain access to the host labor market. For most non-EU immigrants, obtaining these permits involves a lengthy, costly, and difficult procedure with a highly uncertain outcome. Which immigration policies or special provisions do European countries implement vis-à-vis high-skilled non-EU immigrants? The following sections provide an overview of these policies in a cross-section of EU and European Economic Area (EEA) member states. In particular, we consider countries representing each of the four distinct migration patterns observed in contemporary Europe: Scandinavian welfare states, the Western European core, newly emerged European cores, and the new member states.

Scandinavian Welfare States

The cluster of Scandinavian welfare states includes Denmark, Finland, Iceland, Norway, and Sweden. This group of countries is characterized by steady inflows and outflows of migrants, economic prosperity, and a generous welfare state based on a social democratic tradition.

Denmark. Denmark grants residence and work permits if labor-market considerations warrant them.[12] In particular, Danish government agencies consider whether professionals already residing in Denmark are qualified for the job in question and the degree to which this job requires specialized training that warrants granting a work and residence permit for an immigrant. A written employment contract in accordance with Danish employment and salary regulations must be presented for immigrants to receive the necessary permits.

Denmark issues work permits for three to four years. A number of policies facilitating easier access exist, for example, for professions on the "positive list," that is, those for which Denmark lacks qualified workers.[13] Other policies aim at foreigners who have been offered a salary above DKK 375,000 (DKK is the abbreviation for the Danish krone, a salary equal to approximately €50,000); employees abroad who are to be temporarily stationed at a company's Danish subsidiary; athletes; religious workers; the self-employed; and highly qualified workers, researchers, teachers, leading executives, and specialists.

Denmark uses a green-card scheme based on a points system. A green card allows a foreigner to stay in Denmark for three years and to seek and subsequently secure employment. To receive a residence permit under this scheme, immigrants must attain at least one hundred points in the points system. Points are awarded for educational attainment, language skills, work experience, adaptability, and age. For the effect of this system on high-skilled immigration to Denmark, the educational criterion is of key importance. Applicants obtain thirty points for holding a bachelor's degree, fifty points for a bachelor's degree followed by a one-year master's degree, sixty points for a master's degree, and eighty points for a doctorate. Graduating from a top university can yield five (top four hundred), ten (top two hundred), or fifteen (top one hundred) additional points. Ten additional points are granted if the applicant's qualifications apply to a profession on the positive list. Depending on proficiency, five to twenty points are awarded for knowledge of any one of the Scandinavian languages, and additional points according to the same rules may be granted for the knowledge of either English or German. An applicant may receive a maximum of thirty points for language skills. Work experience is rewarded by fifteen (ten) points if the applicant has had three to five (one to two) years of work experience within the last five years as a researcher or in a field listed in the positive list. For three to five years of experience over the past five years in any other occupation, applicants are awarded five points. Adaptability is measured by the number of years of study or work in an EU or EEA country or Switzerland. Five additional points are awarded for knowledge of Danish. Young applicants up to thirty-four years of age earn fifteen points; those between thirty-five and forty years of age receive ten points.

A special tax regime applies to expatriates employed by Danish-resident employers. Under this regime, employees are allowed a flat rate of 25 percent, instead of the standard progressive taxation (39–59 percent), applied to salary income for a maximum of thirty-six months. The requirement to pay labor-market supplementary pension-fund contributions, labor-market contributions, and special pension savings is unaffected. To be eligible for this provision, foreign expatriates must earn more than DKK 57,300 per month (approximately €7,640) after deducting labor-market supplementary pension fund contributions, labor-market contributions, and special pension contributions, and must reside in Denmark. Deductions or personal allowances are excluded in this case.

Finland. Residence permits for employees, which are typically tied to a certain professional field but not to a specific employer, are required for non-EU nationals who intend to work in Finland.[14] The needs of the labor market are considered before a residence permit for employees is granted, and the adequacy of a foreigner's means of support needs to be guaranteed before a permit is issued.

A number of permits in Finland, other than the residence permit for employees, carry the right of employment.[15] A non-EU national has an unlimited right to work based on a permanent- or continuous-residence permit based on grounds other than employment or a temporary-residence permit based on the need for temporary protection or other humanitarian grounds for immigration. High-skilled immigrants may qualify for a fixed-term Finnish-residence permit, which also carries an unlimited right to work on the grounds that the immigrant-applicant works as a professional athlete or trainer; works for a religious or non-profit association; works professionally in either science, culture, or the arts; works as a company executive or in a mid-level management position; holds an expert position that requires special skills; or works as a professional in the field of mass communication.

A number of specific groups of foreigners may be granted a limited right to work in Finland. These include residence permits for study purposes; for various teaching, lecturing, and research assignments (maximum of one year); for work related to, for example, a contract of delivery of a machine that includes the installation of the machine or training in the use of it (maximum of six months); for work covered by interstate agreements or operated through educational institutions and students' associations supported by the EU, international work-camp operations, or other equivalent work; practical training that lasts for a maximum of one year; and for work as an au pair. Finally, several categories of non-EU citizens are permitted to work in Finland for up to three months without a residence permit (but with valid entry documents). These include interpreters, teachers, experts, referees, professional artists or athletes, artists' or athletes' assistants who work upon invitation or under contract, certain categories of sailors, pickers of berries or fruits, and permanent employees of a company operating in another EU or EEA country who perform temporary acquisition or subcontract work in Finland (provided that such aliens have appropriate and valid residence and work permits for the other country). Foreign students are allowed to stay in Finland for six months to look for a job after graduation.

In an attempt to address demographic challenges, the Finnish government started phasing in the Migration Policy Programme in 2007, which is intended to foster labor migration by, among other things, tying work rights to every residence permit and forecasting labor-market needs more precisely.

Finland applies several tax exemptions for high-skilled workers. If staying in Finland fewer than six months, foreign workers are considered nonresidents for tax purposes and are taxed at the source at a 35 percent flat tax rate after deducting €17 per day. Special provisions apply to students, artists, and athletes. Based on bilateral agreements, teachers and researchers from certain countries are fully tax exempt. This exemption may extend beyond the six-month period, provided they do not stay in Finland longer than the stipulated maximum (two years for most countries). Key foreign personnel staying in Finland longer than six months are eligible for a 35 percent flat tax rate if they work as researchers or teachers at a Finnish institution of higher education or if they possess special skills and their cash earnings exceed €5,800 per month, and they have not resided in Finland at any time during the five-year period preceding the beginning of their respective employment.

Sweden. All foreign workers in Sweden are required to have work permits; any staying in Sweden for more than three months are required to have residence permits as well.[16] Prior to the December 2008 passage of a new immigration law, the Swedish labor-market authority reviewed requests for work permits only after giving preference to Swedes; other EU, EEA, or Swiss citizens; and foreign people already living in Sweden. As part of this policy, jobs had to have been advertised for at least ten days in Sweden and other EU countries before an application for a work permit was made. The new law has adopted a philosophy of demand-driven immigration, which presumes individual employers can recognize the best employee for a given job opening better than anyone else. The Swedish Public Employment Service can no longer block the employment of a foreigner based on the argument that there is an alternative match in Sweden, another EU or EEA country, or Switzerland for the position. The agency's emphasis has shifted instead to ensuring that all terms of employment comply with Swedish standards, as established by collective agreements, including salary and insurance protection.

Work permits are issued for the duration of the employment, to which they are tied for a maximum of two years. It is possible to extend work permits multiple times, but not for more than four years in total. After four years, a permanent-residence permit can be granted. A novel provision that facilitates the employment of high-skilled young workers in Sweden is that visiting students with at least thirty higher-education credits or who have completed one term of research education at an institution of higher education in Sweden are allowed to apply for a work and residence permit from within Sweden, meaning they do not have to leave Sweden before submitting their applications. Self-employed foreigners are required to have residence permits but not work permits.

Certain categories of non-EU nationals do not require work permits, including postsecondary (college or university) students with a residence permit and visiting researchers with a special residence permit to conduct research. In addition, a number of occupational categories are exempt from the requirement to have a work permit. These include certain high-skilled occupations, such as company representatives; visiting researchers or teachers in higher education (maximum duration of three months within a twelve-month period); performers, technicians, and other tour personnel; and specialists employed by a multinational corporation who will be working in Sweden for a total of less than one year.

High-skilled foreigners (experts and scientists) with an expertise scarce in Sweden may be entitled to a special tax regime under which no taxes are paid on the first 25 percent of their income for the first three years of their employment in Sweden.

The Western European Core

Austria, Belgium, France, Germany, Luxembourg, the Netherlands, and the United Kingdom constitute the Western European core. Like the Scandinavian welfare states, this cluster of countries is wealthy. These countries have traditionally been a main focal point for immigration heading into Europe.

Austria. To be legally employed in Austria, non-EU nationals are required to have either an employment or a preemployment permit and a permit to reside in Austria.[17] Acquiring these permits is a considerable task with an uncertain outcome.[18] Certain residence permits directly entitle their holders to work in Austria, however. According to the Austrian Aliens Employment Act (*Ausländerbeschäftigungsgesetz*), non-EU nationals can obtain such residence permits if they qualify as high-skilled key staff members (*Schlüsselkraft*). To qualify for this status, employees have to possess special skills or expertise in demand in the Austrian labor market, and earn at least 60 percent of the upper limit of the income base for social-security contributions from their prospective Austrian employer (at least €2,412 per month in 2009). In addition, their employment must be described by at least one of the following: (i) special importance for a region or a segment of the labor market; (ii) creation of new or safeguarding of existing jobs; (iii) significant influence on management and leadership (of the employing company); (iv) facilitating transfer of investment capital; or (v) university or polytechnic education or other stipulated qualification. Self-employed non-EU nationals can also qualify as key staff members if they demonstrate that the proposed self-employment involves a transfer of investment capital or the creation or safeguarding of jobs and affirm the objectives of the proposed self-employment in a business plan.

Quotas stipulated by the effective federal-settlement decree regulate the issuance of these residence permits. Key staff workers receive a special residence permit (*Niederlassungsbewilligung–Schlüsselkraft*), which is valid for a maximum of eighteen months and permits the holder to work for the employer stipulated in the permit without an additional work permit. Thereafter, a residence permit allowing unrestricted employment (*Niederlassungsbewilligung–unbeschränkt*) can be issued if the employee has worked at least twelve of the previous eighteen months as a key staff member. Such permits are usually issued for twelve months. Spouses and children of key staff members can receive residence permits within the same regulation, and the conditions under which they can stay and work in Austria are less strict than for other non-EU nationals. For example, key staff members and their dependents are exempt from the Integration Agreement (*Integrationsverein-barung*), which requires non-EU nationals to learn or prove sufficient knowledge of German within five years of receiving their first or extended residence permit.

Researchers also constitute a special category. A researcher is defined as a person with whom a university or an equivalent institution concludes a hosting agreement. Private enterprises may also conclude hosting agreements if they demonstrate that the employment is dedicated to scientific research. It is, thus, the employer who decides who will be considered a researcher. For stays exceeding six months, three possible residence permits can be considered: the settlement permit for researchers; the settlement permit for special cases of paid employment (neither of which is subject to quotas); and the settlement permit for key staff members (subject to quotas). If the intended stay is fewer than six months, certified research institutions can provide letters of invitation for future employees, researchers, who can then obtain short-term visas (Visa C and D) permitting this employment. Austria is also currently considering implementing a red-white-red card intended to foster immigration of qualified workers with a good knowledge of German.

High-skilled workers often qualify for fiscal incentives to immigrate to Austria. Individuals who have temporary contracts not exceeding five years with Austrian employers, who have not been Austrian residents in the past ten years, and who keep their foreign residence as their primary residence are entitled to a tax deduction of up to 35 percent of taxable income for expenses incurred keeping a household in Austria, educational expenses, and leave allowances.

Belgium. Non-EU nationals who wish to work in Belgium under an employment contract must hold one of three available types of work permit.[19] Type A work permits offer non-EU nationals unlimited access to the Belgian labor market, both in terms of eligible duration and employer, and can be granted to foreign nationals who can prove four working years under a type B work permit, during a maximal and uninterrupted residence period of ten years.[20]

Type B work permits are valid for one employer and are issued for one year. According to a June 1999 royal decree, the type B employment permit is granted only when it is not possible to find an available domestic worker eligible and capable of filling the vacant position in a satisfactory way and within a reasonable term, possibly even after receiving professional training. Certain categories of high-skilled workers are exempt from this requirement, however. These include:

- Highly qualified or managerial workers who pay social security in Belgium and possess a higher-education degree and have an annual gross salary greater than €35,638 or work in managerial positions with an annual gross salary greater than €59,460 (amounts valid as of January 1, 2009);

- Highly qualified or managerial workers posted in Belgium who continue to be employed by a foreign company and pay their social security abroad;[21]

- Researchers providing documentation of a detailed full-time research program; the amount of the salary or scholarship;[22] an invitation letter from a university, institution of higher education, or acknowledged scientific institution; and proof of doctoral or other academic degrees;

- Visiting professors invited by a university, institution of higher education, or acknowledged scientific institution and proof of a salary (from either the professors' home or visiting institution) in accordance with applicable wage scales for teaching staff of universities or institutions of higher education;

- Specialized technicians who work for foreign employers and come to Belgium to install, initialize, or repair an installation produced or delivered by their employers (for a maximum of six months); such technicians must provide Belgian authorities with assignment letters specifying the terms of their assignments, contracts, and notes specifying the sector and field of activity of the foreign company posting its employee that confirm the purpose of the assignment.

A type C work permit is intended for workers whose stay in Belgium is temporary. It is valid for all salaried professions and all employers and has a maximum validity of one year, after which it can be renewed.

Fiscal provisions for high-skilled temporary immigrants, such as executives, specialists, and researchers, include a special tax regime that treats them as nonresidents by calculating their taxable income by adjusting their taxable earnings according to the number of days spent outside Belgium. Furthermore, reimbursement of employees' expenses incurred in connection with their stay in Belgium is exempt from personal income tax.

France. In France, work permits are issued by the local branch of the Departmental Directorate of Labor, Employment, and Education (*Direction Départmentale du Travail, de l'Emploi et de la Formation Professionnelle*).[23] Before a work permit is granted in France, an employer must prove that no worker in France or the EU is able to do the job.

France issues two types of work permits: temporary secondments and full work permits. Temporary secondments serve foreign companies posting their employees onsite with their clients in France. The maximum duration of these permits is eighteen months, and they may be extended for an additional nine months thereafter. To receive temporary secondments, workers must earn a gross minimum of €3,835 per month. Full work permits are required for any company to employ non-EU or EEA workers in France. These permits do not have a time limit.

Full work permits are also a selection tool favoring high-skilled immigrants, as to obtain a full work permit, candidates must be cadres (that is, working in a managerial position or as another high-level professional), generally with high-level work experience and a university degree. Moreover, candidates must earn more than an equivalent French worker, at least €3,835 per month.

To obtain a permit as a self-employed foreigner, applicants must be able to demonstrate serious intent and the ability to generate revenue in the country.

France has adopted some fiscal incentives for foreign professionals. These include tax deductions for social security, health insurance, and pension payments that expatriates make to countries other than France, as well as tax exemptions for bonuses that are directly related to their assignment in France. Foreign professionals may claim this tax exemption for up to five years.

Germany. Work permits in Germany are usually issued only in connection with a specific job position and only in cases when no German or other EU (or EEA) national is able to fill the position.[24] Furthermore, foreigners must obtain consent from the Federal Employment Agency to work in Germany, unless an exemption is granted by an international treaty. In foreign nationals' initial years of residence, work and residence permits are temporary and can be transferred into unlimited ones only after a minimum stay of five years. Immigrants can also be required to attend special integration courses if they lack sufficient knowledge of German language and culture.

Recently, Germany has made several steps toward more liberalized access for high-skilled, non-EU labor immigrants, including the aforementioned immigration legislation that came into effect January 2009. Non-EU immigrants with university degrees, and their family members, are allowed to work in Germany if they have a job and they receive the consent of the Federal Employment Agency. Highly qualified foreigners may be permitted to work in Germany without the consent of the Federal Employment Agency if they are integrated into German society and independent from the public social system. Highly qualified workers primarily include scientists with special professional knowledge, high-ranking teachers and researchers, and specialists or senior executives with specific professional experience and a salary at least equal to the contribution ceiling of the public-pension insurance (€63,600 in 2009). Residence permits for research purposes can be granted, provided foreign nationals can provide documentation of a contract between the researcher and a legally recognized research institution. In addition, the research institution must commit to assuming any expenses that public institutions might incur in connection with living expenses or deportation of the foreigner in the case of an illegal stay in the EU within six months of the termination of the contract.

Additional provisions apply to specific categories of high-skilled immigrants. Family members of researchers, scientific personnel, immigrants in leading positions, or immigrants with special qualifications can also obtain work permits without the otherwise obligatory assessment of the Federal Employment Agency. Immigrants who have lawfully resided in Germany for at least four years without interruption, as well as those beginning officially approved job training, are similarly exempt from this assessment. Immigrants who arrived in Germany before their eighteenth birthday and completed their education in Germany do not need to obtain work permits. Students are permitted to work full time for up to ninety days per year or part time for up to one hundred and eighty days. The self-employed are granted permits if their proposed businesses are expected to have a positive effect on the German economy, will meet specific local needs, and already have secured financing. The two former conditions are usually assumed to be fulfilled if a self-employment business is expected to generate at least €250,000 of investment and create a minimum of five jobs.

Germany had attempted to attract information technology (IT) and high-tech specialists through special policies. The German green card was introduced in 2000 with the objective of attracting much-needed IT specialists. Within fixed quotas, it permitted holders of degrees in relevant fields already living in Germany and those who were able to provide proof of a job offer in Germany securing a minimum annual gross income of €51,000 to obtain residence permits. The maximum duration of stay was limited to five years, and the loss of the job tied to the green card resulted in the loss of the residence permit as well, unless a transitional job-search period was granted. The green card was discontinued in 2004, at which time Germany enacted a new immigration law. The German green-card pro- · gram fell short of attracting the desired numbers of skilled immigrants.

The Netherlands. In the Netherlands, foreign nationals outside the EU, EEA, and Switzerland may seek work permits only after submitting a residence-permit application.[25] Applying employers must demonstrate that attempts have been made to fill the position from the Dutch, EU, or EEA labor markets, and the employment office initiates its own attempts to find a suitable employee through the European Employment Service (EURES) network. While the application process for new arrivals is considerably strict and the work permits are tied to a single employer, after living in the Netherlands for three years with a work permit, foreign nationals may obtain a residence permit allowing any lawful employment.

Since 2004, the Dutch Immigration and Naturalization Service has applied simplified procedures for high-skilled immigrants.[26] Well-paid workers with higher vocational or academic qualifications and those who play a catalyzing role in the innovation process are considered high skilled. In particular, high-skilled immigrants must earn at least €49,087 (or €35,997 if they are under thirty years old) per year, as of 2009. This income criterion does not apply if employment is in an educational or research institute, or if it concerns a postgraduate student or university lecturer under the age of thirty. Since December 2007, graduates who finished their studies in the Netherlands have also been able to obtain residence permits as high-skilled immigrants if their annual wage is at least €25,800. Furthermore, high-skilled immigrants with permanent contracts can be granted renewable residence permits, which have a maximum duration of five years, in contrast to regular residence permits, which are issued for a maximum duration of one year, and high-skilled immigrants' family members can be included in the same application process. Finally, high-skilled immigrants are not subjected to labor-market testing.

Under certain conditions, expatriates may be entitled to a special tax provision that allows employers to pay employees with an assignment in the Netherlands a tax-free allowance of up to 35 percent of regularly received earnings and a tax-free reimbursement of school fees for children attending international schools.

The United Kingdom. The United Kingdom overhauled its immigration system in 2008 by implementing a points-based system for immigrants from outside the EU, EEA, or Switzerland.[27] This system is based on five tiers. Tier one is intended for high-skilled immigrants, entrepreneurs, investors, and graduate students. Tier two regulates the immigration of qualified workers who have job offers. Tier three covers less-skilled workers who fill temporary shortages in the labor market. Tier four is intended for students, and tier five for youth mobility and temporary workers. Applicants for immigration are required to score a sufficient number of points according to a tier-specific grading system to demonstrate that they comply with the immigration requirements for a particular tier. Sponsorship from a licensed sponsor (an employer or educational institution) is required under tiers two through five.

Tier one is the main policy tool to channel high-skilled immigrants to the United Kingdom. It replaces the Highly Skilled Migrant Programme and is based on a points system rather than any kind of employer sponsorship. Doctors, engineers, scientists, and other educated workers who have at least a first degree (bachelor's), can speak English, and earn a relatively high income in their country of origin qualify for tier one immigration. Tier one applicants must attain at least seventy-five points. Bachelor's degrees, master's degrees, and doctorates are rewarded with thirty, thirty-five, and fifty points, respectively. Earnings in the country of origin, which can yield five to forty-five points, are converted to pounds sterling and adjusted for the differences in price and income between the United Kingdom and the country of origin by so-called uplift ratios. Applicants under twenty-eight years of age are given twenty additional points, those between twenty-eight and twenty-nine years old receive ten points, and applicants between thirty and thirty-one years old receive five points. Prior work experience or a qualification obtained in the United Kingdom is rewarded with five points. Evidence of the successful completion of a standardized English proficiency test, a degree taught in English, or origination from an English-speaking country fulfills the requirement of language proficiency, for which applicants receive ten points. Finally, applicants who can provide proof that they will be able to support themselves and their dependants earn ten points.

Skilled workers may also enter the United Kingdom through other tiers, but the conditions may be less favorable. Within tier two, for example, applicants are required to have concrete job offers, and if they do not come as intracompany transfers, athletes (or athletes' associates), or religious workers, their employment must also fill a gap that cannot be filled by a worker already settled in the United Kingdom. Within this tier, the shortage occupation list is compiled by the Migration Advisory Committee, which comprises occupations in which there are shortages and for which immigrants qualify without the need to prove their prospective earnings and qualifications. Within the tier system, international students who study in the United Kingdom receive preferential treatment upon graduation.

Expatriates who have an assignment in the United Kingdom and declare that their intentions in the United Kingdom are temporary may claim tax exemptions on their housing and traveling costs as well as for days worked outside of the United Kingdom.

Newly Emerged European Cores

Several countries in Europe have recently experienced a remarkable economic upgrading and undergone a radical change from providers of emigrants to receivers of immigrants. This distinct migration pattern is observed in Southern European countries such as Spain, Italy, and Greece, but also in

Ireland. Together, these four countries form the cluster of newly emerged European cores.

Ireland. Ireland applies a work-permit scheme to applicants who are ineligible for an Irish green card and, as a rule, who earn a salary of €30,000 or more.[28] Applicants are also required to have adequate qualifications, skills, or experience for the intended employment to receive a work permit. Irish legislation requires firms to first post vacancies locally in Ireland and within the Irish National Training and Employment Authority and EURES employment networks before they are permitted to open the position to applications from non-EU, EEA, or Swiss nationals. Work permits are tied to specific occupations and can initially be issued for up to two years, after which time it is possible to extend the permit for up to three more years. An indefinite work permit can be issued after five years of residence in Ireland.

The Irish green card is a policy tool intended to fill shortages in the Irish labor market with suitably qualified foreign workers. After an initial validity period of two years, green cards can be extended indefinitely. A green card entitles its holder to apply for family reunification immediately. Eligible applicants for green cards are exempt from a prior labor-market assessment. The eligibility criteria are a gross annual salary of at least €60,000 a year, without bonuses, or between €30,000 and €59,999, without bonuses, if the green card is tied to a stipulated strategically important occupation. These occupations include IT professionals; health and associated professionals; professional engineers and technologists; construction professionals; researchers and natural scientists; business, financial, and associate professionals; and specialist managers (European Migration Network 2007).

Ireland facilitates further mobility through a policy permitting intracompany transfers, which entitles foreign senior managers, key personnel, and trainees to move between foreign and Irish branches of the same multinational company. To qualify for an intracompany transfer, an employee must earn a minimum annual salary of €40,000 and must have worked for the company for at least twelve months prior to the transfer. In addition, Ireland's policy toward so-called third-level graduates entitles graduates who obtained a tertiary-level degree in Ireland to stay and seek employment in

Ireland for six months after graduation. Upon finding appropriate employment, they are eligible to apply for either a work permit or a green card.

Greece. The Greek Ministry of Employment and Social Security (together with the Ministry of Interior and Ministry of Foreign Affairs) regulates the entry of non-EU workers into Greece.[29] The ministry stipulates labor-market needs for foreign (non-EU) nationals by occupation, prefecture, and employment type and duration based on regional reports from special committees and the current demographic and labor-market situation. The ministry then forwards the labor-market needs to Greek consulates, which subsequently post the stipulated job opportunities and administer the application process for foreign nationals. Based on the lists of applicants sent back to regional authorities in Greece, employers apply to hire new employees.[30] In coordination with the consulates, an appropriate visa is issued to foreign nationals selected for employment. They must have applied for a work visa from their country of origin and for a residence permit for work purposes after arrival. As it typically takes twelve to eighteen months to complete the process, it works best for seasonal immigrants, who are prioritized by the authorities and whose needs are relatively easy to predict.[31]

In addition to this general system, Greece applies several provisions for high-skilled workers. Foreign nationals who are scientists and researchers, university professors, artists, and intracorporate transfers may be issued special visas for employment. Further, Greece distinguishes three types of high-skilled workers. The first type includes board members, managers, and company staff; they are entitled to a residence permit with the right to work in Greece that is issued for a year and can be extended for an additional two years if they hold a work contract in Greece and document their occupational status. The second type includes foreign workers who serve the "public interest." Employers of such workers must prove that the considered employee is qualified to promote the public interest. Permits for this type of worker are issued for one year and can be renewed every year. The third type includes affiliates of archeological schools. Their employment must be connected to the school's activity. Further provisions apply to foreign nationals employed in other EU member states and posted to Greece. All individuals in these categories of high-skilled immigrants are entitled to immigrate with their family members. Immigrants in all other categories can bring their family members only after two years of legal residence, as long as they provide evidence of a stable and regular income to support them (Kanellopoulos and Cholezas 2006).

Specific regulations apply to intellectual creators such as writers, authors, directors, painters, sculptors, actors, music artists, choreographers and scenographers, and specialized personnel of foreign companies employed in Greece within the framework of a service contract. The self-employed and sole proprietors who deposit €60,000 in a Greek bank and whose business plans pass the feasibility evaluation by the responsible Greek consulate and are accepted by a special committee in the destination region may also be permitted entry with a special visa. Greece does not grant high-skilled immigrants any special tax provisions.

Spain. To be permitted to work in Spain, non-EU nationals must obtain a work permit.[32] In 2005, Spain offered a general amnesty for illegal immigrants, who were then able to legitimize their presence in Spain. More generally, foreigners can obtain the first work permit for Spain in one of two ways. Foreign nationals who are direct employees of a Spanish company may be granted work permits for a maximum of twelve months (type B); this permit may be extended for up to two additional years. The application for a type B work permit must be made by the employer, whereas the extension can be demanded by the employee. Seconded workers—that is, foreign nationals who temporarily work on behalf of a host company but generally remain on the payroll of their original home employer, who is providing some service to the Spanish host company—can obtain a type A work permit for a maximum of nine months. With respect to qualification, applicants for type A permits must demonstrate sufficient experience to fill the position and must demonstrate that they have at least six to twelve months of experience with the company providing services to Spain. Preference is given to candidates who can provide evidence of a link with Spain, including a Spanish grandparent or having studied in Spain, and to Latin American citizens. In addition, each year the Spanish National Employment Institute (*Instituto Nacional de Empleo*) issues a list of occupations (and geographic areas) in which immigrants are especially needed and for which work-permit quotas (*contingentes*) are assigned. Specific provisions apply to entrepreneurs, researchers, academics, and very high-skilled workers.

New Member States

The new member states that joined the EU in 2004 and 2007 have been experiencing migrant outflows. However, with a gradual strengthening of their economies, some of them are experiencing their first patterns of immigration.

Bulgaria. Non-EU workers are entitled to employment in Bulgaria provided they possess a work permit issued by the Bulgarian National Employment Agency.[33] Work permits are valid for a predetermined period of time and tied to a particular work placement; these can be granted to individuals who possess skills or specialized knowledge that is in demand but not available in the Bulgarian labor market.

While a maximum term of one year generally applies for Bulgarian work permits, executive personnel qualify for an extension of up to three years, and managerial-level professionals can be granted extensions of more than three years. In addition, certain groups of high-skilled workers enjoy easier access to the Bulgarian labor market. These include:

- Internationally renowned scholars and intellectuals;

- High-level managerial personnel of companies established by foreign legal entities in Bulgarian territory;

- Foreign-company specialists engaged in the assembly, repair, and installation of imported equipment;

- Specialists in production quality assessment;

- Foreigners whose employment in Bulgaria originates from the implementation of international treaties.

Estonia. A work permit is required for non-EU nationals intending to work in Estonia, whether they are employees, sole proprietors, or in any activity that may result in gaining profit or any other benefit.[34] Work permits are initially issued for a maximum of two years and can be extended for up to five years at a time. Work permits are not required for foreign nationals who have long-term residence permits, residence permits for employment, or residence permits for settling with a spouse or a close relative who permanently resides in Estonia, nor are they required for foreign nationals working in a number of other stipulated categories, such as on locomotive crews.

Foreign nationals may be issued residence permits tied to particular job postings only if the openings are not filled through the state employment mediation service within a three-week period of open competition. While Estonia does not explicitly categorize high- and low-skilled workers for immigration purposes, Estonian immigration policy entails elements that foster positive selection of immigrants. Specifically, applicants must have the qualifications, education, health, work experience, special skills, and knowledge required for the job. Furthermore, a residence permit is issued only if the agreed wage ensures subsistence in Estonia. Specifically, the wage must be at least 24 percent higher than the average yearly wage most recently published by Estonia's statistical office. Estonia also has specific immigration provisions for scientists and researchers.

Hungary. Foreign, non-EEA nationals and their family members coming to Hungary for work must have a work permit.[35] Employers apply for work permits, and Hungarian authorities grant the permits if no Hungarian or EEA national is available for the considered position. The Ministry of Employment Policy and Labor sets quotas that limit the numbers of foreigners in any occupation, regionally and nationally. The agreed remuneration must be at least 80 percent of the average wage in the given sector and occupation and above the minimum wage. Upon being granted a work permit, foreign nationals are required to obtain appropriate long-term visas and temporary residence permits (issued for up to three years and renewable). Seasonal workers can be issued special visas for up to three or six months of employment. Nonnationals are not eligible for employment or work in numerous positions in the public sector.

Certain groups of non-EEA workers do not need work permits to legally work in Hungary. Aside from top representatives of branch offices of foreign companies; those performing commissioning, warranty repair, or similar work under temporary service contracts; diplomats; and employees of international organizations, this exemption applies to certain groups of high-skilled workers. These include foreign nationals who are (i) recipients of appointments at the postdoctoral level or of research scholarships; (ii) enrolled in apprentice training programs organized by an international student organization; (iii) pursuing full-time studies at vocational schools, secondary school, basic art schools, or institutions of higher education; or (iv) to be employed in accredited programs at elementary, secondary, or higher educational institutions as foreign-language instructors or lecturers. Other occupational groups are exempt from having to consider the situation in the Hungarian labor market prior to granting work permits to foreign nationals. These include foreign nationals employed in key positions; those employed in a company with a foreign majority ownership, provided the number of foreign nationals employed in the company does not exceed 5 percent of the company's labor force; professional athletes; and internationally recognized foreign nationals in the fields of education, science, or art.

Policies Applied at the EU Level: The EU Blue Card

To date, immigration policy in the EU has been in the hands of national governments. However, the European Commission is one of the more active proponents of managed immigration with an emphasis on high-skilled immigration. In 2007, the commission proposed an EU work permit, the so-called blue card, to facilitate the entry—for residence and work—of high-skilled non-EU citizens into EU labor markets. The blue card was proposed with a validity period of two years with the possibility of renewal, and was intended to facilitate intra-EU mobility as well.

The blue card was endorsed by the European Parliament in November 2008, and the EU adopted plans for its implementation in May 2009 (European Commission 2009a). The twenty-four signatories of the scheme will have to transpose it into national law within a period of two years. Denmark, Ireland, and the United Kingdom opted out of this policy tool, so it does not facilitate entry for high-skilled immigrants into those three countries. The blue card is based on common criteria: a work contract, professional qualifications, and a minimum salary level equal to at least 150 percent of the annual average wage in the country, with a possible derogation to 120 percent of the annual average wage for individuals in professions in high demand. Applications can be made from within or outside the EU. However, member states reserve the right to regulate the national details according to their own standards.

Holders of the blue card and their family members may, after eighteen months of legal residence in an EU member state, move to another EU member state participating in the blue-card scheme for the purpose of high-skilled employment. The movers need to apply for an EU blue card to the authority responsible in this other member state within one month after entry. The EU blue card also ensures equal treatment of foreigners and nationals in terms of working conditions, including pay and dismissal, freedom of association, education, training, and recognition of qualifications. It further ensures that foreigners and nationals will have equal access to some social and welfare rights, freedom of movement within national boundaries, and the right of access to goods and services for themselves and their family members.

What Is Europe Doing to Attract High-Skilled Immigrants?

As the above review demonstrates, national and EU-level immigration policies aimed at high-skilled immigrants tend to have been implemented recently. This means their likely effects are difficult to evaluate at this point. In addition, these policies often involve many institutional and administrative barriers, even for intra-EU migrants, and in many cases, project reservations toward potential migrants. Given the temporary nature of most permits and the discretion involved in their renewal, immigrants often are not provided with a clear outlook concerning their future ability to stay and work in the country to which they have immigrated, including with respect to any future right to citizenship in the host country. While recent policy efforts targeting high-skilled immigrants are commendable (such as the EU blue card), they may have come too late, and it remains to be seen whether they will achieve their desired objectives. In particular, the current blue-card implementation plan is a watered-down version of the European Commission's original proposal, and national-specific regulations are still in place. Furthermore, the blue card may instead lead to discrimination against workers from the new EU member states, who still face transitional arrangements in some of the old member states in regard to intra-EU labor mobility (while blue-card holders will not be governed by these arrangements).

Nonetheless, there have been some positive developments. A number of countries have realized the need for especially high-skilled immigrants and have enacted legal provisions to facilitate their selection and entry. Several countries have defined certain high-skilled categories of workers for whom simplified administrative procedures apply. Another group of countries set minimum salary levels or investment quotas for self-employed immigrants in order to distinguish high-skilled immigrants who are entitled to preferential treatment. Some countries apply an explicit points system to select and facilitate the entry of high-skilled foreign labor. For workers from the new EU member states, the initially imposed transitional arrangements are being phased out. A distinct pattern emerges in table 9-4, which summarizes the main policy approaches across Europe and prevailing migration patterns. Specifically, countries with no or only recent a history of immigration are significantly less likely to apply more elaborate policies to attract high-skilled immigrants. Another observation is that applied policies vary significantly across Europe. The recent shift away from kinship-based immigration policies and toward an emphasis on skills and labor-market–related criteria in many EU countries suggests that the European policy debate on immigration is not driven by ethnic politics.

Conclusions and Policy Implications

Given Europe's position in a globalized economy, and in spite of the current financial and economic turmoil, Europe will most likely remain an important destination for international immigrants for the foreseeable future. Whether Europe can stand up to its internal and external challenges will depend on the quality of policies EU member states apply to manage internal mobility and flows of international immigrants. The required policies need to address two key areas: internal mobility to improve the allocative efficiency of EU labor markets, and immigration from outside the EU to strengthen the EU's labor force.

Based on the analysis from the ESHSLI, a unique expert opinion survey, we confirm the need for skilled immigrants in Europe. In fact, the survey results indicate that Europe is likely to experience a mismatch between the demand and supply of high- and low-skilled labor in the coming five to

TABLE 9-4

EUROPEAN COUNTRIES' IMMIGRATION POLICIES BY REGION OF ORIGIN, EU AND NON-EU/EEA/SWITZERLAND

Policies in Place for Immigration, by Immigrant Origin

Policies by Destination	EU Nationals	Nationals Outside EU, European Economic Area, and Switzerland							
	New member-state nationals	Educational or skill threshold to qualify as high-skilled	Salary or investment threshold to qualify as high-skilled	Market-assessment exemption	Positive list of occupations or sectors	Points system	Provisions for researchers and academics	Provisions for staying students (transition to work)	Tax exemptions
Scandinavian welfare states	Free access	DK, FI, SE[1]	DK	DK, SE	DK	DK	DK, FI, SE	FI, SE	DK, FI, SE
Western European core	Mixed (some restrictions for EU2 and EU10)	AT[2], BE, FR, DE[3], NL, UK	AT, BE, FR, DE, NL, UK	AT, BE, DE, UK	UK[7]	UK	AT, BE, DE, NL, UK	DE, NL, UK	AT, BE, FR, NL, UK
Newly emerged European cores	Mostly free access (some restrictions for EU2)	IE, GR, ES	IE	IE	ES[4], GR[4]		IE, GR, ES	ES[5]	ES[6]
New member states	Free access	BG, EE, HU[2]	EE	HU	HU[4]		BG, EE, HU		

SOURCE: Authors' compilation based on the sources cited in the section of this chapter titled "Current Approaches to High-Skilled Immigration in Europe."

NOTES: 1. Sweden applies a demand-driven policy. 2. With quotas. 3. For those who are self-employed (in the past, also for high-skilled). 4. A list of desired occupations with regional (in Hungary also national and sectoral) quotas applied. 5. Having studied in Spain makes it easier to obtain a work permit. 6. Only applies to exceptionally skilled individuals, such as star football players or very high-level executives. 7. Within tier two. Refer to box 9-1 on page 269 for country codes.

twenty years, characterized by a shortage of high-skilled labor and excess supply of low-skilled labor. Interestingly, the ongoing crisis may alleviate this mismatch to some extent. A promising finding from the survey is that, among the high-skilled immigrants, temporary and permanent immigrants are expected to constitute significant shares. Whether these will suffice to fulfill the objective of efficiently circulating human capital between source and host countries remains to be seen, however.

Our research indicates that past and current immigration policies have not taken advantage of the potential of the international pool of immigrants. To the contrary, and with the exception of a few recent, commendable initiatives, Europe still sees itself much as a fortress protecting its family silver from undeserving immigrants. Europe's internal and external projection has a repellent effect on international immigration flows and results in the diversion of immigrants most valued by labor markets to countries like the United States, Canada, and Australia.

The surveyed experts confirmed this view and generally rated Europe's immigration policies as hostile to immigration, and therefore not effective for preventing labor-market shortages. There is some indication, however, that European immigration policies discourage low-skilled immigration more than high-skilled immigration, which may help reduce the mismatch between the demand for high- and low-skilled labor.

Finally, our results indicate that while high-skilled immigrants are more welcome in EU member countries than their low-skilled counterparts, a general aversion toward immigrants persists in Europe. This aversion is strongest among trade unions, works councils, and other employee associations, and among the general public; it is less pronounced among national governments, the European Commission, and, especially, employers and employer associations. This indicates potential frictions between these native groups on this issue in the political arena. In particular, this finding highlights that while reaching an agreement on less-restrictive general-immigration policies may lead to political deadlock, policies encouraging high-skilled immigration may be considerably more viable. In light of our results on the meager attractiveness of European countries vis-à-vis their global competitors, immigration policies may need to address improving potential immigrants' perceptions of Europe as a destination. Continuing as "Fortress Europe" is no longer a viable option, given labor-market conditions and the globalized economy.

Notes

1. The so-called old member states of the European Union (EU) prior to the 2004 EU enlargement (Austria, Belgium, Denmark, Finland, France, Germany, Greece, Ireland, Italy, Luxembourg, the Netherlands, Portugal, Spain, Sweden, and the United Kingdom) may be referred to as the EU15. EU10 denotes the "new" member states that joined the EU in 2004 (the Czech Republic, Estonia, Hungary, Latvia, Lithuania, Poland, Slovakia, and Slovenia, from Central and Eastern Europe, as well as Malta and Cyprus from Southern Europe). The EU15 and EU10 together are referred to as the EU25. Currently, the EU has twenty-seven members (EU27), including Romania and Bulgaria, which joined in 2007; these are referred to as the EU2.

2. Different distributions of immigrant skill groups across countries may be due to differences in institutional and historical contexts. For example, transitional arrangements applied vis-à-vis natives of new member states seem to have diverted flows of most skilled migrants away from Germany and to the United Kingdom and Ireland (see Kahanec, Zaiceva, and Zimmermann 2010; Zimmermann 2005; Kahanec and Zaiceva 2009; and Zaiceva and Zimmermann 2008). Contrasting the findings of Cohen-Goldner and Paserman (2006) with those of Bauer and Zimmermann (1999), it seems that the educational attainment of immigrants from the former Soviet Union was higher in Israel than in Germany.

3. The Expert Survey on High-Skilled Labor Immigration (ESHSLI) was conducted for the purpose of this study by the authors in 2009 at the Institute for the Study of Labor (IZA), Bonn, Germany (ESHSLI, 2009).

4. Whereas all of the other old member states have since removed the barriers to immigrants from the member states that joined the EU in 2004, Germany and Austria have stuck to the so-called transitional arrangements preventing these immigrants from labor-market access; however, many member states still apply such measures to immigrants from Bulgaria and Romania, both of which joined the EU in 2007.

5. IZA research fellows are generally leading economists, but the group of IZA research fellows also includes a number of sociologists and other social scientists, contributing to the broader field of labor. Research fellows are appointed by IZA's internal committee of directors on the recommendation of incumbent research fellows or research staff for a period of three years with the possibility of renewal. IZA's network of policy fellows includes influential representatives from business, politics, society, and the media, thus complementing the academic network of IZA research fellows. IZA research affiliates are junior labor economists and Ph.D. students, who are appointed initially for a period of two years. After receiving their Ph.D.s and demonstrating an adequate publications record, they may be promoted to research fellows.

6. In most contexts, non-EU nationals of the European Economic Area (EEA) (that is, natives of Iceland, Liechtenstein, and Norway), as well as Swiss nationals, are treated as EU nationals.

7. Ireland, Sweden, and the United Kingdom granted access to their labor markets to workers from the new member states immediately following the 2004 EU enlargement. Finland, Greece, Italy, Portugal, and Spain decided to lift restrictions in 2006; Luxembourg and the Netherlands lifted them in 2007; France in 2008; and Belgium and Demark in 2009. Germany and Austria have simplified their procedures or have relaxed restrictions in some sectors and for some occupations. Ten EU25 member states (Cyprus, the Czech Republic, Estonia, Finland, Latvia, Lithuania, Poland, Slovakia, Slovenia, and Sweden) opened their labor markets to Bulgarian and Romanian workers within two years after the 2007 enlargement. Denmark, Greece, Hungary, Portugal, and Spain granted free access to EU2 workers in 2009. Restrictions and procedures have been reduced in some sectors and for some professions in most of the remaining EU25 member states.

8. Bonin and others (2008) argue that language differences, culture, and labor legislation, as well as the fact that the United States is a federal country and that free movement within the EU is only a recent phenomenon, are behind the difference in mobility rates. The observed gap diminishes if internal mobility rates in the United States are compared to regional mobility rates in the EU, that is, when mobility rates are calculated for geographical units comparable in size to U.S. states.

9. Further practical difficulties arise, such as in the case of waiting lists for specialized medical treatment: positions in these lists are not transferable between countries.

10. In Germany, for example, if one spouse works in another member state, that spouse's earnings may increase the marginal tax rate for the spouse who works in Germany, despite the fact that his or her income has already been properly taxed in the other member state.

11. Although significant efforts have been made in Europe to facilitate recognition of foreign professional qualifications, the procedures developed may still involve significant costs in terms of time and fees, and, thus, still lead to the down-skilling of immigrants. Dustmann, Frattini, and Preston (2007) document this problem in the European context; see also Bonin and others (2008), Chiswick and Miller (chapter 4 of this volume), and McDonald, Warman, and Worswick (chapter 6 of this volume).

12. Information in this section provided by the Ministry of Refugee, Immigration and Integration Affairs, "Ny I Danmark.dk" [New to Denmark.dk], available at www.nyidanmark.dk; and the Ministry of Taxation, "SKAT," available at www.skat.dk.

13. In 2009, the "positive list" included professions in the following fields: academic work; construction; information technology and telecommunications; management; educational, social, and religious work; sales, purchases, and marketing; health, health care, and personal care; freight forwarding, postal services, storage, and engine operation; and education and tuition.

14. Information provided by the Finnish Immigration Service, "Maahanmuuttovirasto: Muut Kuin EU-Kansalaiset Ja Heihin Rinnastettavat; Työntekijän Oleskelulupa" [Finnish Immigration Service: Residence Permit for a Non-EU Employee], available at www.migri.fi/netcomm/content.asp?path=8,2473,2707,2500;

and the Finnish Tax Administration, "Taxation of Employees from Other Countries: Bulletin for Taxpayers," publication 277e. 10, January 1, 2010, available at www.vero.fi/nc/doc/download.asp?id=2873;67467.

15. Residence permits are issued for a maximum of one year or for the duration of the employment or study to be conducted. A residence permit is initially issued for a fixed period. A permanent-residence permit can be acquired after four years of continuous residence in Finland. Separate residence permits are reserved for entrepreneurs and own-account professionals (self-employed professionals without paid employees).

16. Information provided by Sweden's Migration Board, "Migrationsverket" [Migration Board], available at www.migrationsverket.se.

17. Information provided by the Federal Ministry of Economic Affairs and Labor, "Help.gv.at: Ihr offizieller Amtshelfer für österreich" [Help.gv.at: Your aid for official channels in Austria], available at www.help.gv.at/Content.Node/93/Seite.930201.html.

18. Special temporary work permits for up to six months (only six weeks for harvesters) are available for seasonal workers. Students can obtain work permits if their earnings from employment in Austria are not their main means of support (that is, less than €357.74 per month in 2009), education remains the main purpose of their stay in the country, and the job opening cannot be filled by eligible Austrian workers.

19. Information provided by the Belgium Federal Public Service Employment, Labour and Social Dialogue, available at www.employment.belgium.be/home.aspx; and Région de Bruxelles-Capitale, "Working in Belgium as a Foreign National," available at www.bruxelles.irisnet.be/en/citoyens/home/travailler.shtml.

20. Shorter periods apply for nationals of countries that have signed bilateral treaties with Belgium and for those legally residing in Belgium with a spouse or children.

21. If the posting involves a service contract with another (Belgian) company, this contract must be provided to the authorities.

22. Salary or scholarship must equal at least the applicable wage scales for research assistants at universities or institutions of higher education.

23. Information provided by Ministère de l'immigration, de l'intégration, de l'identité nationale et du développement solidaire [Ministry of Labor, Social Relations, Family and Solidarity], available at www.immigration.gouv.fr.

24. Information provided by the Bundesministerium für Arbeit, Soziales und Konsumentenschutz [Federal Ministry of Labor, Social Affairs, and Consumer Protection], available at www.bmsk.gv.at; Bundesamt für Migration und Flüchtlinge [Federal Office for Migration and Refugees], available at www.bamf.de/DE/Startseite/home-node.html?__nnn=true; and Bundesministerium der Justiz [Federal Ministry of Justice], available at http://bundesrecht.juris.de/index.html.

25. Information provided by Immigratie- en Naturalisatiedienst [Immigration and Naturalization Service], available at www.ind.nl.

26. In practice, Dutch immigration policy favors Western immigrants over immigrants from less-developed countries because immigrants are required to present birth certificates and, if married, marriage certificates. These certificates are not regularly issued in many less-developed countries.

27. Information provided by the UK Border Agency, "Working in the UK," available at www.ukba.homeoffice.gov.uk/workingintheuk.

28. Information provided by European Migration Network (2007) and Department of Enterprise, Trade and Innovation, available at www.deti.ie.

29. Information provided by Kanellopoulos and Cholezas (2006); and Ελληνική Δημοκρατία: Υπουργείο & Κοινωνικής Ασφάλισης [Greek Democracy: Ministry of Employment and Social Security], available at www.ypakp.gr.

30. Employers who wish to hire workers from outside the EU have to apply in their municipality by September 30 of the respective year, specifying the number, specialization (profession), and nationality of workers needed, as well as the intended duration of their employment.

31. We thank Anna Triandafyllidou for this insight.

32. Information provided by Ministerio de Trabajo e Inmigración [Ministry of Labor and Immigration], available at www.mtin.es/en/index.htm.

33. Information provided by the Ministry of Labour and Social Policy: National Employment Agency, available atwww.az.government.bg/eng.

34. Information provided by Politsei ja Piirivalveamet [Police and Border Guard], available at www.politsei.ee.eng.

35. Information provided by the Magyar Köztársaság Külügyminisztériuma [Hungarian Ministry of Foreign Affairs], available at www.mfa.gov.hu/kum/en/bal; and Országinfó: Kormányzati Portál [Country Info: Government Portal], "Magyarország" [International Projects], available at www.magyarorszag.hu.

References

Bauer, T., and A. Kunze. 2004. The Demand for High-Skilled Workers and Immigration Policy. *Brussels Economic Review/Cahiers Economiques de Bruxelles* 47 (1): 57–75.

Bauer, T., and K. F. Zimmermann. 1999. Overtime Work and Overtime Compensation in Germany. *Scottish Journal of Political Economy* 46 (4): 419–36.

Bonin, H., W. Eichhorst, C. Florman, M. O. Hansen, L. Skiöld, J. Stuhler, K. Tatsiramos, H. Thomasen, and K. F. Zimmermann. 2008. *Geographic Mobility in the European Union: Optimising Its Economic and Social Benefits*. Institute for the Study of Labor (IZA) Research Report no. 19. Bonn, Germany.

Brenke, K., M. Yuksel, and K. F. Zimmermann. 2010. EU Enlargement under Continued Mobility Restrictions: Consequences for the German Labor Market. In *EU Labor Markets after Post-enlargement Migration*, ed. M. Kahanec and K. F. Zimmermann, 111–29. Berlin: Springer Verlag.

Chiswick, B. R., and P. W. Miller. 2009. Educational Mismatch: Are High-Skilled Immigrants Really Working at High-Skilled Jobs and the Price They Pay if They Aren't? IZA Discussion Paper no. 4280, Bonn, Germany.

Cohen-Goldner, S., and M. D. Paserman. 2006. Mass Migration to Israel and Natives' Employment Transitions. *Industrial and Labor Relations Review* 59 (4): 630–52.

Dustmann, C., T. Frattini, and I. Preston. 2007. *A Study of Migrant Workers and the National Minimum Wage and Enforcement Issues that Arise*, Center for Research and Analysis of Migration, London: University College London.

ESHSLI. 2009. The Expert Survey on High-Skilled Labor Immigration, IZA, Bonn, Germany.

European Commission. 2009a. Council Directive 2009/50/EC, of 25 May 2009, on the Conditions of Entry and Residence of Third-Country Nationals for the Purposes of Highly Qualified Employment. *Official Journal of the European Union* L155/17–29. Available at http://eur-lex.europa.eu/LexUriServ/LexUriServ.do?uri=OJ:L:2009:155:0017:0029:EN:PDF.

———. 2009b. Five Years of an Enlarged EU: Economic Achievements and Challenges. *European Economy* 1/2009, European Commission, Brussels.

European Migration Network. 2007. *Conditions of Entry and Residence of Third Country Highly-Skilled Workers in the EU*. Report financed by the European Commission.

Eurostat. 2006. *Population Statistics*. Luxembourg: Office for Official Publications of the European Communities.

———. 2008. *Europe in Figures: Eurostat Yearbook*. Luxembourg: Office for Official Publications of the European Communities.

Kaczmarczyk, P., M. Mioduszewska, and A. Zilicz. 2010. Impact of the Post-accession Migration on the Polish Labor Market. In *EU Labor Markets after Post-enlargement Migration*, ed. M. Kahanec and K. F. Zimmermann, 219–54. Berlin: Springer Verlag.

Kahanec, M., A. Zaiceva, and K. F. Zimmermann. 2010. Lessons from Migration after EU Enlargement. In *EU Labor Markets after Post-enlargement Migration*, ed. M. Kahanec and K. F. Zimmermann, 3–46. Berlin: Springer Verlag.

Kahanec, M., and A. Zaiceva. 2009. Labor Market Outcomes of Immigrants and Non-citizens in the EU: An East-West Comparison. *International Journal of Manpower* 30 (1–2): 97–115.

Kahanec, M., and K. F. Zimmermann. 2008. Migration, the Quality of the Labour Force and Economic Inequality. IZA Discussion Paper no. 3560, Bonn, Germany.

————. 2009a. International Migration, Ethnicity, and Economic Inequality. In *The Oxford Handbook of Economic Inequality,* ed. W. Salverda, B. Nolan, and T. M. Smeeding, 455–90. Oxford: Oxford University Press.

————. 2009b. Migration in an Enlarged EU: A Challenging Solution? European Economy, Economic Paper 363, European Commission, Brussels.

Kanellopoulos, C. N., and I. Cholezas. 2006. *Conditions of Entry and Residence of Third Country Highly Skilled Workers in Greece.* Centre of Planning and Economic Research (KEPE), Athens, Greece.

McDonald, J.T., C. Warman, and C. Worswick. 2010. Earnings, Occupations, and Schooling Decisions of Immigrants with Medical Degrees: Evidence for Canada and the United States. In *High-Skilled Immigration in a Global Labor Market,* ed. B. R. Chiswick, ch. 6. Washington, DC: AEI Press.

United Nations Educational, Scientific, and Cultural Organization (UNESCO). 1997. *International Standard Classification of Education.* Paris: UNESCO.

Zaiceva, A., and K. F. Zimmermann. 2008. Scale, Diversity, and Determinants of Labour Migration in Europe. *Oxford Review of Economic Policy* 24 (3): 427–51.

Zimmermann, K. F. 2005. *European Migration: What Do We Know?* Oxford/New York: Oxford University Press.

————. 2009. Labor Mobility and the Integration of European Labor Markets, IZA Discussion Paper no. 3999, Bonn, Germany.

Zimmermann, K. F., H. Bonin, R. Fahr, and H. Hinte. 2007. *Immigration Policy and the Labor Market: The German Experience and Lessons for Europe.* Berlin: Springer Verlag.

Appendix:
The Policy Panel

The closing session at the conference was a policy panel. The panel consisted of:

Stuart Anderson, National Foundation for American Policy
Steven A. Camarota, Center for Immigration Studies
Barry R. Chiswick, University of Illinois at Chicago
Demetrios Papademetriou, Immigration Policy Institute
and, as the chair of the policy panel, David Frum, then of the
American Enterprise Institute.

The following summary of the discussion is based on the edited transcript. It attempts to follow faithfully the order and sense of the discussion. Any errors of omission or commission are, however, attributable to the editor of this volume. The session began with opening comments from the panelists, followed by a general discussion.

Stuart Anderson spoke favorably of the H1-B temporary worker visa (up to two consecutive three-year periods) as a mechanism for employers to hire high-skilled foreign-born workers who are primarily graduates of U.S. colleges and universities that they attended on student visas. An H1-B visa can often be obtained quickly, in contrast to the long queues and time delays in employment-based permanent resident visas. He called for a reduction in the restrictions on the use of H1-B visas and an increase in the annual quota. He also advocated an increase in the number of permanent resident visas issued through the skilled employment categories in current immigration law.

315

Steven A. Camarota made several points. He commented on the tax-benefit balance for immigrants, emphasizing that the fiscal balance is much more favorable among highly educated than among less educated workers. He also stressed that the lower-skilled American population experiences more difficulty in the labor market if immigrants are predominantly low skilled. He expressed concern that the immigration of high-skilled workers decreases the incentive of the business community to advocate for higher-quality schooling for Americans. He felt that there is an attitude regarding the highly skilled, that if we can import them we do not need to produce them here. He also raised national security concerns in the event that a large fraction of the nation's science and engineering workers are not U.S. citizens, and argued that the arrival of immigrants in these fields discourages American students from entering them. He then raised the political issue: that the public seems less supportive of increased immigration than the nation's so-called elites. He closed his comments by asking how one enforces immigration law, and mentioning the public skepticism that the government has the political will to enforce employer sanctions.

Demetrios Papademetriou commented on the many opportunities for high-skilled immigrants to enter the United States under a permanent-resident visa, but especially under a variety of temporary visa programs. He noted that the current system has essentially been in place since 1965—that is, for about forty-five years—and that there is widespread agreement that the entire immigration system needs to be "fixed." To end this political dead-lock he called for the establishment of a permanent or standing commission on labor markets and immigration that would "do systematic ongoing research," including developing baseline estimates. The commission could then answer questions regarding the appropriate number of visas in various categories instead of the current practice of picking numbers out of the "deep blue sky."

Barry R. Chiswick also commented that there is wide agreement that the immigration system needs to be fixed, but this has not happened because of a lack of agreement on how it should be fixed. He argued immigration policy reform should be concerned with the future, not the past, and that the future depends on high-technology workers in science, engineering, and management/administration. These workers need to be able to work both independently and as part of a group, and will need decision-making skills. Moreover, whereas in the past the income distribution effects of immigration policy seemed to be of limited concern, this is no longer the case given the widespread public assistance programs for those in economic distress. He believes that the issue is not an either/or: whether to increase the number of homegrown high-skilled workers by improving the U.S. educational system or to import them from abroad. Rather, the United States can increase both sources. He went on to comment that part of the failure to reform immigration policy regarding low-skilled workers is due to the government's failure to enforce the employer-sanctions provisions of the 1986 Immigration Reform and Control Act (IRCA), and part is due to ethnic politics and competing economic interests that have retarded the emergence of a national consensus.

David Frum then criticized current immigration policy as attracting lower-skilled workers and thereby having a negative effect on the skill level in the labor force. This has negative effects on the economy.

B. Chiswick agreed with Frum's point and commented on how the initial post-1965 amendments resulted in very high-skilled immigration from Asia, with subsequent immigration from Asia being less skilled as the share of family migrants increased. He followed by remarking that only in immigration policy is nepotism (favoring relatives) a prominent feature of public policy.

Papademetriou countered that the United States has moved toward a skill-based immigration system when one considers the variety of nonimmigrant visas, such as the H1-B for high-skilled and technical workers. Yet he feels that one builds immigration on the family and we should "honor the family unification" principle. He views immigration as a tripod, with the three legs being family unification, refugees, and skilled migration.

Camarota expressed concerns regarding the declining skill level of immigrants with the increase in immigration from Mexico. He also expressed concern regarding the lower educational attainment of the U.S.-born children of Mexican immigrants.

Carmel Chiswick (University of Illinois at Chicago) commented that potential high-skilled immigrants are concerned with the quality of the education that their children will receive in the United States. Higher-quality schooling here would help attract high-skilled immigrants.

An Unidentified Female commented that the incentive to bring in high-skilled immigrants may arise from this being less expensive than educating our own population, especially disadvantaged minorities.

B. Chiswick, responding to a question, commented that in the city in which he lives he has witnessed a decline in the relative economic status of the low-skilled native-born population as a consequence of the large increase in low-skilled immigration. He added that we want to see an increase in the income of the low-income population not merely for altruistic reasons.

Camarota picked up the theme by reporting data on the decline over time in the real income of those with little schooling. He noted that there is no labor shortage in this group, but rather a "glut" of unskilled labor. He commented on the National Academy of Sciences report that concluded that the net fiscal benefit was negative for those with little schooling and positive for those with a college education.

Papademetriou then argued that the United States needs to integrate schooling and work training and prepare people for lifelong learning. He criticized the current immigration system as being unpredictable for both potential immigrants and their employers.

Örn Bodvarsson (St. Cloud State University) inquired as to what the panelists felt were the most pressing research questions on high-skilled immigration, given that the research to date was not definitive.

Papademetriou responded that he felt there needed to be much more research at the level of the firm, especially about how firms actually respond. This would include studies of the behavior of global companies with operations in several countries.

Camarota responded that he would like more research on the effects of immigration on wages and why American youth are less interested in high-skilled jobs in science, engineering, and the medical professions.

B. Lindsay Lowell (Georgetown University) was not as pessimistic about the American educational system as were many others. He argued that one reason for increasing the number of high-skilled immigrants is to offset the large increase in low-skilled immigration. Another reason is that they are "job creators." He asked the panel if the United States needs more high-skilled immigrants.

B. Chiswick responded that it is a question of gains and losses rather than "needs," and he believes that the U.S. economy would gain, in terms of aggregate income, a more favorable distribution of income and a more favorable fiscal balance (taxes net of benefits) from more high-skilled immigration.

Papademetriou agreed with this overall assessment, but offered that no one knows the right number.

Camarota replied, "We have the most generous skill-based immigration system in the world." He raised the issue of the effects of high levels of immigration on the aggregate U.S. population in the future and the effects of crowding. He felt too little thought has been given to the question of the absolute size of the U.S. population. He noted the lower fertility rate among high-skilled immigrants compared to those with lesser skills.

Index

About the Authors

Barry R. Chiswick is a distinguished professor in the department of economics at the University of Illinois at Chicago and program director for migration studies at the Institute for the Study of Labor. He is a former president of the European Society for Population Economics and a former chair of the American Statistical Association Census Advisory Committee. His primary area of research for the past three decades has been on various aspects of international migration, the economics of language, and the economics of minorities. His 1978 *Journal of Political Economy* article, "The Effect of Americanization on the Earnings of Foreign Born Men," is recognized as seminal. Two of his most recent books are *The Economics of Immigration* (Edward Elgar, 2005) and, coauthored with Paul W. Miller, *The Economics of Language: International Analyses* (Routledge, 2007). In addition to numerous print and electronic media interviews on immigration issues and policies, he has provided testimony to both the U.S House of Representatives and the U.S. Senate and to the UK House of Lords. He has received numerous awards for his research on immigration and racial and ethnic minorities, including an honorary doctorate from Lund University, Sweden, in 2009. Mr. Chiswick edited two previous conference volumes on immigration for AEI: *The Gateway: U.S. Immigration Issues and Policies* (AEI Press, 1982) and *Immigration, Language, and Ethnicity: Canada and the United States* (AEI Press, 1992).

Sarit Cohen-Goldner is a lecturer at Bar-Ilan University in Israel. Her main areas of research are the economics of migration, labor economics, and econometrics. She previously held a research position at Boston University and a teaching appointment at Tel Aviv University and is currently a member of the Young Scientists Forum at the Israel Academy of Sciences and Humanities. Her research has been published in numerous academic journals, including *Economic Quarterly,* the *International Economic Review,* the *Journal of Population Economics,* and the *Journal of Econometrics.*

Joseph P. Ferrie is a professor of economics and history at Northwestern University and a research associate at the National Bureau of Economic Research. He is the author of *Yankeys Now: Immigrants in the Antebellum U.S., 1840-1860* (Oxford University Press, 1999). His research on the mobility of immigrants and the native born in the United States has appeared in the *Journal of Economic History,* the *Journal of Economic Perspectives,* the *American Economic Review,* the *Economic Journal,* and *Research in Labor Economics.* He pioneered the creation of large, nationally representative longitudinal datasets through the linkage of census manuscripts from the nineteenth and early twentieth centuries.

Volker Grossmann holds the chair for macroeconomics, growth, and industrial policy at the University of Fribourg. He is also a research fellow at the Institute for the Study of Labor and a research affiliate at the CESifo Group. Previously, he was an assistant professor at the University of Zurich. His main fields of research include human-capital formation, international mobility of labor and capital, innovation and growth, distribution and growth, development economics, and taxation of capital and estates. His work has been published in numerous academic journals, including the *Journal of Economic Growth,* the *European Economic Review,* the *Journal of Macroeconomics,* the *International Journal of Industrial Organization,* the *Journal of Economic Psychology,* and *Oxford Economic Papers.*

James F. Hollifield is a professor of international political economy and director of the John Goodwin Tower Center for Political Studies at Southern Methodist University. He previously held faculty appointments at Auburn, Brandeis, and Duke Universities. In 1992, he was associate director of research at the Conseil National de la Recherche Scientifique and the Centre d'Etudes et de Recherches Internationales of the Fondation Nationale des Sciences Politiques in Paris. From 1986 to 1992, he was a research associate at Harvard University's Minda de Gunzburg Center for European Studies and cochair of the French study group, and in 1991–92, he was an associate at Harvard's Center for International Affairs. He has worked as a consultant for the U.S. government as well as several organizations, including the United Nations and the Organisation for Economic Co-operation and Development. Mr. Hollifield has been the recipient of grants from private foundations and government agencies, including the Social Science Research Council, the Sloan Foundation, and the National Science Foundation. His most recent work looks at the rapidly evolving relationship between trade, migration, and the nation-state.

Martin Kahanec is an assistant professor at the Central European University and a senior research associate, deputy program director of the migration program area, leader of the European Union enlargement and labor-markets research subarea, and former deputy director of research at the Institute for the Study of Labor, with which he has been involved since 2005. He is a member of several professional associations and a founding member and fellow of the Slovak Economic Association. His main research interests are labor and population economics and policy, ethnicity, and migration. He has published in refereed journals, has chapters in edited volumes including *Oxford Handbook of Economic Inequality* (Oxford University Press), and has edited journal special issues and scientific volumes, most recently *Ethnic Diversity in European Labor Markets: Challenges and Solutions* (Edward Elgar). Mr. Kahanec has held several advisory positions and participated in a number of scientific and policy projects with the World Bank, the European Commission, the Organisation for Economic Co-operation and Development, and other international and national institutions.

Pramod Khadka is a graduate student in the department of economics at Georgetown University.

Linda G. Lesky is an associate professor of medicine and health policy at George Washington University. Previously, she was an assistant vice president in the division of medical education at the Association of American Medical Colleges. From 1996 to 2004, she served as vice head for medical education and residency program director for the department of medicine at the University of Illinois–Chicago. From 1988 to 1996, she was an associate firm chief in the department of medicine at Beth Israel Hospital in Boston and an associate for clinical faculty development in the Office of

Educational Development at Harvard Medical School. She has been on the leadership councils of the Association of Program Directors in Internal Medicine and the Clerkship Directors in Internal Medicine. Her academic interests include medical education reform at the undergraduate and graduate levels and the economic and educational implications of physician workforce expansion. She works clinically as an academic hospitalist.

B. Lindsay Lowell is director of policy studies at the Institute for the Study of International Migration at Georgetown University. He was previously director of research at the congressionally appointed Commission on Immigration Reform, where he was also assistant director for the Mexico/United States Binational Study on Migration. He has been research director at the Pew Hispanic Center of the University of Southern California and a labor analyst at the U.S. Department of Labor, and he has taught at Princeton University and the University of Texas–Austin. Mr. Lowell coedited *Sending Money Home: Hispanic Remittances and Community Development* (Rowman and Littlefield, 2002) and has published over one hundred articles and reports about immigration policy, labor force, economic development, and the global mobility of the highly skilled.

James Ted McDonald is a professor of economics at the University of New Brunswick in Fredericton, Canada. He has published papers on a variety of topics in labor economics, including the labor-market outcomes of immigrants. His work on this topic has appeared in the *Journal of Human Resources,* the *Journal of Political Economy, Industrial Relations,* the *Industrial and Labor Relations Review,* and *Applied Economics.* He has also worked extensively with Human Resources and Skills Development Canada on various facets of the employment-insurance system. The main focus of his more recent and ongoing academic research is on the health outcomes, health-service use, and health behaviors of immigrants and minority groups in developed countries, with a particular focus on cancer incidence and prevention. His research in this area has been published in *Social Science and Medicine* and the *Journal of Immigrant and Minority Health.*

Paul W. Miller is currently professor in the department of economics and finance at Curtin University, Perth, Australia, and previously held an

Australian professorial fellowship in the business school at the University of Western Australia. His primary research interest is labor-market performance, particularly as it relates to educational attainment, gender, and ethnic and racial origin. He was formerly the head of the department of economics at the University of Western Australia (1994–2001) and the inaugural head of the School of Economics and Commerce, formed in 2003. In 1997, he was elected as a fellow of the Academy of the Social Sciences in Australia. He has also received numerous honors for his papers, including the Milken Institute Award for Distinguished Economic Research, and the Economic Society of Australia's prize for the best paper published in the *Economic Record*. He has over 140 publications about labor-market issues in refereed journals.

David Stadelmann is currently a doctoral student and research assistant at the University of Fribourg. His main research interests include the effects of international migration on fiscal policy and economic growth, the role of fiscal variables for property values in the context of regional and international factor mobility, and the political economy of tax competition. More generally, he is interested in combining sound theoretical foundations with sophisticated empirical methods.

Casey Warman teaches in the department of economics at Queen's University in Kingston, Ontario, and is a part-time research analyst for Statistics Canada. He received his doctorate in economics from Carleton University in 2006. His research interests include earnings and income inequality, gender differences in earnings, the economic integration of immigrants, temporary foreign workers, and mandatory retirement.

Yoram Weiss has been a professor of economics at Tel Aviv University since 1980 and has held the Daniel and Grace Ross Chair in Labor Economics since 1993. He was a member of the Committee of the Determination of Wages in the Public Sector from 1985 to 1989 and a member of the Committee on the Absorption of Skilled Immigrants in 1994. He has been the editor of the *Journal of Labor Economics* since 1993 and an editorial board member of the *Economics of Education Review*. Mr. Weiss has published in numerous economic journals, including the *Journal of Economic Theory*, the

American Economic Review, the *Journal of Political Economy,* the *Economic Journal,* and the *International Economic Review.* He joined the Institute for the Study of Labor as a research fellow in December 2001.

Carole J. Wilson is executive director and fellow at the John Goodwin Tower Center for Political Studies at Southern Methodist University. Her main research interests center on questions of political behavior in Latin America and Europe and on the study of regional integration in both of these areas. Her work focuses on the themes of attitude formation with an emphasis on the way electorates and political parties respond to large-scale political and economic changes (particularly the processes of regional integration and globalization), and how exogenous factors (like political institutions and electoral context) affect public opinion and voting behavior. Ms. Wilson's work has been published in a number of academic journals, including the *American Journal of Political Science,* the *British Journal of Political Science, Comparative Political Studies, European Union Politics,* and *Political Behavior.*

Christopher Worswick is an associate professor in the department of economics at Carleton University. His main areas of research are labor economics and development economics, with a particular focus on the economics of immigration. He has published research on the earnings, unemployment, use of social programs, and labor supply of immigrants in Canada, Australia, and the United States.

Klaus F. Zimmermann has been director of the Institute for the Study of Labor and full professor of economics at the University of Bonn since 1998. He is also president of the German Institute for Economic Research (DIW Berlin, since 2000), honorary professor of economics at the Free University of Berlin (since 2001), and honorary professor at the Renmin University of China (since December 2006). He is also chairman of the Society of the German Economic Research Institutes (since 2005), adviser to the president of the European Commission (2001–2003 and 2005–2009), economic adviser to the prime minister of North Rhine-Westphalia (2008–2010), and a member of the World Economic Forum's Global Agenda Council on Migration. Since 1988, Mr. Zimmermann has been editor in chief of the *Journal of Population Economics*. He serves as associate editor for various scientific journals and is author or editor of forty-four books and over 230 papers in refereed journals and collected volumes. His special research interests center on labor economics, population economics, migration, industrial organization, and econometrics.